Bioethics

This book is a philosophically-oriented introduction to bioethics. It offers the reader an overview of key debates in bioethics relevant to various areas, including organ retrieval, stem cell research, justice in health care and issues in environmental ethics, as well as issues surrounding food and agriculture. The book also seeks to go beyond simply describing the issues in order to provide the reader with the methodological and theoretical tools for a more comprehensive understanding of current bioethical debates. The aim of the book is to present bioethics as an interdisciplinary field, to explore its close relation to other disciplines (such as law, life sciences, theology and philosophy) and to discuss the conditions under which bioethics can serve as an academically legitimate discipline that is at the same time relevant to society.

As a systematic and methodologically rigorous overview, *Bioethics: Methods, Theories, Domains* will be of particular interest to academics and students in the disciplines of law, medicine, ethics and philosophy.

'This is a book that embraces neither a single ethical theory nor a pragmatic melange of just-so-principles. It is a thoughtful and engaging analysis of diverse theoretical foundations in Bioethics. It is also an enormous step towards conceptual and philosophical clarity in this fascinating area.' (Professor Christian Illies, Chair for Practical Philosophy at the Otto-Friedrich University Bamberg, Germany).

Marcus Düwell is Professor of Philosophical Ethics at Utrecht University, director of the Ethics Institute of Utrecht University and until 2012 director of the Netherlands Research School for Practical Philosophy. His research concentrates on questions concerning the foundation of morality and on applied ethics in its relation to ethical theory and political philosophy.

Biomedical Law and Ethics Library
Series Editor: Sheila A.M. McLean

Scientific and clinical advances, social and political developments and the impact of healthcare on our lives raise profound ethical and legal questions. Medical law and ethics have become central to our understanding of these problems, and are important tools for the analysis and resolution of problems – real or imagined.

In this series, scholars at the forefront of biomedical law and ethics contribute to the debates in this area, with accessible, thought-provoking, and sometimes controversial ideas. Each book in the series develops an independent hypothesis and argues cogently for a particular position. One of the major contributions of this series is the extent to which both law and ethics are utilised in the content of the books, and the shape of the series itself.

The books in this series are analytical, with a key target audience of lawyers, doctors, nurses and the intelligent lay public.

Available titles:

Human Fertilisation and Embryology (2006)
Reproducing regulation
Kirsty Horsey & Hazel Biggs

Intention and Causation in Medical Non-Killing (2006)
The impact of criminal law concepts on euthanasia and assisted suicide
Glenys Williams

Impairment and Disability (2007)
Law and ethics at the beginning and end of life
Sheila McLean & Laura Williamson

Bioethics and the Humanities (2007)
Attitudes and perceptions
Robin Downie & Jane Macnaughton

Defending the Genetic Supermarket (2007)
The law and ethics of selecting the next generation
Colin Gavaghan

The Harm Paradox (2007)
Tort law and the unwanted child in an era of choice
Nicolette Priaulx

Assisted Dying (2007)
Reflections on the need for law reform
Sheila McLean

Medicine, Malpractice and Misapprehensions (2007)
Vivienne Harpwood

Euthanasia, Ethics and the Law (2007)
From conflict to compromise
Richard Huxtable

Best Interests of the Child in Healthcare (2007)
Sarah Elliston

Values in Medicine (2008)
The realities of clinical practice
Donald Evans

Autonomy, Consent and the Law (2009)
Sheila McLean

Healthcare Research Ethics and Law (2009)
Regulation, review and responsibility
Hazel Biggs

The Body in Bioethics (2009)
Alastair V. Campbell

Genomic Negligence (2011)
An interest in autonomy as the basis for novel negligence claims generated by genetic technology
Victoria Chico

Health Professionals and Trust (2011)
The cure for healthcare law and policy
Mark Henaghan

Medical Ethics in China (2011)
A transcultural interpretation
Jing-Bao Nie

Law, Ethics and Compromise at the Limits of Life (2012)
To treat or not to treat?
Richard Huxtable

Regulating Pre-Implantation Genetic Diagnosis (2012)
A comparative and theoretical analysis
Sheila A.M. McLean and Sarah Elliston

Bioethics (2012)
Methods, theories, domains
Marcus Düwell

Forthcoming titles include: (2014)

The Jurisprudence of Pregnancy
Concepts of conflict, persons and property
Mary Ford

About the Series Editor

Professor Sheila McLean is International Bar Association Professor of Law and Ethics in Medicine and Director of the Institute of Law and Ethics in Medicine at the University of Glasgow.

Bioethics

Methods, theories, domains

Marcus Düwell

Routledge
Taylor & Francis Group
LONDON AND NEW YORK

Original German language edition: Marcus Düwell, Bioethik: Methoden, Theorien, und Bereiche (ISBN 978-3-476-01895-3) Published by J.B. Metziersche Verlagsbuchandlung und Carl Ernst Poeschel Verlag GmbH Stuttgart, Germany. Copyright 2008

First published in English 2013
by Routledge
2 Park Square, Milton Park, Abingdon, Oxon OX14 4RN

Simultaneously published in the USA and Canada
by Routledge
711 Third Avenue, New York, NY 10017

Routledge is an imprint of the Taylor & Francis Group, an informa business

British Library Cataloguing in Publication Data
A catalogue record for this book is available from the British Library

Library of Congress Cataloging-in-Publication Data
Düwell, Marcus, 1962-
Bioethics : methods, theories, domains / Marcus Düwell.
p. cm.
Includes index.
ISBN 978-0-415-60991-3 (hbk) — ISBN 978-0-203-08420-5 (ebk) 1. Bioethics—Philosophy. I. Title.
QH332.D89 2013
174.2—dc23 2012016491

ISBN 978-0-415-60991-3 (hbk)
ISBN 978-0-203-08420-5 (ebk)

Typeset in Garamond
by Cenveo Publisher Services

MIX
Paper from responsible sources
FSC® C004839
www.fsc.org

Printed and bound in Great Britain by
CPI Group (UK) Ltd, Croydon, CR0 4YY

Contents

Preface

The aim of this book is to provide an introduction to a broad range of discussions in bioethics. However, its purpose is not merely to outline debates on cloning, gene therapy or environmental biotechnology. Rather, this book endeavours to put up for discussion the profile of the discipline of bioethics and its multifaceted methodological and theoretical preconditions. Bioethics takes place in interdisciplinary contexts with the participation of legal professionals, biologists, physicians, theologians and philosophers. Yet bioethical questions also arouse considerable interest among the general public, in the media and in politics. Nonetheless, bioethics is an academic enterprise which is organised in research institutes, for which professorships are established and in which students gain degrees. Like other academic disciplines, bioethics is accountable for its research standards, its academic self-conception and its place within the collectivity of academic disciplines. For that reason, this book will introduce and critically discuss positions that are important for a methodological understanding of the discipline. In the course of these discussions it should also become clear which approach to bioethical questions I deem appropriate.

I understand bioethics as a philosophical subdiscipline which is concerned with normative questions that confront us in the domains of medicine, biosciences and related fields (regarding the matter of the precise demarcation of domains see Chapter 1). The aim of bioethics is to formulate, scrutinise and justify criteria, in order to answer the question 'What actions are morally defensible?' in a philosophically solid manner. In order to attain this, a comprehensive engagement with the life sciences as scientific, technical, political and social phenomena is required. Therefore, interdisciplinary collaboration is indispensable for bioethics. Yet questions of bioethics form a challenge for ethics insofar as they confront moral traditions and perceived matters of course with their boundaries. Many of the practices that are currently the centre of attention were once not even considered morally relevant in the first place. Moreover, all recommendations and statements in bioethics are put forward in a situation characterised by a plurality of moral convictions and ethical theories. Bioethics discusses concrete moral questions, but in doing so it must consider the whole range of ethical theories. For that reason, engagement with the moral-philosophical aspects of bioethics is of great significance.

Chapter 1 is aimed at a more detailed description of the situation of the life sciences and bioethics, as a reflection on these academic developments. Chapter 2 discusses the relation of bioethics to moral philosophy. Chapter 3 addresses cultural, social and humanities-based perspectives relevant to bioethics. Chapter 4, to conclude, attempts to provide an overview of the most important bioethical discussions. The exposition of these discussions obviously cannot be exhaustive. Rather, the most important objective is to evoke an awareness of the questions and problems that confront any attempt to reflect on the ethical aspects of the biosciences and their application. In light of the political, economical and societal meaning of the life sciences, I believe that this theme is central to our contemporary culture.

Since the relation of bioethics to moral philosophy is key to my understanding of bioethics, a discussion of some more general issues in philosophical ethics cannot be avoided. This presents the author with the unfortunate choice between either writing in such an advanced manner that only those who already have a solid basis in philosophical ethics can follow or, in addition to providing an introduction to bioethics, also giving a general introduction into ethics. Forgoing a critical portrayal of moral-philosophical discussions would, however, lead to a situation in which the author would introduce his moral-philosophical presuppositions underhandedly, to some extent, rather than – as philosophical honesty requires – confronting them with competing approaches and arguing for the cogency of his own position. The present volume aims to solve this problem by, on the one hand, choosing to bring up a few questions of metaethics and normative ethics but, on the other hand, presenting these debates principally with a view to their relevance for bioethics. I hope that the results will be of interest to specialists and laypersons alike.

When writing this kind of introduction, one cannot be neutral. Whoever would make a claim to neutrality for himself would be rightly suspected of trying to conceal his own standpoint. Therefore, I do not in the least wish to beat around the bush about the fact that my personal position is part of a Kantian tradition, and is informed by a strong emphasis on human dignity and individual rights. I do not, however, consider us merely morally obligated to respect the personal rights to freedom of the individual. Rather, it is the *empowerment* of the individual to an autonomous way of taking up his or her life that is, to me, the most important moral starting point (see Chapter 2).

Currently, bioethics poses a challenge to this position inasmuch as developments in the biosciences have made both the proper subjects of moral rights and the contents and scope of legitimate moral claims all the more difficult to determine. From a metaethical point of view, I am rather sympathetic to transcendental philosophy as a point of departure for ethics in general. Still, I have made an effort to deal fairly with competing standpoints. The point of this book, however, is not primarily to defend my personal bioethical standpoints, but to clarify in what ways bioethical assertions, theories and positions are dependent on moral-philosophical premises. Reflection upon these premises is, I believe, the essential 'ethical' element of bioethics. In this way, bioethics can make a fundamental contribution to the transparency of the way moral judgments are formed in a situation of moral pluralism, and thus, moreover, be exceptionally conducive to understanding and constructive communication in public debate.

This book reflects, in multifarious ways, my bioethical work over the last 20-odd years. As an academic coordinator of the Interdepartmental Centre for Ethics in the Sciences and Humanities in Tübingen I have collaborated on a number of academic projects. Particularly exciting were the many doctoral projects of the research training group 'Ethics in the Sciences', the broad interdisciplinary team as well as the European research projects. I have learned much, in particular, from liaisons with Dietmar Mieth and Klaus Steigleder. For over 10 years now, my working context has been the Department of Philosophy at Utrecht University, where I am director of the Ethics Institute, and from where I directed for the last 7 years the Netherlands School for Research in Practical Philosophy. The move to a new country and the encounter with a different academic culture has certainly disclosed a number of new perspectives. The intensive contact with students of philosophy and the students on our international MA programme in Applied Ethics, and the collaboration with the doctoral students of the institute and the research school has been the most enriching challenge.

I thank Sigrid Graumann and Micha H. Werner for their numerous comments on the concept and individual sections of the manuscript. My gratitude also concerns the comments and corrections I gained from a discussion in the colloquium of the Ethics Institute at Utrecht University, in particular from Marcel Verweij and Jan Vorstenbosch. Robert Heeger's detailed enquiries have – as always – taught me a great deal. This book is the English version of an introduction into bioethics that was first published in German in 2008. I thank Metzler publishing house, especially Ute Hechtfischer, for the support when writing the German manuscript and for the permission to translate it into English. I thank Routledge, especially Katherine Carpenter and Stephen Gutierrez, for their support and patience in the publishing process, and Sheila McLean for the willingness to consider the manuscript for publication in the *Biomedical Law and Ethics Library*. I thank Candice Cornelis for various suggestions concerning the English text, Gerhard Bos and Andre Krom for literature suggestions. But first and foremost I have to thank Naomi van Steenbergen. Naomi has translated the whole manuscript from German into English. She did a really wonderful job and I am very grateful for her scrupulous and reliable edition of the text. Sabine Antony, to conclude, has critically read the entire manuscript and has supported its development. For this I am grateful and for much more.

Utrecht, Spring 2012
Marcus Düwell

1 What is bioethics? An introduction

1.1 An introduction to bioethics?

Since the end of the 1950s, physicians have been able to use heart-lung machines to keep people alive for whom previously there was no prospect of recovery. Shortly thereafter, it also became possible to remove their organs for transplantation purposes. For many physicians, however, this raised the question whether it could be morally right simply to take away organs from living, breathing people. Interesting is the way in which an answer to this moral conundrum was sought: a number of medical practitioners asked the pope to pass judgment. This is an instance of a very early bioethical discussion. Another example would be the debate on the conduct of doctors in concentration camps in the Third Reich, as held in the Nuremberg Doctors' Trial. Since then, developments in the life sciences have led to numerous discussions about cloning, embryo research, genetic diagnosis and selection, xenotransplantation and interference with the human brain – to highlight but a few themes. The contexts of these debates are no longer restricted to individual domains of medical practice, but have a far-ranging influence on the entirety of medicine and on everyday life. In addition, there is no universally accepted moral authority which could provide definitive answers. Bioethical discussions are partly held with considerable public participation and against a backdrop of extensive pluralism of moral convictions.

These are the circumstances and the very diverse contexts in which bioethics has established itself globally over the last 40 years. There are bioethics committees affiliated with parliaments, ministries, churches and scientific organisations. There are numerous research institutes engaged in bioethics, and enormous numbers of books, journals and other publications. In this respect, an introduction to bioethics is confronted with an unwieldy abundance of materials. It would seem positively implausible if a single author were to claim to possess an overview of all these different debates, positions and publications. Moreover, bioethical debate can change at such a speed that an introduction like that would see its expiry date pass in the blink of an eye.

For these reasons, the objective of the present introduction is not in the first place to provide an overview of the entirety of concrete discussions. Rather, the point is to provide an overview of the *range of methodological problems* and *theoretical viewpoints* that play a role in bioethics. It is important to keep in mind from the start that an introduction to bioethics is confronted with a variety of particular difficulties; in opposition, for instance, to an introduction to quantum physics, which presumably would not be an easy undertaking either. The difficulty of gaining an overview of bioethics is connected to the fact that bioethical debates take place *on the boundary of academic and public-political discourse*, that academic bioethics has an *interdisciplinary* character and that there is *no agreement on what exactly bioethics is in the first place*. In order to close in on the question of what 'bioethics' means, or should, or could mean, I shall first of all (in 1.1.1) take a look at some forms of institutionalisation and (in 1.1.2) elaborate on the interdisciplinarity of bioethics. Subsequently (in 1.2), I shall discuss the role of bioethics in the context of developments in the biosciences and, finally (in 1.3), I shall comment on a number of efforts to determine the meaning of the concept of 'bioethics'.

1.1.1 Institutionalisation of bioethics

Bioethics, as I have indicated above, came into existence in the context of public debates about issues in (bio)medical science. The *institutionalisation of bioethics* is mostly a consequence of the increasing need of parliaments, governments and churches to obtain advice on ethical questions in the light of developments in medical science and biotechnology. Numerous ethics committees have been formed to fulfil this need. The functions of these institutions vary. Some committees were established merely to advise on concrete, well-defined questions; others are permanent advisory boards concerned with a whole range of societally relevant questions in the domain of the biosciences or other new technologies (i.e. the European Group on Ethics in the Sciences and New Technologies, the advisory board of the European Commission). While varied in assignment, they are also varied in size and composition. As a rule, these committees are interdisciplinary (with physicians, jurists, philosophers and theologians) and they usually consist not only of academics, but of representatives of relevant parties in society as well (churches, disability rights advocates, etc).

Besides ethical advisory boards affiliated with political institutions, committees have also been formed to advise *researchers* and *hospitals*. These so-called *'ethics committees' at medical faculties* are geared towards verifying that the protection of medical test subjects with regard to risks and informed consent is guaranteed. The title 'ethics committee' for these bodies is somewhat misleading, since their intention is not to carry out ethical reflection on the research project at issue, but merely to certify that the relevant codes of conduct are observed. These committees are standardly composed of physicians, complemented by a (theological or philosophical) ethicist and a jurist.

In recent years *clinical ethics committees* and institutionalised forms of *ethics advisory boards in hospitals* have also been created, to which doctors, nurses and patients can turn in case of conflicts and difficult decisions in treatment and nursing. The task of these advisory services is geared towards individual cases, and is typically not very well defined. Mainly, the point is to create a space within the clinical praxis in which conflict situations can be dealt with transparently with regard to both argumentation and procedure. It may be that, as a rule, these committees are forums that are partially about conflict moderation and the protection of decision-makers. But in any case they are places that should make it possible for difficult practical situations to be dealt with in morally responsible ways.

With these three types of committees, the contexts in which bioethics emerged have already been laid out. From the start, the objective of bioethics was to advise and reflect on *complex decisions in politics, research and clinical practice.* In the domain of medicine, more and more situations arose in which the traditional ethical guidelines of the discipline were not helpful, for which moral intuitions were not prepared, and in which there were no (or insufficient) legal arrangements to guide a decision-making process. In these contexts, the expression 'bioethics' signalled first and foremost a need for reflection on the moral and legal standards regulating medical practice, as well as a need for guidance on the part of decision-makers. It is still undefined, however, in what ways this specific form of advice and reflection differs from other kinds of conflict moderation. And it is even less clear how the advisory task of these boards relates to what has been established as 'bioethics' in academic spheres.

In addition, this advisory task turns out to differ greatly between the forms of institutionalisation discussed. A *clinical ethics committee* is confronted with *particular cases*. As a rule, these particular cases are settled against a backdrop of legal regulations, established practices and widely shared moral convictions. However, the great need for ethical advice indicates that ever more practices are becoming problematic, and ever fewer moral convictions can be taken for granted as shared. Nonetheless, no comprehensive ethical theories are called upon when such conflict situations are being dealt with in medical practice. Rather, those involved tend to fall back on medical knowledge, somewhat familiar standards of medical and nursing practice and moral principles that are (rightly or wrongly) considered to be unproblematic. Incidentally, the customs of medical practice are based only in part on the question whether those acts could meet with general approval in the public sphere. The medical profession has simply been successful in asserting certain standards of medical practice within its strongly hierarchically organised and legally regulated domain. In any case, factual observance of a given standard and its moral acceptance are two different things. Whenever the call for ethical advice arises in the clinic it is never enough merely to assess the *particular case* in light of established practical standards and moral convictions. These *standards and convictions* themselves must also be considered. The call for ethical advice is thus also an indicator for the necessity to think about established forms of practice.

Discussions of bioethical themes that are widely held in the *public sphere*, on the other hand, are characterised by the fact that in this sphere there are no collectively shared moral convictions; there is at best partial consensus. To an extent, that may be a consequence of the fact that many areas of research, for instance stem cell research, are rather inaccessible to day-to-day experience. Moreover, on many bioethical topics people's moral intuitions are extremely varied. In these cases, a much more systematic kind of ethical guidance is called for. Discussions in media and politics, as well as institutionalised ethics committees, therefore, fall back on academics who inform participants about scientific, legal, sociological and ethical aspects of new forms of practice and new technologies. These informatory tasks then fall to biologists, jurists, sociologists and ethicists. This means that *academic ethical discourse* plays a role in *public discussions* as well. Yet the relation between the academic discipline and public bioethical debates is remarkable in several respects. First of all, the academic discipline did not exist until the need for reflection on its subject arose in practice. Now that is not all that surprising. Ever since Aristotle, ethics in general has been understood as a philosophical reflection on practices, and has conceived its task as guidance towards a good *praxis*. But there are some further particularities of bioethics compared with other debates on the boundary of academic and public discussion. For one, it is striking that many debates – for instance those on cloning – are largely defined by academics but disseminated by public media. It has thus been possible to read articles containing elaborate philosophical argumentation in national newspapers. Occasionally, philosophers and theologians will speak out and express their standpoints on cloning in the press before engaging with the subject in academic journals. Sometimes, philosophers and theologians will even present themselves publicly as bioethicists, despite the fact that their academic publications are in very different areas. Those practices, of course, evoke the question of exactly what competencies a bioethicist may be expected to have.

The relation between bioethics as a *topic of public debate* and as an *academic discipline* is thus unclear in many respects. In a public debate, every citizen can vocalise his own moral intuitions. Is the bioethicist then something like an official who receives a salary for expressing her moral beliefs? If bioethics is a practice of advising politics, is it merely a rhetorically pretentious way of making one's own standpoint heard? Is the establishment of bioethics a product of some strategy to evade the plurality in the battle of opinions by grounding a pseudo-expertocracy? Is incapacitation of the public sphere impending?

This relation between academic bioethical debates and the public and political spheres makes it difficult to provide a systematic introduction to bioethics in the first place. Yet insofar as bioethics constitutes a reflection on the *praxis* of medicine and the development of the life sciences, *ethical consultation* of politicians, physicians, etc. is only possible if there is a background of *academic debates* as well. Bioethics as an academic activity is therefore also presupposed in the established practices of various kinds of ethics committees, if their claim to provide guidance is in fact taken seriously.

For this reason, considering the academic profile and the expectations for bioethics is necessary in light of the public debate as well. But given the *interdisciplinarity* of bioethics it is not easy to identify a clear-cut profile of the field (Green 1990; Holmes 1990; Pellegrino 2002). As a branch of ethics, bioethics seems to have a special connection to philosophy (and theology), yet as an institutionalised subject it is often part of medicine or interdisciplinary centres. Opinions regarding the methodological and professional roles of the different disciplines in bioethics vary greatly. Below, I shall work out *one single proposal* for understanding the interdisciplinarity of bioethics by way of the example of 'enhancement'.

1.1.2 Interdisciplinarity: judgments in bioethics are mixed judgments

For a few years now there has been a discussion of the question to what extent it is morally defensible to use the possibilities of medical science not only to cure people from disease, but also to improve their physical or mental capabilities (Parens 1998; President's Council on Bioethics 2003). These 'improvements', which are known as 'enhancements', range from plastic surgery to memory-improving pharmaceuticals. The range of applications is broad and the boundaries with therapy are fuzzy. The same medication can be used to slow down the loss of memory in people suffering from dementia or to boost the mental capabilities of students shortly before an exam. Enhancement is morally controversial, since traditionally, the task of medicine has been formulated in terms of therapy, diagnosis and prevention of *disease*. Yet the question what exactly health and disease are in the first place is itself disputed in medical science (Murphy 2009). If one understands the medical task of healing to be the rectification of dysfunction in order to enable a functioning that is typical for the human species (Daniels 1985: 26ff), the applications mentioned above do not necessarily qualify. But why should this definition of disease be our guiding thread? And what right would we have to deny people medical possibilities that would improve their lives? So-called 'transhumanists' even claim that one should free oneself as much as possible from the arbitrary limits to which humankind is evolutionarily subject (see e.g. Bostrom 2005). I shall return to the subject of *enhancement* (see Chapter 4) shortly. At this point, I merely want to differentiate between some questions and topics in order to make the division of the roles of the various disciplines within bioethics a little more transparent.

1.1.2.1 Scientific and technical possibilities

First of all, no bioethical reflection will be able to say anything about enhancement without being informed about the possibilities that are currently technically possible and implemented. In terms of plastic surgery this is not difficult to establish; in terms of pharmaceuticals it is significantly more problematic. In this respect, it is of course important to survey the relevant effects – both direct and lateral – and the limits of our knowledge of those effects. Not only are the facts relevant; it is also important to reflect critically on the question how these facts were generated and which theoretical conceptions led to their establishment.

1.1.2.2 *Prognosis of future possibilities and uncertainties*

What technical possibilities can we expect? What issues are being researched? What research aims are there? Why is there a desire to fulfil these aims? How realistic are they? Are there alternative ways in which these aims could be reached? If bioethics is to avoid losing itself in passing judgment on completely irrelevant future scenarios, these are essential questions. They might sound trivial, but they are in fact very hard to answer. Scientists themselves usually have difficulties making claims about the development of their research. As a non scientist, one is inclined to overestimate the predictive capabilities of those in the field.

1.1.2.3 *Social and psychological reality*

What do we know about dealing with these technical possibilities in 'real life'? How often does cosmetic surgery fail? What do patients say: are they actually happier afterwards? What hopes do these possibilities arouse in people? What impact does the presence of these technical possibilities have in the media? How do different cultures handle these possibilities? (Plastic surgery, for instance, seems to be employed predominantly in the USA and Brazil.)

1.1.2.4 *Possibilities for legal regulations*

To what extent does interaction with enhancement technologies allow for regulation? What regulative possibilities are there? What could be said about the expected effectiveness of these regulative possibilities? Do these regulations have further implications for, say, the protection of private information and the over abundance of regulations in the domain of medicine? What effects do these regulations have on legal policy? What is the symbolic meaning of the prosecution or authorisation of these technologies?

1.1.2.5 *The meaning of the notion of disease in medicine*

Traditionally, medical practice is legitimated on the ground that the physician's task is to cure disease. This duty to cure determines the professional self-understanding of physicians. The financial facilitation of medical research and the solidary funding of health benefits are justified on the same grounds.

In a sense, even the moral meaning of medicine is connected to this duty to cure: we understand the development of medical science not just as a technical challenge but also as a moral duty. When, however, parts of medical science are no longer based on curing disease but on the 'improvement' of human capabilities, it must be considered what this means for the legitimacy of medicine or the (non-)legitimacy of these technologies.

1.1.2.6 What qualities are important to people?

If the goal of 'enhancement' is to improve human qualities, any assumption in this field is connected to an idea of what exactly is important to people. Some say, for instance, that every person should decide for himself which capacities he wants to enhance. Technically speaking, there is no reason to consider merely the possibility of a longer life or improved mental capabilities. It is conceivable that qualities could be improved, apart from the performance-enhancing drugs that are currently available, that would lead to considerable advances in athletic performance or even military skill. Critics fear that the hope for technical refinement itself might lead to an illusory human lifestyle. Whatever one's take on the matter, these are relevant philosophical-anthropological questions.

1.1.2.7 What are we to do?

Finally, there are moral-philosophical questions to be considered. The provision and development of enhancement technologies are morally relevant practices. They evoke moral claims: as soon as it is technically possible for people to improve their opportunities in life, we are morally obliged to provide these possibilities. Or is it a moral duty to develop technologies that allow humankind to escape the contingencies of natural evolution? Or is it morally indefensible for people not to accept their physical and mental boundaries? It is unjustifiable to spend money on researching such technologies if at the same time there are no means to ensure basic medical supplies for everybody. All of these moral claims presuppose a justification, which is typically a task for ethics.

The preceding survey of possible questions is not complete, and the questions that have been mentioned are particularly relevant to the issue of enhancement. A different bioethical topic evokes different moral questions. Yet at least the list shows that knowledge and research methods from different disciplines are pertinent to bioethical questions. First, one must attempt to gain an overview of what is *scientifically and technically* possible. The point of such an attempt is not merely to retrieve existing knowledge, but also to understand and critically discuss the scientific assumptions grounding this knowledge.

Secondly, it is necessary to try to formulate a prognosis of future technical developments; something for which the discipline of *technology assessment* has developed several tools. Not only are current technical possibilities at stake;

research and development are also in the matrix. Research objectives, including their plausibility and moral acceptability, are up for debate. It is, however, just as important to establish what means are necessary for achieving these objectives, and what alternative ways of attaining them might be possible. These questions are not trivial, for in many research areas (for instance stem cell research) hopes for research achievements represent fundamental moral standpoints. With regard to enhancement technologies, on the other hand, it is important to ascertain what implementations will be realised in the foreseeable future in order to assess what regulations need to be put in place. If enhancement technologies are regulated *today*, it is important to know what technologies will need to be reckoned with in the near future.

Thirdly, it is essential to have some idea of the social circumstances in which these future technologies will be used. This is a task that *social sciences* could contribute to. What do we know, for instance, about the motives of people who undergo plastic surgery? What can be observed empirically in terms of changes in social circumstances? What are the experiences in other countries? It is not only important to generate empirical data, but also to interpret these data sociologically. Why are certain needs relevant for people? Which cultural horizons play a role in that?

Fourthly, with regard to the legal aspects it is essential to apprehend the possibilities for regulation with respect to these technologies at large. In addition, fifthly and sixthly, there are questions in the domain of medicine, as well as philosophical questions; in these cases questions concerning the concept of human nature (see Chapter 3). Finally, because bioethics, like ethics in general, is a normative discipline, bioethical questions are always accompanied by *moral normative statements* – assessments of the question whether any given contact with the possibilities made available by the life sciences is morally good or bad. In that respect, *philosophical ethics* is required as a discipline which considers the fundamentals and principles of moral judgments.

The questions I have distinguished here are considerably diverse in nature. A large number of them are *descriptive questions*, that is, questions about what is the case. Other questions are prognostic in nature – they aim to make predictions concerning future developments. However, what bioethics itself is concerned with is neither what *is* the case nor what *will be* the case, but rather *how* we are to act. In that respect, bioethics is not a *descriptive*, but a *prescriptive* discipline. At its core, bioethics is about the question of the morally right way to deal with possibilities offered by biology and medical science (and a more precise delineation of the domain will be discussed below in this chapter). With respect to enhancement technologies, the question would thus be whether it is morally defensible to develop and offer these technologies. In order to answer this question, however, every one of the questions outlined above is relevant. That is to say, to answer the normative question one needs to discuss a number of descriptive aspects. It is impossible to discuss the moral permissibility of enhancement technologies without knowing what they involve and in which direction they will likely develop.

Moreover, one must know how these technologies can be regulated and how they influence society, relations between people and the human self-image.

My proposal is to consider the judgments developed in the context of bioethics as *mixed judgments*. This proposal is not a new one. Its roots can perhaps be discerned in Aristotle's practical syllogisms, but that is not of further relevance here. The proposal means, in our case, that the *most important bioethical question*, the *normative moral question*, is: is developing and offering enhancement technologies morally defensible? The judgment concerning this moral question, then, is: offering enhancement technologies is morally defensible, not defensible or only defensible under certain circumstances. This judgment, however, is based on a series of *partial answers* to descriptive and prognostic questions. The reasoning underlying such judgment could – very schematically – look something like the following: (1) We know what can be done with enhancement technologies, and the effects of these known possibilities can be identified. There is (2) no evidence that the near future will see implementations of these technologies that are entirely different in nature. We can (3) establish that these technologies can be legally regulated and (4) it is not evident that these technologies lead to fundamental social change or that they have a negative impact on those who remain uninvolved. (5) On the basis of a normative theory that states that we are to ensure and protect as large a scope for human freedom as possible, the conclusion could be that offering enhancement technologies is morally acceptable.

As indicated, this line of argument has only illustrative meaning, and I take it that I do not have to point out explicitly that it is not an expression of my own moral judgment. Also, it would be easy to add further perspectives to the ones noted. What is important for the *theory of mixed judgments* is that the cogency of the argumentative stages 1–5 is justified by very diverse disciplines. Stage (1) is a question for scientists. Whether or not we are in fact able to establish the effects of technologies is not dependent on the question whether the normative theory of stage (5) is right in stating that we should protect as large a scope for human freedom as possible. Disagreements regarding the moral judgment could also be based on the fact that one does not agree on one of the premises. Party A could be of the opinion that the normative theory (5) is valid, but that the assessment of the state of affairs on the research front (1) and legal regulability (3) is flawed. B, on the other hand, might think that the judgments in (1–4) are correct, but does not share the moral normative theory in (5). Proponents of the same moral theory can thus come to completely different conclusions in this particular matter, and likewise it is possible for people to agree on the assessment of the relevant practical facts, but to diverge with respect to the criteria for moral judgment.

The term *mixed judgments* also indicates that the justification of these judgments takes place in different disciplines and discourses. Perhaps the explanations sound trivial. The possibilities for mutual understanding would, however, be greatly improved if this fundamental notion of interdisciplinarity were common ground. Four possible misunderstandings must be pointed out briefly before proceeding.

1. For the *praxis of interdisciplinary discourse*, it is important to understand that all that has happened so far is the identification of different questions and the competencies for answering them inherent in different disciplines. Nothing is said or implied about the appropriate method for the interdisciplinary conversation. As a rule, it is not very productive for a philosopher merely to be told by physicians what the current technical possibilities are. It is often necessary to have at least a rough idea of the functioning and theoretical presuppositions of the other discipline if the meaning of this information is to be assessed and discussed critically.
2. The differentiation of mixed judgments does not imply any assumptions about the *relation between facts and values*. It is not a presupposition that the establishment of facts can be value-free. Rather, it is the task of ethical discourse to problematise such presuppositions. In the same vein it must not be presupposed that values exist independently of the social world, that there is a dualism of mind and body, or anything of the sort. However, it is understood that a correct description of *what is the case* and the judgment that we *ought to do* something are two different things.
3. Despite the fact that several different subquestions have been identified and the necessity of interdisciplinarity has been emphasised, bioethics gives *methodological priority to normative ethics* over all other disciplines. For the decision which empirical and prognostic questions are to be investigated is dependent on the judgments of normative ethics. If one, for instance, defends a moral position according to which the physical appearance of people may not be technically altered (for example on religious grounds), most of the aforementioned empirical questions are simply irrelevant. From an extremely libertarian point of view, on the other hand, in which restraints to personal freedom are only held to be legitimate if they directly infringe upon fundamental rights to freedom of others, perhaps a sociological investigation of cultural and societal consequences of enhancement technologies would not be relevant in the first place. From such a point of view, risk assessment would probably suffice. Normative ethics thus determines in bioethics which further questions are relevant in the first place, and how urgent they are.
4. Lastly, one could feel that such an impressive list of relevant questions hopelessly overburdens bioethics. One can never hope to find an answer to all questions, which means that there are some urgent moral questions that will never be resolved. This complex problem will return later in this book (see in particular Chapter 3). For the moment it will suffice to emphasise that the fact that we know very little about the effects of many technologies can in fact be a moral ground to view their application as morally impermissible or as permissible only under special circumstances. In cases where the answer to individual empirical

questions is particularly important for a certain moral question, this would be a reason to call for research of these aspects on moral grounds.

Whatever the circumstances may be, any judgment in the domain of bioethics involves moral-philosophical presuppositions. It is impossible to conceive of a moral judgment regarding developments in the life sciences or the practice of biomedicine in which no morally contestable assumptions are made. It is, therefore, simply no option not to consider the validity of these assumptions. This is why Chapter 2 of this book discusses the moral-philosophical aspects of bioethics so elaborately. In addition, almost all domains of bioethics involve presumptions about philosophically complex concepts such as 'life', 'nature', 'humans', 'society', the meaning of 'gender' or 'technology'. The conceptual side of bioethics will be discussed in Chapter 3. Only after this, in Chapter 4, shall we come to concrete areas of bioethical discussion. First of all, however, this introduction should discuss the *scientific developments* on which bioethics reflects, provide a brief introduction to the *history of bioethics* and present some of the *possible definitions of the notion of 'bioethics'*.

1.2 Biosciences – biomedicine – bioethics

Even if bioethics does *not merely* act as a science, bioethical discussions in the public realm do make a claim on participants' reflective competencies. It is up to academic bioethics to develop and foster these competencies. This task is not easy, since within ethics (or moral philosophy) we are already confronted with multifarious theoretical concepts, to which the necessary interdisciplinarity of bioethics constitutes an enormous additional challenge. This challenge is connected with developments in the life sciences and with the corresponding political and public reactions. Therefore, it will be necessary briefly to address these developments, which are internally connected to the emergence of bioethics. The point of this exercise is not to provide an overview of scientific developments in a narrow sense – as a philosopher, I lack the knowledge such a task would require. Rather, the goal is to identify the challenges these developments pose for bioethics.

In the debates on brain stem death alluded to above, the established doctors' ethos appeared to have hit a boundary. Apparently, people still took this ethos to offer sufficient moral orientation, and supposed that it simply had not anticipated certain situations. After the Second World War, a different debate was of drastic importance for bio- and medical ethics. In the aftermath of the Nuremberg Doctors' Trial, which brought home the possibility that medical research can assume an inhuman character, people started to ask the question what the general conditions for morally acceptable experiments on humans might be. This debate ran parallel to the development of the universal and European declarations of human rights, and to a new estimation of the rights of individuals. Consequently, this led to a reorientation of medical ethics. Medical acts are no longer solely legitimised by the physician's duty to cure, as was the dominant understanding in the Hippocratic tradition. Rather, medical acts nowadays are legitimised explicitly by the patient (or, in the case of medical experiments on humans, by the test subject). The World Medical Association expressed this paradigm shift in its declarations of Helsinki (1964) and Tokyo (1975) by stating that the legitimacy of medical acts is made dependent upon the 'free and informed consent' of the persons concerned (on informed consent see Faden and Beauchamp 1986; O'Neill 2002; Beyleveld and Brownsword 2006; Manson and O'Neill 2007).

This paradigm shift has been important for bioethics in a number of respects. On the one hand, almost all *bioethics declarations* emphasise the normative validity of informed consent (see for instance the UNESCO declaration: UNESCO 2006). Academic bioethical literature, on the other hand, is characterised by a significant concentration on questions surrounding informed consent. Researchers carry out *conceptual differentiation* and formulate *conditions* regarding when consent can truly count as *free* and *informed* (see Chapter 4). Some of the demands thus formulated are that medical information is to be conveyed comprehensively, that physicians are not allowed to misrepresent important information, that risks and alternative treatment options must be mentioned, and that information about the patient needs to be communicated in a way that is understandable for laypersons. In the previous decades a large number of empirical studies have investigated how consent is granted in practice, and to what extent this practice accords to the demands on informed consent (see e.g. Molewijk et al. 2004).

The emphasis on informed consent is not merely a detail in the transformation of the medical practice. The issue signifies a fundamental change of direction in the entire medical and bioethical debate. It has become a central question in bioethics of how to deal with patients who are unable to grant such informed consent, for instance because they do not have the mental capacities required to comprehend the relevant medical information. Furthermore, the fact that the Helsinki/Tokyo declarations on informed consent are professionally binding has contributed significantly to the fact that nowadays it is a worldwide requirement for 'ethics committees' to appraise any medical experiment on humans.

Moreover, many documents single out informed consent as the most important concretisation of notions such as human dignity, autonomy and individual rights. The protection of autonomy, for instance, is concretised almost universally by way of protecting informed consent. With regard to the protection of human dignity and human rights it is generally accepted that these involve more than the individual's freedom of decision-making; another common demand is that every person should have access to medical care. However, it can certainly be observed that the bioethical literature is dominated by the idea that the protection of autonomy and human dignity is to be secured by protecting informed consent.

The transition from a paternalistic medical ethos to a paradigm of informed consent was a radical one. Yet all the same, the increased focus on informed consent and patient autonomy constitutes a reduction of morally relevant viewpoints. For both paternalism and patient autonomy remain to a large extent geared towards the existing state of medical practice. They do not even touch upon questions concerning which technologies are to be provided, which therapies should be offered, and what should be the basic research paradigms. By contrast, the decisive developments on which bioethics is to reflect are influenced by developments in scientific research and the technologies resulting from such research. Therefore, bioethical discussions do not merely pertain to the protection of individual rights with regard to already existing medical practices. They also concern developments in a domain that greatly influences medical practice at large: the life sciences.

The development of the life sciences was intended, from the very start, to have a revolutionary impact on medical practice. The initial underlying thought was that medical science had always essentially been symptom control, acting to a large extent reactively, predominantly relying on experiential knowledge which is at best statistically verifiable. Medical science was hardly capable of establishing the causes of diseases, since the corresponding causal relations were unknown. It was hoped that the gene technologies that were being developed would be able to generate fundamental changes in this respect. If only the genetic causes of diseases were known, prevention, diagnosis and therapy of an entirely different kind would be in reach. In the 1960s and 1970s, the expectations regarding the significance of gene technology were through the roof. It was expected that the foreseeable future would bring the deciphering of the human genome, and consequently access to the causes of disease. This expectation was shared among proponents and critics of the development alike. While the former assumed that this would result in the ultimate instrument towards the elimination of many diseases, the latter saw the danger of ultimate control over the human body. Nonetheless, the two standpoints did not differ in terms of the *estimation* of which development was to be expected, but solely with regard to the *assessment* of this expectation.

In the meantime the human genome has been sequenced, but expectations have radically changed – or at least this can be observed academically; scientific-political rhetoric has not been affected to the same extent. First of all, the notion of *genetic determinism* was radically mitigated (Neumann-Held and Rehmann-Sutter 2006). 'Genetic determinism' denotes the idea that there is a causal connection between genotype (the genetic information of an organism) and phenotype (the observable features of an organism) that is unambiguously determined and can in principle be understood. Genes determine what happens in the human body. Once the location and function of genes is known, then, bodily phenomena can be predicted with confidence and, by intervention on the genetic level, also changed. In the domain of gene diagnostics rapid results were expected. Gene therapy was considered to be a long-term possibility.

The developments in molecular genetics and the refinement of diagnostic devices have indeed opened up a wide range of gene diagnostics. So far, the possibilities are limited to a handful of disease patterns that are unequivocally connected to specific genetic anomalies. As a rule, these diseases can be accounted for monogenetically; that is, they are associated with the mutation of a single gene. The vast majority of diseases, however, are induced by complex interactions between gene constellations and environmental factors. The result of this correction of the idea of genetic determinism is that the significance of gene technology is not in the first place located in unequivocal prediction and control of genetic causality. Rather, one could make probability statements regarding phenotypic phenomena on the basis of certain gene constellations. For physicians it has become a difficult hermeneutic task to inform their patients about what these gene constellations mean with respect to their lives. Since diseases often only manifest in the course of a life and since their emergence is not certain, diagnostic findings can remain inconclusive or ambivalent.

As a result of molecular-biological technology, the last few years have seen the rise of a complex of techniques that are discussed under the header *genomics*. Behind this term are developments in medicine and pharmaceutics that base therapeutic (mostly pharmaceutical) treatment – but also prevention and diet – on knowledge of genetic correlations. All of these therapeutic possibilities are subject to highly complex cause-and-effect relations. Relevant to our understanding of these relations are not merely developments in molecular human genetics, but also developments in information technology and in the nonhuman domains of the biological sciences. Detailed knowledge of molecular genetic correlations, information-technical ways of handling these complexities, and pharmaceutical and biological insights can therefore provide individually targeted pharmaceutical offerings and therapeutic dietary advice. The range of applications thus clearly goes beyond the medical domain, and could have far-reaching effects on several areas of life (food production, individual lifestyle).

I shall return to specific discussions of gene diagnostics and therapy in Chapter 4. At this point, the relevant question is whether the discussed paradigm shift in medical ethics is sufficiently prepared for these discussions. Bioethics can no longer restrict itself to the question how patient autonomy with regard to available treatment options can be protected from the paternalism of physicians. Rather, it will have to develop a moral assessment of the very existence and expansion of such treatment options. While the array of conflicting moral positions on early diagnosis is still relatively uncomplicated, the complexity of standpoints in more recent genomics discussions has become increasingly unmanageable. After the *conception of genetic determinism was dismissed*, a very different challenge emerged: the problem that the explanatory power of genetic information is becoming ever more uncertain. Statements regarding genetic information are generally probabilistic – they say something about genetic dispositions to diseases and the probability of their occurrence. For that reason, the accruing treatment options are often not transparent to anyone, including the patient. This makes the interpretation of genetic information a particularly important challenge. Making genetic information meaningful to the patient's everyday life is a challenging hermeneutic task. In the domain of *gene therapy*, the complexity of genetic correlations leads furthermore to the complication that the effects of genetic interventions can for the most part be predicted only with limited certainty. A targeted control of these interventions would, however, presume a transparency of the whole of relevant cause-and-effect relations. For many operations such a transparency would be rather unlikely.

The complexity of genetic information, the diversity of possible courses of action and the discrepancy between biological information and everyday experience constitute an often underestimated challenge for ethical evaluation. Some older discussions still presuppose clarity of the medical meaning of genetic information. Peter Sloterdijk's 'Rules for the human zoo' (Sloterdijk 1999/2009), for instance, assumes that the problem of human genetics comes out in the selective breeding of people with specific characteristics. The problem of justification would pose itself merely as the task of taking up this possibility responsibly. In other words, we should hope that the human zoo be managed by responsible zoo staff. This presumes that the moral problem is the result of the successful realisation of possible control over the genetic basis of the human body. Having abandoned the idea of genetic determinism, this scenario is rather improbable. The more central challenge seems to lie in the fact that an unequivocal prediction of the relation between the genetic and the phenotypic level is only possible to a limited extent. The question, then, is how to deal with the ambiguities and uncertainties of genetic knowledge in a morally responsible way.

However, the project concerned with the deciphering of the human genome is only one of many projects in the life sciences. A further project, which has caused extensive discussions in bioethics since the 1970s, concerns emerging techniques in *reproductive medicine* (see Chapter 4), especially artificial impregnation in a test tube or in vitro fertilisation (IVF). When in 1978 the first baby conceived with the aid of this technology was born, the legal liberalisation of abortion had in most Western countries only just begun or indeed not even yet occurred. In that respect, the IVF discussion was largely overshadowed by the debate concerning the moral status of embryos and foetuses in the context of pregnancy termination. At present the IVF debate is still significant, but over the last three decades there has also been much discussion of many rather concrete points regarding the application of IVF. On the one hand, IVF technology makes it possible for countless couples to realise their desire for children, and the initial reluctance with respect to the mechanisation and resultant 'artificiality' of reproduction has ceased to be an urgent subject. On the other hand, the meagre success rate of IVF (doctors still have to send large proportions of their patients home without a child), the physical and mental strain on the women involved, the high rate of multiple pregnancies and similar issues are still subject to ethical controversies. Because of its low success rate and high impact, the women concerned are still thoroughly ambivalent about the technique. With regard to the children conceived via IVF, the debate on risks associated with multiple pregnancies and increased mortality is still ongoing. In the 1990s the most important subject of discussion was the possibility of combining artificial impregnation and genetic diagnosis and selection; so-called preimplantation genetic diagnosis (PGD). This technology promises the possibility of carrying out prenatal diagnosis before the pregnancy starts, and thus of avoiding a possible decision to abort the pregnancy. Nevertheless, critics assert that the selective character of this technology is different from that of prenatal diagnosis (see Chapter 4).

However, no subject engrossed the public bioethics discussion in the last decade, however, as much as the possibility of *cloning*, particularly since the successful cloning of Dolly the sheep in 1996. Like to gene diagnostics and therapy, the morally disputable point was considered to lie in the possibility of identically reproducing humans. The moral problem was deemed to lie in the possibility of cloning another person as a replacement for a deceased child, or as a genetic duplicate of oneself. The moral problem would then be that the genetic structure of one person is designed according to the interests of another. According to Jürgen Habermas (2001/2003), this would lead to a form of dependence between generations that would threaten to undermine the basic conditions of a free societal and social order (for the details of this argument see Chapter 4). Relevant here is that Habermas deems the morally problematic aspects to be associated *only* with the successful production of an identical replica of a human being. In the debate on cloning, a difference is usually made between reproductive and therapeutic cloning. However, this difference is conceptually unfortunate, since hardly any therapeutic application is currently possible, and because the two operations are technically identical. Yet in terms of Habermas's reservations it seems more problematic that his description severely restricts the range of possible applications that require ethical discussion; even before we know which possible applications might appear on the horizon.

The last bioethical topic that will have to be surveyed briefly at this point is *organ transplantation* (see Chapter 4). Since the 1960s organ transplantation has become widely established. In the first instance, the initial debates focused on the status of and regulations regarding brain-dead patients. The most important problem was coming up with legally acceptable regulations (Is the patient's explicit advance directive required? Or does approval by relatives suffice? May the absence of a living will be considered implicit consent?). In the meantime, however, other ethical questions have emerged. Criteria for the *allocation of available organs* are discussed, as is the moral defensibility of live organ donation. Beyond these questions, however, the discussion focuses mostly on the possibilities for alternative ways of obtaining organs, either by recourse to animal organs (xenotransplantation) or through organ *production* from embryonic stem cells. Not infrequently, however, it is also asked how organ transplantation influences the tasks of medicine and the corresponding expectations of patients. For instance, people use the catchword 'repair medicine' to refer to these operations. Furthermore, it has become a question whether there might be a subtle tendency towards people considering themselves to have a 'right' to other persons' organs.

This cursory glance at the life sciences shows the entire domain to be very dynamic, even without taking into account the developments in animal biotechnology, in the domains of crops and food or in neurobiology. By now it is evident that debates regarding developments in the life sciences are becoming increasingly interrelated. While in, say, the 1980s human genetics, organ transplantation and reproductive medicine were discussed mostly independent of each other, new debates on PGD and embryonic stem cells show that there are numerous connections, and that these are important for the ethical side of the debate as well. Likewise, it is clear that developments in other areas will be highly significant for the dynamics of the life sciences. Since gene technology requires the handling of extremely large amounts of data, *information technology* is one of the obvious examples. For researchers, access to large amounts of genetic information of large parts of the population would be very attractive (see Chapter 4). However, the question arises how the existence of such DNA databases can be combined with successful protection of individual privacy. Practically, implementation of informed consent is all but impossible in this case. The emerging practice of *nanotechnology* offers another reason to believe that the life sciences will see an increase in potential implementations.

The developments in the life sciences are accompanied by numerous public, legal and ethical discussions. In the first instance, people are generally sceptically disposed towards these developments, and show considerable ambivalence in their attitudes. Initially the public sphere was dominated by sweeping pledges of hope and horror scenarios. Certainly, it is always difficult for the uninitiated to have a sense of what is at stake in these debates in the first place. Most people find it very hard to picture a gene, and the question whether a fertilised egg in the four-cell stage should be said to have human dignity is a question which to most people simply does not mean anything at all (which as a fact does not yet say anything about the problem of the ascription of human dignity). Many scientists and physicians consider the central difficulty to lie in informing the public about the technical details of their research. What is often overlooked, however, is that the relevant questions are not in the first place technical, but questions of valuation – a matter in which scientists are not specifically equipped to contribute.

In the political domain, these discussions have involved complications that are not insignificant. For one thing, legal systems are sometimes not capable of dealing with the developments at hand. Moreover, bioethical questions are highly ideologically sensitive. Churches, feminists, animal activists, the doctors' lobby, the pharmaceutical industry, disability rights advocates, patient organisations and other groups are easily enraged by these issues. At the same time, the international competition pressure on research institutes is enormous. Economic and social pressure is significant and, in addition, the field is very tense. These facts surely contribute to the large number of committees, counsels and other advisory bodies.

Yet even beyond politically strategic considerations, politicians are baffled by many of these developments as much as their electorate is. What attitude should one have towards the production of embryonic stem cells? What to think of the possibility of diagnosing an embryo's gene that increases the chance that the future person will at some point fall ill with breast cancer? Most people do not have clear moral intuitions with respect to these questions. There is no long tradition in the history of ethics to turn to for guidance. The history of moral rules of conduct is, for all the differences in concrete guidelines, relatively constant with respect to the question which kinds of conduct are to be morally regulated. Traditional morality is about prohibitions of killing or deceiving, guidance on leading one's personal life, regulations concerning sexuality, etc. Dealing with technology or responsibility for scientific developments has never been a central theme of ethical thinking. These days we are faced with the moral appraisal of new technologies that radically change our lives, and that will decisively influence the lives of future generations as well. Of course, technological innovations have always been associated with promises of salvation and expectations of doom. Currently, however, we are part of a process that will be very long, that involves very fundamental technical change and that has decisive implications for a large variety of factors shaping everyday reality. In many respects, this process can be influenced from within. The developmental potential of the life sciences is frankly not completely unpredictable; if it was, there would be no grounds at all to pursue certain technological possibilities and give up on others.

We are thus forced to make moral assessments without knowing exactly how the corresponding technologies will develop, which risks they will entail and how they will influence our lives and the lives of future generations. However, as a rule we find it easier to formulate moral judgments in relation to clear-cut acts: punching an innocent person is morally bad; helping an elderly lady across the street is morally good. Naturally, moral casuistry also involves more complex situations and comparative judgments: punching a person is morally good if he is about to commit a murder. Not only helping an elderly lady across the street, but also carrying her groceries home is morally even better – unless there are more pressing moral needs one could help with, etc. Such forms of moral judgments do, however, show that these judgments basically concern actions of which we more or less know the consequences or effects – or at least we think we do. In the political domain, things are no different: genocide in Rwanda is bad, supporting a dictator is at least dubious, and so on.

The developments in the life sciences, by contrast, are such that in many respects we can hardly oversee their consequences. We frequently have to adjust our expectations. Applications of different technologies often have very different implications. Moreover, these technologies are implemented in very diverse cultural contexts. However, researchers have only recently began to investigate how cultural background influences perception, action and judgment in a (bio)medical context. It is altogether unclear, for instance, what the explanatory value of the notion of a gene is in the context of African conceptions of the human body. Similar considerations hold for numerous Asian societies, in which the individual is understood first and foremost in terms of family relations (Becker 2008). Not only is the perception of biomedicine affected by these insights, but also the idea of moral protection. This is, for instance, clear from the central position of patient autonomy in Western medical ethics. Facilitating a patient's free decision is either considered a normative argument in favour of the development of certain technologies (people are to be provided with the possibility to decide to have a child, or for it to be 'healthy') or, on the other hand, as a central form of protection (patients are to be asked for their permission before they are subjected to medical procedures). If, however, in Asian communities family relations are considered central, individual autonomous decision will be valued differently. The role of autonomy in the legitimation of medical conduct and as a stronghold of moral protection will then change accordingly. At least one could wonder whether the concept of informed consent might be a Western concept, and what its role in non-Western societies could be. If biomedical techniques are employed globally, the discussion of the moral legitimacy of these techniques will have to accommodate these diverse contexts as well.

These cursory remarks have indicated the range of problems of contemporary bioethics. Bioethics deals with the moral legitimation of questions that are essentially connected to life. The development and application of new technologies in the domain of the life sciences are central; not the application of technologies in well-defined situations. On the contrary: bioethics is faced with the difficulty that its subject matter involves the development of technologies of which the potential long-term applications, including all of their (physical, psychological and social) implications, are not readily foreseeable, and which will be introduced in a large variety of cultural contexts. Moreover, bioethics is faced with the challenge of providing moral legitimation against a backdrop of moral pluralism. Many of these new technologies confront us with possibilities that have not been validated by long moral or legal traditions, and about which we usually do not even have shared intuitions. It is clear that bioethics, if it is to accommodate this situation, will have to make specific academic efforts in order to reach justifiable answers to the question of moral legitimation.

1.3 Bioethics – history and concept

As pointed out above, since the 1960s bioethics has been institutionalised in the form of ethics committees. Nevertheless, the notion itself owes its establishment to the formation of research institutions, in which bioethics was practised in an academic manner. Of those early institutions, two American ones were particularly important: the Institute for Society, Ethics and the Life Sciences, founded in 1969 and now known as the Hastings Center and, since 1971, the Joseph and Rose Kennedy Institute of Human Reproduction and Bioethics, now known as the Kennedy Institute of Ethics. (For a detailed history of bioethics see Jonsen 1998.) The notion of 'bioethics' appeared in the name of the Kennedy Institute as an abbreviation of 'biomedical ethics'. Parallel to that use, the notion was used by the oncologist Van Rensselaer Potter in the title of his 1971 monograph. Potter's book entitled *Bioethics – Bridge to the Future* refers to a sort of ethics of the future; a moral system that is designed with the aim to secure the long-term survival of the human species. (On the history of the concept of bioethics see Reich 1995.)

Since then, bioethical research expanded so quickly that no later than 1978 an *Encyclopedia of Bioethics* could be published (reissued in 1995 and 2004 in fully revised versions). The subsequent years saw the publication of a series of books that would become important reference points for bioethical discussion: Peter Singer's *Practical Ethics* (1979), Hans Jonas's *Das Prinzip Verantwortung* (1979, in English: *The Imperative of Responsibility* 1984) and, also in 1979, the first edition of the *Principles of Biomedical Ethics* by Tom Beauchamp and James F. Childress. In 1986 the first edition of *The Foundations of Bioethics* by H. Tristram Engelhardt, and in 1988 Albert Jonsen and Stephen Toulmin published their *The Abuse of Casuistry*. From the mid-1980s onwards the bioethical debate also established itself in Europe, mostly because of the formation of political advisory bodies and research institutions devoted to ethics (for instance in Copenhagen, Maastricht, Tübingen and Utrecht). Before long, courses and doctorates emerged that offered academic degrees in bioethics.

Alongside the increasing establishment of bioethics came the expansion of institutionalisations, methodological standards and issues under discussion. Since the notion of bioethics will be important for the rest of the book, it will be necessary to explore the meaning of this term, even if quite briefly. Part of what is to be determined are *merely terminological issues* that are of no systematic relevance. Whether one chooses to use 'bioethics' as a broad term to refer to medical, animal and environmental ethics, or as a narrow term that is restricted to medical ethics and concerns environmental and animal ethics as independent ethical domains is, to an extent, nothing but a question of labelling. Nevertheless, the description of the domain of bioethics does to some extent imply *theoretically relevant predispositions*. A field such as bioethics can be expected to reflect explicitly on these predispositions. In a sense, therefore, what is at stake is at the same time the delimitation of the respective domains of these different bioethical discussions.

I shall sketch the problems of delimitation in three cases. These are:

1. Bioethics as an academic discipline
2. The concept of ethics
3. The domain of application

1.3.1 Bioethics as an academic discipline

On the one hand, the term 'bioethics' is used to indicate the discourse on moral, legal, social and political issues concerning fundamental questions of life and the life sciences. In this sense, 'bioethics' is an overarching term for certain debates in the media, politics and science. Yet 'bioethics' is also used to refer to a particular academic discipline in which journals are published, degrees awarded, doctoral dissertations written and professorships endowed. Now there are other domains as well – medicine, for instance – in which a term is used to refer to an academic discipline and a certain practice at the same time. And to be sure, the academic side of medicine does at times provide occasion for controversy. Yet in the case of bioethics it is still a question of whether it can be considered an academic discipline in the first place, or whether it merely denotes a certain subject of public discourse. This question even precedes the question of what exactly defines this discipline and where it is to be located. The same question applies mutatis mutandis to other domains of applied ethics – ethics of technology, medical ethics, ethics of science, or whichever terms one chooses to use.

The consequences of this question are very extensive. It is, for instance, pertinent to the legitimation of the establishment of professorships, master's degrees and doctorates in bioethics (or in any other domain of applied ethics) (Rasmussen 2005). Similarly it affects the legitimation of ethical advisory activities in the political domain. It can be justified that academic degrees in bioethics are awarded and that specialists in the subject provide advice to politicians only if bioethics presents itself as having particular academic validity. If the legitimacy of the role of bioethics as an academic activity and as expertise in the public realm depends on a defence of bioethics as an academic discipline, then intellectual honesty requires bioethicists to reflect on this academic self-conception in a scholarly way, and to fashion their academic and public appearance accordingly. In any case it seems hardly acceptable that a bioethicist would proclaim his personal ideological convictions in the guise of a bioethicist.

Now this is a problem that characterises the whole of bioethics – a problem that is pertinent even beyond the specific role of bioethicists. In bioethical debates, moral normative judgments are expressed. This means that the different parties take a stand with regard to the moral quality of certain acts, attitudes, institutions, etc. Without this, there could not even be ethical discussions. However, the bioethicist is not the only person to raise moral claims. Physicians, jurists and sociologists formulate claims and moral judgments in the discourse as well: they consider patient autonomy good, euthanasia bad, abortion legitimate, informed consent important, civic participation desirable, etc. It is almost impossible to imagine a bioethical discussion in which none of this would occur. Therefore, the bioethicist is not the only one who has a burden to justify in the name of which authority he presents his moral judgments. If a sociologist endorses civic participation, or a doctor patient autonomy, the very same questions of legitimation arise. The physician or sociologist is equally responsible for the legitimation of any normative position she defends when acting as an academic or scientist. Nonetheless, ethics is the discipline which, as a profession, questions, considers and grounds the preconditions and assumptions of moral judgments. In that respect, it is bioethics which has the responsibility of making these assumptions explicit and verifying whether they can be justified. Therefore it is reasonable to expect of a bioethicist that he will take particular care in reflecting on his own moral statements, and that he will publicly state only those beliefs which he is able to justify philosophically. It is an embarrassing experience to hear a philosopher defend the claim that moral standpoints are always relative to one's culture, yet at the same time demand universal respect for the autonomy of the individual. In any case, a professional bioethicist will not be able to avoid granting that bioethics is an academic (sub)discipline. Otherwise it would not be clear in virtue of which authority he spoke at all.

However, despite all reflexivity, a certain tension remains between the academic side of bioethics and the public and political expectations. After all, the questions at hand are matters that rightfully agitate the public, and on which people would like to see clear-cut positions being taken. Academic respectability and critical modesty are not always compatible with these expectations. This warning is, of course, meant neither a plea for the ivory tower nor a praise of linguistic inaccessibility. Rather, it constitutes an attempt to determine the role of my own discipline in an academically appropriate way.

1.3.2 The concept of ethics

If it can be agreed that bioethics has a role as an academic (sub)discipline, or at least that it has particular academic validity, a question that immediately presents itself is how this discipline relates to other domains of academic 'ethics'. The issue is not yet whether one's bioethical position is informed by preference utilitarianism, Christianity, contractualism, etc. Rather, we first need to answer the more basic question of where to place bioethics within the field of ethics at large. A related discussion deals with the question of whether bioethics is a 'special' ethical approach or not. Early on in the discussion on bioethics, there was a tendency to think that 'bioethics' denotes a *specific substantive moral belief*, one that was frequently attributed to Peter Singer. And many 'liberal' bioethicists have attempted to suggest that bioethics is bound to a particular ethos, for instance of informed consent or patient autonomy. To put their point succinctly: while the Catholic church protects (unborn) life, bioethicists protect a patient's space for autonomous decision. Others have proposed that bioethics should formulate normative judgments on the basis of the established 'doctors' ethos' or that it should base itself on 'shared moral beliefs'. Against the 'doctors' ethos' one could, for a start, argue that bioethics concerns itself mostly with questions that relate not only to the conduct of physicians, but to the ways in which new technologies are regulated in society; an issue for which the doctors' ethos is not directly relevant. Moreover, bioethics usually deals with moral questions, for which the 'doctors' ethos' has equally few transparent judgments to offer as our 'common morals'. The proposal to understand bioethics as an ethics of responsibility for the future, which was made early on by Van Rensselaer Potter (1971) would be another example of an account in which the domain of bioethics is determined by a specific substantive moral belief.

It seems problematic to me to defend the idea that bioethics is an academic discipline and, *at the same time*, to think that everyone working in this discipline should share a conception of ethics or certain moral beliefs (a doctors' ethos, a common morality, a religious or a liberal ethic). The latter could only be defended if the relevant beliefs were uncontroversial; but then a large portion of the questions that bioethics intends to consider would already have been answered. My plea does not aim to obligate the bioethicist to be morally neutral (which seems fundamentally impossible). Quite the contrary: I believe that it can be expected of a bioethicist that she will express normative judgments and that she will defend these. This should, however, happen *as part of* the discipline of bioethics, and not in the constitution of this discipline. That is to say, bioethics should be a domain that is constituted by the pursuit of sound defences of moral judgments. This is also the reason that it is not a valid criticism of bioethics to object that representatives from different disciplines are in disagreement. On the contrary: if they did agree, there would be few reasons to pursue the discipline any further. At the same time, however, it can be expected of a bioethicist that he will not merely express opinions about some biopolitical issue that he may have as a citizen, yet with the authority of an academic. Every bioethicist will therefore have to be able to show that the standpoints he takes are open to academic scrutiny. Of course, this issue is very directly connected with fundamental questions in the philosophy of science. For if one advances an empiricist or positivist view, according to which only empirically verifiable (or at least falsifiable) statements can claim to be scientific, things do not look very good for ethics. However, moral philosophy is able to offer alternatives to such empiricist or positivist perspectives, as will be discussed in the next chapter.

Whichever standpoint in the philosophy of science or moral philosophy one adheres to, it will not be possible to imagine a form of bioethics that does not, with respect to its normative fundaments, clearly situate itself in the range of moral-philosophical perspectives. There are no normative claims concerning bioethical questions that are not made on the basis of certain philosophical standpoints. These moral-philosophical suppositions can be made explicit and examined, or they can be blindly presupposed. Since ethics is traditionally the very discipline that reflects on the fundamentals of moral judgments deliberately and critically, we may also expect bioethics to reflect on its own moral-philosophical presuppositions. That does mean, however, that any academic form of bioethics can only be conceived in relation to philosophical discussion. Because of the 'mixed judgments' introduced above, bioethics will not *merely* be moral philosophy and its application, but will draw on insights generated by other disciplines as well. Nonetheless, whenever bioethicists issue moral judgments they will have to appropriate the philosophical foundations of those judgments. And this is no less true when bioethics is not based in philosophy departments, but incorporated within medicine or law. The status of bioethics as an academic discipline can only be determined by philosophical ethics in general, even if bioethics, because of its interdisciplinary character, is not reducible to any particular subject. That is the reason why the next chapter discusses moral philosophy so elaborately.

1.3.3 The domain of application

The expansion of the range of topics of bioethics and the expansion of applied ethics in general have made it increasingly difficult to identify the precise subject area of bioethics. Initially, bioethics was basically an abbreviation of 'biomedical ethics' (Reich 1995). Meanwhile, however, questions of justice in the health care system or animal ethics are being discussed under the heading of 'bioethics' as well. In addition, subject-specific discourses have established themselves in areas that overlap with bioethics: 'ethics of technology' for instance. Now it seems rather unhelpful to me to strive for some sort of terminological purism in this area, primarily because the domain of applied ethics simply does not lend itself to segmentation very well. This is true both for the methodology of the discipline and for the knowledge it strives to generate. When considering the issue of, say, preimplantation diagnosis, no difference is made between considering the relevant questions from the perspective of medical ethics, bioethics or ethics of technology. Moreover, it should be noted that terminological divisions within bioethics are frequently motivated by the politics of funding allocation. Yet all the same it will be helpful to seek terminology that is at least somewhat transparent.

All in all, I understand each one of these ethical subdomains (or 'ethics of ...') as part of *applied ethics*. The latter differs from metaethics and normative ethics, which reflect on questions concerning the fundamentals of ethics (and are, therefore, occasionally referred to as 'fundamental ethics'). Parts of applied ethics, then, are all discourses in which ethical reflection is applied to concrete practical moral questions. However, within applied ethics, bioethics can mean different things. I shall consider four different possibilities:

1. *Bioethics as medical ethics.* Bioethics is understood as a reflection on those changes in medicine that are the result of developments in the biomedical sciences. This way of understanding bioethics brackets the role played by discussions of nonhuman subjects from the discourse of bioethics. Moreover, all rather traditional discussions (such as those concerning the doctor-patient relationship) are excluded. This is possible, but does not

seem very sensible, given the factucal meaning of these debates in the current bioethical discussion.

2. *Bioethics as an overarching term for medical, animal and environmental ethics (including public health ethics and food ethics).* This exceptionally broad term encompasses all areas of applied ethics that are, in the broadest sense, concerned with intervention in the living world. Against this use of the term it can be argued that it makes the discipline very hard to delineate, and that the individual domains that it brings together have relatively little to do with each other. Moral questions regarding ecology and the treatment of newborn babies do not have much in common. Nevertheless, this use of the term seems to have become widespread.
3. *Bioethics as ethics of the life sciences.* Since the better part of bioethical problems is formulated in response to the dynamics of the life sciences, some authors consider reflection on the ethical aspects of the life sciences *the* central subject of bioethics. One could share the view that the debate on the life sciences is central in bioethics. Yet on the other hand, it seems that if bioethics were reduced to this topic, this would not do justice to the current debate.
4. *Bioethics as the ethics of dealing with the phenomena of life.* This conception is closest to the literal meaning of the notion of bioethics. It also offers a very good reflection of the range of themes that were initially central to the debate: bioethics was dealing with ethical questions 'of life and death' in particular with 'moral problems of abortion, artificial insemination, organ transplantation, brain death, and euthanasia' (Leist 1990). Considering more recent debates, however, it would seem misleading to restrict the bioethical discussion to these exact themes. Doing so would, for instance, exclude all issues related to human genetics. At the same time, an extension of bioethics to 'phenomena of life' would go too far, since such a formulation could easily be argued to include a subject such as war, which is quite clearly a matter of 'life and death'. Discussing wars under the heading of bioethics would, however, not make much sense.

Yet unlike the debates concerning the academic side of bioethics and the conception of ethics, which both are truly central questions in the self-conception of bioethics, I deem the question concerning the area of application first and foremost a pragmatic issue. The understanding of bioethics that has emerged historically began with central questions of bioethics and expanded as time went on. For that reason, I shall understand bioethics in the second sense – as an overarching term for medical, animal and environmental ethics. In this book, however, I am only able to discuss a much smaller number of specific discussions than usually play a role in the different domains. Issues such as clinical ethics and nursing ethics will not be touched on here. On the other hand, discussions about moral questions in relation to the life sciences will be particularly urgent. From a systematic perspective, however, it is problematic to understand bioethics exclusively as a reflection on the life sciences. For it is hardly possible for bioethics to pass moral judgment on the life sciences without reflecting somewhat elaborately on the practices that are changed and affected by those sciences. One cannot consider transgenic animals in an isolated way – that is, without keeping an eye on the practices of breeding, keeping and feeding livestock and of animal experiments. Yet it should be emphasised one last time: the question of the appropriate methodology is not connected to the question of whether one thinks, say, that the moral permissibility of biotechnology falls within the domain of the ethics of technology or rather of bioethics – as long as there is a shared understanding of how these notions are used.

In terms of the domain of application, the term 'bioethics' is, in any case, used as a hybrid of the conceptions outlined above. The main objective of this book is to take a methodological stand on the question of how bioethics should proceed. In view of this methodological objective, the areas of application that are discussed in Chapter 4 will be primarily relevant as exemplars.

2 Bioethics and moral philosophy

2.1 The tension between moral philosophy and bioethics

In the Preface to this book, three things should have become clear.

Firstly, bioethics reflects on the moral dimension of the way in which we deal with life and in particular on the consequences of the *life sciences* and *medical science*. This is a challenging task, especially since new technical possibilities generated by the life sciences have a great impact on the shape of *medicine*, *pharmaceutics*, *agriculture* and the *protection of the environment*, with possibly serious consequences for the economy, society and (international) politics. However, in many respects we are able to assess neither the technical possibilities nor their further consequences. The boundaries between bioethics and other ethical subdomains (environmental ethics, medical ethics, ethics of technology, etc.) are blurred.

Secondly, bioethics has *academic standing*. Issues of the life sciences are widely discussed in society, politics and the media. In the context of this biopolitical discourse, bioethics offers academic reflection on the validity of moral claims about issues regarding life and our ways of dealing with it. However, not only the academic institutionalisation of bioethics, but also the practice of bioethicists advising politicians is legitimate only if the bioethical claim to academic validity can be substantiated.

Thirdly, the questions of bioethics can only be answered in *interdisciplinary collaboration*. Methodologies from technology assessment and the social sciences, for instance, are needed in order to assess technological or social developments; juridical methods are required to identify the necessity for legal regulation and the possibilities for codes of conduct in the life sciences. It is a central task of bioethics to assess to what extent the possibilities opened up by the life sciences or corresponding developments are morally acceptable. With respect to this normative dimension, bioethics must employ normative theories that are developed as part of philosophical ethics. Yet moral judgments in bioethics are always *mixed judgments*, based on both descriptive and prescriptive assumptions. The interdisciplinarity of bioethics originates from the fact that these assumptions must be justified on the basis of the standards and methods of different academic disciplines.

It will therefore be vital for bioethics to understand what kinds of goals are pursued in the life sciences and what its developments mean for medicine, the economy and society. In doing so, bioethics must always draw on methods and insights of other disciplines. The special relation between bioethics and moral philosophy is based on the fact that bioethics makes *prescriptive claims*. It is the goal of bioethics to make explicit statements about the question of whether certain developments or acts are morally defensible. The normative dimension of bioethics is not predominantly characterised by the fact that it is a discipline in which normative moral problems are considered – this is true for the social sciences as well. However, in bioethics normative moral claims are made and justified; claims, that is, about the moral rightness of certain acts, the moral permissibility of the development of certain technologies, euthanasia, embryonic research, etc. The point in doing so is not to lay down doctrines. Nor should these judgments be simple answers, along the lines of 'Dolly yes, euthanasia no' (or vice versa). Most bioethical judgments will contain provisos and differentiating conditions. Normative judgments in the domain of bioethics therefore tend to be unlike moral judgments that occur in everyday morality. In everyday morality we say: it is immoral to kill an innocent person. Or: we have a moral duty to help starving people in Africa. Moral judgments in bioethics, on the other hand, are judgments that, so to speak, take place on a higher level of reflection: they reflect on the conditions of moral judgments with respect to the ways in which we take up possibilities facilitated by the life sciences. In order to elucidate the methodological process (once again), I shall repeat the individual elements of the formation of bioethical judgments in a very schematic manner using an example:

1. The *normative question* is: is it morally justifiable to develop and offer enhancement technologies?
2. This question aims at a *moral judgment*, which has the following structure: it is morally prohibited, necessary or permissible to develop or offer enhancement technologies. This judgment can be made with a plethora of reservations (that is, it is morally permissible if informed consent is guaranteed, or: it is permissible only if the development of this technology remains controllable, etc).
3. This judgment is a *mixed judgment*. That means that it is dependent on presuppositions that must be justified on the basis of a variety of disciplines. The first task at hand is therefore to clarify which *ancillary* judgments are required in order to arrive at the moral judgment.
4. These ancillary judgments of the moral judgment constitute *questions for research*. What can be done with the help of enhancement technologies? What will likely be possible in the future? What effects will the presence of these possibilities have on people's experience of physical and mental 'deficits'? On the basis of which moral perspective can it be resolved whether the development and provision of this technical possibility

are morally justifiable? The list of possible questions can of course be expanded.

5. The list of questions would have to be probed with respect to *completeness* and *relevance*. Have we captured all ancillary questions that must be answered in order to come to a moral judgment? Are there reasons to consider some questions as more important than others?
6. In order to proceed from these questions to judgments, a large variety of academic disciplines is relevant. Some judgments are *descriptive judgments* that can be advanced mostly by physicians, physicists and sociologists:
   - What kinds of things can currently be done with these technologies?
   - What objectives are supposed to be met with help of these technologies?
   - What alternative possibilities are there to meet these objectives?
   - What kinds of effects do these technologies have on people's experience of their bodies, on systems of social interaction and on the behaviour of those involved?
7. Some questions aim at *prognostic judgments*, with which physics and technology assessment might be able to help:
   - What further technologies can be expected for the future?
   - What are the likely consequences of the applications of these technologies?
   - How will these technologies affect our perception of our bodies, capabilities, etc?
   - How much can we know about possible future scenarios?
8. Some questions aim at descriptive judgments of regulations and regulability, with which jurists might be capable of helping out:
   - To what extent are enhancement technologies already regulated by existing rules and standards?
   - What forms of regulation are conceivable and possible?
   - Which international regulations exist or would be relevant?
9. *What is the relevance of these technologies for our understanding of disease and health?* That question is one that has a central place in medical science and philosophical anthropology. Insofar as anthropology does not merely have descriptive objectives ('What is our understanding of health?'), but also makes normative claims ('What conception of health is philosophically defensible?'), these judgments are once again descriptive-prescriptive mixed judgments.
10. In bioethics, a *moral judgment* about enhancement technologies will thus have to evaluate numerous descriptive and prognostic ancillary judgments in the light of a moral perspective, for which it is dependent on ethics.

In the process of bioethical reflection, interaction with a large variety of disciplines is thus relevant. Insofar as bioethics is a *prescriptive discipline*, however, it is part of ethics or moral philosophy. Bioethicists will therefore have to justify that they do not merely make descriptive and prognostic judgments, but also advance prescriptive claims to the effect that these technical developments and medical offerings are morally permissible or impermissible. This is, in any case, the task that bioethics has and that is expected from it by society. But once again, in view of the complexity and openness of the development of new technologies, this task can only be fulfilled if a variety of ancillary judgments are considered, which cannot be done in philosophy alone.

The aim of the preceding considerations was to sharpen the profile of the role of moral philosophy in the context of the interdisciplinary task of bioethics. Nothing, however, has been said so far about the appropriate ethical theory emerging from the framework of bioethics.[1] So far I have, quite deliberately, only talked in a very vague manner about 'moral standpoints' that legitimate a prescriptive dimension to a moral judgment. I have also not spoken of 'moral principles' or *a* 'moral principle'. Doing so would have meant that I had already restricted myself to those ethical traditions that start from such principles. We can neither assume that consensus regarding a suitable moral-philosophical theory is possible, nor that the standpoints relevant to a moral assessment of, say, enhancement are undisputed.

I do, however, start from the assumption that in the domain of bioethics it is imperative to reflect on any underlying normative presuppositions. It can be expected of any bioethicist that he will indicate which moral-philosophical presuppositions underpin his prescriptive judgments. This form of self-reflection is the ethical aspect of bioethics. Ethics is characterised by the fact that ethicists do not merely assert moral judgments, but also disclose moral-philosophical presuppositions by means of which the corresponding judgment can be legitimated. This feature of self-reflection on the validity conditions of moral judgments signals the decisive difference between everyday moral claims and moral judgments in the context of ethics. In that sense, bioethics does not differ from other fields of ethics. The only way bioethics distinguishes itself is through its specific subject matter.

1 I use the concepts 'ethical theory' and 'moral philosophy' synonymously. Bernard Williams and John Rawls, on the contrary, propose to distinguish 'ethical theory' and 'moral theory' from the notion of 'moral philosophy'. The latter would be understood as a comprehensive doctrine, by which Rawls means a comprehensive ethical, anthropological and metaphysical model. In the same sense, Habermas's ethics – an 'ethics of the good life' – differs from a 'discourse theory of morals', that is, from a universalistic ethics as it is usually understood. We will return to the substantial questions that are evoked by these differentiations. At this point, however, it is important for methodological reasons to *refrain* from making any further theoretical decisions. For that reason, 'moral philosophy' and 'philosophical ethics' will for the moment be used as synonyms (cf Habermas 1991/1994; Rawls 1993; Williams 1985).

This pertinence of reflection on the validity conditions of moral judgments, therefore, still says nothing about the appropriate ethical theory. However, the way in which the *role of moral philosophy* has been described does have consequences for the relation between bioethics and moral philosophy. For a start, these consequences should be pointed out explicitly.

Bioethics makes prescriptive moral claims. Bioethics makes assertions about the moral rightness of the way we deal with life and living things. Insofar as bioethics is part of ethics, one cannot imagine this discipline forgoing its prescriptive dimension. A form of bioethics that merely describes what is technically feasible, what will be possible in the future, how things are regulated legally and what people think of all that, would simply not be 'ethics' anymore. Moreover, the interest of society in bioethics is also based on its prescriptive dimension. The reason for the institutionalisation of bioethics has always been that people wanted to know whether new technologies could be morally justified. It has – to be fair – been speculated time and again that strategic reasons could have played a role in the institutionalisation of bioethics. The official reason, however, has always been the desire for insight into the moral permissibility of new technologies.

This prescriptive dimension of bioethics is not neutral in a moral-philosophical respect. Moral judgments in the field of bioethics constantly make presumptions that are grounded in metaethics and normative ethics. It is characteristic of the reflexivity of bioethics as a part of ethics that these presuppositions are made explicit and that they are justified philosophically. There may of course be *convergences*, that is, different philosophical starting points could lead to the same moral judgments. Such convergences do not, however, release the bioethicist from the responsibility of justifying his own judgment.

The pluralism of ethical theories is reflected in bioethics. If the justification of moral judgments is made dependent on ethical theories, this has the inevitable consequence that bioethical discourse is burdened with debates about the foundations of moral philosophy. This is exactly what most bioethicists try to avoid. They fear that complicated debates on principles from over 2,000 years of philosophy will be discussed anew in bioethics. If, however, philosophers have not been able to reach a consensus on a form of ethics so far, what reason would there be to hope that they would succeed in the realm of bioethics? The plurality of positions that play a role in moral philosophy will therefore inevitably reoccur in the context of bioethics. That does not mean that individual bioethicists cannot commit to a specific tradition. In fact, such commitment is almost a necessity if bioethicists are to come to normative statements at all. For bioethics as a discipline, however, this means that it can quite easily make itself dependent on a normative or metaethical theory, but that it must be possible in principle for all standpoints at play in ethics in general to occur in bioethics too. This is not a plea for a form of relativism. But if in bioethics all standpoints that are relevant for the moral assessment of the life sciences must be scrutinised, then it must also be possible in principle to represent these standpoints within bioethics. Some metaethical standpoints – those, for instance, that contest any academic validity of bioethics – will lean towards rejecting bioethics altogether. This is an attitude that instantly exhausts the possible contribution of those standpoints.

To outsiders, this may all sound somewhat trivial. But that is really not the case. In fact, a bioethical mainstream strives towards the establishment of a basis for bioethics that should emancipate it from moral-philosophical debates on principles. At this point I shall simply give two examples, which will crop up again later on.

First, the most famous book in bioethics is *Principles of Biomedical Ethics* by James F. Beauchamp and Tom L. Childress (6th edn 2008; see also Düwell 2006). Since its first publication in 1979 the book has appeared in six editions and has been revised and expanded continually. The book proposes a concept that has become known as *principlism*. The starting point of this concept is the idea that there are four principles (autonomy, beneficence, non-maleficence and justice), which can be agreed on by all participants in moral discourses. These principles thus embody partial consensuses that are considered to be legitimate reference points for moral argumentation. The most important task of bioethics, then, is to explicate the consequences of these principles in light of concrete bioethical questions and to determine their relative weights. Such a standpoint can of course be adopted, yet it cannot be that *principlism* is without discussion presumed as the normative basis for the whole of bioethics. The choice for this concept already implies numerous philosophically controversial decisions.

Secondly, something similar is true for a *common morality approach* (Gert 1998) and for *intuitionist concepts* (see for instance Audi 2004; Roeser 2002; Stratton-Lake 2002). *Common morality* is the idea that certain moral convictions can be construed from everyday morality. These moral convictions underpin a variety of moral judgments and form a shared moral basis of everyday morality. Gert gives several examples of acts condemned by everyday morality, such as deception, killing innocent people, etc. He ventures that these shared convictions are not a historical and unchangeable, but they nevertheless provide for so much stability that they can be viewed as an inventory of common beliefs. An indicator for the fundamental status of common morality is the fact that one cannot openly defend moral judgments that are at odds with these basic moral principles. An *intuitionist ethics* would hold that these common beliefs have the status of basic moral principles that cannot be further justified, and which indeed do not require any further justification.[2] Empirically, it can be debated whether it is possible to identify a perfectly common cross-cultural morality. Perhaps there are sufficiently common beliefs that allow for the solution of morally disputed problems.

2 Robert Audi, who is currently representative of the most-discussed intuitionist concept within bioethics, is more nuanced in the sense that he attempts to combine the status of these basic intuitions with a theory of a Rawlsian reflective equilibrium (see Chapter 2).

However, even if this were the case, the existence of such a cross-cultural morality would not (yet) say anything about its legitimacy. Even a morality that assumed slaves to have inferior human worth was widely shared for centuries. That a system of moral beliefs has a certain pervasiveness is not in itself a reason to consider it justified.[3]

Apart from principlism and the common morality approach, we could elaborate on methods based on the so-called 'reflective equilibrium' (cf Daniels 1996 and Chapter 2 of this book). On the whole, however, there are no arguments relevant to those methods besides the ones that have been discussed so far. All notions that have been mentioned can be held as standpoints within bioethics. But there is no reason to believe that any one of them can provide a foundation for the discipline 'bioethics' as a whole. Within bioethics, basic intuitions, the idea of a common morality and consensus views are all merely possible grounds on which to justify moral judgments; grounds that one can set out to defend, but that always call for validation. Likewise there will be bioethicists who choose different moral-philosophical starting points – who defend, say, a utilitarian moral principle, or an attempt to derive moral judgments from prudence, or who assume a substantive principle of human dignity. A choice for any of these concepts already involves certain theoretical decisions that are not self-evident, and which will strongly influence the outcome of moral considerations. Since these choices are not self-evident, it can be expected of bioethicists that they will be transparent about the metaethical and normative presuppositions that form the basis of their prescriptive judgments and that they will point out the importance of these. In order to conduct this discourse adequately, it is vital for bioethics as a discipline to leave room for these questions of validity to be asked systematically. This openness to moral-philosophical debates on principles is, in a sense, a relevant precondition for the possibility of dealing in a philosophically reflected way with the various possible ways of understanding morality and substantive moral beliefs. In the end, the meaning of applied ethics depends on this. Methodologically, this means that bioethics cannot avoid moral-philosophical discourse. Casuistry and principlism may be held as positions within bioethics, but adopting them does not allow one to

3 A further question is to what extent Gert's concept will be at all helpful for questions in bioethics. For it is one of his starting points that common morality does not provide us with an orientation in the case of controversial issues such as abortion. Gert writes: 'I realize that there are many controversial moral issues, such as abortion, [...] where each side claims that the position held by those on the other side is morally unacceptable. One of the most important, and perhaps unique, features of the account of morality presented in this book is that it does not decide genuinely controversial moral issues, but rather admits that both sides to the dispute have morally acceptable positions' (Gert 1998: 4). This feature would make his theory particularly less helpful with respect to questions of bioethics. In a way, this consequence is plausible: since such questions are relative newcomers in the history of our moral beliefs, no stable patterns of judgment have yet had the time to emerge.

circumvent complicated debates on principles of moral philosophy. In addition, bioethics must, as a matter of principle, leave room for all positions that are held in those general ethical debates. Again, this is not a plea for arbitrariness in the choice of theories, or for a form of relativism. Quite the contrary: if there are different theories, then the choice between them must be argued for. To the extent that decisions about theories influence the formation of moral judgments, a principled decision for relativism would mean that moral judgments in bioethics are fundamentally impossible. Yet if the discipline of bioethics would, as for instance Beauchamp and Childress stipulate, base itself on consensus views that are more or less applicable to different ethical theories, then the battle of theories would be settled – it would be removed from the discourse. This would deprive bioethics of the possibility of critically assessing which concrete normative judgments stem from different normative points of departure. For this reason, it must be methodologically possible to take on different philosophical-ethical positions within the discipline, since otherwise their validity could never be discussed. That does not mean, of course, that every single bioethical discussion should be burdened with every imaginable debate on principles. There are numerous debates in which the relevant disagreements are on an explicitly concrete plane, and in which debates on principles hardly play a role at all. In the context of 'mixed judgments' it has already been indicated how these different disagreements can be localised (see Chapter 1). What I have said does not mean that every bioethicist must at all times imagine the consequences that every single possible ethical theory would have for his topic. But it does mean that, as a discipline, bioethics does not have the option not to confront the multifaceted and controversial debates on principles of moral philosophy. In the thicket of bioethical discussion there are no shortcuts that would avoid fundamental moral-philosophical controversies.

2.1.1 Morality and ethics – conceptual differences

The rest of this chapter concentrates on a more thorough investigation of some theoretical presuppositions that are relevant to the relation between bioethics and moral philosophy. For a start, however, it is important to introduce some conceptual distinctions. It must be noted that throughout philosophical ethics the following concepts are used in different ways.

2.1.1.1 Morals, values and norms

The most fundamental conceptual distinction is between 'morality' and 'ethics'. As a rule, 'morality' is taken to be the name of the subject matter, while 'ethics' denotes the mode of reflection. With regard to subject matter, the concept of *morality* is used both in opposition to *immoral* and to *amoral*. For the distinction *moral/amoral*, the question is whether something belongs to the domain of morality or to a different domain, for instance factual knowledge or aesthetics. We do not say that the weather is morally good or bad – it falls outside the domain of moral evaluation. Morality is about the assessment of *actions* or *attitudes*, but also of institutions, etc, which are identified as *moral* or *immoral*. When calling a certain action moral, we can deem the action to be a morally *right* action (an action that is demanded by morality) or a morally *good* action (stemming from a morally good disposition). Sometimes, a 'morally good action' is simply called 'moral action', and a 'morally bad action' an 'immoral action'.

Morality predominantly evaluates *actions*, which are assessed as good or bad. As an *action* we understand – ever since Aristotle – any deed that is characterised by *intentionality* and *freedom*. That means that actions are not simply events in the world. For something to be called an action we presuppose that the agent aims at a certain goal, and that he at least had the possibility of doing otherwise – that is, of refraining from doing the action, or of doing some other action. In addition to these fundamental distinctions there are numerous discussions of the question of whether we are actually free, what the range of our freedom is, and so on. Since our acting is purposeful, the *goods* and *values* at which our actions are aimed are relevant. The concepts 'goods' and 'values' indicate things that appear *good* or *valuable* to the agent, which gives him a reason to *strive* for them. However, we also speak of goods and values in a *nonmoral sense*, in the sense that these goods and values can be deemed good or valuable independent from moral criteria. It is possible to speak of *aesthetic values* or of *instrumental goods*, things that seem good to us because we want to achieve something else. Values and goods do not always have to be the objectives of actions – aesthetic values, for instance, may not. When talking about *moral goods and values* one must, therefore, always add the adjective 'moral' – otherwise nonmoral values and goods could be meant as well.

Norms, unlike *values*, are always aimed at actions: you shall not kill, you shall honour your mother and your father, etc. Norms identify certain actions as *demanded*, *prohibited* or *permissible*. Not all norms are 'moral' norms. We do, for instance, have *professional* norms – actions that must be performed by those in certain jobs (a physician needs to comply with his duty of care, a priest cannot break the seal of confession, etc). In addition, there are matters of *etiquette* or *decency* (not picking one's nose during dinner), *conventional expectations* of social interaction (if I invite my neighbour for a barbecue, I expect that he will invite me back at some point) and *moral norms* (it is bad to lie to others). A specific class are *legal norms*, which gain their validity from the fact that they have been authorised in a certain institutionally regulated procedure. The validity of legal norms is fully dependent on the fact that these norms are legally stipulated. This is not the case for informal or moral norms.

Moral norms, of course, also develop historically and are subject to culturally induced change (cf on the concept of morality Frankena 1966; Gert 2011; Skorupski 1993; Wallace and Walker 1970). However, moral norms always involve a claim to validity that transcends the specific social context. In that way, we are able to formulate moral criticisms of social norms (the way we deal with the environment is morally indefensible). Or we can criticise legal systems that do not implement certain moral norms (introducing the death penalty is immoral). When making such judgments, we evaluate social and legal norms from a moral perspective. Important distinctions between different forms of norms can be found in Kant's *Groundwork of the Metaphysics of Morals*. Kant distinguished between *hypothetical* and *categorical imperatives* (Kant 1785/1996:67ff. see also Habermas 1991/1994). *Hypothetical imperatives* are normatively binding in relation to certain goals. Certain actions are compulsory for us in virtue of their character as necessary means through which certain ends can be reached. Kant differentiates between two forms of hypothetical imperatives. *Technical imperatives* are those that express the necessity of a certain action and can apply to any kind of goal. 'If you want some fresh air, you have to open the window' would be an example of such an imperative. As soon as the end (fresh air) is no longer desired, the necessity for attaining the means (an open window) disappears. Such ends can be entirely amoral but, given the ends, there is a necessity for realising the corresponding means (if you want to rob a bank, you have to get yourself a gun). The other forms of Kant's hypothetical imperatives are called *pragmatic imperatives*. These are imperatives that express a normative judgment about what is required for us to live a happy life (you have to exercise regularly if you want to stay fit; if you do not want to become depressed, you will have to drink good wine every day). These normative hints for a good life are also discussed under the heading 'ethics of the good life' (Chapter 2).

The *categorical imperative*, on the other hand, is valid for all actions. Without going into the details of Kant's moral philosophy, it can be added that this concept of the categorical imperative has had a profound effect on the shape of modern ethics. As a rule, we take it that the moral quality of actions has to do with the fact that they are demanded without restriction, independent of the question of whether they may benefit us, or yield social status. We view it as morally required to help those in need, even if we will not gain any advantage from it. At this point, the question is not whether we do in fact have such obligations towards those in need. It should merely become clear that according to the Kantian moral philosophy, the moral quality of actions consists in the fact that they are required independently of our benefit. (We will come back to this discussion later.) Moral judgments are thus *assessments of actions*. The specific moral evaluation of actions centres on the question of which actions we are morally obligated to do, and which ones are morally prohibited. Attitudes, motives, intentions and norms for actions (of individuals or institutions) can also be the subject of moral evaluation. However, such evaluations will always refer back to the evaluation of actions (cf Gert 1998: 25ff). When we deem an attitude to be morally good or virtuous, we believe that actions done on the basis of this attitude will normally be morally right. When we assess a motive for action as morally good, we take it that the motive involves an orientation towards the moral rightness of the action it is aimed at. And we can only give a moral evaluation of intentions if we interpret them as intentions towards certain actions that do themselves have a moral character. We call norms right insofar as they specify morally right conduct. And we say institutions are morally good or just insofar as they provide a framework for morally right interaction between the members of a community. That actions are in fact the *primary* subject of moral evaluations becomes clear from the fact that these relations cannot be reversed: actions that stem from a morally good attitude or motive, or that are done with good intentions, may very well turn out to be morally wrong. Along the same lines, general norms and social institutions can never guarantee morally right conduct.

2.1.1.2 What is ethics?

The concept of *ethics* generally denotes *reflection on morality.* Morality is thus the subject matter on which ethics reflects as a form of deliberation. This, in any case, is what is meant when people speak of 'philosophical ethics'. Bioethics, economic ethics or political ethics are also (sub)disciplines that deliberate on certain aspects of morality. That means that, strictly speaking, actions and attitudes cannot be 'ethical' or 'unethical', but merely 'moral' or 'immoral'. In what follows, the terminology will be used in this way.

However, the formulation 'reflection on morality' is very broad and unspecific. We can think about the phenomenon of 'morality' in very different ways. *Ethical* reflection is centred on the question of whether claims and demands that occur in morality are *justified.* When the point of morality is to appraise certain ends as 'good' ends, or to claim that we are obligated to act in certain ways, this immediately evokes the question of *why* such-and-such an end would be better than another one, or whether we are, for instance, *really* obligated to help others, not to torment animals, etc. The point of ethics is thus to *verify* the justification of moral statements and moral demands.

This form of ethical reflection takes place in everyday life as well: when we give *reasons* for moral claims, we tell someone *why* they should perform or refrain from certain actions. Ethics thus asks for the *justification* of moral claims or demands. In that respect, philosophical ethics does not do anything fundamentally different from everyday moral communication, in which reasons are also called for. Philosophical ethics merely does so more systematically and methodically. In addition, ethics systematically questions moral beliefs that are hardly ever made an issue in everyday morality. Disciplines outside ethics thematise questions of morality as well, but in such cases different kinds of questioning are at stake. From a *psychological* perspective, for instance, one can ask about *motives* for action: why has someone done a certain thing? Why does a certain action appear morally obligatory to someone? Or one can ask from a *historical* perspective how certain moral convictions have *emerged*: how have we come to view torturing animals as morally reprehensible? Or we can compare moral beliefs of different cultures from a perspective of *cultural anthropology*: what is the status of the family in Asia and Europe? Considering the development of moral convictions is relevant for ethics as well. The central ethical question, however, is a normative question: are we really obligated not to torture animals? Is this particular action actually a good thing to do?

The central difference between 'morality' and 'ethics' is thus a difference between the domain or subject matter and the mode of reflection. I do want to point out, however, that the concept of 'ethics' is sometimes used differently as well.

Firstly, the concept of 'ethics' is sometimes used as an expression of the entirety of certain ideas of value, for instance in the sense of a 'Christian ethics' or a 'Buddhist ethics'. What is meant in these cases is the entirety of moral convictions in Christianity or Buddhism (as opposed to, for instance, the concept of a 'theological ethics', which denotes the reflection and teaching of ethics in the context of the theological sciences). This concept of 'ethics' is confusing insofar as it is not customarily used to refer to 'academic disciplines'. There cannot be an academic discipline that is the 'entirety of certain ideas of value'; an academic discipline can only be the teaching of, or reflection on, certain ideas of value, morality, etc. For that reason, it would appear rather helpful to speak in the above cases of 'Christian morality' or 'Buddhist morality' (if such a thing exists).

Secondly, Habermas proposed to reserve 'morality' as a term for universalisable codes of conduct and to use 'ethics' as a name for subjectively or culturally variable concepts of the 'good life' (cf Habermas 1991/1994; Williams 1985; Forst 2001). Even if this distinction is warranted in terms of the difference it makes, it still seems problematic to use the concepts 'morality' and 'ethics' to denote this particular opposition, since doing so creates confusion in light of the usage of these concepts introduced above. Habermas himself runs into this kind of terminological problem in the sense that the concept of 'discourse ethics', which is strongly influenced by his work, does not fit into this new conception of 'ethics'.

2.1.1.3 Ethical theories – different levels

So far, the concepts 'ethics' and 'ethical theories' have been used interchangeably. At this point, some differentiation is necessary. It is common to distinguish between four levels of ethical theories:

- metaethics
- descriptive ethics
- normative ethics
- applied ethics

Metaethics is both a fundamental part of ethics and a form of *reflection on ethics*. Metaethics deals with fundamental concepts of ethics, that is, with questions such as: what is morality? What distinguishes a moral judgment from other forms of judgment? What is moral communication? What is an action? What is an agent? What is moral identity? At the same time, however, metaethics deals with the preconditions of ethical reflection, communication and theory formation. Is moral communication about power or (also) about knowledge? Can there be such a thing as moral knowledge? What possibilities are there for justifying moral demands? The boundaries between metaethics, philosophy of language and epistemology are fluid, as are the boundaries between metaethics and normative ethics.

Traditionally, the task of *descriptive ethics* was to describe and reconstruct moral beliefs, moral attitudes and systems of morality. At the moment, however, this undertaking is largely considered a task for the social sciences, which develop a whole set of methods for empirical research. It is currently a much-debated question to what extent ethics should refer back to empirical research (see Chapter 2). In any case, it should be noted that ethics does not have its own methodological instruments for empirical research, meaning it is dependent on the social sciences for conducting such research. But at the same time, it should also be considered to what extent the social sciences themselves make presuppositions that require verification through normative-ethical theories.

Normative ethics investigates criteria of morally right conduct. An example of a normative ethical theory would be 'utilitarianism', which takes the maximisation of collective utility – the sum of everyone's happiness – as the criterion for morality. While metaethics reflects on the preconditions of morality and ethical theory formation, normative ethics deals with the specific substantiation of the moral. For normative ethics, the goal is to clarify why a certain criterion for morality or a certain moral viewpoint should in fact guide and orient our conduct. Normative ethics, then, does not investigate which norms we do in fact follow, but rather asks which norms *should* be guiding us. Correspondingly, Kant formulated the basic question of ethics as follows: what ought I to do? Normative ethics is a *prescriptive or normative discipline* not because it reflects on norms, but because it makes and justifies specific claims regarding what is normatively right. If it is the case that within normative ethics moral convictions are described or reconstructed, then this is done with the expectation that such reconstructions of our factual beliefs will yield orientation for other cases. When ethicists investigate how people generally feel about exceptions to the prohibition of killing (that is, self-defence, war), they hope to gain normative understanding of what should be done in different, morally contentious cases (that is, epidemics). Such approaches do, however, assume that our moral common sense is 'valid' and that our moral judgments can thus rightly be based on it.

Nevertheless, normative ethics is not independent of metaethics. The formulation and justification of normative statements can only take place within the framework of what can be metaethically grounded. For that reason, *metaethics* is sometimes confined to the identification of the presuppositions of ethics disclosed by epistemology and philosophy of language.

The justification and identification of criteria (or a criterion) of morality are then considered the task of a so-called *fundamental ethics*. In such a situation, metaethics would be the analytic part of ethical reflection on principles, and fundamental ethics the prescriptive part.

What is important to keep in mind is that metaethics reflects on the theoretical presuppositions of ethical theory formation, while normative ethics asks about valid moral criteria; that is, the criteria of right ways of acting. Corresponding to different metaethical assumptions, there are different conceptions of the ways in which prescriptive statements can be justified.

Applied ethics is the generic term for any subdiscipline of ethics that is concerned with *more specific* ethical questions. I already indicated in the Introduction how a division of domains within ethics could be imagined. Bioethics is part of applied ethics, and perhaps the part that has thus far been developed most.

2.1.2 *Normative ethics and the good life: criticisms of normative ethics*

The most fundamental question of normative ethics is: 'what ought I/we to do?' – 'ought' being a *moral* imperative. Correspondingly, the most fundamental question of bioethics is: 'what ought I/we to do in dealing with the life sciences?'. With this formulation of the task of the discipline, we have already settled on the concept of a *moral obligation* as the most fundamental notion in bioethics. This means that bioethics is about the reflection and justification of moral obligations. However, it is precisely this focus on the concept of obligation that is the topic of a heated debate in ethics.

From a historical perspective, it is in fact far from self-evident that ethics would be about 'obligation'. For a large part of the history of ethics, 'ethics' meant *virtue ethics* (cf Crisp and Slote 1997; Taylor 2002). The central point of Aristotle's virtue ethics is not to determine what we are obliged to do or what we owe to others. Aristotle instead observes that humans strive to lead a happy life, but that they are unsure how this happy life can be attained. His virtue ethics thus attempts to come up with fitting ways to realise the happy or felicitous life. Therefore, we sometimes speak of an *ethics of the good and successful life*. Since the success or perfection of human life is at stake, this tradition is also called *perfectionism* (cf Hurka 1993). This perfectionist tradition was leading in antiquity, but also shaped Christianity. In the Middle Ages, however, happiness or felicitous existence was not conceived merely as a quality of the worldly life. Rather, the aspiration had become to identify ways to attain eternal life.

It is not uncommon in present times for the obligation-centred orientation of ethics to be criticised under reference to virtue ethics. In bioethics this criticism is particularly vehement, since several authors express the suspicion that the commitment to an idea of moral obligation unavoidably leads to the centralisation of the rational person or agent who can subject himself to obligations. This focus on rational persons and agents capable of action will, however, – according to the opponents – have considerable (and problematic) consequences for the status of embryos, comatose patients and animals. Therefore, this criticism of the notion of obligation, the central notion of normative ethics, must be addressed.

Criticisms of normative ethics come in several forms. First and foremost, fundamental critiques of the obligation-oriented character of *modern moral philosophy* have existed for several decades. The critique of the universalistic ambitions of modern ethics that Alasdair MacIntyre put forward in his book *After Virtue* (1981) became particularly well known. Yet, as early as 1958, Elizabeth Anscombe criticised the fact that the significant players in modern moral philosophy (Hobbes, Mill, Kant and Hume) presuppose that the idea of a moral obligation is the pivotal point of ethical thinking (Anscombe 1958; also see O'Hear 2004). The notion of a moral law is a residue of a form of morality based on the idea of a divine legislator, yet this legislator can no longer be given a systematic place. In an 'abstract' morality of obligations, morality is taken to be a self-contained sphere, independent, in a way, from a comprehensive philosophical understanding of personhood. In a similar vein, Hegel had criticised Kant's allegedly abstract conception of morality a century and a half earlier. Like Hegel's, MacIntyre's critique is aimed at the supposedly devastating consequences of this abstract ethics for moral life. As morality is seen as a self-contained sphere and moral obligations are anchored in an idea of impartiality and rational personhood, morality becomes a critical instance against moral traditions handed down through history (in religions, customs, practices). MacIntyre particularly feared the destructive effects of the ethics of rationality on the moral traditions. If nothing but the authority of rationality can justify moral obligations, the entire wealth of moral traditions becomes ideologically suspect. Anscombe and MacIntyre submit a fundamental criticism of the universalism of modern ethics, and attempt to establish an alternative based on an Aristotelian doctrine of the felicitous life. The resultant ethics is a virtue ethics, which must take leave of the modern notion of morality altogether.

Secondly, the critiques of Anscombe and MacIntyre result from a relatively conservative background, which in a way is deeply suspicious of the modernity and liberality of modern moral philosophy. Relatively similar criticisms, however, have come from other directions as well. From the side of the 'ethics of care', there have also been criticisms of intrinsic exclusion mechanisms associated with modern ethics (cf Kittay 1999; Noddings 1984; Rudnick 2001). Central to the 'ethics of care' is not merely the idea of caring for others, but the balance between care for oneself and care for others.[4]

4 A brief philosophical remark may be helpful: this concept is also not identical to Heidegger's notion of 'care' in *Being and Time*, for in Heidegger's work 'care' is ontological rather than ethical.

The ethics of care has received very decisive impulses from psychological and pedagogical discussions on moral development. This debate goes back to Carol Gilligan's critique of the empirical model of moral development devised by Piaget and Kohlberg (Gilligan 1982). Their staged model, which has been widely discussed since the 1970s, takes its start from the idea that the individual and collective genesis of moral beliefs involves a progression towards higher forms of moral sense. In individual terms, the egocentric perspective of a small child becomes increasingly decentred and is universalised through intersubjective role reversals. In the first instance, only direct, close relations (that is, family, peer groups) provide reasons for moral considerateness, until more abstract norms of social communities and eventually even universal principles of justice become reference points for moral judgment as well. Gilligan's criticism was that the empirical data were obtained predominantly from research with young people and that the validity of this research was uncritically generalised. The debate that sprang from this criticism does not, however, address only the interpretation of these empirical studies. A question that is equally important is whether our basic ethical principles are determined by gender-specific prejudices, and why abstract notions of justice and an orientation on principles are allocated a central role within ethics. Against the orienting role of abstract principles, proponents of the ethics of care assert that morality is about relations to concrete others, and that it should therefore be shaped by the attitude of 'caring' for others. The idea of an ethics of care has ties with the tradition of virtue ethics. Nevertheless, many advocates of the ethics of care certainly do develop universalistic notions according to which the attitude of care commits people to very extensive assistance and support, without specifically arguing for the validity of these universal demands. The aim of the focus on 'caring' is to avoid a unilateral concentration on liberal rights to freedom – a practice of which care ethicists accuse traditional forms of ethics that centralise rights and duties. The ethics of care is furthermore motivated by the concern that a one-sided focus on rational persons will have the adverse result that exactly those groups that are particularly vulnerable (for instance children, or the elderly, ill or disabled people) are excluded from moral protection. The term 'ethics of care', in any case, does not identify a unified theory, but refers to a whole host of positions. These different positions relate to the idea of moral obligations and thus to normative ethics in a variety of ways. In principle, the following ways of relating are imaginable:

1. The ethics of care is considered to involve a fundamental rejection of the idea of moral obligations and is thus viewed as an alternative to normative ethics.
2. The attitude of caring is conceived as a framework for normative ethics. In this case, the question of what this attitude should be directed towards – the question of the object of care – is one that is to be determined in normative discourses.

3. Caring can be conceived as an approach – that is, a version of normative ethics – in which the analysis of caring yields the contents of normative obligations.
4. Deontology (ethics of duty) and ethics of care are thought of as mutually complementary; the ethics of care being the side that emphasises forms of assistance overlooked by duty-oriented forms of ethics. This is also how certain Kantian approaches, for instance in the work of Onora O'Neill, emphasise the connections between virtue on the one hand and justice or rights on the other (O'Neill 1996).

However, the emphasis on the necessity to expand rights-based ethics or theories of justice with obligations to assist and support does presuppose that rights-based ethics take their start exclusively from liberal rights to freedom, which does not hold for many current variants (see for example Shue 1980; Gewirth 1996; Chatterjee 2004).

Perhaps there are further ways in which the relation between the ethics of care and normative ethics can be understood. Overall, however, it will be possible to conclude that the relation between the two is theoretically underdetermined.

Thirdly, *Martha Nussbaum* and others have proposed to bridge the gap between virtue ethics and normative perspectives by way of a so-called 'capabilities approach', in which fundamental concerns of the ethics of care are addressed (Nussbaum 2006; for a critical discussion see Claassen and Düwell 2012). The capabilities approach regards the capabilities that every human needs for a successful life as a cornerstone of moral protection. In other words: we are morally obligated to enable every human being to lead a successful life. The basic capabilities are envisaged very broadly: every person needs bodily integrity, a certain level of safety, the possibility of education and social contact – irrespective of the question of which concrete ends they may value. The idea of human rights is thus understood in terms of the basic capabilities that are to be morally protected. In her book *Frontiers of Justice* Nussbaum develops a theory of the protection of dignity. The protection of dignity, in her account, means ensuring that each person has the possibility to develop him- or herself. Nussbaum also attempts to expand the protection of dignity to animals. Her concept, however, is haunted by a number of unclarities. It is not evident, for instance, why being dependent on certain goods in the development of our capabilities would justify a claim to other people's support. In addition, Nussbaum considers the different capabilities to be equally fundamental aspects of a successful life; aspects that cannot be ordered hierarchically. Now it is indeed plausible that having access to education or social contacts is important for each and every person. Yet for a concept that aims at justifying moral obligations it is vital that some ranking of the urgency or importance of capabilities is possible. Nussbaum's attempt to tie in with virtue-ethical traditions thus factically presupposes a particular theory of normative ethics, one for which the possibility of a successful life for every person is a criterion of morally right conduct. To what extent Nussbaum is right to assume that this can be part of an interpretation of the virtue-ethical tradition from Aristotle onwards is, however, open to doubt.[5]

Finally, apart from criticisms of normative ethics or virtue-ethical expansions, one can adopt the idea of a complementary relation. To an extent, this approach corresponds to the differentiation between universalisable questions of morality and questions of an ethics of the good and successful life that has already been noted in connection with Habermas (Habermas 1991/1994), or to the Kantian distinction between hypothetical and categorical imperatives. Hans Krämer has developed this idea in considerable detail. Krämer differentiates between an 'ethics of ought' and an 'ethics of striving for the good life' (Krämer 1992). While the 'ethics of ought' refers to the ethics of moral obligations and mutual recognition that has been dominant since modernity, the 'ethics of striving for the good life' was developed mostly in ancient philosophy. The ethics of the good life provided people with advice for dealing with their bodies, needs and friendships in such a way that a successful life would become attainable.[6] The ethics of the good life aims to equip people with techniques and therapeutic perspectives that help them lead their lives. Nevertheless, Krämer emphasises that these ethical considerations cannot be carried out in isolation, but are always based on the assumption that the basic conditions of political justice and the protection of individual autonomy have been secured.

Needless to say, criticism of the normative-ethical concept of obligation fundamentally affects the profile of bioethics. The different forms of critique do, however, have very different consequences. An expansion of normative ethics along the lines of an ethics of the good life may be largely unproblematic, but would in the first place be relevant for the personal lifestyle of the individual and no directly for moral discussions in society. This expansion would thus have limited relevance in the domain of bioethics. Nussbaum's proposal and certain forms of the ethics of care could quite easily be taken as suggestions relevant to normative discussions of the appropriate ways of dealing with our living environment. More problematic are criticisms that deem the justification of duties and norms a hopeless modernistic endeavour. From this perspective, the project of pursuing a discipline in which the aim is to develop systematic theories and frameworks for the discussion and justification of demands will seem mostly meaningless. Before we can discuss theories within the domain of bioethics at all, we will therefore have to resolve

5 A variant of such a virtue-based normative ethics would be the virtue ethics of Michael Slote, who seeks to locate moral criteria in the motivations of the agent (Slote 2001).

6 In contemporary ethics, these discussions are conducted under the heading of perfectionism (Hurka 1993) or in connection with the historical studies of Michel Foucault (see in particular Foucault 1976/1998).

whether the question of moral obligations is a meaningful one in the first place. All calls for the protection of informed consent, individual autonomy and the protection of human dignity and individual rights presuppose that we are confronted with moral 'oughts' in the first place. An ethics of care will have to determine its relation to this matter. On the conservative side, in contrast, there are attempts to avoid the conflict about what is morally right by recourse to traditions. In *After Virtue*, Alasdair MacIntyre seeks to bring value consensuses within small communities into play. The praise of the holy Benedict at the end of the book makes it clear which ideals are to be propagated within the bounds of these value consensuses. MacIntyre's and Anscombe's invocations of moral traditions are supposed to protect the Christian-occidental ethos from the corrosive force of the Enlightenment. If bioethics is to take itself seriously as an academic enterprise, it will have to resist giving in to that temptation.

2.1.3 Metaethical presuppositions

Whenever bioethics deals with the discussion and justification of normative claims, a whole range of metaethical questions becomes relevant. At this point, these questions can be discussed only in a very rudimentary way. However, a few fundamental metaethical aspects of the ethical debate will be sketched.

First of all, we are confronted with the basic question of what the goal of ethical deliberation might be in the first place. Is the goal of ethics *knowledge of what is morally right*? In metaethics a distinction is made between *cognitivist and non-cognitivist ethical theories*. Cognitivists defend the standpoint that what is morally right can be the object of rational knowledge (whatever this knowledge is taken to be at any given time). Non-cognitivists deny this possibility. In any case, the question immediately arising is what the status of such knowledge could be. What exactly is it that we know in such cases? What seems to be clear is that it only makes sense to speak of *knowledge* if what is known is valid for others as well. Epistemologically, we will therefore have to presuppose that we will only be able to defend a form of cognitivism in morality insofar as we start from the assumption that the validity of any moral judgment is not restricted to the person making the judgment. In a sense, this means that moral judgments must hold independently from the judger. This is exactly what non-cognitivists disagree with. The classical version of non-cognitivism, called *emotivism*, asserted that moral claims are nothing more than judgments of taste or expressions of emotions (classical texts are Ayer 1936; Stevenson 1944; Blackburn 1993). It is relatively clear that it is not very plausible that moral convictions could be justified with arguments if a moral judgment is no more than the expression of certain feelings – in other words, if the assertion 'embryonic research is morally objectionable' could be translated, without loss of meaning, as 'embryonic research – boo!'. The only thing one can do is hope that others will share these feelings. The emotivist was thus forced to consider large parts of the bioethical discourse as rather senseless, namely all parts that deal with arguments for normative-ethical assertions. Nevertheless, the traditional emotivists who worked in the first half of the 20th century were in an easier position than those in the current bioethical debate. The early emotivists may have believed that moral judgments are essentially judgments of taste, but they also assumed, at least to an extent, that our emotional reactions to glaring injustice are somewhat stable. Intuitively, we find the killing and torture of innocent people, lying and deceit, simply not pretty (and, evidently, this is true for very many people). In the contemporary bioethical debate, however, we are often confronted with issues that do not evoke immediate and univocal emotional responses, perhaps because we have no long moral tradition of dealing with those issues. Or we have very strong emotional reactions (for instance in relation to the protection of embryos or animals), but these reactions are very different for different people. On the basis of an emotivist metaethics, however, the gap between different emotions cannot be bridged by argument. The development of bioethical theories would therefore seem a largely senseless endeavour.

There are also reasons to think that *bioethics only makes sense if ethics is in fact about moral knowledge*. This idea evokes a number of further questions; for instance, what in that case would be the status of the object towards which such moral knowledge is directed. Are we, for instance, to assume that moral knowledge is only possible if the object of this knowledge (what we would know about) exists independently from the subject (the one who has the knowledge)? Sometimes such a standpoint is called moral realism (Blackburn 1993; McDowell 1998; Shafer-Landau 2003). Now if the object of moral knowledge, the moral good, were to exist independently from the knowing subject, then what form of knowledge could be directed at this object? All of this is further complicated by the fact that we cannot define the moral good by referring to certain natural properties. This was G. E. Moore's critique of the 'naturalistic fallacy' (Moore 1903). That is, we cannot gain moral knowledge by pointing out certain natural facts in the world, as we can with other forms of knowledge. However, the question is, then, in what ways we *can* arrive at knowledge of the moral good. One of the classical answers of cognitivist ethics was *intuitionism*, the theory that in forming moral judgments we are forced to fall back on basic moral intuitions. According to intuitionism, these intuitions cannot be further justified, nor do they require any further justification. An example would be the basic intuition that life or autonomy constitutes valuable goods. In contemporary metaethics, intuitionism has regained a certain status (Audi 2004; Roeser 2002; Stratton-Lake 2002). There are, however, a number of difficulties with this theory, for example the question of how to deal with the fact that, in actuality, people have different intuitions (which appears, at the very least, when one has an intercultural perspective). Most bioethical questions, after all, come up in relation to issues for which the difference in moral intuitions is glaring. How can intuitionism arrive at answers in the face of moral controversies? Is intuitionism not, a way of breaking off moral disagreements dogmatically?

Some more recent intuitionist approaches attempt to connect intuitionism with a theory of reflective equilibrium (Audi 2004) or with a coherentist epistemology (Daniels 1996; van der Burg and van Willigenburg 1998; Timmons 1999). The theory of reflective equilibrium was developed by Rawls (1971) in order to extract from our intuitions about a just society exactly those of which we may think that they deserve general approval. In order to do this, Rawls proposes a procedure in which we must imagine ourselves behind a 'veil of ignorance', where the details of our personal position in society (wealth, gender, disability, etc.) are unknown to us. Those principles that we can agree to in this situation deserve general approval. Since the outcome of this thought experiment depends on intuitions about justice, Rawls assigns the procedure a central role in his approach. Rawls uses this thought experiment, which systematises our intuitions concerning justice, in order to justify his moral theory. In justifying this procedure as a central axis of his theory, Rawls employs the concept of a 'reflective equilibrium'. This concept denotes the procedure by which moral intuitions and the formulation of principles of justice are brought into a mutually critical relation. We are neither to infer our principles simply from intuitions, nor should we simply revise our intuitions on the basis of philosophical considerations. Rather, a reflective equilibrium is reached by a deliberative process in which our pre-theoretical intuitions play an important role, but are open to critical reflection that may lead to changes, modifications and revisions. By now, numerous expansions of Rawls's theory of reflective equilibrium have been proposed. Noteworthy is, for instance, Norman Daniels's theory of a 'wide reflective equilibrium', according to which the balance is not only between principles of justice and intuitions (Daniels 1996). Rather, Daniels suggests that we work with a range of relevant beliefs that is much broader, and that we include assumptions about nature and society or anthropological suppositions in the process of mutually corrective reflections. In newer editions of their book *Principles of Biomedical Ethics*, Beauchamp and Childress also draw on the theory of reflective equilibrium as a methodological background for their concept of *principlism*. Both Daniels and Beauchamp and Childress consider the most important advantage of such a theory that concrete moral judgments are neither deduced top-down from an abstract principle of morality, nor gained bottom-up from empirically available moral beliefs. Rather, the development of a moral judgment must be thought of as a complex process of mutual critique between all relevant viewpoints: principles of justice, moral intuitions, anthropological assumptions, etc. The task of ethics would then first and foremost consist in explicitly developing all of these factors, and verifying their internal coherence and consistence. In the factical process of the development of moral and political opinions, ethics could thus take on a sort of 'maieutic' role, a term that originates from the Greek word for midwife. The role of the midwife was an inspiration for philosophy as early as Plato: the philosopher ought to identify the relevant viewpoints that are already implicitly present in the moral discussion, and he should work out what a coherent moral solution based on these viewpoints could look like. This theory presupposes a coherentist epistemology. That means that the justification process does not start from fundamental ethical assertions from which further moral judgments are deduced; rather, moral beliefs are justified as part of a coherent system of beliefs in which no particular belief or assumption is privileged as a foundation. For this reason, a coherentist approach strikes many as an attractive method for bioethics, since it allows debates in society to tie in with beliefs that people actually have, without being committed to approve them.

There are numerous different versions of coherentism. While I will not be able to elaborate on these any further, it is important that two problems are pointed out. First of all, coherentism presupposes that our fundamental moral intuitions must play an essential criteriological role in a coherently formulated concept of moral judgments. In other words: when an ethical theory conflicts with fundamental moral beliefs, there must be something wrong with the theory. A theory, for instance, that leaves no room for *individual rights* would be a casualty for this criterion. Our moral convictions become criteria for the question of whether a certain ethical theory could be right (see for example Timmons 2002: 271). Coherentist theories thus inherently presuppose a certain form of intuitionism. Consequently, the connection of coherentism and a reflective equilibrium with an intuitionist theory – such as made by Robert Audi – readily suggests itself. This means, however, that a coherentist theory cannot fully disengage itself from the problems of intuitionism. Why would we be justified in assuming that our intuitions are morally right? Moral intuitions also held slavery to be good. Or let us take recent discussions concerning headscarves. Many Muslims consider the way in which Western women dress in public immoral, while many Westerners regard this as a fundamental part of their civil liberties. A similar case is the assessment of homosexuality, which the majority of religious people in Christianity and Islam probably consider morally problematic even today, while for liberal-minded people it is fully acceptable. Even so, a worldwide enquiry into people's intuitions concerning the moral permissibility of homosexuality would quite possibly turn out rather sobering. Of course, this is not yet a fundamental argument against intuitionism, but it does remain a question of why we should take moral intuitions to be criteria for morality and how we should deal with the plurality of intuitions.

The second question leads in a very similar direction: when is a coherentist argument successful? When is the reflective equilibrium a 'good' one? Do we not need a 'success criterion' in order to decide that? After all, even totalitarian ideologies cannot always be denied a certain degree of internal coherence. This point of criticism is not at all meant polemically. Particularly in the light of bioethical discussions it is a truly fundamental problem, since very different suggestions can be imagined coherently, regardless of their starting points. Can this problem be addressed within coherentism? Or will it have to simply to come to terms with a coexistence of different coherent ethical theories?

Exactly these questions, however, lead to a discussion with a long tradition in moral philosophy: is it possible to find a basis of assessment of our moral judgments that has not been chosen arbitrarily and that does not simply spring from 'a' cultural tradition – a basis of assessment, that is, which ought to be philosophically accepted? Such a basis does seem to be indispensable if moral claims are considered categorical claims. A bioethical example will clarify this. Someone asserts that it is immoral to harm animals unnecessarily. If for the sake of the discussion we disregard the otherwise necessary specifications – exactly which kinds of harm would be 'unnecessary', say – the first issue that arises is the metaethical question of what kind of assertion this is in the first place. The emotivist would say that this is a case of someone expressing repugnance in the face of conduct associated with unnecessary animal suffering. Others would say that this is someone expressing his own opinion regarding the kinds of conduct he happens to prefer. From the perspective of an extensive tradition in modern moral philosophy, however, it would be said: what is asserted here is that actions that harm animals unnecessarily are unacceptable and that nobody may act in such a way. This means that morality is associated with a claim that is aimed at all other agents: we expect that each and every moral agent ought to accept this. Furthermore we expect that moral claims should determine our conduct even if we, as agents, are not benefited by such conduct, and that we should abide by them even if no law requires us to. The assertion 'it is immoral to harm animals unnecessarily' would then be identical to the statement 'nobody ought to harm animals unnecessarily, even if it is to their advantage and even if it is not legally prohibited'. Of course, several restrictions and modifications of this principle could be imagined. It would for instance be possible to have the reservation that the protection of human life has a priority. In that case the prohibition to kill animals would only hold prima facie, and could be mitigated by other perspectives, which would however have to be moral as well. In addition, the judgment that such conduct is immoral would not necessarily lead to a demand for legal prohibitions. Following this discussion, several questions would remain. First and foremost, however, we are confronted with the fact that *advancing a moral claim* involves *asserting an 'ought'* that is *universally addressed* and that demands *prioritised observance*. Now this seems a correct description of the claims of morality – arguably, this is the only sense in which the moral claim to respect human rights can be understood. If that is right, it does not seem exaggerated to demand of the theoretical part of ethics that it identifies this basis of assessment in such a way that the legitimacy of its moral claims becomes apparent, and to expect that this basis of assessment is not arbitrary, but demands acceptance by anyone. Within ethics there are some attempts to do exactly this. To illustrate such an attempt, let us briefly touch on the theories of Emmanuel Lévinas and Immanuel Kant, both of which play an essential role in bioethics.

Lévinas has argued in several important publications that we can only properly appreciate our self-understanding, our connections to the world around us and our social relations if we acknowledge the fundamental demands that originate from the 'other' (see above all Lévinas 1961/1969). The other confronts us with a demand to assume our responsibilities prior to any reflection. The 'face' of the other confronts us with the unconditional obligation to respect his fundamental vulnerability, and to not kill or harm him. This obligation does not become apparent to us by use of our rational capacities, but is immediate. Lévinas develops a substantial theory that engages critically with Husserl and Heidegger, and tries to establish that this obligation is so fundamental that we could not even understand the possibilities of subjectivity, language, knowledge and intersubjectivity without reverting to this fundamental experience. Lévinas sees 'ethics as first philosophy', without which all other domains of philosophy remain incomprehensible.

Now there are a number of objections that could be raised against this theory. One question is whether the encounter with the other can be understood at all without the constitution of a subject already being presupposed. Will I be able to conceive of the encounter with a 'concrete' other if there isn't already something like an 'I'? How can we proceed from the level of pre-discursive experience to the level of moral demands? Numerous discussions could emerge from these questions, and even the very fact of Lévinas's popularity within bioethics evokes a number of questions. In any case, Lévinas provides an example of a theory that attempts to make clear how the categorical demand of morality can be understood and how its legitimacy can be justified.

Another example would be *Immanuel Kant* and several *transcendental philosophical theories* that were developed in a Kantian tradition. The basic idea in this tradition is that moral duties can only be justified by considering the necessary preconditions of moral obligations. Kant takes *us*, as autonomous beings that are capable of determining their actions and assigning themselves moral responsibilities, as his starting point. Morality can only exist insofar as there exist beings – such as ourselves – that are capable of action and self-determination. For that reason our autonomy, our moral capacity, forms the basis for human dignity. The notion of morality and moral obligation cannot be conceived in any other way. The idea of transcendental philosophy is thus that we should first consider the necessary preconditions for morality and, on the basis of that, identify moral duties.

This topic will return in a more elaborate form later in this chapter. In the current context, the only thing that is important is that there is an internal connection between the interpretation of the status of morality and the theoretical form of ethics. The first question this brings up is what characterises a moral judgment and a moral demand in the first place, and the next question is what possibilities are available to ethics for thinking about the justification of such judgments and demands. Depending on the answers to these questions, the expectation that one has of bioethics will change. Furthermore, since all of these questions are debated in metaethics, bioethics as a discipline will have to deal with a multiplicity of metaethical positions. Of course, every individual bioethicist will be able to – and will in fact have to – commit to a metaethical standpoint. Certain metaethical standpoints, such as emotivism or radical non-cognitivist positions, declare any attempt at knowledge in bioethics to be gratuitous. In that case, we must wonder what the task of bioethics as an academic discipline *could* be.

2.1.4 *Case studies – experience – narrativity*

In the last section I showed that ethics is about moral normative questions, although in the context of an 'ethics of the good life' other ethical questions might emerge. Furthermore, two things have become clear: trying to understand the status of moral claim-making requires discussion, as does the theoretical pertinence that ethics, as a reflective discipline, claims to have. All of these discussions provide a basis for the expectations that can be had of bioethics. I will now proceed to discuss bioethical methods that are based on the presumption that the best way to deal with normative claims is not to consult normative theories and moral principles, but rather to turn to exemplary individual cases and life experience.

2.1.4.1 *The renaissance of casuistry*

In the context of bioethics, *casuistry* has made an unexpected career (for literature see Arras 1999; Kuczewski 1999; Wildes 1993). When in 1988 Albert Jonsen and Stephen Toulmin published their book *The Abuse of Casuistry*, they were able to draw upon a moral-theological tradition of dealing with individual ethical cases, which had enjoyed its heyday from the 15th to the 17th centuries. In the moral-theological tradition, casuistry was deployed primarily in an attempt to provide pastoral workers with some orientation in taking confession. Now for medical ethics, considering particular cases does indeed suggest itself. In many journals of medical ethics this practice has become well established,[7] and for educational purposes case studies are useful too, since they make it possible to present a moral problem in a concrete and didactically meaningful way. One might for instance sketch the situation of organ scarcity in relation to a variety of possible beneficiaries of organ transplantation in order to discuss, by means of a concrete example, which arguments are pertinent for and against prioritising which patients.

However, casuistry is not only of interest from a didactical standpoint. In fact, Jonsen and Toulmin's attempt was to establish casuistry as a general method in bioethics. As a method within bioethics, casuistry starts by carefully *describing* the case at issue, and identifying the moral *peculiarities* of

7 Several journals, for instance, regularly publish anonymised cases from clinical practice, on which ethical comments are solicited.

the case. Subsequently, its task is to *compare* the case to similar, *paradigmatic cases*, in order to propose a moral judgment in light of this comparative assessment. Casuistry thus fundamentally depends on *paradigmatic cases* and the formation of *analogies*. When, for instance, it becomes clear in the description of a medical case that the moral issue involves patient autonomy, the withdrawal of medical treatment or the improvement of the patient's quality of life, we ask ourselves what kinds of judgments have been made in analogous cases and in what ways the present case might be different. In short, casuistry starts from paradigmatic cases for which a relatively comprehensive consensus can be achieved and uses a comparison to the paradigmatic case as a basis for the moral judgment at hand.

Jonsen and Toulmin consider this method to have a number of advantages compared with rather theoretical approaches in bioethics. In casuistry, the moral judgment is based on paradigmatic everyday moral understanding and thus on familiar forms of moral consensus. While philosophical engagement with moral issues always results in considerable discrepancies, we seem quite capable of coming to agreements on a pre-theoretical level. Regardless of whether we are religious or secular, Kantians or utilitarian, we consider the killing of innocent persons morally problematic. By describing particular cases and building analogies to a paradigmatic situation where the moral evaluation is unambiguous, casuistry aims to tie in with this common moral knowledge.

Moreover, one might point out in favour of casuistry as a moral-philosophical method that it is a kind of systematisation of everyday forms of moral argumentation. In everyday life, after all, we are more likely to try to come to moral judgments by forming analogies than by appealing to big theories. When discussing the issue of abortion, people might say: 'But it's not OK to kill a small child either, is it!' Everyday moral reasoning is familiar with casuistic methodology, and casuistry as a bioethical method is a systematic development of this common manner of reasoning. This continuity with everyday practical reason has a long tradition within ethics. Aristotle pointed out that in ethics we cannot have knowledge in the same way as we do in the domain of science in the natural world. But in ethics – according to Aristotle – gaining knowledge is not the main point. Ethics is about guiding our actions. While knowledge is about something general, acting always has to do with a particular case. In acting, knowledge does play a role, but the actions themselves are always situated in a concrete setting and it is the task of ethics to provide guidance in these concrete situations. For that reason, Aristotle strongly emphasises the significance of 'phronesis' or practical wisdom – the ability to act rightly in a concrete situation in the light of available practical knowledge. Jonsen and Toulmin draw upon everyday logic of argumentation when they tie in with Aristotle's *Rhetoric*. 'Rhetoric', in this case, is not a strategy for manipulating others, but a systematisation of the argumentative structures that are familiar to us through everyday use. Rhetoric will, for instance, identify the argumentative sources we draw upon in everyday life (tradition, life experience, etc). It is this broad range of methods and sources of knowledge of which casuistry makes use.

2.1.4.2 Critical remarks

However, the establishment of casuistry as a methodology in medical ethics has sparked criticism as well. From a practical perspective it can be asked whether casuistry is able to meet the requirements of modern moral discussions. Casuistry, for instance, assumes that particular cases can be described in *a more or less isolated way.* However, that is only true for a very restricted fraction of bioethical discussions. It is not a coincidence that the casuistic method was initially used for discussions in clinical ethics. A clinical setting is where cases occur according to paradigmatic patterns: two patients are eligible for an organ transplantation, but there is only one organ – who should receive it? The situation can be described, the case can be isolated. Of course more complex cases are conceivable as well. Indeed, in medical practice there often are 'paradigmatic cases' – treatment situations that occur repeatedly with only minor variations. And the method of casuistry corresponds in many respects to the ways in which, in medicine, experiential knowledge is handed down and taught. However, there is a whole range of bioethical questions that are not about particular isolated cases, but about understanding structural and institutional coherences. Political discussions about organ transplantation, for instance, are not primarily about decisions in concrete cases, but about the question of how organs can be allocated justly within an institutional context. In those discussions, the issues are waiting lists, allocation formulas, legal arrangements, etc. 'Eurotransplant', for instance, is an institution active throughout Europe which has to deal with different legal regulations in different European countries. An important question is also which research strategies can be developed in order to resolve the lack of donor organs. Pertinent is how the consent of organ donors is to be arranged, and what the role of organ transplantation in future medicine will be in the first place. All of these are, of course, questions for which it is vital to be aware of the consequences of different regulations for the concrete situation at the patient's bedside. What is important, then, is first and foremost to understand the structural context that has a bearing on that situation, rather than relating it to paradigmatic individual cases. For all questions that involve complex situations, therefore, casuistry has *clear limitations.*

Moreover, it is strongly disputed what the paradigmatic individual cases are in the first place, and whether constructing comparisons does at all advance our understanding of the moral problem. In the case of abortion, for example, comparisons are frequently drawn between the termination of a pregnancy, the killing of newborn babies and the prevention of pregnancy through impeding nidation (implantation). Reinhard Merkel (2002), for instance, expands this field of analogies with a large range of fictive cases. One of his examples is: a fire breaks out in an IVF laboratory. The only person present is forced to choose between saving either a child, or a large number of fertilised ova. What to do? Merkel's point is, of course, that no sensible human being is able to treat embryos and born humans on equal terms. To illustrate this, he presents a number of cases with great imagination. The opposition, however, has got its cases ready as well. Robert Spaemann (2001/2006), for one, is no less imaginative when presenting analogies about abortion and euthanasia. Spaemann argues that anyone who denies an embryo the right to life cannot sustain any good grounds to grant this right to a newborn baby or comatose patient. In fact, he concludes that from the denial of the right to life to embryos it is only a small step to debating the right to life of Jews. Spaemann's contributions to the discussion are rich in individual cases and appeal – quite like Merkel's – to the immediate plausibility of the individual case. In all fairness, it must be noted that neither author restricts himself to presenting case studies; both have much to offer theoretically as well. However, we should ask whether the fervent deployment of exemplary cases has actually been conducive to the illumination of what is at issue. One might feel that, above all, the effect of such cases is on the emotional plane.

With Merkel and Spaemann, I have – quite intentionally – introduced two particularly antithetic exponents of the German embryo protection debate. Their example shows that there are limits to casuistry, particularly when there is no commonly shared view of the moral issue in question. Casuistry cannot produce any new moral consensus; it can only test whether a certain individual case can be interpreted convincingly against a background of existing moral agreement. In a situation in which there is a plurality of assessments of fundamental questions, the method cannot contribute anything towards overcoming such pluralism. Moreover, casuistry is not capable of providing any critical assessment of the justification of our moral convictions. The method remains altogether silent about the question of whether or not certain basic convictions that are articulated in paradigmatic cases are good and justified. However, in the two aspects of *moral pluralism* and the question of *moral justification*, two central challenges of the contemporary bioethical debate have come to light.

Casuistry functions best when – as is true in many clinical cases – the problem at hand is situated within an institutionalised context; that is, if its situation is one in which it is possible to look back on relatively long traditions of 'good conduct' and in which a large number of circumstantial conditions has already been clarified legislatively. It seems, therefore, that casuistry is a helpful approach for *clinical ethics*; not, however, for the discussion of issues for which there is a strong pluralism in opinion and assessment. The debate on whether a paradigmatic case exists by which to judge abortion is particularly misleading. And that is not because there is no hope of ever coming to an agreement – *that* aspect is a danger that will always be present in this discussion. Rather, the problem is that it does not help the transparency of the debate when people endeavour to discuss analogous cases at the cost of all other considerations. For casuistry has less potential to identify and propose *morally relevant aspects* than methods that draw upon normative ethical theories and which explain and verify the conditions under which corresponding moral judgments can be justified.

2.1.4.3 Casuistry as an ethical method?

The foregoing considerations bring up another central issue: the relation between the *casuistic method* and *ethical theories*. This is a divisive matter, for casuistry can be seen either as an *heuristic approach*, compatible with a further discussion in the context of normative ethical theories, or as an *alternative to ethical theories*. For a proponent of *casuistry as heuristics*, one could for instance turn to Baruch Brody (1988). According to him the accomplishment of casuistry is that it offers an entrance into the moral complexity of individual cases. While a normative ethical theory usually focuses on only one morally relevant matter (avoidance of suffering, autonomy, etc.), the description of individual cases can do justice to the multifaceted nature of concrete situations, and emphasise their complexity better than any approach that takes its start from an ethical theory. What this leaves out is that the description of a case will lead to questions and disagreements that can only be discussed with the help of ethical theories. As a *heuristic instrument*, casuistry can thus make use of the existence of moral consensuses by describing individual cases and forming analogies to established paradigms. At the point where it discovers moral disagreement, however, it will turn over further discussion to theory-based discourse. When, on the other hand, casuistry is understood as an *independent approach*, that is, as an *alternative to ethical theory formation*, this can take two forms, both of which have far-reaching implications. A first possible starting point is the belief that the particularities of individual situations of action can be done justice only if all abstract generalisations of morality associated with, for instance, Kantianism and utilitarianism are set aside. This is in line with the parallel between casuistry and Aristotelianism suggested above. Yet having or lacking a preference for an Aristotelian type of ethics is not only a matter of how one is disposed towards the role of rules and principles in ethics. The available options are not 'Aristotle for the individual case' versus 'Kant/utilitarianism for ethical theory'. Moreover, it is significant that Aristotle develops no notion of individual rights and categorical moral obligations. Rather, in the context of the distinction between normative ethics and ethics of the good life, Aristotle is concerned with providing practical guidance towards a successful life. His concentration on common moral beliefs and practical wisdom is subservient to the development of this guidance. If the practice of starting from individual cases and practical moral knowledge were to be interpreted in an Aristotelian framework, this would have to entail that one depart – much like MacIntyre or Anscombe – from the modern notion of morality. That is of course a standpoint that can be defended, although not with the arguments central to the bioethical casuistry debate. Casuistry is not merely concerned with taking individual cases seriously, or doing justice to the particularities of concrete situations. A decision in favour of casuistry would require an argument against the modern notion of morality that would have to be theoretically much more profound than that.

Another way of understanding *casuistry as an ethical theory* could be metaethically characterised as *particularist*. It was Jonathan Dancy, in his book *Ethics without Principles* (2004), who introduced particularism as a general ethical method (there are some changes in the recent position in Dancy 2009). In his book, Dancy argues that it is possible to identify moral obligations without drawing upon moral principles. It is only in the light of concrete situations that we know that it is morally reprehensible to murder someone, or not to help him. Dancy thus fully commits to a Kantian notion of moral obligation, but questions the idea that rules and principles can contribute in any significant way to our knowledge of these obligations. It is inherent in the very structure of moral knowledge that it is concrete, situated and context-bound, yet it is knowledge of the existence of moral obligations all the same. Therefore, the most crucial aspects of moral reflection for the purposes of moral communication and forming judgments about complex moral problems are reflection on individual cases, developing an understanding of their particularities and applying this knowledge to new cases. For Dancy, the particularities of individual cases do not divert from what is really important; they are not disruptions. In particularism, it is not the case that moral knowledge can be found on a general level and is secondarily applied to the individual case. Rather, moral knowledge can only be attained in individual cases, and generalised perspectives are always generalisations of such individual cases, meant only to serve the assessment of other individual cases.

It is to Dancy's great credit that he has developed a systematic account of the concept of a particularist ethics. His achievement is clearly stronger than many similar conceptions, which reject the use of moral principles without making any effort to develop a systematic defence of the corresponding implications. However, his approach is still vulnerable to the weaknesses of casuistic models outlined above. How one can do justice to complex moral questions situated in an institutional context, how individual cases can be described in such a way that their morally relevant aspects come to light unambiguously, and how it is possible to provide moral orientation in a context of moral pluralism – these questions remain open in Dancy's account as well. His conception is also dependent on there being factical moral consensuses on which we can draw. When dissent in a controversial moral debate is quite deep, particularism does not aid the justification of moral judgments. Moreover, it is largely unclear how it is possible to arrive at knowledge of moral obligations in individual cases without the use of moral principles.

With respect to the relation between casuistry and ethical theories, three possibilities emerge: first, casuistry as a heuristic instrument, compatible with theoretical ethical debates; secondly, casuistry as a form of situation-dependent practical wisdom in an Aristotelian sense; and, thirdly, a particularist theory *à la* Dancy. Given the complexity of modern bioethical discussions and the internal problems of particularism, only the first form seems plausible to me.

2.1.4.4 Narrative ethics

In the context of casuistry, one last domain that should be noted is that of narrative approaches, which over the last decade and a half have also gained some attention in bioethics (Jones 1999; Verstraeten 1994). Several different forms of the narrative approach to ethics can be distinguished:

Some bioethical approaches draw upon *narratives* along the lines of casuistic approaches in clinical ethics. In a compact and accessible form, narratives provide an entrance into patients' biographies, present patients' value systems, and are able to disclose unsolved tensions and dilemmas. Examples from novels can make the clinical experience and the encounter with new technologies accessible to us. Such stories show, to an extent, how medical research and technologies are reflected in people's experiences. In recent years, the function of literary works has increasingly been performed by film. Narratives and films are suitable instruments for presenting a case in didactic contexts. With regard to the meaning and limits of narrativity in the context of bioethics, what has been said about casuistry holds for narrativity as well.

In addition, however, there have long been attempts to develop a 'narrative ethics' (Kleinman 1989; Nelson 1997; in the German-speaking world, a narrative ethics had already been developed in the 1970s in Mieth 1976). Compared with actual patient biographies, literary narratives are denser and richer in reflection. Yet literature is not only a concentration of life experience; it is itself a form of reflection. Literature does not simply mirror human life experiences, but in many ways reacts on them, alienates and surpasses them, etc. On the one hand, art is very close to life experience; it echoes people's individual and particular experiences, human suffering and the tensions of life. At the same time, the narrative structure is a form of critical thinking about experiences in life. This fundamental meaning of literature as a way of dealing with the world becomes important mostly in the domains of life experience for which we lack interpretative models. Literature, film and other aesthetic forms develop possibilities and proposals for the interpretation of our experiences. Pedro Almodóvar's film *All About My Mother* (*Todo Sobre Mi Madre*), for instance, is an important contribution to the development of models for interpreting and dealing with transsexuality. Something similar can of course be said of the numerous contributions to possible ways of dealing with cloning and gene technology (from *Gattaca* to *The Island*) or to the presentation of problems surrounding euthanasia, as in the film *The Sea Inside* (*Mar Adentro*) by Alejandro Amenábar. Art can sketch fictive future possibilities and bring human fears to light. Art has hands-on ways of showing what a world would look like in which a certain technology was being developed.

But art can also present tensions without offering resolutions. A film such as Almodóvar's shows possibilities, hopes, fears, emotional and social abysses that can open up in the context of transsexuality. Yet the film is not forced to draw conclusions, as one would in real life. A film can end without resolve and is not compelled to moral judgment. (I have developed this theme more elaborately in my book on ethics and aesthetics (Düwell 1999).) For that reason, literature and art form a special reflective medium that is important for ethics. This is especially true since our fears, wishes, hopes and utopias play a central role in bioethics. It is hardly possible to understand the social dynamics of dealing with gene and biotechnologies without reference to our hopes for cures, utopias of physical improvement and fears that society will take control of our bodies. Art provides our emotional interaction with medicine and technology with an authentic mode of expression and makes it possible for this dimension to be thematised and communicated.

The meaning of literary and aesthetic presentation for the public debate, however, remains ambivalent. Art can manipulate, fixate certain impressions and direct our reflection unilaterally. Take the film *Gattaca*. It depicts a world in which genetic diagnosis allows for extensive control over people. People are born after preimplantation genetic diagnosis and are, as a rule, the result of careful selection: the best life prospects must be guaranteed for every child. Here life is characterised by governmental control over human genes. The drama of the protagonists is developed through the tension between the incidental moments of their lives and the attempt at total genetic control by society. In reaction to this conflict, the protagonists try to cut their own paths, both in quite different ways. Now the meaning of this film is not to be relativised. Without being able to go into detail at this point, it may well be said that the film develops a perspective in an aesthetically coherent manner, and depicts the drama of the protagonists clearly and successfully. All the same, the film presents a very one-sided view of the potential dangers of human genetics and remains rooted in the Orwellian and Huxleyan tradition of state dystopias. The message it sends is that we must figure out how to avoid the peril of governments using human genetics to control citizens genetically. Such a suggestion, however, steers the image of gene technology in a very particular direction; quite similar, actually, to Sloterdijk's discourse on the human zoo, in which he also presumes that this kind of control is what forms the threat. If, however, we consider the developments in the life sciences as sketched in the first chapter, then this perspective is actually very improbable. It seems more likely that the most significant problem resulting from human genetics will be not state control, but the uncontrollable nature of these developments themselves. That the broad application potential of genomic technologies might be threatening is not so much because governments could use them to control their citizens. Rather, the question is whether in a globalised society governments will still have enough power to ensure the protection of individual rights against numerous actors who want to use the available information. How much power do governmental bodies have to force health insurance companies and industries to respect individual rights? Surely *Gattaca* also suggests that the only thing we must make sure of is that governmental control is ruled out and that this is the problem to which the ethical discussion should restrict itself? The point here, however, is not so much whether or not the *Gattaca* scenario is accurate but the observation that the film directs people's imagination, fears and expectations towards a state dystopia. When it appeared in 1997, *Gattaca* attracted quite some attention and, as a result, it influenced the way in which people picture gene technology. In a sense, the film thus pre-structured the ethical discussion on the opportunities and risks of gene technologies. Films, stories and art exercise influence on the directions in which the subsequent ethical discussion will move. They are capable of opening up new horizons, but can also mask complexities and uncritically steer people's collective imagination in one direction.

This makes it clear that the relation between narrativity and ethical discourse and theory formation is *ambivalent*. On the one hand, it is relevant for ethical reflection that aesthetic media provide a space for the expression of human life experiences, feelings and fears. On the other hand, the aesthetic potential for manipulation must not be disregarded. Any form of narrative ethics that draws on art in the sense of an anti-theory is subject to this potential for manipulation. Extreme precaution is thus required insofar as narrative ethics aims to be an independent approach within ethical theory formation. This would threaten not only the independence of ethical reflection, but also the autonomy of aesthetic experience and composition, which can be ensured only if art is not employed directly as an embodiment of ethical reflection. (In Düwell 1999, I develop a systematic overview of the different ways in which the relation of ethics and aesthetics can be determined. Also see Seel 1991.)

2.1.5 Empirical research and ethics[8]

Over the last few years people have, in several contexts, considered the question regarding the relevance of empirical research for bioethics. Partly, this discussion was held under the heading 'empirical ethics' (Arnold and Forrow 1993; Borry, Schotsmans and Dierickx 2004, 2005; Callahan 1999; Haimes 2002; Molewijk et al. 2004; Musschenga 2005; Nijsingh and Düwell 2009; van der Scheer et al. 2004; de Vries and Gordijn 2009. That title, however, is misleading in a number of ways. On the one hand, it simply is the case that

8 For a large part, the following considerations reflect discussions in the Netherlands School for Research in Practical Philosophy and knowledge gained in the context of the multi-year research project 'Challenges of biomedicine', funded by the European Commission, in which sociologists and ethicists held focus groups on gene testing and organ transplantation, and engaged with the methodological questions concerning collaborations between ethics and sociology. See http://www.univie.ac.at/virusss/cobpublication.

ethics – with all the differences in methodological standards advocated by different bioethicists – is not an empirical discipline. The term 'empirical ethics' is therefore about as useful as the expression 'biochemical church history'. At the same time, however, the notion raises very misleading expectations. Albert Musschenga, who played a leading philosophical role in the development of this subject in the Netherlands, has introduced the alternative term 'empirically informed ethics' (Musschenga 2004), which is clearly more appropriate. In any case, the topic opens up a vast thematic spectrum. For that reason, this discussion is one that we should address.

The call for empirical investigations in the context of bioethics has different causes, and the kinds of empirical research suggested are diverse. As I explained in the introductory chapter, bioethical judgments are always mixed judgments, based on both normative and empirical presuppositions. In order to verify the soundness of the empirical presuppositions, bioethicists draw on the outcomes of empirical research. In the early decades of bioethics, the interdisciplinary discourse involved mostly biologists and physicians. At that time, important topics were the understanding of technological developments, risk assessment and scientific questions associated with the life sciences. More recently, the discussion with social and cultural sciences has been most prominent. This discussion comprises a variety of issues. On the one hand, bioethicists seek to improve their understanding of the situations in which moral decisions are made. Yet it is also important to understand how new technologies are being perceived by people. After all, technologies are not used independently of their valuations. They are perceived in concrete contexts of people's lives and integrated into concrete value systems, and they change these value systems and the self-understanding of those who use them. A central aspect of the bioethical conversation with social theorists is the attempt to understand these value systems and the changes propelled by new technologies.

Another motive is *acceptance assessment*. Social rejection of, for instance, nuclear energy, or a sceptical public attitude towards genetically modified foods poses a significant problem for researchers and developers of these technologies. Economically speaking, it is of course disastrous to develop technologies that large parts of the population simply do not want. In that sense, different parties are interested in developing insights into the public attitudes regarding new technologies, with the aim of changing them where necessary. Not infrequently, this coincides with an attitude on the part of the scientists that the public are not at all capable of having any adequate understanding of new and complex technologies. Therefore, it is imperative that measures are taken to improve the public understanding of science.

A further motive in the discussion is the connection of the technical-political debate with the desire for *public participation*. This is a change that can be traced in the history of technology assessment. While in the 1970s technology assessment roughly followed the model of the early warning system, and considered its task to be the presentation of technical and scientific data on the impact of new technologies, the more recent technology assessment debate is concerned with models of citizen participation. A variety of models are used for this purpose. Partly, the discussion concerns concrete decisions in the technological-political realm. Other modes of participation are focus groups in which a group of citizens is informed extensively about a certain new technology, after which participants are asked to comment on its desirability. New forms of research on scientific and technological developments often do not consider themselves as disciplines that merely investigate people's beliefs and attitudes about technology or parallel developments in technology and life worlds ('co-evolution'). Rather, investigating those beliefs and attitudes is combined with a sociological aim to assist society in articulating its standpoints (cf for instance Schweda and Schicktanz 2008, 2009; Felt and Fochler 2008).

To date, there is still hardly any theoretical framework for the collaboration between ethicists and sociologists. The discussion is clearly still in its infancy and it is, for a number of reasons, not a simple one either. First, the attempt of many ethicists to conduct their own sociological research is not unproblematic. Doing so requires a methodological apparatus that is not usually available at institutes for medical ethics or philosophy departments. Moreover, it may be asked whether it can ever be the task of ethicists to carry out sociological studies. In the domain of medical ethics this question is particularly pertinent, since the topics at issue often put a considerable emotional strain on participants in empirical studies. When, for instance, people who are ill are being asked what they think of advance directives, this is by no means a morally neutral procedure. The moral legitimation of such a study requires at the very least that the project meets all methodological standards and that its research aim is of high importance and cannot be attained by any other means (this, at least, is the standard that would form the basis of the assessment of scientific human subject research for an ethics committee).

There are, however, further difficulties for the dialogue between bioethics and the social sciences. For a start, the possibility of such a dialogue presupposes that the social sciences perceive bioethics as a discipline with which they can interact in the first place. Yet, as a rule, the social sciences consider bioethics rather as a research subject than as an interlocutor and, quite often, the distinction between the technical bioethical discourse and the biopolitical discourse is disregarded altogether. Moreover, there are numerous difficulties regarding the establishment of theoretical compatibility. Many scientific and technological studies are committed to certain basic theoretical concepts that *eo ipso* render ethical enquiries difficult, if not impossible. To name but two examples: in his version of systems theory, Niklas Luhmann tries to replace the perspective of action theory with a perspective of higher-level observation. Luhmann has actually personally authored contributions to the sociology of morality (Luhmann 1988/1991). Yet it remains a very fundamental question of how problems regarding the validity and justification of standards of conduct can be understood from the perspective of systems theory at all. In effect, Luhmann can only observe the claims of different actors and discourses of legitimation – he can not enter such discourses himself. The same problem emerges in an even more serious form in the context of Bruno Latour's actor-network theory (2005), which is very influential in areas of scientific and technological research. The basis of this theory is a notion of 'actor' that is systematically rid of all intentionality. Actors, for Latour, are persons, institutions, artefacts and natural objects which affect their environments. The distinction between an action and an event is systematically nullified. Such a theory, it is hoped, furthers an understanding of the influence of all these factors on different events, since the theory can take into account both human and nonhuman parameters. It does, however, introduce a concept of 'actor' in which 'mere' events cannot be distinguished from actions for which people can be held responsible. This makes all basic ethical notions utterly groundless. Without agents who can be held responsible for their actions and who formulate and justify standards or rules for this responsibility, or who wonder whether certain actions contribute to their life goals, ethics has lost its *raison d'être*. In order for any conversation between bioethics and the social sciences to be possible, it is therefore imperative to clarify certain basic theoretical notions that are required for the formulation of questions and methods in both fields.

In addition, it must be asked what bioethics wants to gain from its interaction with the social sciences. A few possibilities would be:

- data regarding people's opinions, preferences and attitudes with regard to life science technologies
- insight into the broader context of situations in which morally relevant decisions are made
- insight into people's perception and interpretations of these technologies

It may be clear that, depending on the interest of bioethicists, very different sociological research methods will be relevant. If the bioethicist wants data on people's opinions, quantitative methods will be pertinent; if the bioethical interest is in perceptions and patterns of interpretations, hermeneutic and qualitative approaches will be helpful.

With respect to the practice of gathering mere information regarding people's opinions and attitudes, there is of course one accusation that particularly suggests itself and which has dominated the debate on empirical ethics. From the fact that people think certain things, ethics cannot simply conclude that the opinion at issue is morally legitimate. 'Empirical ethics' is therefore vulnerable to the accusation of committing an 'is-ought fallacy'–the accusation that it justifies value judgments by reference to empirical matters of fact. Whatever one may think of the pertinence of the is-ought problem in general, simply referring to people's factual beliefs when assessing the validity of a moral norm is not a valid procedure in ethics. An opinion is not justified simply by the fact that it is *someone's* opinion nor by the fact that a large number of people share it.

In the context of an investigation into the relevance of public responses for utilitarian ethics, Dieter Birnbacher (1993: 66, translation N.v. Steenbergen) has pointed out a way in which people's factual beliefs might be indirectly significant. He writes:

> [W]hen considering different outcomes, the utilitarian must give the same weight to the standpoints that cannot be justified according to utilitarian principles, but are instead akin to rival positions or based on reactions and attitudes to these, as to those that can be grounded on a utilitarian basis. Appropriate consideration of these reactions simply follows from the demand for impartiality. I personally, for instance, do not deem the decisive argument against embryonic research to be that this research violates certain 'rights' of the human embryo or that it fails to respect the supposed fact that human life is worthy of unrestricted protection. I see it simply in the social non-acceptance of this kind of research on the basis of strong and evidently stable feelings of repulsion and fear.

The normative assumption underlying this argument appears to be that hidden behind people's reservations about embryonic research lie concerns that are said to be somehow respectable and that can be included among the range of positions that can be seriously held in principle, even if the evaluator does not share them. If that assumption is at play, it means that there would be something worthy of protection about embryos entirely independently of anyone's fears or feelings of repulsion. If not, then the only thing that supposedly matters is the simple satisfaction of people's preferences. The latter would be perfectly coherent from a utilitarian point of view. In that case, the mere fact that people display 'stable feelings of repulsion and fear' is already a reason to accord more weight to those feelings when trying to determine what is morally right. That would be no different in the case of people's negative feelings towards embryonic research than for female circumcision or other issues. In the matter whether immigrants should be allowed entrance, the strong feelings of repulsion in nationalists should be weighed in a similar way. Through such a procedure, ethics would surrender rather uncritically to people's most hollow reactions. For the question is never what reasons are offered for these preferences, but merely whether or not the preferences exist.

Very *different* kinds of empirical questions could, however, be relevant for a broader range of normative ethical theories, extending beyond variations of utilitarianism. Such questions pertain to understanding morally relevant decision-making situations in the first place. If we hold that individual freedom of decision is something that should be morally protected, and if we fear, for instance, that in decision-making situations regarding abortion there is often pressure on the pregnant woman, the latter is an empirical assumption that should be verified. If we fear that decisions concerning euthanasia are made under social pressure, then we ought to know more about the circumstances in which these decisions are made. When we discuss whether live organ donation amongst family members is morally defensible, we should attempt to find out empirically what the experiences of donors and recipients have been in the past.

In a broader sense it could also be important to gain insight into patterns of perception and interpretation of technologies. This is pertinent for several different forms of ethical argumentation. If someone deems it a moral obligation to facilitate people's self-fulfilment, that person ought to know first which possible circumstances might threaten this self-fulfilment; and such threats cannot be formulated independently of the question of whether those concerned consider and experience it as a threat. Someone who wishes to protect individual rights has to know when technologies are experienced as a threat to individual rights, and to an extent must identify which goods are candidates for moral protection. Someone who points out in favour of reproductive technologies that they can help women realise their life goals must try to understand how these technologies influence the lives of affected women.

For almost any moral judgment, therefore, it is important to be acquainted with the range of possible courses of action. Before we can judge whether a certain action is morally defensible, we have to know what alternatives there are. To an important extent these alternatives are, however, determined by social factors and by affected agents' perceptions of the range of possible things to do. In this respect too, social sciences are an indispensable conversational partner for bioethics.

All of these questions are not only interesting for our understanding of individual decision-making situations in the context of new technologies, but also for political discussions of bioethics. If these technology-specific political discussions are not to be mere attempts to manipulate citizens or 'produce' consensus, it seems to be of utmost importance to understand the horizon of perceptions and interpretations of new technologies. For the standard of bioethics, it is a vital question to what extent it manages to conduct normative discussions against the background of an adequately sophisticated understanding of the perceptive and interpretive patterns of 'users' of this technology. Moreover, it is imperative to have at least a somewhat sophisticated picture of arguments concerning biotechnology used in the non-academic world. But of course none of this has anything to do with 'empirical ethics'. Ethics remains a discipline that employs philosophical arguments in its attempts to justify normative demands. The theory of 'mixed judgments' proposed early on is a much more productive model for a methodologically transparent discussion between social sciences and bioethics than the systematic obfuscation of the relations between normative and empirical claims which currently characterises the discussion on 'empirical ethics'. In political contexts too, bioethics should protect itself from the illusion that reverting to empirical research methods could help us deal with the confusing diversity of moral opinions and ethical theories. The complexity of modern discussions cannot be evaded and this should never be presented as a possibility, neither in politics nor in the public debate.

2.2 Bioethics and normative ethics

It is clear that with the advancement of the life sciences the field of bioethical topics that are controversial or require discussion has become exceptionally diverse. Nevertheless, the central endeavour of bioethics remains to investigate morally permissible conduct with respect to living creatures, as explained in sections 2.1.1–2.1.3. The discussion of casuistry (section 2.1.4) and so-called 'empirical ethics' (section 2.1.5) showed that these methods do not provide an alternative to normative ethical theory. Therefore, we have come to a point where we must discuss the range of normative ethical theories in more detail. Before doing so, however, some preliminary remarks are in order.

Especially with regard to the bioethical topics that are particularly controversial, there are fundamental differences between the proponents of different ethical theories. At the same time, there are large areas of overlap. A preference utilitarian and a Kantian will both judge killing innocent people to be morally impermissible. Indeed, it is certainly a task of bioethics to identify such areas of overlap. At the same time it is in the interest of transparency in bioethics that relevant differences are not played down, but explicitly worked out. Clarifying the differences is what makes it possible to discuss them in the first place. In the same vein, *convergences* of isolated concrete judgments across theories do not mean that one can randomly use any normative ethical theory with that particular outcome, or that different theories can be combined at will. To name but one example: traditional utilitarianism demands the maximisation of the total sum of all pleasure or happiness. The demand of this theory is taken seriously only if one accepts in a discussion that for a utilitarian this demand is the only criterion of morality. All the same, it can be shown that utilitarianism will *converge* with other theories on many concrete moral judgments, so that in content it will arrive at the same or similar demands as other normative theories. It is, however, a different matter altogether to propose a normative ethical theory that is modelled on utilitarianism, but attempts to avoid certain weaknesses. In such a procedure one would propose a *new* normative ethical theory, which would involve having to *justify* this new theory. Unreflected syncretism in combining ethical theories neither takes seriously the pertinence of those theories nor does it contribute to their development.

Normative ethical theories propound one or more criteria by which to judge the moral defensibility of actions and attempt to justify why these are the right criteria. The *application* of normative ethical theories to concrete bioethical discussions is nevertheless always a complex step. If my aim here is to emphasise that bioethical judgments are bound to normative ethical theories, I am not pleading that concrete judgments are simply *deduced* from normative theories. Even less relevant is what Kant or Mill himself would have thought about concrete normative ethical questions. The normative ethical theory merely identifies the foundation for a concrete ethical assessment. That is something completely different from the reduction of a concrete moral judgment to its theoretical origin. Moreover, even authors of identical ethical theories can arrive at different moral judgments if they differ in their assessment of other aspects that are relevant for the judgment, for instance the prognosis of certain technical developments or the interpretation of ethically relevant feelings or attitudes of those concerned. The underlying normative ethical theory and its application to concrete moral discussions are therefore *two different levels* of ethical discussion.

Finally, it should be pointed out that the *classification of normative ethical theories* presents certain difficulties as well. The category of utilitarianism, for instance, involves a whole range of ethical theories. The classical utilitarianism of John Stuart Mill and the preference utilitarianism of Peter Singer are divided by numerous important differences. Even larger are the differences in the application of great metaethical concepts for the classification of ethical theories. For that reason, I will start by providing a brief overview of the differences in the formation of these concepts.

2.2.1 Classifications of normative ethical theories

Normative ethical theories are theories that propose a criterion or multiple criteria for the assessment of the moral permissibility of actions. This means that in the overall domain of the issues with which ethics concerns itself, normative ethics is a central area, but does not span the entire field. An important way of determining the difference between normative theories was proposed by William Frankena. Frankena defines 'teleological ethics' as theories that define what is morally right as a function of what is good in a nonmoral way, and 'deontological ethics' as theories that determine the moral right not merely or not principally in dependence on the nonmoral good. 'Nonmoral good' in this context does not denote something that is immoral, but rather *a moral*: something that is not morally qualified at all. Frankena (1973: 14ff, emphasis in original) writes:

> A teleological theory says that the basic or ultimate criterion or standard of what is morally right, wrong, obligatory, etc., is the nonmoral value that is brought into being. [...] Deontological theories deny what teleological theories affirm. They deny that the right, the obligatory and the morally good are wholly, whether directly or indirectly, a function of what is nonmorally good or of what promotes the greatest balance of good over evil for self, one's society, or the world as a whole. They assert that there are other considerations that may make an action or rule right or obligatory besides the goodness or badness of its consequences – certain features of the act itself other than the *value* it brings into existence, for example, the fact that it keeps a promise, is just, or is commanded by God or by the state.

Let us take a moment to consider this central definition, since it requires a number of elucidations, and because it has been of great importance for the subsequent ethical discussion. The concept 'teleological' hails from the Greek word *telos* (aim or purpose). The concept 'deontological', on the other hand, stems from the Greek expression for duty. It would seem natural to conclude that teleological ethics acts in pursuance with the aim or purpose of human action, just as it does for Aristotle, for whom the point of ethics is to provide guidance towards a happy and successful life. Deontological ethics, on this interpretation, is restricted to moral obligations. Yet this is not what Frankena had in mind. Nor is his the distinction that Max Weber marks by the concepts *ethics of responsibility* and *ethics of conviction*, according to which the ethicist of responsibility factors the long-term consequences of an action into his consideration, while the ethicist of conviction lets herself be guided solely by what she imagines herself to be obliged to do in response to a concrete situation (Weber 1988/2004). A further possible misunderstanding could arise in the context of medical ethics where, in a somewhat archaic manner the term 'deontology' is used to mean *professional code of conduct*. It used to be the case, for instance, to speak of deontology when denoting a model of duties for physicians. This, however, is something quite different from the use of the concept in the context of normative theories.

Frankena distinguishes different forms of normative theories that aim to determine what is morally right. 'Teleological ethics' are thus not tutorials for a happy life, but rather, just like deontological ethics, theories for the identification of moral obligations. The characteristic feature of teleological ethics is that they start from the assumption that we need a conception of what is nonmorally good before we can determine our moral obligations. 'Nonmoral good' refers to goods and goals of human action that we consider desirable without striving for them on the basis of a moral obligation. We consider education, pleasure and quality of life worthwhile in themselves, but we do not usually feel morally obliged to strive for these goals. A teleological ethics thus has an axiological (valuing) and a normative (prescriptive) component. Axiologically, the first step is to formulate a concept of a nonmoral good, to which a normative perspective is then functionally matched. A classic example of such an approach is utilitarianism, which in its classical form says: morally right are those actions that realise the greatest amount of pleasure (or happiness) for the greatest number.

The concept of deontological ethics, on the other hand, is described only negatively: Frankena says only that this form of ethics does *not* straightforwardly understand what is 'morally right' as a function of what is 'nonmorally good'. An example could be rights to freedom, which are pertinent even when observing them is not conducive to happiness (or when this is questionable). Rights to freedom are subject to more principled bounds. But Frankena formulates the concept 'deontological ethics' negatively only to the effect that it is *not* functionally aimed at a nonmoral good. It is not very easy to map every existing type of ethics onto one of these categories. Many theological ethics, which hold that the criterion for morality is the realisation of a religious good, would for instance have to be classified as teleological. At the same time, a religious ethics that simply says that morally right is what God has commanded would actually much more appropriately be called deontological. Teleological ethics appear to be less complicated and they leave room for balancing things out, since part of their methodological apparatus is the notion of a more or less. Striving for the greatest happiness for the greatest number always involves comparing different possible ways to increase happiness. Deontological ethics, in contrast, appear to involve strict prohibitions. However, deontological ethics often entail clashes of duties, while teleological ethics assume that it is possible to determine a maximum in the realisation of nonmoral goods. But those are all just matters of application. For Frankena, the central question is whether what is morally right is, or is not, exclusively identified as a function of a nonmoral good.[9]

There is another central distinction within the field of normative ethical theories: the distinction between *consequentialist* and *non-consequentialist ethics*. Some use the concept 'consequentialist ethics' as a synonym for 'teleological ethics' in Frankena's sense (Sense 1998). But that is not as easy. The concept is introduced into the debate by Elizabeth Anscombe's article 'Modern Moral Philosophy', which we have come across earlier in this chapter. In the recent debate the concept is understood in the following way: *consequentialist* ethics measure the moral rightness of an action exclusively based on whether the action results in the best possible outcome. For these theories it does, for instance, not matter at all what motives an agent has, or what goal he wanted to obtain. Rather, there is only one relevant question: what would the world look like after action A, and what would it look like after action B? Which of these would be a better world? For consequentialism in this sense, the *outcome of the action*, often combined with the idea of *maximisation* are decisive (see for example Pettit 1997).

Nonetheless, the use of these concepts may lead to confusion. For one thing, one might gain the impression that deontological ethics, as opposed to consequentialist ethics, emphasise the agent's motivations at the cost of taking the result of his action into consideration, or that they assess actions without regard for their consequences. In fact, this does not hold for most

9 John Rawls made a proposal which further differentiates things. He also formulates teleological ethics as those ethics that specify what is morally right in terms of a nonmoral good, but says then that any form of ethics is deontological 'that either does not specify the good independently from the right, or does not interpret the right as maximizing the good' (Rawls 1971: 30). That means that even forms of ethics that are based on the maximisation of something they determine to be good can be deontological, if the judgment of what counts as good already involves a moral perspective. For the purposes of this introduction, however, we will take Frankena's account as a starting point.

forms of deontological ethics, including Kantian ethics.[10] Almost all deontological ethics also involve judging the consequences of an action.

On top of all that, it is a rather confusing fact that the oppositions 'consequentialist' versus 'deontological' and 'teleological' versus 'deontological' are two distinct pairs that sometimes mean the same thing and sometimes have different meanings. In the first case, the question at issue is how the consequences of actions are taken into account, while in the second case the question is to what extent the criterion of morality entails the maximisation of a nonmoral good. A teleological form of ethics (in Frankena's sense) is *always* consequentialist, yet not all consequentialist ethics (in the sense of an exclusive focus on consequences) are teleological.

A final remark on the use of the concepts 'consequentialist' and 'deontological' is in order. So far, these concepts have been used within bioethics in order to characterise isolated arguments. With respect to cloning, for instance, arguments that take human dignity or the prohibition to kill into consideration are classified as 'deontological', while arguments that focus on balancing interests and assessing consequences are called 'consequentialist' (Gordijn 1999). This is misleading in several ways. On the one hand, people assume that deontological theories imply 'absolute' boundaries, that is, that they leave no room for exceptions. It is along these lines that Kant is accused of rigorism, although it is debatable whether this rigorism is an implication of the Kantian categorical imperative (cf for example Herman 1993). However that debate may turn out, though, rigorism is not a characteristic of deontological ethics per se. The concepts 'deontological', 'consequentialist' and 'teleological', moreover, only make sense as characterisations of ethical theories, not as classifications of isolated ethical arguments. The prohibition on killing, for example, is justified by ethical theorists both based on the idea of respect for human dignity and for reasons of its long-term or overall consequences. Many individual arguments can be constructed within different normative theoretical frameworks. Whether a specific point belongs to a certain type of normative theory can only become clear in the context of the broader argument in which it occurs.

10 When Kant formulates the categorical imperative as the demand to act only on the maxim that one can at the same time will as a universal law, he makes it necessary to consider the consequences of a certain action in order to be able to assess whether one could will the corresponding maxim as a universal law. Kant asks, for instance: could we accept someone promising something with the full intention not to keep this promise? No, says Kant, because if we were to accept that, then the consequence would be that the institution of promising would be ruined, and a world in which that is true is not one we could wish for. That means that in the implementation of the categorical imperative, the assessment of the consequences of an action plays a central role. However, those consequences come into view only with respect to maxims and not as independent descriptions of states of affairs.

2.2.2 Utilitarianism and balancing interests

According to Frankena's classic definition, 'teleological ethics' are characterised by the fact that they understand what is morally right – what action is morally required – exclusively as a function of the nonmoral good. The standard example of a teleological ethics is utilitarian. The term 'utilitarianism', however, is used for a whole range of ethical theories. In the late 18th century and during the 19th century, utilitarian battled first and foremost for liberation from religious paternalism, and were particularly beholden to the idea of equality. Utilitarianism considers us to be morally obligated to improve happiness and good chances in life for everyone. Behind this was mainly an emancipatory impulse to understand morality not as a mechanism that aids the implementation of religious and civic restraints, but as a way of obligating people to minimise suffering and maximise chances of happiness. Central to utilitarianism is the universalistic idea of taking *anyone* into account. This universalism must be emphasised in particular because, colloquially, utilitarianism is often talked about as sheer 'benefit calculus', economic rationality, or even egoism. Those characterisations are markedly misleading, since what is specific about utilitarianism lies not in the defence of economic rationality – even if utilitarianism shows an unmistakable affinity with it – but in the universalistic claim that everybody has to share in the benefits of an action.

Even if the term 'utilitarianism' denotes an entire family of normative ethical theories, it might be worth attempting to formulate a standard version of utilitarianism. The classic formulation of utilitarianism is: the greatest happiness for the greatest number. That is, if there are multiple things that can be done, then we are morally obligated to choose the action that entails the most happiness (or negatively, the least harm) for the largest number. Therefore, the consequences of multiple possible actions must be compared, and the actions must be evaluated in relation to each other. In characterising this standard form, it seems useful to me to distinguish between two aspects, which I would like to call the *axiological* and the *normative aspect* of utilitarianism (cf Smart and Williams 1973). On the one hand, utilitarianism makes *statements about the value* (axiology) of goods that are to be maximised and distributed; on the other, there are *normative statements* concerning how these goods are to be dealt with in a moral regard.

2.2.2.1 Axiology: the assessments of utilitarianism

Utilitarianism attempts to find a basis for the evaluation of moral judgments that requires as few theoretical and debatable presuppositions as possible. Without any strong presuppositions, it should still be possible to show that different states of affairs resulting from different actions can be evaluated differently. To do so, only a single value appears to be necessary – that one value being required because otherwise there would be no point of comparison at all. If I want to compare two situations, but use two different standards,

I will never be able to indicate which situation is better. This fundament leads to three solid facts: (i) utilitarianism has a *'single good axiology'* in which *'utility'* is the only good; (ii) this good is characterised, in the sense of teleological ethics, as a *nonmoral good*; and (iii) at the same time, utilitarianism only evaluates (probable) consequences of actions. It must be emphasised that this holds only for the classical form of utilitarianism, and that there certainly are versions of utilitarianism that assume multiple values (pluralistic theories).

The fact that 'utility' is considered the *only* value that plays a role in the utilitarian evaluation has led to innumerable criticisms. The insight behind this decision is that different people judge differently. 'Utility' is more or less open to the different preferences of those affected. At the same time, 'utility' is not completely dependent on subjective preferences, since the fulfilment of any preference presupposes the satisfaction of certain basic conditions. Whether the scope of 'utility' is determined exclusively on the basis of preferences, or whether 'objective' goods come into play as well, is settled differently in different versions of utilitarianism. A pure preference orientation would mean in practice that it must be determined 'empirically' which preferences people actually have, so that it can then be assessed how the best result can be achieved in light of this evaluative basis. Such a procedure, however, would discriminate in favour of the present generation and those who are able to articulate their preferences. As a rule, *preference utilitarianism*, in which utility is based on individual preference, would refrain from taking a stance on what is useful and what contributes to happiness. *Hedonistic utilitarianism*, on the other hand, asserts that only happiness in the sense of pleasure is a good that ought to be striven for by literally everyone. A *pluralistic utilitarianism* would hold, in contrast, that certain states of affairs, for instance those in which certain basic needs are met for everyone, are worth striving for. The latter would have to let go of the idea of a 'single good axiology'. Preference utilitarianism is economical in its presuppositions, and does not make itself vulnerable to being challenged on its axiology. Yet it does have the consequence that all preferences, however questionable, must be considered on an equal footing. Hedonistic or pluralistic forms of utilitarianism, on the other hand, would certainly be able to make substantive presuppositions as part of their axiologies, but these axiologies will then be subject to disagreements. In any case, it is of fundamental importance that any basic value is understood as a nonmoral good. This means that it is never the case that the utility is 'moralised'. The question is thus not whether certain 'goods' are worth striving for in a moral regard. Rather, the moral perspective is brought into play by the maximisation and distribution of goods.

Finally, utilitarianism merely assesses the results of actions, not intentions or motives. If action A would lead to a world in which utility X exists and action B to a world with utility Y, then the task of utilitarianism is to compare X with Y. This leads to at least two problems: (i) how can these results be compared if the only pertinent criterion is more or less? Even if a 'single good axiology' is presupposed, surely this would require that the utilities (the 'goods') are quantifiable? Pluralistic theories are furthermore confronted with the problem of the standard for comparison mentioned above: action A leads to more musicality in the world, while action B protects a landscape. How to compare such possible outcomes? (ii) The comparability of consequences of actions presupposes that the consequences are known, or at least that probability assessments can be made. The less we know about the consequences of actions, the fewer possibilities we have to evaluate them.

2.2.2.2 Normativity: utilitarianism and the obligation to act

In the light of these evaluations, utilitarianism says that the choice between different actions must favour the action that will (probably) result in as much utility for as many parties as possible. Or negatively: the action that will cause as little harm for as few of those involved as possible. There are two aspects to this demand: *maximisation* and *universality*.

Maximisation means that there is a normative obligation to act so as to realise as much value (utility) as possible or as little adversity as possible. That means that utilitarianism has the concept of a 'more or less' of value that can be realised; harm, for instance, can be done to a greater or lesser extent. The moral demands of utilitarianism are thus predominantly comparative: one action is better than another. Connected to this is the idea that one ought to bring about 'as much value as possible'. This has often evoked the criticism that utilitarianism demands 'too much' of people. In an extreme case, it could require someone to annihilate himself in order to increase overall utility. The more pressure put on the idea of 'maximisation', the stronger the call for an ethical justification of the corresponding principle. It may seem intuitively plausible that I am morally obligated not to harm anyone. Yet even this demand requires justification if the notion of harm has not been specified. Someone may feel harmed when I build a garage across from his house, but that this is morally relevant is something that must be argued for. And it is even much less plausible that I would be morally obligated to do anything to maximise a certain value.

The central 'moral' point of utilitarianism is that any moral assessment must involve the benefit and harm to *all* affected parties. The *universality* of utilitarianism consists in the demand to take into account *all of those affected by an action*. To an extent, this is the reason why utilitarianism reserves such a central place for the common interest, for collective goods. The point is not to advance the collective as such, but to give due consideration to the perspectives of all of those concerned. This evokes a number of questions. First of all: what is the scope of 'affected parties'? Utilitarianism demands that animal harm be avoided, on the assumption that animals belong to the circle of creatures deserving of moral consideration since they can be harmed. Moreover, there is the question to what extent we are to consider the interests of future generations. It is relatively unambiguous, however, that utilitarianism does not require or allow special treatment of those who are geographically near to me, such as the members of my family or nation. The only relevant argument for such differentiation in treatment may be that those who are further away are not directly affected by my actions – an argument that has limited pertinence in times of globalisation. There are, however, critical questions to be asked. If our moral assessment or calculation involves the consequences for all parties, then would it be conceivable that some individual's right to life were up for debate if the advantages for others were significant enough? In other words, would we be allowed to sacrifice a human life for the sake of considerable common utility? Several versions of utilitarianism have responded positively to this question. Most contemporary utilitarian, however, are not prepared to draw this conclusion. Connected with this is the question whether utilitarianism has its own *concept of rights* – the idea, for instance, that an individual is morally entitled to certain goods and that these *rights* are to be excluded from moral weighing, or that they may be weighed only when colliding with other rights. And there is the metaethical question of *why* we are to consider the interests and utilities of all. The fact that all people have certain interests is not itself a moral reason to require from me that I accommodate those interests. There may be reasons of prudence for me to accommodate other people's interests, but in those cases the underlying hope is that they would accommodate mine in return. But then my motive is not a utilitarian one. The demand that we are morally obligated to value everyone's interests equally even if we are the stronger party who has nothing to fear from any others is plausible only if the moral obligation is independent from self-interest. This is a problem that utilitarianism, in my opinion, has not yet been able to answer convincingly.

2.2.2.3 Utilitarianism and bioethics

Since utilitarian approaches play an essential role in virtually all bioethical debates, we shall return to this topic. At this point, I merely want to indicate briefly why, and with respect to which themes, utilitarianism strikes many as an attractive bioethical approach.

What makes utilitarianism attractive are perhaps not so much strictly philosophical reasons, but the secular and liberal attitude associated with the approach. Utilitarianism presents a form of ethics that is ideologically and religiously neutral and that claims to arrive at universalisable moral judgments without big metaphysical presuppositions. Since a range of themes with a religious connotation (such as embryonic research and the protection of life) plays a central role in bioethics, the non-religious perspective of utilitarianism has appealed to many secular thinkers. This is amplified by the fact that, in its basic form, utilitarianism has no fundamental prohibitions and demands. Instead, utilitarianism is characterised by the weighing procedure. The central role of the common good and the possibility of weighing interests strike many as attractive assets for bioethics. This means that there is a trend towards understanding the interests of affected parties as preferences that are not themselves up for discussion or justification.

Yet classical utilitarianism also involves the notion of a maximisation of opportunities for happiness and a strong universalism, which would, for instance, entail that research and technology are obligated to contribute to the well-being of people in developing countries. In an economical-ethical regard, moreover, utilitarianism involves the demand that the differences in welfare between poor and rich parts of the world be rectified. Peter Singer has emphasised the latter point time and time again (Singer 2002a). If the utilitarian principle of equality is combined with the notion of a maximisation of opportunities for happiness, as Singer does, this entails that we are obligated to spend the better part of our financial possessions to improve the situation in the so-called 'third world'. These days, however, it is easily observed that none of the topics mentioned are generally discussed along utilitarian lines, but rather with appeals to rights to freedom, obligations to solidarity and human dignity. In this debate, Peter Singer's emphasis on equality with regard to our obligations towards those poorer than us is received with considerable scepticism.

In the context of embryos and euthanasia, utilitarian arguments do occasionally crop up. In the case of embryos, a common utilitarian-type argument might run as follows: if our central criterion is the avoidance of pain, then morality is to take into account only those creatures that can experience pain. Yet this is not true for embryos. Euthanasia, again, is sometimes argued to be permissible because it furthers the avoidance of pain. Much more often, however, the argument for euthanasia is centred on the notion of patient autonomy – a notion that is not exactly utilitarian. For most authors, the reason to consider euthanasia acceptable has nothing to do with a teleological sense of ethics in which happiness must be increased and pain reduced; their point is, in other words, not to further nonmoral goods. Yet even here, the more recent bioethical debate is concerned with the question of which normative consequences for euthanasia follow from the respect for an individual's dignity and autonomy, rather than with a utilitarian assessment.

Utilitarianism plays a much stronger role in the context of animal ethics. Demands to protect animals can be found as early as Bentham, who argues that moral recognition should not be based on the question of whether a creature is a member of the human species or whether it possesses rational faculties, but rather on the question of whether it can suffer or experience pain (Bentham 1780/1970: 283). The development of utilitarianism in the 19th century was not initially concerned with animals. Yet at the basis of the breakthrough of the later animal protection movement was a utilitarian impulse – Singer's book *Animal Liberation*. Here too, however, it can be observed that the more recent discussion centres on the question of whether the concept of 'rights' should be extended to animals, rather than on the notion of the reduction of pain in the sense of teleological ethics. Singer does not attempt to grant animals rights. Tom Regan, Martha Nussbaum and others, on the other hand, argue that concepts such as 'rights' and 'dignity' are to be interpreted in such a way that they can be applied to animals too, at least to certain animal species. With such arguments, however, the context of utilitarianism has clearly been left unresolved.

2.2.2.4 Peter Singer's practical ethics

Within utilitarian bioethics, a special position is surely occupied by Peter Singer. Always written incisively, Singer's publications have played a significant role in the development of the discipline of bioethics, and have resonated in the academic bioethical debate as well as in the public sphere in a very powerful, if divisive manner. In this light it must be kept in mind, however, that amongst utilitarian approaches Singer's concept of 'preference utilitarianism' is a rather idiosyncratic notion. In Germany in particular, Singer's performances of the late 1980s and early 1990s led to fierce protests and I will comment on this shortly (Düwell 2008a). Representatives of the disability rights movement felt exceptionally threatened by Singer's theses, but those in religious circles, too, found that his work transgressed the boundaries of what could be publicly defended. In particular, Singer was criticised for putting the right to life of disabled persons up for discussion, and it was argued that his ideas contained parallels to Third Reich practices. This situation was complicated by the fact that the very idea of 'bioethics' was hardly known in late-1980s Germany. The impression arose that 'bioethics' was not a particular ethical domain, but an ethical approach – intent on assaulting embryos and disabled people – for which Singer was especially representative. This impression was reinforced by the fact that at the same time the Council of Europe was in the process of preparing a so-called *bioethics convention*, a set of rules and standards concerning bioethical issues, which many interpreted as an attempt to 'dissolve' moral criticism of biomedical progress in the context of European harmonisation. In this situation, Peter Singer was repeatedly precluded from holding lectures and discussion meetings. (Singer presents his own views of these incidents in the second edition of *Practical Ethics* – see Singer 1993: 425–51.)

All things considered, however, these events must be seen in the context of the emerging German debate on bioethics. The beginnings of this debate stood out, for one thing, for the fact that there were very few opportunities for discussion between the official ambassadors of the genetic engineering lobby and their critics, representatives of the disability rights movement and physicians. On top of that, very few attempts were made to organise shared conventions and workshops. Representatives of the disability rights movement and non academic critics felt marginalised in these discussions and, compared to their academic adversaries, they were generally disadvantaged in terms of resources and status. In Germany, this situation has changed radically. The number of workshops and discussions with a diversity of attendants has grown exponentially over the last two decades. Occasionally, there was even almost an 'overkill' of educational events, media coverage and conventions of church academies on bioethical topics. What these developments have led to is that anyone interested in the debate is now aware that Singer is only one voice in the bioethical discourse and not *the* bioethics representative. Certainly, many an established physician has had to learn how to move about in this kind of discourse. The conditions for a more realistic bioethical discourse have improved, and the fact that Singer has been able to hold a number of public lectures in Germany confirm this.

In his book *Practical Ethics*, which first appeared in 1979, Singer broadly sketches his approach (Jamieson 1999). He asserts that the 'ethical point of view' consists in the 'equal consideration of interests'. As varied as our moral intuitions may be, and as varied as the ways are in which we delineate the domain of creatures that ought to be taken into account in ethical considerations, still, impartiality in considering interests is always the hallmark of morality. Whether, for instance, in antiquity only free men were relevant, or whether in patriarchal societies only males count – what makes a certain code of conduct ethical is the 'equal consideration of interests'. Without proposing his own constructive concept of morality, Singer notes that impartiality is the characteristic that designates all conceptions of morality.

Singer notes further, however, that in the context of our existing moral beliefs this 'ethical point of view' will come across as very distorted, because our everyday morality is influenced by a prejudice: speciesism. Analogous to racism or sexism, speciesism is the belief that the interests of the members of a certain species should be given more weight than on those of the members of other species. Singer asserts that the biological fact that a given creature belongs to a certain species is in itself in no way a moral reason to treat this creature differently than other creatures. The matter of species membership is morally neutral. Were we to endeavour to liberate our moral beliefs from this speciesist prejudice and thus to develop, to an extent, a morality that would meet the 'ethical point of view' without any prejudice, morality would look like this: all interests count, and all interests count equally (Singer 1993: 20). It does not matter to which species a creature belongs; the only thing that matters is that it has 'interests'. The minimum condition for having interests is the ability to experience pain. Animals have this ability to experience pain, embryos and comatose patients do not – as far as we can ascertain (in the case of comatose patients there may be some doubt). These interests must then be weighed; the race, nationality, gender or species of the interested parties being entirely insignificant in the weighing process. Morally relevant distinctions between creatures result from the differences in their *interests*. The relevance of this lies, for instance, in the fact that animals, while able to experience pain, are not capable of developing a future-oriented perspective, for which self-awareness is a requisite. In that light, animals have an interest not to be hurt, but it does not harm their interests to be killed painlessly (although the question of whether it can be in an animal's interest not to be killed is answered in a variety of ways (Kaldewaij 2008)). Singer, in effect, does not value animal interests differently from human interests, yet in an essential respect, the interests that animals have are different – or so he presumes. Thus, it follows from the prejudiceless development of the moral criterion that it is morally unacceptable to hurt creatures that can experience pain, even if they are not self-aware. Creatures that can experience pain and are also self-aware should not be hurt and, moreover, they ought not to be killed.

This description of the moral framework results in far-reaching revisions of common moral judgments. It would, for one thing, be permissible in principle to kill animals, but almost all common practices of livestock breeding would be morally impermissible, since they are hardly conceivable without animal suffering. This holds in particular for animal experiments, which, after all, explicitly involve studying the behaviour of animals on which pain is inflicted. At the same time, it would not be clear that embryos would play any role in moral considerations, since they have not yet developed interests. The practice of abstaining from killing severely impaired infants who will not be capable of developing self-awareness is another victim of Singer's critique. The fact that we still cling to strict embryo protection measures and to the prohibition to kill critically ill people has, according to Singer, to do with the doctrine of the sanctity of (human) life – a doctrine that is not ethically justifiable, but must be viewed as a mere Christian prejudice (Singer 2002). However, Singer certainly does accept reasons for granting moral status to people who are not capable of developing full personhood. His stance regarding so-called 'marginal cases' is much more nuanced than criticism of his position has allowed for (cf Dombrowski 1997). To a large extent, Singer's books are a development of this idea of 'equal consideration of interests'.[11] Elements of this development are the explanation of the consequences for animal and environmental protection and for medical ethics, but also questions of global justice (Singer 2002a). Ultimately, Singer argues, for instance, that we have an obligation as individuals to part from large percentages of our income as long as there exist significant inequalities worldwide.

Singer has been criticised extensively and a few points of criticism ought to be briefly addressed here. Klaus Steigleder and Anne Maclean noted very early on that one of Singer's central metaethical presumptions is flawed: his assertion that the 'equal consideration of interests' is *the* moral perspective (Steigleder 1991; Maclean 1993; see also Düwell 2008a). This is neither factically nor conceptually true. *Factically/historically*, there certainly exist conceptions of morality that are not egalitarian. Different forms of morality have valued the interests of women, slaves, Christians, feudal lords, etc. differently. Whether non-egalitarian valuations are flawed cannot be determined by introducing a conception of morality that already contains all sorts of normatively laden presuppositions. Such presuppositions should first be argued for. Identifying any conceptual necessity for Singer's conception of morality also seems impossible. In extreme cases, we could even imagine an

11 This applies only to his books on ethics. Singer also published on sociobiology, Marx, Hegel and other topics.

ethical egoism; that is, the position that everyone is obliged to cultivate his or her own interests. That may not be a very attractive ethical standpoint, but it is a possible one. Much more plausible from a metaethical perspective is the notion that morals are characterised by the fact that they express a categorical idea of obligation, although the contents of such moral obligations can differ greatly, and not all forms of morality are bound to the 'equal consideration of interests'. This means that it is certainly possible to represent and defend the normative position that morality ought to be based on the 'equal consideration of interests', yet it cannot be said that every form of morality does already do this either factically or conceptually. This criticism strikes me as convincing. That does not mean that I have decided that Singer's normative demands for universal equal consideration of interests are altogether wrong. Yet Singer tries to justify these demands by simply introducing a normatively laden conception of morality, as opposed to arguing for it. Rather than showing that other conceptions of morality are wrong, Singer eliminates them from the domain of morality altogether. And he does not show his conception of morality to be necessary – that is simply taken for granted.

On top of this, the meaning of the *criticism of speciesism* seems insufficiently clear to me. The part that one must grant Singer without reservation is the critical observation that membership of a *biological species* is not a ground for special moral treatment. Species membership as such is not a moral reason. Yet in all of the moral-philosophical tradition, this has never actually been the decisive reason for the idea that there is an 'exceptional position of humanity' in the cosmos. Humans were considered special for being 'Imago Dei' – God's image; for being rational; for being capable of self-determination; for being able to act, to think, to establish goals, etc. In the ethical tradition, the membership of a biological species has never been the relevant *reason*. However, it is important to distinguish reasons from practical *criteria*. For the practical (especially juridical) establishment of the question of which creatures are subject to the prohibition to kill, the criterion of species membership has indeed played a role. Human dignity and human rights, however, have never been justified by means of species membership. We shall return to the question of moral status (Chapter 3.1). Relevant at this point is that Singer's criticism of speciesism is unclear, as all forms of special treatment of humans are criticised under this heading. The criticism is only valid, however, insofar as it comes down to the observation that species membership cannot itself be an argument for any special moral treatment.

Entirely exaggerated is also Singer's criticism of the doctrine of the 'sanctity of (human) life'. I do, to be sure, agree with Singer that this notion is not particularly ethical in nature and certainly not a defensible moral criterion. But through his focus on this notion, Singer has made a significant contribution to a massive distortion of the ethical debate. One gets the impression from him that the demands for the protection of embryos, comatose patients, dying people, etc. can only be defended through the doctrine of the 'sanctity of life'. The options, then, would be: either 'sanctity of life', which can only be understood religiously, or abandoning the protection of life in all relevant cases. Participants in the discussion on the American coma patient Terri Schiavo found themselves confronted with this alternative. Interestingly, Peter Singer's analysis of the morally decisive difference is fully in line with those of Josef Ratzinger and George W. Bush. Just like those two devout Christians, Singer wants to force us into an alternative that misappropriates all nuanced bioethical positions. None of the standpoints on human rights and human dignity that are at all sophisticated simply aim to taboo human life. In that sense, when it comes to bioethics the assertion that the 'sanctity of life' marks a parting of the minds is wrong.

The fact that the balance so far is critical may be unfair in many respects. It could give rise to the impression that Singer's demand for a species-transcending egalitarianism is wrongheaded and that his criticisms of speciesism and the 'sanctity of life' are ungrounded. That is not my intention. I explicitly grant Singer that an appeal to biological species as such does not constitute a moral argument and that the 'sanctity of life' cannot be employed as a moral criterion. And it has not been my aim to show that we do not have any obligations with respect to animals. I will come back to specific questions concerning embryos and animals (see Chapters 3 and 4). Aside from the indicated weaknesses of the conception, it should be pointed out that a utilitarian version of egalitarianism reduces moral considerations to the application of equality considerations. It seems to me that such an approach shuts out a fundamental part of the meaning of moral considerations, namely the foundation of moral obligations and the recognition of moral subjects.

For many, Singer's viewpoint was particularly attractive in the context of the bioethical debate for its secular disposition and the willingness to question traditional prejudices. And of course it was appealing for the elements of animal protection and the liberal stance regarding embryo protection and euthanasia, which resonated with the intuitions of many contemporaries. It must, however, be noted that in terms of global justice, the idea of equality has not had a substantial impact on the bioethical discussion. With respect to questions of international solidarity, for instance, Singer is mostly criticised for his allegedly overstated demands. Moreover, the majority of recent bioethical debates is not all that concerned with the utilitarian idea of the avoidance of pain, but rather with conceptions of rights to freedom and autonomy and obligations to solidarity. This is mostly true for discussions of animal ethics as well. The central idea of teleological ethics – the moral right is to be understood as a function of the nonmoral good – plays only a limited role in bioethics.

2.2.3 *Dignity and rights*

We have already seen that in bioethics there are frequent references to dignity and rights. According to the usual classification of ethical theories, this section could also be grouped under the heading 'deontological ethics', as the concept of dignity in the Kantian tradition is commonly thought of as the conceptual counterpart to utilitarian forms of ethics. Yet the concept of 'deontological ethics' – as we have seen earlier in this chapter – is imprecise. For one thing, Frankena defines the concept only negatively as 'non-teleological ethics', so that it is underdetermined. Sometimes, moreover, it is assumed in the distinction between deontology and consequentialism that deontological forms of ethics are those that leave the effects of actions mostly out of the equation. This would mean that in deontological forms of ethics, the moral evaluation is always of actions 'as such'. Lastly, it is thought that deontological forms of ethics are characterised by a special rigour that rules out the consideration of context. Particularly characteristic for this discussion is the debate on Kant's prohibition against lying (Kant 1797/1996). As is well known, Kant did not allow for lying for the sake of kindness, since this would undermine faith in truthfulness. Participants in this discussion do not tire of pointing out examples in which refraining from lying has results that are morally extremely counterintuitive – the situation, for instance, where lying could have saved Jews from Nazi persecution. This debate does not need to be discussed in detail here. What does need to be asked is whether this controversy and the criticism it contains are at all relevant to deontological forms of ethics *as such*. In the terminology introduced by Frankena, it is not essential that certain actions are prohibited 'as such' and 'without exception' (an approach that is also known as 'absolutism'). Rather, the decisive question is whether or not the obligation is determined completely independently of nonmoral goods; in other words, whether the central moral criterion refers only to happiness or (long-term) self-interest, or also to something containing inherent moral value or simply non-instrumental validity (see section 2.2.1).[12]

It is exactly the latter that the notions of 'dignity' and 'rights' stand for in a special way. We do not make the protection of 'dignity' dependent on the question of whether this protection advances the happiness of other people or serves our own interests, nor is our respect for the dignity of others dependent on the fact that this respect makes them happy. Even a misanthropist who does not think much of life at all does not by virtue of this attitude lose any claim to the protection of his dignity. Dealing with dignity, therefore, inevitably leads to very fundamental ethical questions.

In bioethics, dignity is mostly discussed in conjunction with euthanasia and the status of embryos. However, much-discussed as human dignity has been in these contexts, an understanding of the ethical questions it involves can only be gained when the notion is discussed at a more fundamental level.

12 Barbara Herman discussed whether Kant's ethics can even be considered deontological in the first place. In her discussion, however, she does in turn rely on a different distinction of normative forms of ethics: teleological ethics determine the moral right in dependence on a certain theory of value, whereas deontological ethics do not presuppose a theory of value. In this sense she shows convincingly that Kant's 'groundwork' cannot be understood without presupposing the absolute worth of persons (Herman 1993).

2.2.3.1 Cursory historical comments on the notion of dignity

The concept of 'dignity' (*dignitas*) was known as a designator of special individual status as early as antiquity. At that time, the term was mostly reserved for the honorary status of the noble and aristocrats. Similar concepts can be found in numerous traditions. Later, the notion became connected with the Christian doctrine of 'Imago Dei' (humans being God's image), although in the Renaissance, the emphasis on human dignity functioned as an emphasis on the special place of humans in the world, with a decidedly emancipatory goal (Bayertz 1996; Trinkaus 1970). However, the concern in the Renaissance was mostly with determining the cosmological status of humans. Humans were seen as creative and inventive, masters of their own fate. The notions 'dignity' and 'rights' both played a role in the early modern doctrine of natural law; our understanding of individual rights developed in the transition from the late middle ages to early modern times (Tuck 1979; Haakonssen 1996; Tierney 1997). It was only in the 18th century that the concept of dignity gained its specifically moral sense. Only since then has human dignity been understood in conjunction with human rights. Kant introduced the formulation canonical for modernity: that we ought to 'always treat humanity, whether in your own person or in the person of any other, never simply as a means, but always at the same time as an end' (Kant 1785/1996: 80). This formulation does not mean that people cannot *also* be conceived as means towards something else; rather the point is that people may not be solely reduced to 'means'.

In Kant's philosophy, the human capacity for rationality, autonomy and human dignity are systematically interlinked. Human dignity has a central place in ethics exactly because people as rational beings are capable of giving themselves moral laws. By virtue of being capable of this, they are autonomous creatures, whom we always ought at the same time to treat as ends in themselves. The central position of humans as bearers of dignity is therefore connected with their special status as moral lawgivers; as beings, that is, without whom moral obligations and moral laws would not even be thinkable. If this is true, then the special moral-philosophical place of human dignity is necessarily connected to the capacity for rationality. The moral status of people (designated by 'dignity'), is necessarily connected with their capacity for giving themselves moral laws. Since human beings are the source of morality, they have the special status that we call 'dignity'.

Even if the specifically Kantian justificational model is often rejected, the normative substance of the notion of human dignity is very largely understood along the lines of the Kantian idea of self-determination. In the 20th century the notion of dignity has entered into many legal and international documents, such as the 1948 Universal Declaration of Human Rights and several national constitutions. In the context of bioethics, the protection of human dignity was not only a crucial motive for the regulation of experiments on human subjects (one might think of the conduct of doctors in concentration camps), but it also entered into most of the international regulations on bioethics.

It can safely be said that the notion of dignity underlies the large majority of bioethical statements; however, the interpretation, status and normative implications of the concept remain subject to countless discussions.

2.2.3.2 *Moral-philosophical questions*

In the following section, I give an overview of a range of ethical questions and problems that are (especially in bioethics) associated with 'dignity'. The point here is not to answer all questions, but to give an indication of the problems that tend to arise in this domain and to do so in such a way that, at the same time, the contours of the concept may emerge (see in this context Beyleveld and Brownsword 2001; Düwell et al. 2013).

2.2.3.2.1 WHAT DOES IT MEAN TO HAVE DIGNITY?

In bioethics, it is often pointed out that the use of the concept of dignity is markedly unclear. If a certain action is not compatible with dignity, the action is in a very fundamental respect immoral. This is particularly significant since dignity is rooted in many constitutions from the very first and/or most important clause. An appeal to human dignity therefore seems to be a discussion-ending argument that trumps any other possible point of view. The constitutional centrality of human dignity has moreover led to several social groups trying to claim the interpretative authority over the concept. Several pressure groups have attempted to employ the authority of the concept of dignity to legally enforce convictions specific to the group in question. Deryck Beyleveld and Roger Brownsword identify two concepts of dignity in the contemporary debate: 'dignity as empowerment' and 'dignity as constraint' (Beyleveld and Brownsword 2001: 9–47). The former concept interprets dignity in the context of obligations concerning those rights that protect the necessary conditions of a successful life. The latter, in contrast, tries to burden the moral content of dignity with ideological intent. If it were not possible to establish the meaning or substance of human dignity – at least in the sense of a principle of dignity – in a philosophically binding manner, the concept of dignity would remain entirely undetermined and therefore vulnerable to being employed in the service of any kind of ideological objective.

At the same time, however, the notion is so fundamental and not further differentiated that many are of the opinion that the conditions under which it can be used do not allow for further description at all. It does seem uncontroversial that certain very fundamental forms of conduct are not compatible with dignity – often mentioned are torture, genocide and other atrocities, with torture, at least, being discussed rather much at present. In this sense, it is worth noting that the notion of dignity – both in constitutions and in international legal treaties – only started appearing after the Second World War; that is, in the context of the crimes of Nazism.

However, it is easy to see that the meaning of the protection of dignity cannot be reduced to the rejection of just these forms of cruelty. In the 1948 United Nations Universal Declaration of Human Rights and several national constitutions, dignity is always employed at a more fundamental level than any particular human right.

In a moral-philosophical respect, we must assume that the normative content of dignity is to be specified in terms of rights. This does not mean that we ought to strive to deduce the entire list of human rights from the concept of dignity. Arguably, however, the moral meaning of dignity should be specified by way of 'moral rights', that is, legitimate moral claims. In order to do this we need not assume that all rights form a basis for individual legal claims against the state. It is part of the specific nature of many moral rights that the possibility of protection by the state simply does not apply to them. Yet we must assume that the demand for legal implementation of basic rights is grounded in the presumption that these rights are based on legitimate moral claims. Even if dignity is legally protected, it still expresses an extrapositive moral claim (a claim, in other words, that demands to be respected regardless of whether it is legally regulated or not). This claim to moral validity, that is, the moral notion of 'dignity', must also allow for explanation in a moral-philosophical context.

However, the precise relation of rights and dignity calls for discussion in a number of respects. It seems clear that dignity cannot be understood as independent of rights. At the same time, it is unclear how this relation is to be conceived. Is the concept of dignity a kind of description of the entirety of an individual's moral rights? Or does the protection of dignity only mean the protection of the most basic rights? Neither of these options, however, would make it clear why dignity would count as the *ground* of human rights. If dignity was only a summary or a subcategory of rights, the entire notion would be redundant. One proposition is to presume that dignity represents a 'human right to rights' (Arendt 1951; see also Forst 1999/2011). In this case, dignity would be the fundamental claim to being acknowledged as a rights-bearing subject. The precise determination of rights would then be left to the concrete historical discourse. Yet this proposition does not give us an insight into how such further determination of rights should be carried out.

In any event we can assume that dignity must have an inherent relation to concrete moral rights. The protection of dignity is not independent of the protection of bodily integrity and certain basic forms of freedom. This does mean, however, that dignity is not only pertinent when torture and other atrocities are at stake, but that the normative content of human dignity is of a different kind than that of individual rights. For this reason, enlisting the protection of human dignity alongside other moral goods is problematic from the very start. It is a mistake to say that moral goods are bodily integrity, autonomy, non-maleficence and then also human dignity. Such a statement is, in a way, an ethical category mistake. For bioethics, this is not trivial, since a significant part of the debate treats human dignity as a mid-level principle between concrete cases and abstract standards; a concept expounded by Beauchamp and Childress in their *Principles of Biomedical Ethics* (particular in the 5th Edition of 2001, see as well Chapter 3) (2001 and see Chapter 3). Kemp and Rendtorff, for instance, suggest that the principles laid out by Beauchamp and Childress are too much an expression of American culture, and they advocate the substitution of the four principles with European counterparts. The four alternative principles of bioethics they propose are integrity, vulnerability, autonomy and dignity (Kemp, Rendtorff and Johansen 2000). Regardless of what else can be said about this conception, at the very least it is problematic because it treats dignity as a mid-level principle.[13] It is not really intelligible how the concept of human dignity could be understood in any way that does not involve an internal connection with integrity and autonomy. Human dignity is always a fundamental concept, inherently connected with other moral goods worthy of protection. The interconnection of rights and morality at stake in this will be further explored below. However, understanding human dignity not as a specific right alongside other rights, but rather as a ubiquitous 'constitutional principle' of human rights also means that it is not nearly as easy to identify when exactly dignity is harmed. However, certain clarifications are possible, even if they are initially only negative.

One first aspect that seems to characterise the essence of human dignity is the fact that dignity cannot be traded against other goods. If the presumption is that there is such a thing as dignity, then this cannot be subject to all kinds of bargaining. At most, what could occur would be a conflict between the dignity of one person and the dignity of another. Of course there is disagreement as to what exactly the substance of the notion of human dignity is, but whatever this substance is judged to be, dignity confronts us with an unqualified moral demand. This is why the difference between utilitarian and Kantian ethical theories is often said to be that in Kantian theories the right to life and the fundamental capacities of freedom and autonomy are not up for discussion anymore; that is, we must take them to be overriding considerations (I presume here that bearers of dignity have a right to life, which, however, still needs to be demonstrated). This does not foreclose that within the field of dignity-based ethics tragic conflicts exist that present irresolvable moral situations. Perhaps the possibility of tragedy in the moral domain is even necessarily conditioned upon the existence of categorical demands. Only when we face demands that are categorical yet cannot be reconciled is it possible to speak of a tragic situation. From a utilitarian perspective, in contrast, conflicting points of view can be weighed in a utilitarian calculus.

However, these considerations do not yet determine which moral goods are protected by dignity, or how the protection of dignity is to be specified.

13 Moreover, it should be noted that while vulnerability is indeed fundamental for morality – in the sense that without our vulnerability there would not be anything requiring moral protection in the first place – this does not make 'vulnerability' a moral notion.

The protection of dignity seems to apply to the absolute moral worth of the bearers of dignity. The question is when exactly this absolute moral worth is threatened. One angle would be to consider the inhibition of fundamental forms of freedom. That means that through dignity, the *negative freedom* of the bearers of dignity is protected. In that case, we are only obliged to refrain from interfering with the way in which the bearer of dignity exercises her freedom. But we would have no obligations to support and aid her (cf Shue 1980).

If, however, bearers of dignity have absolute moral worth, it could be argued that they have *positive rights*, which involve obligations of others. That would mean that the bearer of dignity has a right to be supported by others to the extent that he can use and develop his fundamental abilities. One way in which this becomes relevant is in terms of the question of what obligations we may have towards people in poor countries (Pogge 2001, 2002; Chatterjee 2004). But the question is just as relevant for the discussion of whether human dignity calls for certain forms of social security, employment opportunities, etc. Whether dignity leads to positive rights depends upon the presumed grounds for dignity. In any case, effective protection of positive rights can only be guaranteed through corresponding measures in society. Even this brief comparison, however, shows that there are very distinct ways in which the normative substance of dignity is actually understood. I would like to summarise them briefly:

- According to the first interpretation, dignity demands that we do not treat bearers of dignity in abhorrent ways. Protection of dignity simply stands for a core domain of moral protection. Dignity is not to be understood as the fundament of the entire range of rights.
- The second interpretation of human dignity calls for respect for the freedom and autonomy of bearers of dignity, and demands that this freedom is not restricted without reason.
- According to the third interpretation, the notion of human dignity expresses a fundamental judgment concerning the moral status of people, which does not only demand that we do not impede the exercise of people's freedom (negative rights), but also that we provide for political participation (political rights) and create the necessary conditions for an autonomous life (positive rights).

This list of possible interpretations is certainly not exhaustive. It does make clear, however, that bioethicists should be expected to specify which moral demands they take to be connected to the notion of dignity; not in the form of a list of concrete rights of protection and entitlement, but by defining the grounding principle for the determination of the substance of human dignity.

Yet an explication of the concept of dignity should also be expected of those participants in the bioethical debate who criticise the vagueness and indeterminateness of the concept. The hackneyed lament of the openness of the notion of dignity has become part of the basic repertoire of bioethical discourse – regardless of the fact that it seems less than obvious that the notion of dignity is used in a more obscure manner than other ethical concepts. Notions such as 'non-maleficence' or 'autonomy' are used in a variety of ways as well. Moreover, it does not constitute a criticism of the concept of dignity to point out that it is used in unclear or ambivalent ways. A serious criticism and even a reason for dismissal, on the other hand, could be constructed if it was demonstrated that the concept suffers from structural weaknesses, or if it was shown that it is impossible to explicate the concept in the sense I indicated. This would, however, require the critic at least to make the effort to start with a more precise investigation of the possible ways in which the notion of dignity could be used.

The problem of the normative substance of the concept of dignity is even more acute in bioethics, where it concerns not only individual claims, but also collective goods. In the context of the debate on cloning, for instance, this has come to the fore in the idea of a human in the sense of the *dignity of the human species* (Habermas 2001/2003). Since in so-called reproductive cloning the generation of the parents decides on the biological design of the offspring's, generation and thus determines – by direct choice – its physiological appearance and potentially also its mental capacities, a previously unknown dependency has been introduced to the intergenerational relation. This raises the systematic question of whether certain acts can harm not the dignity of a single individual, but the dignity of free, autonomous, rational beings as such. Similar questions could be asked with regard to the protection of collective goods such as natural assets, which we consider worthy of protection in the light of the quality of human life. One could hardly claim to respect the dignity of humans while destroying their living environment. What is at stake in such cases is not the dignity of specific individuals, but of all people.

2.2.3.2.2 WHY DO WE HAVE DIGNITY AND RIGHTS?

Under the heading of 'dignity', we grant a creature autonomy, or self-governance. This means that it is not the case that a creature has dignity because it is useful or instrumental for other purposes. As we have already seen, Frankena deemed it a characteristic of teleological forms of ethics that they determine the moral right as a function of the nonmoral good; the paradigmatic case of teleological ethics being expressed in the formula that the moral right is to be understood as the maximisation of the utility of all affected parties taken together. Deontological forms of ethics, on the other hand, were characterised by the fact that they do *not* take the moral right to be a function of the nonmoral good.[14] While that only gives us a negative definition of the

14 A reminder: earlier, I distinguished the conceptual pair 'teleological versus deontological ethics' from 'consequentialist versus deontological ethics'. In both oppositions, 'deontological ethics' has a different meaning.

term, the formulation according to which each person ought to be regarded as an 'end in itself' is considered a classical example of a deontological ethics. The claim that people are subject to dignity and rights means that what is morally protected in such an approach is not dependent on the question of whether the granting of such rights advances nonmoral goods. In a very fundamental way, dignity cannot be thought of as instrumental. That is, the notion of dignity will not arise in the process of a weighing of interests. Rather, the bearer of dignity is to be thought of as a being who has this 'inner worth', regardless of whether this is in the interest of all. What is at stake here is a necessary moral judgment in which every bearer of dignity is granted inalienable moral worth.

Such a commitment does, however, preclude certain forms of moral argumentation. Dignity cannot be justified by way of utility calculations and the weighing of interests. Rather, the accordance of dignity seems to express that the moral domain itself is, in a certain way, an end in itself. So how could we justify that every creature should be accorded this moral worth? One answer that seems to suggest itself is that only a religious context can provide an adequate justificatory horizon for an 'ethics of dignity'. And it does appear that, in fact, many Christian authors draw upon the notion. Historically and systematically, however, this conclusion is not necessary; in fact, it is not even compelling. It is true without a doubt that Christianity has had a very significant role in the development of our moral notions, and this certainly holds for the concept of human dignity as well. And we do find the beginnings of similar conceptions in other religions too. Yet the idea of an inalienable dignity of the individual that can be unfolded in individual rights is a modern idea, which has come to occupy an important place in the history of moral philosophy only since the 18th century. Christian authors have played a role in the development of the notion, but so have others. From a systematic perspective, however, the question arises why the religious explanatory horizon would provide the appropriate context in the first place. This is not to say that there cannot be religious interpretations of dignity. Dignity can be accorded for religious reasons. Yet when it comes to the justification of the universal validity of human dignity, it must be asked whether the religious context will suffice. Along Christian lines, dignity would either be grounded in a Christian conception of natural law, the convincingness of which would have to be defended separately; or the accordance of dignity is understood as an expression of God's commands, as could be argued in the context of a 'divine command theory'. But such a theory will argue that humans have to do whatever God commands, which *can* imply respect for the dignity of humans, but it does not have to. Or, at the very least, divine command theorists will justify the very existence of moral obligations to their being commanded by God (Van den Beld 2006).[15] This would, however, mean no

15 I thank Anton van den Beld for illuminating suggestions on this topic.

more than that moral obligations exist only where there are divine commands. Like natural law, this stipulation is purely formal. Both theories say merely that there is such a thing as objective moral obligation, and justify such obligations along religious lines. Yet this does not specifically entail that human dignity or individual human rights are part of this divinely commanded morality. A justification of human dignity through divine command theory is moreover not very plausible because it does not provide an argument for granting humans a special status in terms of dignity, if their nature is simply to obey God's commands.

In this context, we need to say a little bit more about the modern notion of natural law, which has been important for the development of the idea of dignity. While natural law has a respectable philosophical tradition to show for itself, it has several fundamental problems. On the one hand, the question arises whether natural law presupposes a normatively laden conception of nature. The conditions of the notion of dignity, in contrast, seem to involve that humans are thought of as free and independent of nature. Historically, the idea of the inalienable dignity of the individual is established right at the time when the teleological conception of nature is disappearing. On the other hand, the reference to natural law cannot raise any claims to justification: the substance of natural law cannot be justified in any binding way, since natural law can only be discovered as such. In principle, the interpretation of natural law is subject to a high degree of arbitrariness. Similar problems confront more recent attempts to argue in the context of intuitionist forms of metaethics that the intrinsic worth of all people is intuitively plausible and does not come across as requiring any further justification. In fact, people do have different intuitions about this. There are people who hold, for instance, that individuals can be sacrificed for collective goals (religion, nation, etc.), while others dispute this. There are people who believe animals to have dignity, while others disagree. Intuitionism does not accomplish much when it comes to justifying dignity.[16]

One more fundamental problem with the justification of morality should be pointed out here. As demonstrated above, the idea of an *intrinsic* moral worth cannot be derived from long-term interests or from any utility calculus. This means that any attempt at justifying morality instrumentally is precluded. However, the notion of dignity is, as indicated above, an extrapositive concept, which cannot derive its validity from any legal decision. Rather, the legal and political debate on dignity presupposes that dignity is to be protected because of its great moral importance. If dignity is central to

16 In one of the most elaborate intuitionist approaches (Audi 2004: 80ff), it is claimed, for instance, that the categorical imperative should be considered the ultimate standard in case of conflicting intuitions. Audi does not, however, provide us with a reason to think so. He rather asserts that in Kant, too, the validity of the categorical imperative should be understood along intuitionist lines, which does not strike me as an apt interpretation of Kant.

such an extent, but can at the same time not be thought of as morally self-evident – since there are rival conceptions of moral normativity – then there are no alternatives to an attempt to justify its pertinence through arguments. At the same time, references to religion, natural law and intuitions can neither provide nor replace this justification. Therefore, we are faced with a problem, one that is known in moral philosophy as the problem of 'ultimate justification'. It seems necessary to justify dignity as the ultimate moral reference point. Yet, according to numerous philosophers, such justifications are fundamentally impossible. Hans Albert, for instance, takes all attempts at ultimate justifications – including all attempts at deriving an ultimate moral principle – to be confronted with the so-called 'Münchhausen trilemma' (Albert 1980/1985: 13). This means that every attempt to establish an ultimate principle in ethics must choose between three alternatives:

1. An *infinite regress*, which means that every justification of such a grounding principle in turn necessitates the justification of the argument used to support the initial justification, so that the process of justification goes on into infinity and thus fails to arrive at any ultimate ground.
2. A further possibility is the *circular argument*, that is, the logically flawed derivation of the principle that has to be justified from another principle, the validity of which is not established, but on which the validity of the other principle – which was to be justified initially – depends.
3. The process of justification could, of course, be concluded with a *decision*. That only means, however, that no justification was found, and the process was halted arbitrarily.

Albert asserts that any attempt to justify a fundamental moral principle is confronted with these three – equally fatal – alternatives. That would mean that a justification of dignity is simply impossible. If dignity requires this kind of justification – if otherwise we cannot show that dignity really does have a morally binding character and if we are unable to determine the normative substance of dignity in any other way – it would have to be assumed that an 'ethics of dignity' is impossible.

A number of authors, however, have shown that Albert's argument only holds for deductive forms of justification and that, besides deductive and (in no way 'binding') inductive forms of justification, another kind of justification exists. Karl-Otto Apel (1973/1980) has attempted to design a transcendental-pragmatic form of ultimate justification – a type of justification that proceeds neither deductively nor inductively but, rather, reflexively. Christian Illies (2003) calls this 'retorsive' justification; Alan Gewirth (1978) and Deryck Beyleveld (1991) speak of 'dialectical necessity'. These approaches have in common that they do not attempt to gain the moral principle inductively from existing moral convictions nor to deduce it from even more general premises (which would indeed lead to the trilemma sketched by Albert). Rather, they try to show that certain moral implications are inherently tied to a *praxis*, which in turn cannot be nullified. This concept of justification is, however, spelled out differently by each of the authors mentioned above. Apel, Habermas and other discourse ethicists have tried to show that the participants in any moral discourse are bound to acknowledge certain substantive moral presuppositions of that discourse, for instance in the sense that they must grant each other, at least implicitly, basic rights to freedom. According to Apel, Kant's categorical imperative can be reconstructed as the idea that the fact that norms in a practical discourse are subject to approval posits a moral criterion that must be accepted by all participants in the discourse. This version of a reflexive structure of justification is not particularly relevant for our present purposes, however, because Apel does not attempt to use it to ground a concept of human dignity.[17] In any event, this kind of reflexive or retorsive argumentation is not vulnerable to the Münchhausen trilemma criticism, since it is not a form of deductive ultimate justification, but rather a reflexive referral to elements of a practice that cannot be nullified.

Now it does seem to me that Kant and Gewirth (1978) offer a concept that provides the framework for a grounding of human dignity that averts Albert's Münchhausen trilemma and that is at the same time capable of making clear why the notion of human dignity expresses the central good requiring moral protection. Kant puts forth a proposition that in a way makes it possible conceptually to unify the *raison d'être* of morality and the content of morality. According to his proposition, moral demands differ from other forms of conduct-related expectations because in the case of moral demands, we are confronted with categorical obligations. The moral point of view obliges even if conduct in accordance with these obligations involves disadvantages, if the conduct does not lead to social esteem and if it is not legally sanctioned. This strict notion of moral obligations gains its binding character from the fact

17 Apel's (1973/1980) aim is to provide an intersubjective reconstruction of Kant's ethics. This means that only the first formulation of the categorical imperative, that is, the formulation of the universalisability of maxims, reoccurs in discourse ethics. For Kant, however, it was essential that the demand for universalisability and human dignity are internally connected. It is only because being a rational person is of absolute moral worth that the maxim of the rational person (the maxim that can at the same time be conceived as a universal law) is normatively binding in the first place. In that sense, the formal perspective of universalisation and the substantive perspective of human dignity were necessarily connected for Kant. This connection is not reflected within discourse ethics. In that sense, discourse ethics also does not provide a concept of human dignity. Considering this, it is already quite astonishing that Habermas, in his bioethics book (2001), nevertheless pulls the notion of a 'species dignity' out of his hat; a notion that he explains nowhere in his *œuvre*. Equally astonishing is the fact that Habermas (1991a/1994) is of the opinion that discourse ethics – of all theories – evades the charge of formalism, a charge he deems justified with regard to Kantian ethics. Habermas does not once acknowledge the problem that human dignity provides Kant with a substantive, material version of the moral principle, which does not reoccur in discourse ethics – and he never grants that, in that respect, discourse ethics is more formal than Kant.

that the content of morality is determined by nothing but the question of whether the guiding maxim of any particular action could be willed by a purely rational being. This account of morality aims to show that there is an internal relation to the concept of strict obligation (rational necessity) by acknowledging the existence of beings gifted with rationality. Kant held that this first formulation of the categorical imperative (in which we are bound to act according to the maxim that we could will as a universal law), the formal determination of the moral law, is identical to a material formulation, which prescribes that humanity, both in one's own person and in the person of any other, ought never to be treated merely as a means, but always at the same time as an end in itself. Whether it is plausible to assume this internal coherence of the different formulations of the categorical imperative and how this coherence is to be understood is widely disputed in philosophy (regarding the Kantian concept of dignity cf Hill 2002; Korsgaard 1996: 106–32; Wood 1999: 111ff; Kerstein 2006). It is hardly possible to make sense of such a coherence if the human dignity formulation is understood as a straightforward application of the general formulation of the categorical imperative – at the very least the stark claim that the different formulations are identical would then be fairly implausible. The coherence can only be made plausible if we assume that the categorical bindingness of the demand for universalisability of conduct-guiding maxims arises from the fact that the categorical imperative constitutes the explication of the willing of a rational being. Categorically binding are exactly those demands that correspond to the first version of the categorical imperative, since it is that maxim whose necessity we – insofar we are rational beings – must acknowledge. However, such an imperative only occurs when the reason that these moral obligations are binding is internally connected to the fact that there is indeed absolute moral worth to *being* such a rational creature. That is, it does not make sense to say that we first of all have moral obligations and that in addition to that, there is moral worth to being a rational creature. Together with the acknowledgement that the principle of universalisability is categorically binding, it is acknowledged that there is worth to being a creature in possession of the capabilities relevant to this moral self-governance. This conclusion is necessary exactly because the reflexive test with regard to rational consistency in the first version of the categorical imperative is nothing but the question of which maxim would have to be acknowledged by a purely rational being. The bindingness of morality is thus not independent from our nature as beings capable of agency and morality. At the same time, this does mean that the contents of morality must be determined by the respect for a being with such properties. That is, the only conduct that can qualify as morally good is conduct characterised by respect for beings possessing this capacity for practical reason. This means that the imperative nature of morality, its content in the testing of the universalisability of maxims and the demand for respect for beings with the capacity for practical autonomy are necessarily interconnected as elements in determining the contents of morality. The object of a morally required act of recognition is, in other words, the dignity of the rational being.

It is striking, however, that Kant only ever formulated the demand for the respect that we owe rational beings in a negative way. We are bound never to use others 'merely' as a means. It could be concluded that the substance of the recognition demanded in this way is limited to leaving others – in the sense of a liberalist or libertarian ethos – to pursue whatever aims they may see fit, in other words, simply not to intervene in their freedom. Recognition would then be limited to a respect for the negative freedom of rational beings (Berlin 1969). If, however, we consider the examples that Kant draws upon for elucidation, the respect for rational beings appears to be much more far-reaching. We are, for instance, bound to develop our own talents and abilities, and it belongs to the obligations demanded by virtue that Kant develops in the *Metaphysics of Morals* (Kant 1797/1996) that we aid and support others in a multiplicity of ways. The recognition of dignity thus entails a very fundamental moral value judgment that is directly connected with the structure of moral obligations. However, any further development of concrete moral demands that would follow from this would have to observe the difference between legal and virtue-ethical perspectives. In legal-political contexts, what is required is predominantly a matter of non-intervention in the freedom of others, while from the perspective of virtue ethics the support of their potential for development must surely be considered a requirement as well. This distinction arises from Kant's view on the possible task of the state. If the moral task of the state is to be determined in terms of what follows from the respect for the absolute worth of practical-rational beings, then the state can only carry out its protective task in a morally legitimate way if in doing so it takes into account the character of these beings as autonomous subjects. Any form of state action that is not geared to this freedom and whose purpose is not the protection of this freedom would fail to observe the core of morally demanded recognition.

It would, however, appear that this register of the state's tasks is somewhat historically conditioned. For if the worth of rational beings is the indispensable morally guiding perspective, it is not really clear why it should not also be a task of the state to ensure the conditions necessary for the personal development and thriving of these rational beings. This means that apart from seeing to the protection of negative freedom and providing a certain degree of security (protection from war, violence, ecological destruction), the state would also have to provide any conditions that rational beings require for the pursuit of their opportunities in life (education, health care) and those that prevent their impoverishment (social security). This would all have to be explored further. For our present purposes, the following consideration is relevant: if the protection of rational beings forms the reference point for moral-normative judgments, it follows by no means automatically that the tasks of the state must be limited to the protection of negative freedom. Rather, what follows is that all state responsibilities must be realised in such a way that the freedom of each rational being is the normatively decisive reference point. The action-guiding perspectives that follow from this express the core of moral recognition.

We must now turn briefly to Alan Gewirth's account, in which the relation between moral obligation, the worth of the subject and moral rights is made the explicit focus of enquiry. Gewirth's conception in his books *Reason and Morality* (1978) and *The Community of Rights* (1996) can be read as a development of Kant's moral philosophy – I shall not dwell on the differences between their accounts on this occasion (see also Regis 1984; Beyleveld 1991; Boylan 1999). Gewirth wants to show that there is a categorically valid moral principle that is obligatory for all agents. The bindingness of this principle should, however, not be understood as a truth that people could recognise independently of themselves and their own agency. Rather, Gewirth presumes, as does Kant, that the validity of this principle is to be thought of as a necessity that arises from the presuppositions of action that any agent must acknowledge, simply insofar as she is an agent.

In order to show the soundness of his argument, Gewirth develops a sequence of judgments that he calls 'dialectically necessary'. In contrast to assertoric judgments, which express something about the object of a judgment (x is red), Gewirth's notion 'dialectic' applies to those judgments that express something about the subject of a judgment (A holds/believes/hopes/fears that x is red). While most dialectical judgments are contingent (I can believe that x is red, but I could also not believe it), Gewirth claims that there are judgments that are dialectically necessary. Dialectically necessary are those judgments that anyone who makes a judgment must make insofar as she makes a judgment in a rational way at all. This leads to a sequence of argument that can be sketched as follows: as judging subjects, we necessarily consider the goal of any of our actions a good (regardless of what this goal consists in). Certain goods can only be considered good in relation to certain specific aims. Yet there are some goods that we must consider goods whatever our actions or aims may be. Gewirth specifies freedom (as the capacity to choose between different aims at all) and well-being (meaning those goods that are necessary for the attainment of our goals) as examples of goods that must always be considered goods, regardless of the particular concrete aim that may be pursued by the action. That is, I am bound to consider these goods necessary simply because I am an agent and the goods are the necessary conditions of agency. They follow solely from the fact that I am a – as Gewirth calls it – prospective agent, that is, an agent who aims to realise a certain goal.

If this is the case, I must also want these goods not to be restricted and, correspondingly, for others not to be allowed to threaten these goods. Insofar as Gewirth argues that I am only compelled to demand that these goods not be harmed or threatened because I am an agent, this demand follows from the capacity for agency alone. If, however, this positive assessment of the necessary goods of agency results from the fact that I am an agent, it follows that I must also grant any other agent that she has a legitimate claim to the goods of agency as well. In this way, Gewirth arrives at a moral principle that makes the protection of the necessary conditions of agency a moral obligation for all potential agents. This principle, which he calls the 'Principle of Generic Consistency', says: 'Act in accord with the generic rights of your recipients as well as of yourself' (Gewirth 1978: 135). The 'generic rights' are goods that acquire their meaning from their relevance to the capacity for agency. If the central good that ought to be protected consists in being an agent, then this implies both the negative right not to be constrained in one's freedom and positive rights to goods that are necessary for the deployment of the capacity for agency. Therefore protection can only be attained by organised state action; the principle also justifies state institutions, which, however, are bound in turn to the protection of the rights that spring from the Principle of Generic Consistency. Moreover, the introduction of such a principle establishes a normative framework in which these rights are not considered a mere list of moral trumps (an interpretation advanced by Dworking 1984), but instead provide a standard for interpreting and assessing concrete weighings of rights. The measure of dependence on the corresponding goods is the general perspective that guides the hierarchisation of competing goods.

Complicated as this argument may appear, its significance for the purposes of this discussion is mostly that it represents an attempt to conceive of a specific coherence: moral obligations are grounded in a value judgment that can be universalised because it *must* be made by any agent. The object of this value judgment is the positive evaluation of being a person capable of agency, and its normative consequences are rights to the necessary conditions of this agency. This implies an internal relation between the specific form of the obligation (dialectical necessity), the circle of addressees (all agents), the object of valuation (being an agent) and the normative consequences in terms of moral rights claims. To me, this seems an appropriate model for understanding human dignity as the basis of human rights (Gewirth 1992).

These elaborations on Kant and Gewirth obviously provide only extremely terse indications of the possibilities for justifying human dignity as a normative principle without falling prey to the problems of deductive attempts at justification expounded by Albert. The point of these forms of justification is that attributing absolute worth or dignity to rational beings is a demand that we are justified to make of every agent, since the claim arises from nothing but a reflection on what it means to be such an agent. If these justifications are indeed sound, that also means that attributing dignity does not presuppose any special ontological assumptions with regard to the status of having dignity. Dignity is an ascription that has to do with self-respect and respect for others. Yet it is – according to the claim detailed above – an ascription we are rationally necessitated to make. Gewirth, moreover, claims to provide a standard in the form of a principle, which makes it possible to specify materially which moral rights follow from this respect for dignity.

2.2.3.2.3 WHO HAS DIGNITY AND RIGHTS?

What is clear from the argument so far is that the justification of dignity and rights has to do with the special capacities of agents. This extends the demand for respect and the attribution of rights to at least all persons. What it means for the moral status of animals and human beings who do not have personhood will be discussed later (see Chapter 3). At this point, I will restrict myself to some brief comments on the relation between the debate about dignity and the matter of moral status. So far, the term 'dignity' has been interpreted rather casually as meaning 'morally relevant'. In that case, moral status and dignity mean the same thing. In some theories, however, (utilitarianism, for instance) moral status is defined entirely independent from the notion of dignity. Among ethics of dignity, some equate moral status with dignity, whereas others presume that dignity expresses 'full moral status', but that there are lesser forms of moral status too. Some theories only attribute dignity to persons. Others also view potential persons as full bearers of dignity, or consider potential persons as beings who have moral status, but not the same moral status as persons. Then, there are theories that want to broaden the scope of the protection of dignity to all sentient creatures, and other theories that attribute dignity only to persons and some lesser moral status to animals. Finally, a recent development has been the argument for a 'plant dignity'. This brief overview is only intended to show that there is a wide range of possible ways of conceiving of the relation between 'moral status' and 'dignity'. What should be noted is that if a theory involves the existence of a 'lesser' moral status than dignity, such a status cannot be understood as 'a bit of dignity'. Between conceptions of dignity it is a matter of debate as to who has dignity, and what the normative consequences are if someone is granted dignity. But the entire discourse presupposes that if a being has dignity, then it is subject to all the rights that are connected to this status. A lesser status than dignity could still be a moral status, but not the status of dignity. However, any theory would have to be able to explain how this lesser moral status relates to the status of a bearer of dignity (cf Chapter 3).

2.2.3.3 Dignity and rights – a summary

In this chapter, I have tried to give an overview of the difficulties that are connected with the notion of human dignity and corresponding moral rights. It has become clear that dignity is a concept that expresses an absolute moral claim and demands respect for the bearer of dignity. The questions of who has dignity, what normative consequences there are to having dignity and how the demand for respect for dignity can be justified are widely discussed in bioethics. In particular, the connection between dignity and (moral and human) rights warrants special attention. This element was discussed in particular detail in order to bring out the complexity of the concept. In the public biopolitical discussion, as well as in many bioethical publications, the dominant impression is that dignity only has to do with embryos and euthanasia.

If, however, dignity is conceived as a fundamental moral concept with a leading function for fundamental rights and the tasks and responsibilities of the state, it becomes clear that such a reduction is entirely inappropriate. The association may be understandable since in the indicated domains it is particularly unclear who should be included amongst the bearers of dignity (embryos, animals, persons?), and because in – for example – the case of euthanasia, it is not immediately evident what exactly respect for the individual demands from us. Even so, an understanding of dignity requires clarity about the place of these domains within the entirety of our moral convictions.

It could of course be concluded that it would be wise to relinquish the notion of dignity altogether. Such a conclusion, however, would have to result from an argument that shows in detail that answers to the above-mentioned questions are impossible. Entirely impertinent, on the other hand, is an attitude that dismisses the notion of dignity because it is allegedly vague or indeterminate, a remnant from Christian ages, and nothing but a discussion-ending argument anyway. Given the complexity of this discussion, such a trite dismissal of the concept of dignity is as impertinent as the attitudes of prim jurists, politicians and church dignitaries who try to use the reference to human dignity to keep all consideration of circumstances, detailed argumentation and the intellectual imposition of bioethical questions at bay.

2.2.4 *Prima facie principles, principlism*

With utilitarianism and a Kantian form of ethics we have encountered two very different kinds of normative ethics, which both have a central role to play in bioethics. Moral judgments in bioethics will always make some presuppositions on the basis of an overarching normative theory. Even the question of how to describe the field of normative-ethical theories is laden with philosophical presuppositions, as are the acts of designating the overarching theory and the metaethical premises grounding its justification. For concrete judgments in bioethics it matters whether the standard for moral rightness is the aggregation and distribution of preference fulfilments, the protection of individual rights to freedom or the guarantee of positive rights for all agents – to name but a few possibilities. And in all of these cases, a number of metaethical premises are involved in the decision for or against a certain theory.

In this way, the business of forming moral judgments becomes particularly complex. Moreover, moral consensus can hardly be expected, as the number of prior decisions over which dissent can arise is enormous. In fact, reflection on all the different philosophical presuppositions makes the dissent greater than it is, even in real life. It does seem, after all, that moral consensus can be found in everyday life, even if it does not exist from a philosophical perspective. It is therefore not surprising that, even in the early bioethical literature, there were attempts to argue that bioethics should not make itself dependent on philosophical reflections on fundamental principles. One of these attempts is – as indicated above – casuistry (section 2.1.4), which forgoes any appeal to moral principles and bases itself instead on paradigmatic cases. A second example would be the concept of what is called *principlism*. This term is a made-up word, coined by Tom Beauchamp and James Childress in their *Principles of Biomedical Ethics*, which has been published in several new, elaborated editions since 1978, and which has gained the status of a standard work in bioethics.

In contrast to utilitarianism and Kantianism, principlism does not draw on *one* moral principle, but on several. Beauchamp and Childress observe as early as the 1970s that bioethical discussions keep coming back to four moral principles: autonomy, non-maleficence, beneficence and justice. The concept of autonomy (in the sense of patient autonomy) refers in a bioethical context to the value of a patient's self-governance. Non-maleficence refers to the traditional stipulation for medical conduct to make sure, above anything else, not to do the patient any harm (*primum nihil nocere*). Beneficence comes from the teleology of medical conduct, the physician's duty to cure as the fundamental legitimation of medicine. Justice, finally, has to do with the systematic aspect of medicine; that is, elements such as equal access to the benefits of the medical system.

The appeal to these principles is said to hold independently of the philosophical theory to which the person who makes the judgment happens to adhere. Beauchamp and Childress argue that the ethical principles should not be interpreted as great normative theories. Rather, they are *mid-level principles*, valid not as alternatives to each other, but because each one has its own relative value. The four principles represent different dimensions of medical conduct, on the basis of which they have their relative weight. The relation between the four principles is considered non-hierarchical. While it has been argued on several occasions that autonomy deserves relative priority, such a standpoint is hardly sound, given the context. The principles are to be understood as criteria in deciding what is morally right; criteria that can only be applied by determining their pertinence in certain situations and by balancing them against each other.

The introduction of these principles resulted from the experience that these particular principles play a central role within the bioethical debate. The authors note the significance of the principles in the work of bioethics committees. In the initial editions of the book, their attempt was first of all to use the principles in the context of concrete bioethical discussions. However, the authors were aware that the mere fact that these four principles are important in the actual discourse cannot replace the question of their legitimation. For that reason, later editions saw the addition of some metaethical reflections. Beauchamp and Childress began by pointing out that in moral philosophy justification of moral principles is impossible both inductively and deductively. *Inductively*, the fact that moral judgments factically involve an appeal to certain moral principles does not warrant the conclusion that these principles are legitimate. In that respect, a 'bottom-up approach' is not an option. But the reverse direction – developing moral judgments *deductively* from a moral principle – is fundamentally foreclosed since it does not do justice to the diversity of moral life. For that reason, a 'top-down approach' is out of the question too. In the context of moral judgments there is thus no alternative either to accepting the contingency of moral convictions or giving up on the possibility of a critical evaluation of their legitimacy. It can be critically noted that this simple alternative of top-down versus bottom-up approaches has widely taken hold in the presentation of bioethics. The current complex ethical debate on principles, however, does not warrant this simple alternative. The methodology of 'mixed judgments' discussed in the first chapter already makes clear that what is at stake cannot come down to the alternative of top-down and bottom-up.

Several authors try to seek the significance of this approach away from the justification of moral judgments. The principles are, in this context, thought to have a mostly heuristic significance in structuring moral problem areas and for the development of ethically relevant questions and standpoints. In this sense, the approach is certainly much less controversial. But it cannot be denied that the 'four principles' concept also involves an attempt at providing justifications. In the earlier versions of their book, Beauchamp and Childress claimed their approach to be compatible with both Kantian and utilitarian conceptions. Later, their emphasis shifted towards the idea of a reflective equilibrium, developed by John Rawls in his *A Theory of Justice* (1971) and subsequently elaborated by Norman Daniels (1996). According to Rawls, the formation of moral judgments is a matter of finding a balance between our considered intuitions about justice on the one hand, and the theoretical explication of principles of justice on the other. That means that the principles of justice are neither gained inductively from intuitions, nor simply deduced from abstract principles. Rather, the justification of the principles and their application in concrete judgments should be thought of as a continual process of restatement and adjustment. In *A Theory of Justice*, Rawls introduces the idea of an 'original position' in the form of a thought experiment. This original position is characterised by the fact that it situates all parties behind a 'veil of ignorance'. Behind this veil, any concrete details of one's own nature and situation are hidden. That is to say, nobody knows whether he will be poor or rich, old or young, man or woman, black or white. In other words, nobody knows what position in society he will occupy. Rawls's claim is that the only principles concerning the organisation of society that can be just are those that would be chosen behind this veil of ignorance, since behind the veil of ignorance our choice cannot be influenced by any perspective that might persuade us to partial decisions. This thought experiment has a particular function in the justification of our social institutions. The idea of a reflective equilibrium, then, is introduced to show that the principles of justice are not deduced from a moral principle, nor gained inductively from empirical beliefs, but that the principles of justice are balanced with our considered moral judgments. In order to test the adequacy of our principles, however, the thought experiment of the original position serves as an heuristic tool. The justification of our principles draws on considered moral judgments that can be understood as stable moral intuitions, and inserts them into a reflexive test process, which results in a balance between intuitions and principles. Norman Daniels has expanded this model and adds the concept of a 'wide reflective equilibrium'. According to this notion, the justification of our moral principles should not merely be concerned with our intuitions regarding justice, but also with other background suppositions, such as anthropological and ideological beliefs. Beauchamp and Childress explicitly referred to the concept of a reflective equilibrium as the model for their concept of principlism (Beauchamp and Childress 5th Edition 2001: 397–407). Their goal is to justify a 'common morality', which could provide an adequate basis for society to make decisions about morally controversial questions.

It should be pointed out that this use of the notion of moral principles has a parallel in the history of moral philosophy, although one that is not identical to Beauchamp and Childress's concept. This parallel is the concept of *prima facie duties* developed by David Ross. Ross was a student of the British philosopher G. E. Moore, whose book *Principia Ethica* is the origin of modern metaethics. In this book, Moore criticises the attempts to develop a naturalist understanding of value concepts. He argues that it is impossible *on principle* to define the value concept 'good' in natural terms. That raises the question of how we can gain knowledge of what is morally right at all. Moore claims that fundamental insights concerning value are intuitively clear to us. His student David Ross is equally indebted to the idea of intuitionism. Ross proposes a deontological form of ethics, but one that, unlike Kant, does not start from the validity of a moral principle, but considers a variety of moral obligations as intuitively plausible (Ross 1930). We know intuitively that murder, stealing, etc. are morally flawed actions. Yet the corresponding obligations (not to murder, steal, etc.) are merely *prima facie duties*. We are 'prima facie' (at first sight) – that is, as long as we have no reason to take up a different moral responsibility – obliged not to steal or lie. It is, however, possible that situations arise in which we are confronted with multiple prima facie obligations. Therefore, developing moral judgments in concrete situations is a matter of determining and mutually weighing the relative pertinence of the individual prima facie duties. It is only as the result of such a balancing process that we can recognise what our actual duties are.

Notions such as principlism and prima facie duties undoubtedly owe their attractiveness to the fact that in cases of partial moral consensus they seek to tie in with the everyday familiarity of the matter at hand. Moreover, many people prefer the relative concreteness of these principles to more fundamental principles such as the categorical imperative or the utilitarian moral principle. However, these concepts are associated with a number of ambiguities and metaethically laden presumptions, which I shall now briefly address.

First of all, it is not immediately clear how the balancing of the mid-level principles or the prima facie duties can be carried out in a nonarbitrary manner. If A believes that patient autonomy deserves priority over the prohibition to harm, while B has his priorities reversed, that is, if in evaluating the principles of autonomy and non-maleficence there is no agreement, then the approach offers no help whatsoever towards establishing such an agreement. The weighing itself and the establishment of priorities remain philosophically ungrounded. Single-principle theories, on the contrary, facilitate a transparent way of organising morally relevant perspectives into a hierarchy. Moreover, the principles of principlism are exceptionally static. Autonomy and non-maleficence are diametrically opposed as conflicting principles. This gives the impression of a certain evaluative conflict. But this way of describing the moral problem or conflict is by no means self-evident. Other forms of conceptualising moral conflict can easily be imagined: the weighing of different degrees of preference fulfilment for affected parties, conflicts between the rights to freedom of those concerned, etc. The recourse to mid-level principles is a form of conceptualisation that in a moral-philosophical respect has particularly weak legitimacy. Where do these principles come from? Why should they conflict? In utilitarianism or Kantianism, the way in which the moral principles are established is much more transparent. Principles such as the Kantian concept of human dignity or Gewirth's principle of generic consistency are also much more open to changes in context, without being empty.

Finally, there is the question of how the validity of these principles can be legitimised. For Ross, the justification of duties is dependent on his intuitionist metaethics. We know intuitively that we have these duties. The duties cannot be justified beyond this, nor do they require any further justification. A certain intuitionist basis must also be presumed by theories that consider a reflective equilibrium as a method towards knowledge of what is morally right. The reflective equilibrium aims to test both our considered intuitions and our principles of justice and subject them to a process of mutual correction. In a way, such an approach presumes that ethical intuitionism is right. By that, I do not merely mean an heuristic function of moral intuitions. I certainly would not want to question the significance of intuitions in the way we build moral judgments and in the way we describe moral problems. Yet this is quite different from an epistemological intuitionism, which at a decisive point in moral argumentation relies on the idea that certain moral insights are shared by all. Certainly, it is still true that in 'everyday moral life' we presume certain intuitions to be valid without questioning them. But surely, our ethical discourses are characterised exactly by the fact that they refuse to take those unquestioned intuitions as self-evidently valid. It seems to me that the reflective equilibrium presupposes the justification of certain fundamental intuitions of equality, whose moral pertinence is, however, far from self-evident. Even if recourse to grounding intuitions is not in principle compatible with the coherentist outlook of the reflective equilibrium, since the latter principally grants epistemic priority to neither of the sides of the equilibrium, I still do not see how, given the epistemological reserve of the reflective equilibrium in controversial cases, one could seek to establish a decision without already presupposing the legitimacy of fundamental intuitions.

For this reason, one of the currently most elaborate intuitionist theories – that of Robert Audi (2004) – rightly tries to connect intuitionism and a theory of reflective equilibrium. But it must be noted that the legitimacy of this presupposition is controversial. This is true for all ethical theories under discussion here, but it simply means that one cannot shirk the justificatory burden of one's normative starting points. A scholar who propagates a theory of mid-level principles does not defend a theory free from moral-philosophical claims or import, that is, one that requires no further justification; rather, he invites moral-philosophical queries.[18] Why should the fact that something seems morally plausible to me be a reason to assume that this plausibility is also justified? How to relate to the fact that there is, for instance, a great historical consistency in the moral condemnation of homosexuality (a consistency wholly incompatible with my own moral intuitions)? How does intuitionism deal with the historical and cultural shifts in moral convictions? How can intuitionism make sense of the idea of a moral learning process at all?

In addition to this, there are questions very specific to the context of bioethics. Concepts such as Beauchamp and Childress's principlism presuppose that there is a broad moral consensus on the foundations of moral judgments. Like intuitionism, they deny the factical existence of moral pluralism. However, in the context of bioethics moral pluralism is generally much sharper than in other domains, since bioethical debates often provide few opportunities for drawing upon moral traditions. H. Tristram Engelhardt, for instance, has taken the matter of pluralism much more seriously than Beauchamp and Childress. In his book *The Foundations of Bioethics* (1996), Engelhardt assumes that we share only some values, and only with 'moral friends'. In modern societies, however, we usually find a variety of communities with different moral perspectives. The relation between these communities is that of 'moral strangers'. Moral strangers do not share a value horizon. While A assumes that we have an obligation to show solidarity and care for people in need, and that we should have a tax system to support this, B finds that there are no such obligations, and that the use of a tax system for goals such as universal health care amounts to theft (an example which rather precisely reproduces the factical debate in the USA). In such situations, what could count as a moral starting point that we can expect to be acceptable to all? In pluralist, secular societies, the basis for dealing with shared issues could be conceivably formed only by a very minimal ethics, which makes sure all actions are legitimated by the consent of affected parties, and refrains from forcing others to acting in ways they have not freely chosen. Engelhardt's constructive proposal can be justifiably called into question. In the most elaborate study on the topic so far, Klaus Steigleder points out that Engelhardt's minimalist ethics is only a presentation of a certain conception of value, which Engelhardt may share with his 'moral

18 The same cannot be said of Rawls's political philosophy. This will be addressed in the next section.

friends', but which he has not satisfactorily shown to be suitable as the starting point for a shared morality (Steigleder 1992: 11–114). Nevertheless, Engelhardt takes the problem of moral pluralism much more seriously than Beauchamp and Childress, who simply assume that their four principles count as the core of shared moral convictions.

Now how does a theory of 'shared morality' deal with the fact that particularly in the domain of bioethics people commonly advance views that adamantly break away from moral traditions? Peter Singer, for instance, argues explicitly that we need to revise traditional ethics. Examples include demands to expand the circle of morally relevant beings to all creatures capable of experiencing pain, calls to limit the prohibition on killing to persons only, or the Swiss proposal to ascribe dignity to animals and plants as well. Especially the claims regarding animal protection, which have a central role in bioethics, would entail a profound revision of traditional moral beliefs. My assertion is not that all of these demands are legitimate (especially with regard to Singer I am rather sceptical). But Singer's demands cannot be rejected merely because they are not supported by shared moral convictions or long traditions. If Singer's theses are to be criticised, then that must be done only on a basis that can show that they are not convincingly justified and not because they are at odds with some existing consensus. Anyone who rejects demands for a revision of our traditional moral *schema* in the name of shared morality relinquishes the possibility for a critical appraisal of the legitimacy of our existing moral convictions. Such an immunisation strategy can neither be understood as a serious engagement with the moral fundaments of pluralistic societies, nor can it be reconciled with the critical attitude that should be expected of serious bioethics. As a paradigm within bioethics, principlism mainly expresses resignation of the demands for reflection with which complex modern societies confront us. Particularly inappropriate, however, is any attempt to present principlism as a kind of reconciliation between different schools of normative ethics. This is simply incorrect. H. Tristram Engelhardt (1994: 507) explains:

> Eschewing foundationalism and embracing intuitions, middle-level principles or casuistry will not help. [...] Middle-level principles function only if persons from sufficiently similar, theoretical commitments reconstruct a similar moral vision. But, if one appeals to the principle of justice to resolve disputes between a Rawlsian and a Nozickian regarding appropriate health care policy, the two will discover how much they disagree, not how to forge common policy. Finally, all casuistry requires a framing tradition or moral perspective in order to know how to identify particular cases and particular practices as guiding, as well as particular individuals as in authority to adjudicate disputes.

The notion proposed by Beauchamp and Childress is not a pragmatic compromise or an open way of connecting different ethical concepts. It is one ethical approach amongst others. There is no reason why this concept should be casually accepted as the starting point of bioethical debates. It must answer to the demand of metaethical legitimation just like competing ethical theories. It is striking that bioethical works commonly and without further justification rely on autonomy or beneficence as mid-level principles, and that moral conflicts are conceptualised by way of these principles without argument. The dominance of these concepts in the bioethical discourse truly gets in the way of a proper debate concerning moral-philosophical differences. It would be a very positive development if people were to take note that the field of moral-philosophical conceptualisations is broader than the four principles approach wants to make it seem.

2.2.5 Contractualism and political liberalism

In the previous section, we elaborated on John Rawls's theory of reflective equilibrium and addressed the problem of moral intuitionism. To what extent the application of the reflective equilibrium presupposes a kind of moral intuitionism depends on what the moral-philosophical import of such a theory is taken to be in the first place. This question plays an important role when it comes to the relation between ethics and political philosophy, and to the question of how bioethics is positioned in this context. With regard to the history of bioethics, it is remarkable that bioethics emerges more or less in parallel with the renaissance of political philosophy. Rawls's *A Theory of Justice* was first published in 1971, the same year in which the concept 'bioethics' was introduced into the debate. Connected to this is the question of how bioethics is located between ethical theory formation and philosophical theories of the political, and what kinds of claims to knowledge are at stake in bioethics.

This discussion cannot be had independently from the idea of contractualism. At this point, it is not possible to elaborate on the different aspects of the history of the social contract. In its traditional form set out by Thomas Hobbes, the idea of the social contract served the legitimation of state violence based on the self-interest and right to self-defence of all. However, if everyone pursues their own interests without any coordination and without there being an institution that has the authority to decide in the case of conflicts, this leads to a situation that is a threat to all agents. Only the establishment of state authority can fulfil everyone's justified interests in self-preservation and security. The legitimation of the state occurs, then, not by recourse to moral grounds, but on the basis that it is the only effective way in which the self-interests of the individual can be guaranteed. Here, what is established is a form of the legitimation of the political that understands itself explicitly as a competitor to moral legitimation. Moral grounds ought to be excluded from the legitimation of the political. In Hobbes's time, of course, this also had to do with the experience that competing conceptions of morality were based on differences in people's religious and ideological outlooks. Exactly that connection, however – between political and religious power – had in the 17th century led to devastating wars. The attempt to legitimate state power without recourse to any ideological or religious basis was therefore also an attempt to find a neutral ground for the legitimation of the state. Such an approach does, however, lead to a foundation for political obligation that is not legitimated in a moral regard, but solely from the idea that the protection that can be provided by the state is so fundamental for anyone's life projects that nobody can do without it – and thus, that everyone's endorsement of the state can be presupposed. In the more recent discussion there are numerous attempts to justify a contractualist ethics solely on the basis of those assumptions that are drawn upon for the legitimation of the social contract. Closest to the Hobbesian perspective is certainly the attempt to reconstruct the legitimation of coordinated state action by means of game and decision theory. David Gauthier developed this perspective most coherently (Gauthier 1986). According to this theory, morally obligated are those actions that allow for the optimal realisation of everyone's rational self-interest. Elaborate concepts of game and decision theory moreover try to avoid the problem that such a contractualist ethics would be forced to presuppose that people only care about the maximisation of their self-interests.

Newer forms of contractualism, however, are more likely to follow a paradigm established by John Rawls's *A Theory of Justice*. As mentioned above, Rawls's business is to put the basic principles of the organisation of our community to the test in such a way as to establish whether they accord with our intuitions about justice. In this test, the thought experiment of the 'original position', in which we are unaware of our own social and economic position, plays a fundamental role. Rawls illustrated this methodological procedure with the image of a reflective equilibrium. The forms of contractualism based on this are of a particular kind. Rawls's method does not aim at knowledge of the moral right, but merely seeks to test the principles of justice on their accordance with our considered intuitions on the just organisation of society. The concept does not aspire to justify the validity of moral claims, but aims to show their acceptability in the context of shared ideas of justice. Later, Rawls expanded his considerations into the concept of a *political liberalism* (Rawls 1993). Political liberalism takes its start from the insight that we face an irreducible plurality of value systems. The objective of political liberalism, then, is to refrain from defending a comprehensive doctrine, since such a doctrine would inevitably compete with other comprehensive moral models. Rawls does not consider these moral doctrines superfluous nor does he reject them. Rather, he shows that they are not self-evidently suitable for forming the basis of the organisation of society, which, after all, should make it possible for people with different value systems to live together. Rawls proposes to explicate shared ideas about justice that can be understood as forming an 'overlapping consensus'. Making such a consensus explicit does not result in a presuppositionless philosophical or metaphysical argument that any corresponding demands are actually morally binding. The aim is merely to show that this basic liberal consensus is compatible with the moral assumptions of competing moral models. In a way, *political liberalism* is the attempt to lay out the conditions of the possibility of communal living for people with diverging conceptions of the moral good. Contractualism in the Rawlsian tradition would thus be the development of a kind of core of justice, which shapes our living together in such a way that this living together fully conforms to moral demands. But the foundations of living together should be formed only by those conceptions of justice that we can suppose have not resulted solely from particular ideological or religious convictions. All the same, this is not a social contract that is only plausible on the assumption that agents act solely out of self-interest.

Some brief critical remarks are appropriate. First of all, overlapping consensuses are, in a way, merely factical consensuses. Thus, if it is argued that the perspectives of several different moral models result in certain duties, this says very little about the validity of these duties. Whether overlapping consensuses can be established depends on the depth and breadth of the moral pluralism at hand. How, for instance, should an overlapping consensus with vegan standpoints be formed? At the same time, however, Rawls also emphasises that there are rational consensuses (also see Scanlon 1998). In order to show their rationality, however, the justification of their claims must be assessed. Yet to do this, it is not enough to show that these claims to validity can be defended on the basis that they are in fact taken to be valid in a certain context. Rather, the question is whether these convictions are themselves rational. In that case, however, we have to return to all of the problems of validity and justification that were discussed in section 2.2.3 in the context of the justification of values and rights. In that sense, the reference to an overlapping consensus does not meet the requirements of ethical justification.

Not infrequently, however, this form of contractualism is drawn upon as a paradigm in applied ethics. This leads to a number of further questions and problems. First, it should be noted that Rawls developed his theory as a theory of the political in light of traditional questions of the granting of freedoms and stipulating demands concerning the distribution of economic goods, access to administrative offices, etc. That is to say, the questions at issue are all questions that are well known from the classical debates on the conception of social freedom, tasks of the state and distributive justice. With regard to all of these questions, long historical processes have resulted in moral traditions that provide frameworks for the discussion of possible overlapping consensuses. Yet all of them leave many problematic (moral-)philosophical presuppositions untouched. For instance, they (almost exclusively) only discuss how agents should organise the ways in which they relate to each other. In bioethics, on the other hand, the predominant question has to do with the moral significance of being or not being an agent in the first place (cf Chapter 3). The vegan demand for equal moral treatment of animals has drastically changed the horizon of expected moral standpoints in a way that political liberalism did not anticipate. This does not make such standpoints irrelevant nor does it mean that its claims are justified. It does, however, raise the question to what extent political liberalism constitutes an appropriate paradigm for applied ethics. If fundamental concepts of moral thought are called into question, for instance the value of freedom, the question of whether we are free, the question of whether we have moral duties only with respect to free creatures, etc, these questions cannot be discussed in the absence of a metaethical justification of the validity of the corresponding assumptions. Perhaps this problem poses itself more sharply in bioethics than in discussions of social justice.

Rawls could, of course, have taken recourse to the claim that with respect to many bioethical questions there simply is no overlapping consensus. To the extent that his approach is bound to factical consensus, bioethical debates provide examples of topics in which this basis is lacking. In matters such as animal rights, then, Rawls's theory would simply not be helpful. As soon as liberalism is not political liberalism, but a bioethical method, it loses, in a very fundamental way, its impartiality. Surely liberalism structurally prioritises one side of the discussion? In bioethics, this can be elucidated by reference to particular confrontations: some take an embryo to be an entity that deserves the same protection as a fully matured person, whereas others consider embryos not, or to a lesser extent, deserving of protection. Some take the interests of animals to be equally relevant to those of humans; others perceive relevant differences. Some find that biotechnologies ought to be developed freely; others deem the influence of those technologies so threatening that even their development should be prohibited, or only allowed under heavy restrictions. From the perspective of a form of bioethics committed to liberalism, the party that puts forward fundamental criticisms is always at a disadvantage. From the perspective of liberalism, a liberal regulation for the treatment of embryos would suggest itself – a development that would not be acceptable to those who consider embryos bearers of dignity. From a liberalist perspective, it would probably be odd to ascribe to animals the same significance as creatures that are bearers of liberal rights to freedom. And liberalism would be unlikely to hinder the development of technologies. All of these conclusions can be argued for, and often convincingly. But if political liberalism turns into a bioethical method, we must ask whether it may not be the case that victories are predetermined by the liberalist conception of the field of discussion, rather than obtained by a philosophical argument for the validity of relevant considerations. Certainly, it can be asked whether political liberalism as such is philosophically neutral; whether it does not necessarily involve metaphysical, anthropological and moral-philosophical assumptions (cf Hampton 1989). For bioethics, in any case, it would be a problematic distortion of the debates if the field of argumentation were prestructured by the horizon of the reflective equilibrium and the formulation of overlapping consensuses. It can only be hoped that bioethics will master the courage to refuse to accept such forms of intellectual self-restriction.

2.2.6 Methodological reflection

In this chapter I have attempted to relate several different methodological perspectives in bioethics to concrete debates within moral philosophy.

My aim was first and foremost to present some important methodological bioethical approaches. At the same time, however, I wanted to clarify that moral judgments in bioethics are always dependent on metaethical presuppositions and assumptions grounded in normative ethics. If, for instance, one shares Elizabeth Anscombe's critique of the modern notion of morality, then the objective of bioethics cannot be to justify moral claims, since the notion of morality itself is under attack. Likewise, if one's aim is to explicate overlapping consensuses in the sense of Rawls's political liberalism, then the underlying argumentative objective is very different from the objective that shapes theories of normative ethics, which aim at knowledge of the moral right. But even if one's aim is to identify the moral right in an ethical context, it makes a difference whether one's normative ethical theory compares and assesses a variety of prima facie duties, or whether one justifies a single normative starting point from the perspective of utilitarianism or Kantianism.

Concrete work in bioethics is not neutral with respect to all of these moral-philosophical distinctions. It may be expected that theoretical alternatives are acknowledged somewhat open-mindedly, and that people are prepared to justify their own course of action after due consideration of the alternatives. Bioethics would be well advised to show itself open to the entire breadth of possible moral-philosophical standpoints. This is not a matter of value relativism – quite the contrary. In principle, however, bioethics must be methodologically open to the different standpoints in the moral-philosophical debate. The decision of many bioethicists to conceive of concrete debates only by means of the most modest theories, such as Beauchamp and Childress's principlism approach, and to acquaint themselves with metaethical and normative-ethical alternatives only in a very truncated form, does not contribute to developing a deeper understanding of the moral dimension of the life sciences.

3 A cross section of bioethical questions

In the first chapter of this book, I introduced bioethics as an interdisciplinary enterprise, and pointed out that all bioethical judgments are *mixed judgments*. The validity of judgments in bioethics depends on the soundness of judgments that must be legitimised within other disciplines. Moreover, all bioethical discussions depend on moral-philosophical presuppositions, since the relevant ethical starting point always calls for moral-philosophical legitimation. In bioethical discussions, however, presuppositions from a variety of backgrounds – philosophy, cultural studies and many others – often play a crucial role. Since bioethics is concerned with the moral aspects of the way we deal with life, philosophies of nature and the concept of human nature are particularly relevant. For this reason, the current chapter will address a cross section of topics that are at play in bioethical debates. The first of these topics will be *moral status* (3.1), which is relevant in both animal and environmental ethics and in all considerations of the beginning and end of human life. The discussion of moral status thematises some questions that have already come up in the previous chapter. Subsequently, several questions concerning the notions of *nature* and *life* (3.2) will be discussed. Then, I shall address bioethical discussions about the nature of *human beings* and *culture* (3.3), subsuming, for the purposes of this chapter, theology and religion under culture. Finally, the discussion will turn to central distinctions with respect to *responsibility* (3.4), a notion relevant for almost all bioethical domains. Since every one of these discussions is concerned with themes that play a huge role in the history of philosophy and the humanities, the aim cannot be to offer a complete overview of all of these topics, but only to address their relevance to bioethics.

3.1 Moral status

The discussion of 'moral status' plays such a crucial role in bioethics because due to the life sciences (amongst other developments) the scope of those on the receiving end of moral conduct and objects of moral protection are put into question. (Adams and Donovan 1995; Bentham 1781/1982; Clarke 1977; DeGrazia 1996; Gaard 1993; Hursthouse 2000; Jamieson 2003; Dunstan and Seller 1989; Lizza 2009; McMahan 2002; Steinbock 2011;

Thomson 1971; Varner 1998; de Waal 2006; Warnock 1985; Warren 1997). It is worth noting, however, that a large variety of questions are gathered under the label of 'moral status'. Demands for the revision of traditional morality emerged in the earliest bioethical discussions in the 1970s, concerning animal protection. The moral status of animals became a central theme early on. At the same time, there are fundamental criticisms of the anthropocentric orientation of the entirety of traditional ethics, as well as the demand to replace this orientation with one more eco- or biocentric. Such demands put the moral status of nonsentient entities up for discussion. This criticism was aggravated by the fact that the ecological crisis was frequently presented as the consequence of the exceptional position of humans and as the result of a one-sided valuation of rational human capabilities. Moreover, bioethics is always concerned with the moral status of human beings or of phases of human existence in which very few personal features can be detected, if any. The matter is often presented as if the discussion about status is solely concerned with the question of whether embryos' lives should be protected or not, in other words: unrestricted protection of life versus freedom to choose for the pregnant woman. This is a serious misjudgment. What is at stake is not just the status of embryos, but a more fundamental question: on the basis of which qualities or characteristics are creatures owed moral consideration? But even with regard to the beginning of life, the question is not simply whether we are allowed to kill embryos. Rather, if we are, the question is first and foremost whether we have a moral responsibility towards embryos, foetuses and newborns, and, if so, why we do. What is striking in this discussion is that many liberals vehemently reject one of the main arguments in favour of the duty to protect embryos, namely the potentiality argument, according to which even the potential to develop into a person is a ground of moral pertinence, while at the same time hardly anyone argues that embryos should be considered morally neutral. From a juridical perspective, all countries that have regulations on biomedicine also have strict guidelines for situations in which embryos are involved. Conversely, radical pro-life activists demand an unrestricted duty to protect embryos, without however being prepared to face all the normative consequences that come with the duty to protect. This all requires further reflection. Four preliminary comments may be helpful:

First, no element of this discussion is uncontroversial, not even the question of whether the discussion is philosophically meaningful in the first place. According to a number of virtue-ethical conceptions, the very fact that moral conduct is made dependent on considerations concerning moral status is a sign of the legalistic myopia of principled ethics. However, whenever the question of moral status is asked, the point is to determine whether, in which respects and to what extent we may or may not owe creatures moral consideration. In this discussion we can differentiate between moral consideration *based on the moral status of the creature itself*, and moral consideration based on the meaning the creature has for other beings, who in turn have moral status. It could be, for instance, that an embryo is important to a pregnant woman, but that does not mean that it has moral worth independently from her valuation of it.

Secondly, the discussion of the 'moral status' of entities takes shape differently within *different normative-ethical theories*. Therefore, certain debates that have been introduced in the previous chapter on moral philosophy return here. Many variants of ethical value or utilitarian theories, for instance, make norms of conduct dependent on the *assessment of situations* and *utility balances*. For many approaches, however, it is of central importance to be able to establish who or what is a subject of intrinsic value, worth or rights. Even in theories that accord the consideration of interests a central place, the question arises who can be subject of interests in the first place, and why those interests are to be weighed in what way. It is important, however, to keep in mind that these theories *do not always mean the same thing* when they state that someone or something has moral status.

Thirdly, it should be noted that, in the literature, the statement that a creature has 'moral status' usually does not intend such an ascription as if it is a particular *quality* that the creature possesses. Moral status is not a quality such as body height or hair colour. That is, a person does not have blonde hair, squat stature and, moreover, a moral status. Talking about 'moral status' does not automatically imply that there exist characteristics with a particular ontological status. Rather, what is meant is that we *ascribe this status* to entities. However, these entities must have qualities or specifics on the basis of which we accord them this status – and on the basis of which we should thus also consider ourselves obliged to accord them this status, otherwise such ascription would be arbitrary. If I speak here of entities 'having' moral status or of this status 'applying' to them, this should be understood to mean that we have sufficient grounds to ascribe them this status.

Finally, with the discourse on 'moral status', it has, moreover, not been established that all creatures that can be said to have such a status have *the same moral status*. Different theories look differently upon this. Some theories work with only *one* moral status; others differentiate between *full moral status* and a lesser moral status. The distinction between these could lie in the belief that full moral status entails a right to be protected, which ascribes the bearer all possible rights and restricts the scope for weighing, whereas a simpler or lesser moral status allows for weighing, but still makes any interaction with the entity at issue fundamentally subject to moral accountability. However, this too is conceptualised in a variety of ways. Moreover, the *determination of moral status* is to be distinguished from *normative consequences* associated with this status. If it is established that a particular creature has moral status, this initially comprises only the judgment that it deserves moral consideration. Formulating moral rights, however, requires determining which goods are to be protected when they are threatened in concrete situations, and the relation of these goods to other goods worthy of protection. In the discussion concerning human embryos and foetuses, which is focused on the issue of status, this question tends to be pushed to the background.

In the following section, several aspects of moral status will be examined in more detail. The questions are: what the *basis* is on which beings are granted moral status (3.1.1), and what the *circle of those beings* possessing moral status is (3.1.2). Finally, I shall address the somewhat more specific discussion on ascribing *'dignity' to animals* (3.1.3).

3.1.1 The justification of moral status

The purpose of asking about moral status is to find out who or what deserves moral consideration. There is an internal connection between this question and normative theories and their foundations. Each normative-ethical theory presents a concept aimed at determining morally right conduct or morally right actions. We saw, for instance, that in the standard version of utilitarianism, which conduct or action is morally right is determined by how much happiness or utility is brought about, while for Kant respect for persons is the decisive perspective. These theories thus show that one or more qualities are decisive for the question of why we owe moral consideration to certain creatures in the first place. If what is morally required is the minimisation of suffering, then the decisive perspective for the determination of moral status is the ability to suffer, or at least to experience pain. I call this relevant quality the *basis for moral consideration*. That is, in light of the respective normative theories, the basis for moral consideration is that quality that accounts for creatures having moral status. A normative theory, however, determines the relevant quality only in a very basic respect. This morally relevant quality only says something about why, in light of a particular normative theory, this is the perspective relevant to the moral evaluation of conduct in the first place. Yet for the concrete application of such a perspective, several broader considerations slip in again. In terms of the ability to suffer, for instance, we could ask whether only the suffering of the current generation plays a role, or that of future generations as well. Or one could ask how we can even know whether a certain creature can actually suffer. All of those are questions that are relevant to the concrete ascription of moral status. For that reason, the *basis* for moral consideration can be distinguished from the *criterion* for determining the circle of those entitled to protection. Such a criterion must, of course, be legitimised in light of the respective basis for moral status, but basis and criterion do not necessarily coincide. The *basis* says something about the perspective that determines why we owe moral consideration. The *criterion*, on the other hand, determines who exactly belongs to the circle of those entitled to consideration. This will be further discussed and clarified later in this chapter, as we come to talk about the moral status of embryos.

In terms of the justification of moral status, we can distinguish between moral consideration for *prudential* reasons, or because creatures are judged to have *intrinsic moral value*. Only in the latter case is moral consideration required in the absence of prudential grounds. From the perspective of certain *contractualist theories*, which understand moral consideration as the egotistically motivated mutual abstinence from aggression, moral consideration only involves those subjects who as independent actors are capable of signing a contract, or who pose a (potential) threat. If the only reason to take others into consideration is that we have agreed with each other to coordinate our actions, because it is the only available way to ward off the latent threat of others, then it is not rationally conceivable why we should take creatures into consideration that do not in any way pose a potential threat. Embryos, comatose patients and animals are then out of the equation as creatures that are to be taken into consideration. However, it is conceivable that from a contractualist standpoint it could be argued that state institutions have the task of ensuring that their subjects feel fundamentally secure. If the intrinsic moral value of persons at the boundaries of personal life is put into question, then this security is challenged. If we start – thus the presupposition – by putting the right to life of embryos, comatose people and people with mental disabilities up for debate, we open the floodgates to a discussion of the right to life, which leads to a situation in which nobody can be sure whether his or her right to life will be put into question as well. On the other hand, this is merely an instrumental argument. Implicitly, such an argument suggests that embryos do not have moral status, but ought to be protected only for the sake of the sense of security of those who are agents. Moreover, the possibility of feeling insecure may be an argument in discussions on the termination of life or the status of people with severe mental disabilities, since any of us could become severely disabled or fall into a coma, etc. Yet, in relation to embryos, such a line of reasoning does not apply. The sense of security in terms of the right to life would be equally established if the assignment of an intrinsic moral status started with the acquisition of fundamental personal capacities, for instance at some point in the first year of life. Such a conclusion, however, is not one that anyone appears to be prepared to reach.

If, on the other hand, moral status is not understood instrumentally, then creatures entitled to protection are ascribed a proper value – a status of their own. The ascription of a *proper moral status* is generally justified by reference to certain morally relevant *qualities* or *characteristics*. In that case, what is at stake is to determine those qualities that form the basis for moral consideration. Three possible candidates should be discussed.

The first candidate for a morally relevant quality would be *species membership*. At first sight, concepts such as 'human dignity' and 'human rights' seem to have exactly this quality as their basis. However, as emphasised above (Chapter 2), the justification for the ascription of dignity almost always lies in characteristics such as the capacity for agency, rationality or speech, and not in the esteem for a biological species as such. In the humanities and also colloquially, the term 'human' was and still is often used as an evaluative notion, expressing esteem for creatures or conduct without intending this in a biological way. When for instance a charitable attitude is said to be very 'human' (or humane), this does not imply that the agent is in fact human, but rather that such an attitude is morally valued. Simply belonging to the species *Homo sapiens sapiens* is not itself a basis for ascribing a particular moral status. The membership of a particular biological species is in itself morally neutral. In that respect, Singer is absolutely right. Yet the basis for the ascription should be distinguished from the extension of the domain of protection. There may be good reasons to include all members of a species under the protection identified by the concept of dignity. These reasons may not merely lie in biological species membership, but also, for instance, in the fact that the members of this species generally develop into persons, combined with the fact that we have additional reasons to extend the protection of persons to all members of this species. In such a case, the species membership is not what *justifies* the scope of the inclusion. But this will be discussed in the next section.

A second candidate would be the capacity for *suffering or experiencing pain*, or creatures' *vulnerability* or *needs*. Another common suggestion is that the capacity for developing *interests* is the precondition for having moral status. Associated with this suggestion are philosophical questions concerning the underlying concepts of 'interest', 'vulnerability' or 'need'. Depending on how ambitiously these concepts are conceived, there are consequences for the circle of creatures that are to be considered. This kind of concept, however, can appeal to the fact that moral consideration makes sense only with regard to beings who can be harmed by the conduct of others, or who can at least be affected. A creature without interests and without the ability to feel pain is simply not affected by the way it is treated. Consequently, taking the interests of such a creature into account would not be required at all, whereas all vulnerable creatures are ascribed intrinsic moral status (Feinberg 1984). It could be said, however, that the reference to a *vulnerability* does not automatically show that the creature is also entitled to having its interests taken into consideration. The reference to vulnerability merely points out that a creature can be affected by the actions of others purely on the basis of its needs and interests, not that others therefore have a reason to take this vulnerability into consideration in their actions.

Thirdly, several deontological conceptions justify – as we have seen in Chapter 2 – the special moral status described by the notions of 'dignity' and 'rights' on the basis of *the capacity for agency, autonomy or rationality*, or the presence of *some features of personhood*. In this context, there is no need to go into complex discussions regarding what persons are, what is special about the capacity for agency or rationality and how the notions of person, action and rationality are internally related. Here, it suffices to note that these terms indicate different concepts, but that we can nevertheless act on the assumption that for the justification of moral status, these differences will not matter significantly (they would, perhaps, play a role in determining the concrete rights and obligations that follow from this moral status). Since we are rational creatures, we are capable of choosing between alternative ways of acting. We have a capacity for rational self-control. This capacity is the most minimal characteristic of the qualities that form the basis of the ascription of a moral status, even if in concrete attempts at justification it may be further qualified, for instance with an eye on moral self-governance (autonomy). In Kant's classical formulation of the concept, rationality forms the basis of moral status as an 'end in itself', which in turn grounds the right to corresponding respectful treatment (Kant 1785/1996: 80ff). This focus on the right to due respect for freedom also forms the core of constitutional systems. In the more recent debate, however, there has been considerable emphasis on the possibility of distinguishing between *moral agents* and *moral patients*, that is, that the circle of subjects who are capable of moral consideration does not necessarily coincide with the circle of those who are to be considered. If it is nevertheless accurate that the capacity for agency or rationality forms the basis for the ascription of moral status, then the circle of 'moral patients' would have to be determined by their bearing a *qualified relation* to rationality.

These three candidates represent three types of grounds for moral status. Obviously, there exist concrete accounts that further qualify the notions of interests or rationality. Reference to one or more of these qualities in the justification of moral status strikes me as inevitable. That does not change when one tries to find an alternative to the conceptions of ethics noted above in an *ethic of care*, a form of *relational ethics* or in *virtue ethics* (see Chapter 2). Rather than of principles or rights, these forms of ethics speak of caring contact, or of empathic attitudes. Such notions indicate morally significant aspects, but the central problem of determining the circle of beneficiaries poses itself for these approaches as well. As soon as needy creatures are at stake, as soon as resources are scarce and choices are necessary, the question inevitably arises which creatures are entitled to caring attention, or who are to be provided for most urgently. Something similar is true for the reference to so-called 'advocatory discourses', which are frequently brought up by discourse ethicists (Habermas 1991a/1994). In this view, the scope of beings to be taken into account is to be expanded beyond the circle of those capable of communication, so that the interests of those incapable of communication – living humans, future generations and animals – are present and advocated within the discourse. Yet this immediately evokes the question of who exactly is entitled to an advocate. If the question of who is advocatorily represented in the discourse is to be decided in a nonarbitrary manner, then prior to any advocatory representation, it must be settled whose interests deserve consideration – in which case the question of moral status has already been decided at the point where advocacy comes into play. The reference to *advocatory discourses* therefore adds no new perspectives to the problem of who is to be included in the circle of 'moral patients'. At best, it suggests a method for inclusion. For the status debate, this is of no further relevance.

3.1.2 The scope of moral status

Within bioethics, the dominant question of moral status concerns the *scope of moral protection*, that is, who ought to be morally protected. In this context, we shall come to take a closer look at the question of the moral status of animals (see also Chapter 3 and 4). Indeed, there are approaches that call for ascribing inherent moral worth to nonsentient nature. But the *protection of nature* can also be justified with a view to the fact that rational beings, persons or creatures capable of suffering are dependent on their environment. Only an extremely libertarian model would perhaps object to the restriction of human freedom for the sake of the protection of nature and the environment. Yet no conception that considers the long-term protection of human (or animal) possibilities important can evade calling for the protection of nature or environment. These demands for protection, moreover, are not to be understood merely in a very narrow instrumental sense. Rather, nature as the space in which people live also has aesthetic qualities, which are valuable and important for human life. For this discussion, however, it is not necessary to assign to natural entities their *own* moral status.

Fiercely disputed is the question to what extent *members of the human species who do not or no longer have any personal qualities, interests or characteristics* – those qualities that form the basis for ascribing human beings a special moral status – do still have moral status in their own right. In this regard, the following standpoints can be distinguished.

First, someone who takes *species membership* as such to be the quality that justifies moral protection will not consider this question morally relevant at all. In this case, the ground for the ascription of moral status and the criterion for the determination of the scope of those entitled to protection fully coincide.

Secondly, someone who only takes *actually present interests and personal qualities* into account will answer this question restrictively. If the actual possession of interests or the actual agency is morally decisive, then this means that a creature either does or does not have these interests and qualities, without any middle ground (Engelhardt 1996). As indicated above, conceptions of long-term self-interest rely on the actual presence of certain properties. If the ascription of moral status ultimately depends on others' expected consideration of me, then it is not clear why an expansion beyond the circle of actual agents should be necessary. In preference utilitarianism, the emphasis is on the consideration of actual interests as well. But deontological positions too can make the ascription of dignity dependent on the actual possession of personal qualities.

Thirdly, from the actualist perspective, one more thing to take into consideration is the '*precautionary principle*', which is discussed in several contexts of applied ethics. In the case of people with severe mental disabilities, comatose patients or people in comparable conditions, one might be unsure to what extent the ability to suffer or personal characteristics are present. In the case of small children, likewise, it could be demanded for precautionary reasons that the point at which they are accorded rights is set earlier than the moment from which we can confidently say, on the basis of the evidence we have, that they indeed possess the characteristics of a person. The precautionary principle would then apply. Similarly, with regard to certain mammals (most notably apes) it may be unclear whether or not personal qualities are present. Depending on the degree of uncertainty, this could be a reason to call for erring on the side of caution, and treating, say, apes as if they were persons. However, we would have to insist that the application of the 'precautionary principle' is guided by empirical evidence for such uncertainties. As Beyleveld (2000) rightly points out, we do not ever have (metaphysical) certainty that the other is a person, an agent, in the first place. This fundamental philosophical uncertainty regarding the existence of others, however, can in this context not be the reason for the application of a precautionary principle. Rather, there would have to be specific uncertainty concerning the actual characteristics and capabilities of creatures for which there is empirically sound evidence – or at least evidence that our relevant knowledge is limited. Yet in the case of human embryos or newborn babies, we have no reason to believe that they are agents. However, they are sentient, even if their sentience is less developed than the sentience of adults of several other mammal species. The precautionary principle, then, should not result in any special moral perspectives (see however: Beyleveld 2000). Also, the precautionary principle does not by itself justify the date of birth as the hard-and-fast beginning of moral status.

However, in the context of the actualist view, one further argument should be made; one that is supposed to justify gradual forms of moral status. This is the *principle of proportionality*, introduced by Alan Gewirth (Gewirth 1978: 121ff). This principle states that if the capacity for agency and rationality are grounds for ascribing a particular moral status, then possessing such a quality only in part must be a reason for ascribing a gradation of this moral status. If property A is a ground for ascribing status B, then possessing A in part must be a ground for the ascription of a corresponding part of B. On this view, rights would increase proportionately to the increase of the capacity for agency and rationality (for a critical perspective see Hill 1984). At first glance, this argument seems to have the problematic consequence that the gradation of morally relevant characteristics implies quantification, and therefore relativisation. This is not what Gewirth meant, nor does it follow from his approach. When it is said that the possession of the capacity for agency is sufficient to justify absolute, unlimited protection of the dignity of persons, the proportionality argument says merely that even creatures possessing those personal properties only in part (marginal cases) are entitled to being ascribed at least limited moral status. However, it would have to be shown why partial possession of the quality at issue would indeed be morally significant. If the possession of a capacity for agency forms the ground of a particular moral status, this does not necessitate that the partial possession grounds another moral status.

Finally, we have yet to touch on an entirely separate class of arguments – arguments that go beyond the restriction to what is actually there. They take there to be reasons for ascribing moral status even if the properties that ground moral status are not yet present. This should be elaborated.

We said that it is impossible not to rely on morally relevant properties or characteristics when determining moral status. Since it is not *eo ipso* clear which creatures have a particular moral status, any possible ascription stands in need of justification. A refusal to identify morally relevant properties would therefore lead to pure decisionism. Now in the case of *embryos and newborn babies*, there is no empirical reason to doubt that they lack a capacity for agency. Furthermore, we saw that pure biological species membership is not a sufficient ground for the ascription of a morally relevant status. Moreover, it is clear that vulnerability and the ability to experience pain do not by themselves justify special moral treatment. This is true not only for embryos, but also for newborn babies. In the case of newborns it could be pointed out that their significance for their parents is usually exceptionally high, but this still is not enough to justify ascribing an independent moral status to them.

A demand for the inclusion of embryos and newborns in the domain of moral protection can appeal to the fact that in these cases there is a special connection to persons. This connection is most frequently discussed from the perspective of *potentiality, identity* and *continuity* relations between the embryo and the later person. The point is then that embryos have the *potential* to develop into persons, that there is an *identity* between the embryo and a future person, and that a *continuity* in this development to persons can be observed. Sometimes, *species membership* is also brought up as an argument in this debate, although this cannot mean that the species forms the ground of the status ascription. In this context, the criterion would rather have to be understood in such a way that a creature has a moral status when it belongs to a species in which the morally relevant characteristics are normally found.

These arguments are used in the context of different theories. They cannot, however, be understood as independent normative justifications of a moral status, but presuppose a normative theory. First it must be indicated what the morally relevant property is, and only then can these arguments play a role. The initial question is whether the capacity for agency, the ability to suffer or another property is morally relevant. Only when this is determined can the potential to develop into a creature with these properties be morally relevant. Something similar holds for the other arguments as well. For that reason, the concept of a person does not necessarily function as a criterion for the determination of the domain of those entitled to protection (Birnbacher 2003) – it is, thus, not first and foremost, exclusory. The concept 'person' indicates the relevant property on the basis of which a creature is worthy of protection. What is at stake here is the connection – sketched in Chapter 2 – between the significance of rationality and personal capacities for the understanding of moral duties. Whether the notion of a person makes sense within bioethics is not decided by the question of whether embryos have a moral status or whether the concept of a person is appropriate as a criterion, but solely by the question of whether personhood, the capacity for rationality and the capacity for agency are suitable for *grounding* dignity and rights (see Chapter 2).

The special character of the potentiality, identity and continuity arguments (and at least one variant of the reference to species membership) becomes clear only after there is clarity about the morally relevant property. These arguments attempt to expand the domain of moral obligations beyond the *actual* presence of these properties. Yet it is neither understandable from the perspective of contractualism nor from that of utilitarianism why we should carry out such an expansion. It is comprehensible only from the perspective of theories that grant persons special protection of their dignity that an expansion beyond the actual presence of personhood is considered in the first place, since otherwise the potential to develop into a person cannot be morally relevant either.

If, however, personhood or the capacity for agency or rationality are the bases for the ascription of a special moral status, it can be considered morally relevant that a creature has the potential to develop into someone with those properties (see Steigleder 1999: 184ff; Illies 2003). The reference to the developmental potential of embryos and newborns strikes me as the only perspective that makes it appear necessary to include them in our moral consideration; at least insofar as one does indeed understand the capacity for agency and rationality as morally decisive. By 'moral consideration' we might mean not only that we do not harm them, but also that we have a duty to care for them, raise them, etc. Similarly, there could be reasons to make fundamental distinctions between the concrete obligations towards embryos and newborns. Yet these questions arise only when we are morally bound to embryos and newborns, that is, when they have a moral status.

A further question would be when this protection on the basis of potentiality starts. Insofar as the potentiality argument is based on the identity relation to a person, there is reason to assume that such a relationship is present only after the completion of all early cell stages that can still lead to distinct persons (regarding this question see Buckle 1988). Since the fertilised egg can still divide into multiple embryos, one could say that the identity relation is of a different kind than after nidation, when an identity in the development to a person is present. This evokes the question of whether the entitlement to protection that is based on potentiality applies from fertilisation or only from nidation; whether, in other words, there is a morally significant difference between pre-embryos and embryos. This discussion, however, is only relevant if it is assumed that the potentiality argument is a valid argument in the first place. Only when the potential to develop into a person entails a sound moral reason to grant a creature moral protection can the difference between the protective status of early embryos before and after nidation be morally relevant in the first place. Incidentally, this is the only moral argument on the basis of which the acceptability of embryo research in the first days after fertilisation could be justified (although there are certainly relevant competing moral perspectives as well). Even a position that demands a different treatment for the first days after fertilisation than for the further stages of the development of the embryo still presupposes that potentiality is a valid argument.

Against the potentiality argument, it is often argued that there is a difference between being a potential person and being an actual person. Any deployment of the potentiality argument will have to acknowledge this. If one wished to argue that even the fertilised egg is already a person, then it would be entirely pointless to revert to potentiality. Potentiality arguments only make sense if the creature that possesses potential to develop into a person is not yet a person. From a moral perspective, the distinction can be a reason for the unequal treatment of potential persons and actual persons. In Peter Singer's classic formulation (2011:138f), this criticism of the valuation of potential persons is presented in the form of the Prince Charles argument: if the king of England has a special status, this does not mean that the future king of England can already claim a special status too. However, this comparison only has the consequence that there is a difference in status between the actual and future king of England. That does not preclude that the crown prince possesses a status, which in turn is different from the status of his valet (were one to wish to remain in the imagery of this example).

This whole discussion only makes clear why, if persons are granted protection of their dignity, there are reasons to ascribe a moral status to potential persons as well. Many questions remain unanswered. If potentiality is to be an argument, then at least the following matters should be clarified: (i) the question regarding the beginning of a moral status; as well as the question (ii) of whether what is meant is full protection based on dignity or a lesser moral status; and (iii) whether the status of these entities allows for balancing and negotiation and, if so, under what conditions; and (iv) how a possible distinction between actual and potential persons would work out in terms of the corresponding legal status.

The entire line of reasoning has so far been exemplified only in reference to embryos and newborns. This does not yet determine the status of people *who will never be agents*. It would also have to be asked what this sketchy discussion means for the moral status of future generations. Similarly, we should consider how the status of sentient but nonpersonal beings is to be determined, if personal properties function as the grounds of moral status. These questions will reappear on various occasions. The distinction between the grounds of moral status and the criteria for determining the circle of those entitled to moral protection is relevant insofar as it makes clear that in extreme cases it is possible for species membership to serve as a criterion for the delineation of the moral circle, even if the ground for the status determination lies solely in personal characteristics. It would not be unreasonable to doubt that such a correspondence can be plausibly defended. Yet for the transparency of the discussion, much would be gained if this distinction were continuously present in the background.

When it comes to the way we treat embryos, these very fundamental considerations regarding moral status would need to be complemented with numerous detailed reflections on concrete situations, such as abortion, pre-natal and pre-implantation diagnosis, cloning, or scientific research on embryos or embryonic stem cells. First, it would have to be determined which rights and entitlements are at play here. In doing so, it must be noted that what is at stake are goods whose protection is crucial, and that there are very profound moral questions associated with the possibility of embryo selection. These general reflections on moral status ought to be distinguished from legal considerations concerning how efficient legal protection in this domain is achievable. It could be asked, for instance, how abuse in the domain of human cloning can be legally precluded. If it turns out to be difficult to ban abuse in this way, that could even be a moral reason to demand that the legal protection should reach beyond what is strictly morally justified. A desire to silence all of these issues by referring to the question of status would hardly do justice to the debate (see Chapters 1 and 4).

However, it is important to emphasise once more that such questions of balancing or negotiation are preceded by the question of whether embryos are entitled to any moral protection in the first place. For it is conceivable that only those actions are to be regulated that have direct consequences for future persons, in other words, that only such treatment of embryos is to be regulated that would or may directly harm or adversely affect the life of the person into whom this embryo would develop. In that case, the actual treatment of the embryo would be morally relevant only if the embryo is also carried to term. Nearly all global regulations concerning the treatment of embryos are based on a different concept of protection. Even the liberal British Government presupposes – as evidenced by the establishment of a statutory body that inspects and regulates experiments on human embryos – that the early embryo has a value which makes any treatment of it require justification, independently of the question of whether the embryo is carried to term or not. This *praxis* can only be understood if it is presupposed that the embryo has some (if only a partial) worth. Yet it is exactly this that stands in need of justification. The reference to the development towards a person has so far been the only argument that is at all convincing on this count.

3.1.3 'Dignity of the creature'[1]

Very briefly now, we shall touch on a particular debate regarding moral status. In 1992, a formulation was introduced to the Swiss federal constitution which stipulated the protection of the 'dignity of creatures' ('Würde der Kreatur' – also 'dignity of living things'). In the corresponding debate, several attempts

1 I owe innumerable suggestions to discussions with Heike Baranzke, Robert Heeger, Frederike Kaldewaij and Peter Schaber.

were made to methodologically articulate an interpretation of this formulation (Balzer, Rippe, and Schaber 2000; Baranzke 2002). The notion introduces a number of ambiguities. First of all, one could have fundamental misgivings about the inclusion of formulations so strongly religiously inspired in a constitution. Since it only makes sense to speak of 'creatures' if there is a creator, this formulation has a meaning that can only be correctly expressed in a theological context. Theologically, however, 'creature' is everything created by God; that is, everything except for God. Yet if everything except God has dignity, this amounts to an inflation of the notion of 'dignity' that could hardly be outdone. If the entirety of creation had dignity without distinction, then such a demand would have nothing in common with the morally substantive notion of human dignity. In Switzerland, the matter has in fact evolved accordingly. According to a statement of the federal ethics committee on nonhuman biotechnology in spring 2008, the ascription of dignity is now extended to plants.

As a rule, however, these kinds of demands are restricted to the protection of 'sentient creatures', and plenty of authors attempt to work out a distinction between the conception of worth in the sense of Kantian human dignity ('inherent worth') and an ascription of intrinsic value to animals. The concept of dignity then strictly implies a prohibition on instrumentalisation and an absolute non negotiability of the individual in the sense of strict prohibitions. The concept 'intrinsic worth' is used in such a way that animals have *more than instrumental* meaning and that fundamental interventions (such as the creation of transgenic animals) are subject to moral accountability.[2] This distinction, however, is not always made. Even if attempts to make the ascription of 'intrinsic worth' fall into line with the Kantian notion of dignity are plentiful, it is hardly ever assumed that respect for animals or their right to life are to be understood as leaving no room for any balancing of interests. With regard to humans, in contrast, it would be incompatible with the idea of human dignity if an experiment were to be conducted that promised great medical progress, but which would lead to the death or expected severe harm of a research subject. The dignity of those affected cannot be balanced even against a significant benefit. The stipulation of a 'dignity of living beings' in the Swiss constitution, in contrast, has – as far as I am aware – not yet led to the termination of animal experiments in Switzerland.

This, however, inevitably evokes the question of whether it makes sense to use the notion of a 'dignity of creatures' at all, if it evidently means something different than human dignity does and if, moreover, the scope of this theological term is so vague. It seems highly desirable to me to abandon the concept. Much more interesting, however, is to place this formula in the context of the debate about the moral status of animals. The attempt to

2 Robert Heeger in particular has made valuable points about the concepts underlying the notion of dignity in the Swiss debate (Heeger 2000; Rutgers and Heeger 1999). See also the contributions in Dol et al. (1999).

ascribe rights and dignity to animals is connected with the desire to discuss animal protection in a non-utilitarian theoretical context. The central utilitarian premise of the avoidance of suffering made animal protection a constant concern in that context. At the same time, many theorists found it unsatisfactory to be forced to accept the normative implications of utilitarianism, most notably the unclear status of individual rights and the lack of strict prohibitive norms. For this reason, there are numerous attempts to expand forms of Kantian ethics towards animal protection. Tom Regan (1983) may be the most prominent proponent of this. Now these attempts are of course confronted with the problem that, for Kant, the ascription of dignity is connected with the capacity for autonomy particular to rational creatures. Therefore, Regan tries to describe concepts such as 'person' and 'autonomy' in such a way that they can be applied to animal behaviour. Not everyone may find his descriptions compelling. Yet regardless of any other upshots, this attempt reveals a difficulty faced by any form of animal ethics that bases itself on the concept of dignity: either it must decouple the ascription of dignity from its connection to autonomy (which then raises the question of what the basis for the ascription of dignity is), or it must show that animals also possess these autonomous capacities. The latter could perhaps be debated when it comes to apes, but for the development of animal protection in a comprehensive sense this path does not result in a truly convincing basis.

In her book *Frontiers of Justice* (2006), Martha Nussbaum presents an attempt to broaden her approach to animals. As indicated above, Nussbaum's version of the *capabilities approach* states that there are a number of basic capabilities, and that any conception of the good life must allow for these capabilities to be enabled. Regardless of the concrete aims we want to fulfil in life, we always need basic security, nourishment, shelter, the possibility of play, mental stimulation, sexuality, etc. Certain basic capabilities necessary for the realisation of fundamental possibilities seem to be interrelated with the conditions of our human existence. Therefore, any just society must allow room for the development of these. In several books and articles Nussbaum proposed lists of basic capabilities. These capabilities are not understood as hierarchically oriented. The ways in which they can be realised are, rather, representative of opportunities that are so fundamental for any conception of a successful life that the justification of their inalienability does not even require a special concept of a successful life.

Nussbaum now adds that the well-being of animals can be described in terms of basic capabilities as well. Her intention is to present a new concept of dignity on this basis. In her book, Nussbaum offers an elaborate critique of the strongly contractualist nature of modern ethics and political philosophy, and their conception of duties as rational persons' mutual obligations of recognition. In this way, animals and people with mental disabilities are excluded from the shared domain of protection. In Kantian approaches, the concept of dignity was unilaterally connected to our rational capacity as well. Now Nussbaum does want to develop a concept of dignity that can live up to the normative achievements of the Kantian concept of dignity (the non-negotiability of the bearer of dignity) in order to evade utilitarianism. At the same time, however, she wants to avoid binding this dignity to rationality and personhood. Her slogan is therefore: 'Dignity, Aristotelian not Kantian' (Nussbaum 2006: 159–60). She says: 'For Kant, only humanity and rationality are worthy of respect and wonder; the rest of nature is just a set of tools'. About her own approach, in contrast, she says: 'the capabilities approach sees the world as containing many different types of animal dignity, all of which deserve respect and even awe' (ibid. 159).

The question, of course, is what the ascription of these different kinds of dignity is based on. In answering this question, Nussbaum tries to avoid the classical choice between utilitarian and Kantians. The point is not to choose between alternatives – the ability to suffer versus autonomy, moral sense versus the capacity to form relationships, but to avoid these alternatives altogether: 'Instead, we should adopt a disjunctive approach: if a creature has *either* the capacity for pleasure and pain *or* the capacity to movement from place to place *or* the capacity for emotion and affiliation *or* the capacity for reasoning, and so forth (we might add play, tool use and others), then that creature has moral standing' (ibid. 362, emphases in original). That is, there are numerous grounds on which a creature could be ascribed a moral status. Why all of these capabilities may serve as grounds for dignity is not further justified. Therefore, Nussbaum's approach immediately evokes the question of what it means for all creatures to be ascribed their own dignity. Moreover, it is striking that the dignity of an animal in no way serves as a prohibition for killing it when it threatens us – although the more desirable option would be to prevent the threat if possible, for instance by sterilisation. Nussbaum adds: 'we may admit the wisdom in Utilitarianism and say that the primary goal should be painless, humane killing, if there has to be killing' (ibid. 371).

The desire to overcome philosophical alternatives and enmities in ethics is of course very understandable. Yet such a form of eclecticism in no way aids the debate. It makes no sense at all liberally grant all creatures the notion of dignity if it is not clear what grounds the necessity of such ascriptions and if, on top of that, it is entirely incomprehensible what normative consequences there are to a creature having dignity.

A final concluding remark: the desire to grant animals dignity is perhaps connected to the fact that in the Kantian conception of dignity we are confronted with an alternative: either something is a person, or it is a thing. Persons have dignity and inherent worth; things in contrast have a price and are replaceable (Kant 1785/1996: 84). *Tertium non datur*. This is not entirely correct, for reflections on animal protection and duties to help can indeed be found in Kant. However, many present the alternatives in the following way: if one wants to protect animals, then one must either reject the Kantian notion of dignity, or declare animals to be persons. This dilemma is so far-reaching that it shapes our entire legal system. Instead of indiscriminately nominating new bearers of dignity, one should consider whether our moral universe may allow for more comprehensive descriptions. Perhaps there are other entities that are neither persons nor things and that are morally relevant without having dignity. However, in the context of a conception based on the notion of dignity, the morally relevant link of these entities to persons would have to be describable. For this purpose, it could be helpful to bear in mind that we are not merely persons with rational and autonomous capacities, but also embodied, vulnerable creatures. On the one hand, this corporeity is the basis of our capacity for moral conduct and, on the other hand, it is the reason why moral regulations are necessary in the first place. As embodied creatures we are moral agents, yet at the same time the vulnerability of our body provides a reason to grant us moral consideration. Now this vulnerability is something we have in common with animals. We know what it means to be vulnerable, and we can conceive what pain and well-being mean. With our own corporeity in mind, there may be grounds to grant moral protection to creatures who share this vulnerability with us. Perhaps we owe it to our own moral integrity not to disregard their vulnerability. This would not mean that we declare animals bearers of dignity, but perhaps we could declare that, for the sake of our own dignity, we owe them moral consideration. For now, however, this is only a thought. To my knowledge, a mature ethical argument to this effect does not yet exist.

3.2 Nature and life

3.2.1 'Naturalness'

Bioethics concerns itself with practices that are aimed at interventions in nature and alterations of living things. It is not insignificant that what is at stake in those practices is nature. The reference to 'naturalness' has always played a large role in bioethics (Birnbacher 2006). It is striking how often arguments of naturalness are put forward, how vehemently they are criticised and how enduring the reference to naturalness nevertheless remains. That indicates that something important is at stake here.

In public debates, people are relatively uninhibited when it comes to drawing on the notion of 'naturalness' for expressing judgments about developments in the life sciences. Transgenic animals, the artificial creation of embryos, a chimera and a mouse with a human ear on its back are considered 'unnatural'. A significant part of the critique of the use of genetic engineering in agriculture and livestock breeding is centred around arguments of 'naturalness'. For someone with a philosophical background it is relatively easy to come up with critical counterarguments against the objection of 'unnaturalness'. The conduct of people and the development of culture and technology are always to some extent 'unnatural'. While in nonhuman nature sick and disabled people mercilessly become the victims of natural selection, human societies implement efforts to make their lives easier. Technology is fundamentally characterised by the attempt to improve people's life circumstances by nonnatural means. Culture and technology can be essentially understood as human devices for compensating the weaknesses of human existence by artificial means (Gehlen 1986/1988). A consistent critique of the unnaturalness of new technologies would have to address not only these technologies, but human technology and culture in general. Now such radical cultural criticism does indeed exist, most prominently in the writings of the French philosopher Jean-Jacques Rousseau, and it is conspicuous that this fundamental cultural criticism, under the header of 'naturalness', has played a role in the most totalitarian and fascist ideologies. Culturally divergent acts and ways of life, such as homosexuality, are also often branded 'unnatural'. A normative conception of nature tends to declare historically developed phenomena, such as marriage or other life styles, natural, thus shielding these practices from their own critiques. A normative notion of nature therefore seems reactionary and highly ideology-prone.

Now these are certainly rather widespread Enlightenment insights that can be picked up quickly by any educated person. What is surprising is the fact that the refutation of arguments from naturalness takes up such a large place in the bioethical debate. Is this due to the fact that the public is simply not capable of understanding the good arguments, so that these have to be explained again and again? Is the naturalness ideology so stubbornly rooted in the 'reactionary mass consciousness' that a great deal of work is needed in order to clear away these prejudices? Why are these debates so enduring? Could it be that there are legitimate concerns underlying the arguments from naturalness after all? It certainly is striking how much time and effort bioethicists have invested in criticising this – supposedly so trivial – argument from naturalness. In many debates one gets the impression that it is very convenient to have pushed the opponent into the 'naturalness-corner'. If critics of genetic and biotechnology have nothing more to offer against the technological changes than the reference to their unnaturalness, then it is easy to dispose of one's reservations simply by pointing out that people have always changed nature around them and even their own nature and that, therefore, the new technologies are not introducing any truly radical changes, but merely represent further strides on well known cultural paths. In any case, it seems to me that the frequency with which the arguments from naturalness are criticised calls for illumination just as much as the lack of willingness to understand what people intend to express with these arguments in the first place.

What exactly is actually criticised when new technologies are said to be unnatural? What seems to be meant is that what is currently happening involves an amount of technical intervention that people no longer deem acceptable. This seems to be a moral standpoint that has its own special character. Take the animal experiment in which a human ear was transplanted onto the back of a mouse, the image of which was published by the media worldwide. If this experiment is deemed unnatural, then this objection cannot be translated into other moral judgments without loss of meaning.

Viewing this experiment as unnatural seems to be independent of the suffering of the animal. Convincing as the scientists' proof that the mouse does not experience the experiment as painful may be, the scepticism is not overcome. It is also not the point that any alleged rights of the mouse are violated, nor those of any third party. It is possible that the critique is concerned with the 'instrumentalisation' of the mouse, that is, with the fact that a sentient being is used as an instrument for our knowledge gain. But why does this criticism arise in reaction to this particular experiment? Surely all animal experiments could be accused of this? Why do people find this type of experiment more unnatural than other types?

Something similar holds for the genetic modification of plants. If a tomato is changed in such a way that it does not turn mushy as quickly as it does, people develop misgivings, which would not be dispersed if it were possible to prove that the change does not give rise to any risks. Of course genetic engineering can be challenged with quite different criticisms too, such as the fact that we have only limited knowledge of the possible consequences of genetic modifications. If the aim is to criticise genetically engineered modifications of agricultural products, there are other arguments available than 'naturalness'. It seems, however, that there exists a kind of reservation that is independent from medical and ecological risks.

This seems to be true particularly with regard to changes that affect human nature itself, for instance in the case of the creation of human-animal composite beings (hybrids and chimeras), in the case of so-called reproductive cloning or for interventions in the human germ line. It is true that the limited nature of our knowledge of possible consequences alone already provides an exceptionally strong argument against these technologies being used. At least in the early stages of their implementation, interventions in the human germ line or reproductive cloning involve such enormous uncertainties for those affected that strong moral reservations could be held against these technologies purely for precautionary reasons. Even so, here too the argument from naturalness does not seem identical with a safety assessment.

A first interpretation of this argument could be that people dislike seeing the stability of their familiar world threatened. Humans are dependent on the world around them allowing for a certain degree of familiarity. We do not want to wonder constantly what a door is and how it is opened. We are not usually confronted with the question of what a sock is and how it is put on. As a rule, we are able to deal with the familiar objects in our environment in such a way that we can move about the world without too much thinking. A certain familiarity with the environment in which we live is also simply necessary for life and, to an extent, it is a precondition for people to feel good and happy. In this familiar life world, mice with ears on their backs do not exist anymore than the aliens that populate the space ships of *Star Trek*. The fate of Gregor Samsa, the hero of Kafka's story *The Metamorphosis* who transforms into a beetle, can serve as a case study of how things go for someone who loses all normalcy. Moreover, it is vital for everyday moral *praxis* that we are competent in using moral notions such as esteem and respect. Part of this entails, for instance, that we must not rack our brains to decide whether a creature we encounter in the street is among those entities to whom we owe moral respect. Rather, we treat people who outwardly appear human to us with respect. If the world were populated by chimeras, this would be significantly harder. For that reason, viewing the natural life world as valuable is not a case of an irrational refusal of modernity.

However, the need for familiarity in one's environment is not yet a decisive moral argument against certain actions. Certainly, an experiment on humans in which the test subjects would be deprived of all spatiotemporal orientation would be morally problematic exactly because those people would be deprived of almost all their possibilities. What is at stake in developments in the life sciences, however, are much more limited experiments, which do not alter the entirety of our life world. As long as people are given the opportunity to adapt to the most recent circumstances, they are still capable of maintaining a deep sense of familiarity with their environment. Moreover, hammering on the familiarity with our environment can also come to exhibit clearly repressive traits. People with a peculiar appearance are humiliated and exhibited as freaks and monsters. The critique of the unnaturalness of homosexuality was also a reaction to the fact that it confronted civil society with a way of life that put familiar norms into question. This form of challenging what is familiar must be possible, not only with respect to the basic rights of homosexuals, but also in order to allow for moral learning processes.

The question is thus to what extent our need for an environment in which we can get our bearings and that is 'natural' to us can become a moral argument. The question is not yet whether such an argument would always be decisive. It is possible that the need for a familiar world does not outweigh the opportunity to find medical cures. Yet the necessity to weight at all only arises if the argument from naturalness can be translated into a valid moral argument in the first place. In the following sections, some possibilities for this will be discussed.

3.2.2 Control over nature and life

A significant group of critics of the life sciences augments this critique with an attack on the modern conception of nature and natural sciences. Their objection is that the newest technological developments merely represent the most recent move in a tendency towards unlimited technical power, which has already shaped the whole of modernity and has now led to an ecological crisis. The technological self-determination of humanity is considered on a par with the development of totalitarian regimes in the first half of the 20th century. The separation of mind and nature in Descartes or Bacon's concept of the natural sciences is seen as the precursor of the new life sciences. This critique exists in quite diverse shapes and forms, and draws on several different traditions of technology criticism, some of which should be mentioned briefly. Martin Heidegger, for instance, views modern technology as the result of a development of Western metaphysics in which the self-mastery of humans turns nature into a piece of matter that is there for them to use at will (Heidegger 1962/1977). In his infamous 'Rules for the human zoo', Peter Sloterdijk aimed to enter into a discussion with Heidegger's theses in order to work out the implications for the way we use biotechnologies. In a similar vein, Max Horkheimer and Theodor W. Adorno's 1969/2002 *Dialectic of Enlightenment* describes humans as searching to liberate themselves, by way of language and rationality, from the dominance of nature and their own impotence in relation to their natural environment. In Horkheimer and Adorno's description, however, the resulting control of nature does not lead to liberation, but to new forms of unfreedom. People initially develop control of external nature, and subsequently subject everything to this demand for control. Both social interconnections and the relation of humanity to itself become power relations. The absoluteness of power is thus prolonged with almost no way out. People try to make everything that is alien similar to themselves, in order to eliminate it as alien. In particular, the relation to nature is shaped by the 'compulsion of identity'. Whatever in nature is unordered, contingent and not determined by humans is slowly subjected to their dominance. Even our 'inner nature', that is, what is natural about our own existence, is forced under the dominion of rationality. It should be noted that both for Heidegger and for Horkheimer and Adorno the development of modern technology is only a consequence of a course that was set in the very early stages of human history. The suppression of nature starts with the development of language, which allows for naming and thus controlling nature; and with the separation of subject and object, which can be understood as the first step towards free access to the resources of nature. It must be said, however, that there is little chance of changing anything about this tragedy of entangled power if new technologies are viewed as the result of conditions that are deeply embedded in human existence. The subject-object division and the use of language simply belong to the human condition. So if totalitarian dominance, the repression of nature and the ecological crisis are the result of the development of language and the separation of subject and object, there is little hope for humanity. We could only avoid these consequences by giving up what makes us human. If people cannot change anything in that respect, then there is no reason to criticise them for these developments.

A variation on this fundamental critique can be found in Michel Foucault's critique of 'biopower', a term that appears ever more often in the most recent criticisms of the life sciences (Foucault 2004/2010). As early as the 1960s, Foucault sought to show in several different studies how subtle forms of power influence social discourses, as well as the relations of people to each other and to themselves. Foucault's main aim is to show that power should not only be understood in the sense of binary power relations in which one person dominates another or in which institutes overpower their members.

Rather, power exists in cultural practices that have developed, such as medicine, pastoral care, sexuality, detention or psychiatry, and which form power constellations in which the individual becomes the subject of dominance, but functions at the same time as an agent of power. In practices such as confession or soul searching, the individual performs practices in which he subdues himself according to prescribed cultural standards. Biopower is – according to Foucault – the process of the development of technologies for controlling human life that stand in the tradition of methods aimed at controlling the masses. In a way, *biopower* and *biopolitics* are cultural strategies for controlling the human body in the service of collective needs. Foucault noticed that even for traditional forms of power constellations the human body cannot be understood as a residue of private existence, as something like a last alcove of authentic existence in which one could escape the pull of power. Rather, the diverse discourses on the body reveal forms of cultural access to the individual. The new biotechnologies more or less introduce a new stage of such access. Biotechnologies are seen as subtle forms of subjecting the biological basis of human existence to methodically targeted access on the body of the individual.

From the mid 1990s, the critique of biopower is mostly taken up in the social sciences. In the wake of Foucault, many authors view *bioethics* as a form of intellectual background music that serves to manipulate people's convictions in such a way that they can be used more easily for biopolitical purposes. Now it can hardly be denied that the bioethical discourse – as any academic discourse – is influenced by power strategies. It is therefore not only legitimate to criticize those strategies, but there are also moral reasons to indentify these strategies as power strategies. It also cannot be denied that bioethics is used as a political instrument, that bioethicists are used and abused for political purposes and that, occasionally, they are quite happy to allow for such use and abuse. I consider disclosing and criticising all of this a task of bioethics itself. However, even someone who understands bioethics as a strategy for the subtle manipulation of moral convictions would have to acknowledge the *task of bioethics* as legitimate. It simply cannot be denied that there exists a plurality of moral standpoints regarding bioethical questions and that, in that sense, it is necessary to debate the justification of these standpoints. Bioethics (at least the academic discipline) is the attempt to understand this justification as an argumentative process in which we demand from the participants that they back up their moral standpoints with reasons. This inevitably puts moral traditions and habits to the test of argumentative criticism. Someone who understands this discourse *eo ipso* as a mere power discourse in disguise is either so convinced of her own moral standpoint that she deems any challenge to it absurd, or she would have to understand any form of debate of bioethical questions as a subtle power strategy (which, however, would then also have to apply to her own critique of bioethics). In the former case, bioethical discourse would be redundant; in the latter impossible. In a situation in which there is a pluralism of moral convictions and in which new possibilities for conduct factically result in different moral answers, the lack of willingness rationally to defend one's own moral answers becomes dogmatism. However, serious participation in the bioethical debate does presuppose faith in the potency of arguments, which can then not be understood as mere power strategies in disguise. Yet this is a precondition that bioethics has in common with every other academic undertaking.

In this context, we will have to address certain attempts to make phenomenology fruitful for the current bioethical debate. This usually happens with reference to Maurice Merleau-Ponty (1945/1962) (sometimes with reference to Hermann Schmitz, 1965); two philosophers who have, in different ways, placed the human body in the centre of their philosophical considerations. In their work, the body is not taken as a material object, something that can be observed, scientifically investigated, or serve as an instrument for the realisation of the human will. Rather, these philosophers attempt to understand all forms of *praxis* from the enactment of human liveliness. According to this insight, a form of biotechnology that considers life only from the perspective of technological ordering would fundamentally miss the nature of the part of life that eludes all kinds of objectifying access. Before we are capable of thinking of nature and life in an objective way in the first place, we already have access to life in our life world, given that we are living beings. Reducing life in general and human life in particular to a technological enterprise would be a misunderstanding of our own status as living creatures. Life is never an object before us; we must first understand ourselves as living beings in and from life as it is lived. This has profound consequences for all types of scientific illumination of life in general and human life in particular. According to this argument, the naturalistic objectifying perspective must always be understood as derivative. Only within the general horizon of our life world can we relate to biological phenomena in an objectifying way. That also means, however, that the natural sciences do not straightforwardly uncover the truth about reality, but that truth is only disclosed through our everyday lived access to reality. The dominance of the life sciences and the cultural hegemony of an objectifying perspective on life would have to be understood as the expressions of a comprehensive cultural misapprehension. In its place, we would have to start by developing a notion of life and the human body, which would take the shape of unfolding perspective of the involved agent.

With respect to Merleau-Ponty in particular, the concept of *corporeity* (*Leiblichkeit*) is used as an expression for the *unavailability* of human nature, which, in a fundamental manner, resists the strivings of technological ordering. The human body can be instrumentalised only at the price of a failure of self-conception. This makes technological intervention in and patenting and commercialisation of the body fundamentally problematic. The notion of corporeity has become a motif that many bioethicists draw upon as a critical source. In this context one could, for a start, point out that it is surely to the credit of the debate to have suggested that many presuppositions of bioethical discussions, both epistemological and with regard to the nature of human beings, are thoroughly blind. It is a justified criticism that in the majority of current bioethical debates the fundamental concept of 'body' and the understanding of 'life' remain wholly unexplained.

Nevertheless, there are a number of manifest weaknesses in this discussion. First of all, this critique tends towards oversimplification and generalisations. Take the widespread criticism that, in the life sciences, the human body is understood – after John Locke – as property in the sense of absolute self-determination. In relation to Locke, such a criticism is simply mistaken. Locke does say that 'every Man has a Property in his own Person', but his refers mostly to the 'Labour of his Body, and the Work of his Hands' as his property. This is a legal statement. Property here is understood as barring the possibility of being at someone else's disposal. For Locke, the point is not to ascribe an unlimited moral right to the individual to do with his body whatever he wants, but to make sure that it is laid down in the law that the individual is the one who determines what happens with his body and nobody else. What is morally defensible in terms of what one does with oneself is an entirely different question.

The reason why phenomenological criticism can be sweeping is connected to the way it builds its theories. It can only accuse technological and cultural developments *in toto* of misunderstanding and misconceiving life. A more sophisticated criteria-based identification of moral boundaries can hardly evolve from this perspective. This objection applies in a similar fashion to Horkheimer and Adorno as well. If our relation to the world is shaped by the separation of subject and object and if this separation determines our relation to our body in its entirety, then this holds fundamentally, and not only after the introduction of specific biotechnologies. If our relation to the world is determined by the way in which our body is at our disposal, why would this be any less true for the farmer who maltreats himself and uses his body in order to cultivate his land (staying with Heidegger's imagery) than for the use of certain performance-enhancing drugs? I am not saying that there is no relevant difference, but I wonder what criteria a phenomenology of corporeity has at its disposal for identifying such differences. Yet criteria are necessary if one is to formulate a criticism of concrete phenomena, such as the commercialisation of the human body.

A further serious point of criticism concerns the concept of *morality*. To what extent is phenomenology capable of formulating a *moral* critique (see also Chapter 3)? Martin Heidegger quite deliberately abstained from writing an ethics. To him, no attempt to formulate an ethics in terms of rights and duties and no form of moral criticism could conceivably be a serious philosophical undertaking at all (see for instance Heidegger 1947/1998: 38). Within the boundaries of his theory, this is only consistent. Yet if this is true, then it is also not possible to formulate *moral* criticisms of the instrumentalisation of the body. This also holds for Adorno and Horkheimer and for Foucault. It seems clear that their critiques of modern society are inspired by

Kant's prohibition of the instrumentalisation of people and that, therefore, they presuppose the central significance of human dignity. It is only possible to criticise modernity's utilisation, instrumentalisation and control over the individual if it is assumed that the dignity of every individual deserves to be protected. But the philosophical conceptions of Heidegger, Horkheimer and Adorno, and Foucault provide no basis for justifying this stipulation. If all conceptions of morality are subject to the universal suspicion that they are mere products of power relations and false metaphysics, then this must also be true of the moral demand that human dignity be protected.

Despite this critical balance, it must be noted that it was phenomenological discourse that put the *notion of life* onto the philosophical agenda. Before, 'life' was a topic for bioethics mostly under the header *'sanctity of life'*. I have already pointed out that this concept had a very distortive effect on the bioethical debate (Chapter 2), as it produced the impression that the question of whether one considers life sacred or not determines one's attitude towards the main bioethical problems. Critics and proponents of such a position have been equally responsible for the emergence of this misconception. However, the 'sanctity of life' has traditionally referred to the protection of human life. Hence the alliance between the notions of 'human dignity' and 'sanctity of life' that can be found in the Christian tradition and in (some) in other religious contexts. In a way, the 'sanctity of life' then provides an interpretive framework for the content of 'human dignity'. The reference to sanctity detaches human life from all practice. But the problems of a religious grounding of human dignity have already been discussed (Chapter 2).

By only contemplating the boundaries of human life, however, bioethics has failed adequately establish the concept of 'life' in the life sciences. However, life has been at issue in many ways throughout the history of the humanities. While an incredible financial investment is now put into making the investigation of 'life' into a scientific topic, an understanding of 'life' in general is supported that is at odds with people's everyday experience. Scientific or technological ways of understanding life are not limited to isolated areas of technical implementation. The proposals for interpreting life developed by the life sciences also influence people's self-understanding. Understanding this development in detail, and providing a description and moral evaluation of the effects on our understanding of ourselves and the world around us is a task that bioethics has not yet truly taken up.

Phenomenology has put these questions on the agenda, asking how we can conceive of a non-instrumental relation to nature, a non-instrumental notion of the human body and an adequate concept of life. However, a philosophical framework for bioethics that manages to reflect on these moral dimensions of the life sciences in a critical and sophisticated manner would require the prior establishment of an adequate theory. In the context of bioethics, it would have to be expected that this is done by developing a normative theory which does have a concept of morality at its disposal, which licenses *moral* critique, and which is able to provide nonarbitrary moral criteria that allow us to determine when moral boundaries are crossed in our dealings with life. So far, the phenomenological tradition has not done this.

3.2.3 ***A teleological understanding of nature?***

In the early days of bioethics, in the late 1970s and early 1980s, a book appeared that attracted a great deal of attention. Hans Jonas's *The imperative of responsibility* (1979/1984) and his attempt to ground a new approach to nature introduced an important paradigm into the debate on new technologies. Following the 1970s we saw the first manifest signs of the ecological crisis and the new developments in biology started to become assessable. While the atomic threat to the world in the cold war was still present, Hans Jonas appeared as a voice of one calling in the desert, urging a change of direction. His critique of the development of technology was radical and at the same time he was – unlike the proponents of the Frankfurt School and Bloch – free from the suspicion of leftist ideologies. In fact, significant parts of his book were devoted to a critique of Ernst Bloch's *Principle of Hope*, another philosophical bestseller at the time.

Hans Jonas calls for responsible ways of dealing with technological possibilities. In his analysis, the threats that developed in modernity are the results of our objectifying understanding of nature. This becomes manifest not only in the ecological crisis and through the unlimited exploitation of nature, but also in the development of medical science. Jonas's critique of modern medical science had a particularly strong influence on the debate about the definition of so-called brain death (Jonas 1974). For Jonas, the introduction of the notion of brain death, which connects the determination of the time of death with the irreversible loss of all brain function, was a sign that we have developed a fully physicalistic-objectivistic understanding of medicine (see Chapter 4). According to Jonas, this development in modern natural science and the corresponding naturalistic understanding of medicine rest on a development in modernity in which the understanding of nature as teleological is abandoned. The premodern conception of nature conceived nature as a comprehensive referential nexus of internal meanings. This internal order of nature already played a role in antiquity, and was modified by Christianity to the effect that God ordered nature through his creation. This conception of nature formed the basis for natural law, which provided orientation for human conduct as well. In the medieval doctrine of natural law people were taken to be capable – aided by the capacity for rational insight – of finding a regulative framework for morally defensible conduct. In premodernity, then, the orientation provided by nature was understood as a structure that could be found in nature or as the order given by the divine act of creation.

The end of the Middle Ages saw the start of a process in which nature loses its internal meaning. In Nicolaus Cusanus and William of Ockham, the natural order no longer appears as an order inherent to the elements of nature, but as an order applied to nature by God in an act of free will. If, however, the natural order is only the way it is on the basis of a decision of God, then there is something arbitrary to it. The consequences drawn from this insight vary widely. On the one hand, the Renaissance emphasised the sovereignty of people. The first texts on the 'dignity of humans' addressed exactly this point (Bayertz 1996). If humans have no preordained goal, then they are at least free and not bound to natural goals. Yet, in this case, the freedom and dignity of people seem to be necessarily connected to the fact that the purposes of nature do not present them with predetermined moral commitments. The reverse conclusion was drawn in the Reformation, which contemplated the radical transcendence of God. If the natural order is grounded in the fact that God established this order, then knowledge of the natural order is not of primary importance for moral orientation. Rather, good human conduct is owed to the mercy of God.

In all of these considerations, however, it is relevant that nature forfeits its natural order. The triumphant dominance of modernity in the natural sciences as well as in the reorganisation of political institutions is fundamentally connected to the fact that nature is no longer conceived as teleologically structured. The tradition of an internal nexus of meanings and references only reoccurs as the symbolic and metaphorical assignment of meaning in an aesthetic framework.

Jonas's claim is that it is exactly this loss of a teleological conception of nature which forms the fundamental ground for the ecological crisis and the loss of boundaries in our use of technology. Since nature no longer provides an ordering framework, people's dealings with nature become solely instrumental, and they grow incapable of finding any boundaries. Nature becomes the object of their unbridled manipulation and the threats resulting from the uncontrollable effects of this manipulation increase. From that point onwards, only the return to a teleological understanding of nature could provide a framework that would reintroduce meaning, sense and boundaries to the responsible conduct of people. This turning point would involve an understanding of the human body as more than a machine-like, calculable matter into which a soul accidentally strayed. Rather, the human body would have to be thought of as an *organism*, a spirited body which even biologically does not allow for unlimited manipulation.

It is not entirely clear what exactly accounts for the impact of Jonas's work. It might be doubted whether the teleological conception of nature was of initial interest to his readers. It might well be that it was the appellative force of some of his texts which impressed readers. In addition, with his *precautionary principle* and *heuristics of fear* Jonas introduced essential ideas to the debate on the ethics of technology. Both of these keywords indicate that we, when facing uncertainties and when facing possible consequences of new technologies, must always act as if the worst prognosis applies. Responsible use of new technologies demands the precaution always to account for the most catastrophic effects from the implementation of technologies. The formulation of the precautionary principle subjected Jonas to a great deal of criticism. It was frequently argued that acting according to the precautionary principle in effect allowed for no actions at all. Someone who actually is as careful as Jonas demands is condemned for not acting at all, which surely involves positive risk itself. This is a legitimate criticism.

Fundamental criticisms of Jonas are also connected to his notion of nature as teleological. First of all, his conception evokes the question of how it could be justified. Surely any attempt to ascribe an internal nexus of meaning to nature is necessarily an ascription by people? And are not all ascriptions by people dependent on the cultural contexts from which they are initiated? And, if so, surely the assumption of an internal meaningfulness of nature is an obfuscation of the fact that these meanings are cultural constructs and that this inevitably makes such a conception of nature ideology-prone?

And even if we were capable of conceiving of an inherent meaning structure in nature, why should this provide a basis for ethics? An argument that seems to suggest itself is that one would thus inevitably expose oneself to the naturalistic fallacy – that is, G.E. Moore's warning that it is impossible to explicate value judgments in natural terms. But this objection is only partly justified. If nature itself had a teleological structure, then it would not automatically be a fallacy for us to understand value judgments as explications of this natural order. The reference to the naturalistic fallacy already presupposes that this inference actually is a fallacy. However, if one has a teleological conception of nature it is unclear where the normative obligation stems from. If nature has an internal order, why would I, as agent, understand this order as morally binding? Does not the idea of a moral obligation already presuppose that there is a constitutive difference between the order of nature and the idea that an agent has moral obligations? And does not the idea of a moral obligation already presuppose that an agent is obliged to a certain norm on the basis of recognising the rightness of this norm? The mere fact that nature itself is ordered in a particular way is not a sufficient ground for assuming an obligation for agents. Even more serious, however, is the fact that Jonas must first show that the idea of a teleologically structured nature is compatible with human freedom. Without the assumption of our freedom, the idea of an obligation could not be justified in the first place. My intention is not to claim that it is impossible to square the idea of a teleologically ordered nature with the notion of moral obligation. But Jonas has not shown that it can be done. And he has shown even less how such a conception of nature could provide the basis for moral obligation.

However, there is another critical point that should be noted, or at least an enquiry that should be raised. In his attempt to formulate boundaries for morally legitimate human conduct on the basis of his conception of nature, Jonas has no real space for the value and rights of the individual. Jonas focuses his hopes so strongly on the ascription of meaning to nature in which the hubris of modern humans is broken, that he has no room for the equally modern idea of an absolute worth of the human person. Despite all criticism, however, Jonas's effort constitutes an important contribution. He offered systematic elaborations of many motives and criticisms of modern technology and the modern life world that still crop up in the public debate. Moreover, he has been one of the only thinkers to attempt to develop the 'argument from naturalness' as a philosophical argument. Jonas wishes to criticise the boundless exploitation of nature by humans. In doing so, he wants to criticise both the unlimited freedom of liberal conceptions and big historical conceptions of utopia as we know them from Ernst Bloch. He puts the responsibility for the ecological crisis and the – to his mind – many aberrations of modernity on the unbounded human fiddling with nature. To him, a conception that does not understand nature as freely available matter would be the way out. Yet Jonas can show neither how we could arrive at such a conception of nature, nor that it forms the basis for a new way of dealing with nature. He does not even show that this notion of nature is compatible with the idea of human freedom and moral obligation in the first place. And, finally, this conception of nature is incompatible with the special position of humans that we must presuppose if we are to ascribe dignity and rights to the individual.

Criticism of Jonas's idea of precaution is still present today. Cass Sunstein (2005) argued that the precautionary principle is paralysing and makes action impossible. Implicitly, the principle presupposes a kind of ideal form of nature that we are afraid to alienate. This is a contemporary repetition of the old criticism of Jonas. One can indeed doubt that the idea of precaution in the contemporary discourse is used in a sufficiently reflected way. Yet it is not a given that reference to precaution always has to take the form we find in Jonas (see for example Beyleveld and Brownsword 2006) and we can doubt that it always has to presuppose a normative concept of nature. But in all forms of moral action we have to presuppose some kind of precautionary reasoning – we always have to ascribe moral value to a range of uncertainties that are accompanying our actions. We simply do not know many of the circumstances and possible side-effects of our actions. The judgment whether driving a car is morally responsible or not given that it may result in the death of some innocent pedestrians is already a moral judgment that involves some assumptions with regard to the degree to which I am obliged to take precautions. Risk assessment and probabilistic reasoning are here only partly informative, because it is very questionable as to whether the statistical information is morally significant (see section 3.4.2 of this chapter). Precautionary reasoning is a central part of moral reasoning, and such reasoning does not necessarily presuppose a romantic view or a normative concept of nature. It will be the task of bioethics to reflect on this role of precaution more carefully.

3.2.4 The aesthetics of nature and contingency

In what follows, we shall discuss a number of positions that might prove helpful in reformulating the intuitions that I think are expressed in arguments from naturalness. I start with the appeal to the idea of an aesthetics of nature and then move to some general considerations regarding human contingency. An appeal to natural-aesthetical arguments is an attempt to assign meaning and intrinsic value to nature without having to rely on strong assumptions regarding a teleological structure in nature. Such arguments play a certain role in discussions on environmental ethics, but they can also be paradigmatically relevant to a methodology for the use of nature-related arguments in bioethical debates (Seel 1991; Wils 1990; Düwell 1999; Kemper 2000).

For a long time, however, aesthetic approaches of nature have failed to play a significant role in the domain of philosophical aesthetics. Aesthetics understood itself as 'philosophy of art'. For the aesthetics of modernity, it seemed crucial that its objects could be understood as expressions, symbols or sensuous manifestations of subjectivity. Art was thought of as either a representation or a critique of society. In any case, only art seemed to be a possible object for aesthetics.

Amongst the classical aesthetic texts of the 20th century, the aesthetics of nature only plays a role in the work of Joachim Ritter and Theodor W. Adorno. Both assign the aesthetics of nature a central role in the context of a philosophy of modernity. In a famous essay entitled 'Landscape' (1974), Ritter points out how the development of an aesthetic approach to nature is connected to the conditions of modernity. Ritter considers the development of modernity a process in which the subject becomes ever more powerful. Through technological control and capitalist economic reform, nature is increasingly brought under human control and loses its threatening character. The development of technology, complex state institutions and division of labour put people at a distance from nature that allows for natural resources to be used efficiently. At the same time, this opens up the possibility of understanding nature as the object of aesthetic contemplation in the first place. Only when one is no longer immediately engaged in the daily battle against the supremacy of nature is it possible to perceive nature as beautiful and sublime. The increasing control over nature and the expansion of technology are thus compensated by the freedom to engage with nature without perceiving it as the object of threat or control.

While Ritter analyses natural beauty as a compensation for the modern world, Adorno views natural beauty as a promise of the utopia of a redeemed or reconciled world (Adorno 1970/2001: 79–122). Surprisingly, however, Adorno largely agrees with Ritter when it comes to the conditions on the emergence of natural-aesthetic experiences. For Adorno, too, natural-aesthetic experiences are only possible in a context of advanced technology, a society based on the division of labour and corresponding experiences of alienation. Yet Adorno does not view the aesthetic experience of nature as compensation for the alienation that is experienced. Rather, natural beauty indicates a situation without alienation. In our ability to perceive nature as beautiful and sublime we get a glimpse of a relation to nature that is free from any compulsion to control it and equally free from fear of its overwhelming supremacy. In an experience of natural beauty, we must neither defend ourselves against all-powerful natural surroundings, nor do we experience nature as trimmed down for human purposes. What is crucial is that natural beauty gives us an intimation of a situation beyond human compulsions, even though it has been created by nobody. In the experience of nature as harmonious or sublime, we get a glimpse of what the world could be like without the dominance of universal alienation. For Adorno, this model of natural aesthetics is so powerful that he even holds that art should strive after the ideal that is expressed in natural beauty. It is clear, of course, that art could never do this, since it is man-made. However, art must strive to become, in its man-made form, what is beautiful about natural beauty. Adorno does not hold that natural beauty is simply a utopian state. But he also does not suggest that there are any guarantees that the utopian state will ever be realised. Natural beauty is the sphere in which humans can experience a situation beyond social compulsion as possible.

The conceptions of Ritter and Adorno are linked in that they pull the notion of natural aesthetics into a philosophical context. Natural beauty is the compensation for the repression of nature or a promise of a situation on the other side of such repression. In contrast, the third approach of understanding natural aesthetics, which I would like to introduce briefly at this point, tries to liberate the aesthetic from such a philosophical-historical perspective. This third approach is discussed in Martin Seel's book *An Aesthetics of Nature*, in my opinion the most important book on aesthetics after Adorno's *Aesthetic Theory*. In many ways, Seel borrows from Kant's *Critique of Aesthetic Judgment*. Seel describes different forms of aesthetic experience and their relations to the world in which we live. In this context, aesthetic experiences have different functions. They can be playful expressions and articulations of a worldview. They can provide opportunities to test new ways of understanding the world. But it is also possible that aesthetic experiences exist in the absence of meaningful interpretations of the world, or that they reflect the impossibility of such interpretations. In aesthetic experience we remain, for the duration of the experience, at a certain distance from our involvement in the necessities of life and from this distance we can relate to the world and discover new perspectives on it. These forms of aesthetic experience are in no way exclusive to the aesthetics of nature. Rather, nature is simply *one* object of aesthetic experience amongst others. Yet the aesthetic experience of nature is special in the sense that it provides a different kind of freedom from other forms of experience. In the aesthetic experience of nature we experience a distance from the interpretive models of culture. The point of this is not to abandon culture. We do not have an experience of getting 'back to nature' in Rousseau's sense. Nor is the point to claim that in natural aesthetics nature is experienced as 'pure', untouched by human hands. What is at stake is a mode of experience in which nature is experienced as non-instrumental, in which it seems to exhibit a meaningful order or in which it allows people, at a distance from culture and cultural interpretations of the world, to perceive their familiar environment in a different way.

In natural-aesthetic experiences we experience a distance from culture which discloses new perspectives, new possibilities, new horizons of meaning; qualities which, in this specific form, can only be experienced in the aesthetics of nature.

Some people have tried to explain the particularity of natural beauty by proposing that the unmade and unpredictable quality of natural-aesthetic experiences corresponds to the experience of our own corporeity. Natural-aesthetic experiences are moments of 'positive contingency' (Kemper 2000: 61ff; Seel 1991: 188ff). That means that in aesthetic experiences of nature, nature is experienced as meaningful, and this meaningfulness is not the result of purposive organisation, but thoroughly contingent. This positive contingency is meaningful in the sense that it corresponds to the contingency of the human corporeity. Outside of himself, the person encounters a form of contingency that allows him to experience an expression of and counterpart to the contingency of his own bodily existence, while the object of this experience is not created for this purpose. If human beings no longer ever discovered anything outside themselves that still showed traces of this contingency, if in their environment they never encountered natural phenomena allowing for experiences of beauty and sublimity, then they would also be no longer capable of understanding themselves in the contingency of their own existence.

But to what extent can these considerations be relevant to bioethics? This rough sketch should indicate the methodological possibility of a reconstruction and an ethical assessment of arguments from naturalness. The usual criticism of arguments from naturalness in bioethics presumes that the reference to the 'naturalness' with regard to humans and the environment aims to assign normative significance to the special, allegedly natural quality of the human form of or some natural part of the environment. In this case, 'naturalness' would be a more or less objective property of nature or of the human body, which has a special quality that ought to be respected by others. The proponents of 'naturalness' – according to the criticism – first single out a particular state of humans and the environment as 'natural', and subsequently withdraw this state from human intervention. Hans Jonas – but many others too – attempted to secure this ascription of naturalness through assumptions about the metaphysical or ontological structure of nature itself. Their critics' point is that the ascription always depends on historically and culturally contingent preconceptions, that the ascription of naturalness does not imply a normative bindingness in nature itself and that it is very difficult to combine the special character and moral relevance of human freedom with this whole image of naturalness. On the other hand, the reference to natural aesthetics indicates that nature is important for humans in terms of their essential needs for self-understanding and self-interpretation. It is claimed that the possibility of aesthetic experiences of nature is important for people's interpretation of themselves and the world around them, since in such experiences they can experience themselves as free and contingent beings and gain a distance from culturally shaped interpretive structures. If Seel and others are right, this possibility for distancing ourselves is an important element of our experiencing ourselves as free beings. Such a claim does not endow isolated elements in nature with an objective, human-independent worth. Rather, the basis of this valuation of nature depends on humans experiencing natural beauty and sublimity in a special way, and on this possible experience being significant for their self-understanding and possibilities in a qualified way.

Elsewhere (Düwell 1999) I have attempted to show that this line of reasoning provides the basis for an argument that is relevant for at least environmental ethics. If we can (i) demonstrate in the context of moral philosophy that our capacity for agency and the necessary conditions for a successful life are subject to moral protection; and (ii) show that the possibility of an aesthetic experience of nature is crucial for people's self-interpretation and possibilities in life; and if (iii) nature as the basis for this possible experience is threatened because of human conduct, then we have the grounds for a moral demand for the preservation of the nature which allows us these experiential possibilities that are so vital to us.

The individual steps in such an argument require more elaborate discussion. Methodologically, however, the preceding considerations have indicated a path on which bioethics has so far trodden only very lightly. This argument does not demand reverence for nature or life, nor is 'naturalness' promoted to a normative criterion. Both seem hard to justify and both – as we have seen with Jonas, for instance – are in danger of making assumptions which undermine the possibilities for moral critique. Instead, the proposal would be to try to reconstruct the way in which nature is meaningful and worthy of protection from its relevance for us as (moral) subjects. Such a reconstruction would not itself justify general obligations to protection or moral prohibitions. Yet it would be a first step towards testing whether there are moral grounds on which we can demand limits on the interventions in nature and alterations of living things, according to which nature ought to be protected independently from functional reasons, risk assessment and ecological considerations.

3.3 Human nature and culture

3.3.1 Concepts and images of human nature[3]

In bioethics, implicit and explicit references to conceptions of humankind are common, although the contexts and functions in which they appear are very diverse. It is often said that a particular notion of human beings underlies the life sciences and biomedicine; occasionally, a specific conception of humankind is proposed in bioethics; or an 'image of the human being' is employed

3 I owe many insights on this topic to conversations with my doctoral supervisor Reiner Wimmer.

as a normative criterion, for instance when people talk of a 'Christian image of humanity'. Mostly, the exact function of talking about conceptions of humankind is unclear. The relation between conceptions of humankind and morality is ambiguous as well. Before I delve into these matters, a terminological oddity must be addressed. When people use the term 'anthropology' in English-speaking countries, they usually mean an ethnology that operates in the domain of social and cultural sciences. In the so-called 'continental' debate, 'anthropology' is taken to mean either the substance of an 'image of human beings' (*Menschenbild* in German) or–in that sense we can speak about 'Christian anthropology' or 'the secular concept of the human person', a 'philosophical anthropology' as a discipline or philosophical approach. Philosophical anthropology has been an attempt to establish philosophy as the investigation of the human being. This endeavour was particularly widespread in mid 20th century German philosophy, when it became connected to names such as Arnold Gehlen, Max Scheler, Nicolai Hartmann and Helmuth Plessner (Gehlen 1986/1988; Plessner 1975; Scheler 1928/2009). The investigation of the human being was, however, never seen as one topic amongst others, in the sense that philosophical anthropology was not a subdiscipline of philosophy, such as philosophy of language. It was seen as a philosophical approach of its own that aims at understanding the human being in all dimensions. This different tradition of dealing with concepts of human nature has to be taken into account in order to understand those debates.

It is frequently claimed that a certain *conception of human nature* underlies the life sciences. In this conception, humans might, for instance, be presented as *having liberated themselves from the shackles of the contingency and arbitrariness of nature*. Just like humans go on a journey to the moon in order to conquer the universe, they also decide to investigate the biological fundaments of their existence in order to be liberated in the long term from hereditary disease, the scourge of humanity. The delay of aging thus appears as a possible perspective as well. It is in this context that Pico della Mirandola's concept of dignity, according to which humans are characterised by the fact that they are not determined in their being (Pico della Mirandola 1448/1998), seems to come to full bloom for the first time. This conception of humans is aggressively advanced in many publicity campaigns for bioscience, championed by trans-humanists and criticised by the adversaries of biotechnology (from the Pope to Greenpeace). It seems, then, that people agree that the life sciences constitute an enormous cultural project towards overcoming natural contingency and thus towards the triumph of humans over natural boundaries. The evaluation of this project only differs to the extent that some judge this goal to be realistic and desirable, and others as an illusionary undertaking, as a denial of human finitude or as the expression of human hubris. Somewhat cynically it might be asked, however, whether it would have been possible to secure such enormous sums of money for the human genome project or stem cell research without these promises of cures.

A different perspective on the bioscience conception of humans argues that underlying the project of the life sciences is a *reductionist conception* of human beings, which defines humanity purely on the basis of its genetic structures and thus necessarily views humans as genetically determined. Being able to change human nature in such a way that it becomes effectively possible to explain the development of diseases on the basis of genetics and to alter human properties for therapeutic purposes would require humans to understand themselves deterministically according to their genetic basis. As the biosciences have become the model for our modern, scientifically defined culture, our entire view of human beings is shaped by this determinist and reductionist conception. People must think of themselves and their own nature as controllable in order to be able to cure and alter themselves. Within bioethics and social and cultural sciences, these questions have also been debated under the motto 'genetisation' (Hoedemaekers 2001). This term describes the phenomenon that models and notions of genetics encroach upon ever more areas of life. Genetic concepts are usually employed for explanations that transgress far beyond what is scientifically realistic and possible.

The *critique of biological conceptions of humans* is often connected with a critique of the expansion of models of evolutionary biology, and specifically of social-Darwinist views, of which it is then said that the events of the 20th century have disclosed their destructive potential. Relevant in this context is not so much the American debate regarding creationism, which is concerned with the compatibility of the theory of evolution with creation according to the Bible. Rather, what is pertinent is the criticism that such efforts seek to use evolution as a source of legitimation of human conduct. In certain variants of so-called evolutionary ethics it is presumed that reference to evolutionary tendencies can serve as a criterion for the rightness of moral conduct. This position is heavily criticised on philosophical grounds, yet as an argumentative motif, the legitimating reference to the developmental tendencies of evolution can be found in countless debates. Such direct moral-normative references to evolution should, however, be distinguished from standpoints that take as their starting point the idea that evolutionary theory is indirectly relevant for identifying what is morally right. Since we can morally demand only those actions that could actually be realised ('ought implies can'), we also have to be aware of the limits to what we can do and how we can live. Yet these limits are co-determined to a considerable extent by evolution. The latter position is neither subject to a naturalistic fallacy, nor influenced by ideology. It is simply right.

In this context, we will have to address the critique of *eugenics*. Without a doubt, social-Darwinist and eugenic conceptions of humankind have played a role in the development of the National-Socialist notion of racial hygiene (Weingart 1989), even if the development of National-Socialist ideology was exceptionally eclectic and never led – even within the movement itself – to any ideology that was at all cohesive. Without wanting to discuss the historical dimension here, the role of the eugenics-objection in bioethics is very particular. Accusing someone of 'eugenics' discredits the adversary without having to engage with her position in any detail. At the same time, however, it can be observed that, recently, people have drawn on samples of eugenic ideologies rather cavalierly; the debates surrounding Sloterdijk's 'Rules for the human zoo' (1999/2009) are informative in this regard.

In the different discourses, then, it is indeed possible to find evidence for specific views on humanity. All of these are defended by some and criticised by others. In the bioethical and biopolitical debates, these references to conceptions of humankind are usually discussion stoppers: someone who fails to appreciate human finitude or conceives of people reductively seems so irredeemable that he is not even worth engaging with. And someone who wishes to refuse people the possibility of conquering disease and disability, someone who rejects the ethics of curing and helping – such a person's good intentions must surely be doubted. The prominence of a recourse to conceptions of humankind in the public debate corresponds to a remarkable lack of systematic reflection on the role of a 'concept of human nature' in bioethics. For that reason, I wish to distinguish between at least four constellations of questions, for which I can at the moment only see the beginnings of an answer: (i) How can we verify which conception of humankind actually does underlie the biosciences? (ii) Is there such a thing as a correct conception of humankind? (iii) What do conceptions of humankind have to do with morality? (iv) How are we to conceive of the relation between bioethics and conceptions of human nature (humankind)?

3.3.1.1 The conception of humankind of the life sciences and biomedicine

The assertion that the life sciences and biomedicine function with a particular conception of humankind is an *empirical assertion*. At the same time, it is so general and across-the-board that it seems impossible to test it empirically. Empirically, we could perhaps say something about the views on human beings of concrete actors and institutions, for instance by studying their public statements and conducting interviews with them. Through social-empirical studies, we could develop hypotheses on the conception of humankind in certain social groups, age groups, professional categories, etc. Yet these statements will always remain connected to particular contexts and areas of life. Assertions regarding *the* 'conception of humankind of biomedicine' thus seem by their very nature speculative and impossible to verify.

Now it is possible to try to gain an image of humankind from the actions of relevant actors, for instance by reconstructing assumptions about humans that can be identified in allocation policies of governmental or private institutions that finance research. This, however, is complicated by the fact that the actions of such institutions are the result of compromises between numerous actors, and as such allow only for very qualified conclusions on these institutions' conceptions of humankind – if it is possible to speak of a shared conception of humankind at all. In enquiries of the public, too, it will only be possible to find different motifs that mirror a spectrum of views on human beings, and that are probably inconsistent and disparate. This certainly does not render the attempt to reconstruct conceptions of humankind and their role in the discourse obsolete. Indeed, it is exceptionally useful to make the images of human beings that are operative in the discourse explicit and to show in what ways certain decisions and positions are influenced by particular conceptions of humankind. It is an important critical task of bioethics to make implicit assumptions explicit and open them up for discussion and critique. Yet in light of the difficulties of reconstructing conceptions of humankind within the bounds of a complex discourse, it seems doubtful that the primary task of science should be to go into detective mode and figure out which implicit assumptions on human beings can be identified for the different parties.

Given the diversity, fragmentation and indefiniteness of factical images of humankind, the most relevant question, I think, is not which conceptions of humankind are *factically held* by different people, but the question of whether the politics of fund allocation and research development *can be understood only under the assumption of a particular conception of humankind*. The question, then, is whether certain ideas about human beings must necessarily be assumed in order to understand a particular research practice as meaningful. We could ask, for instance, whether 'genetic determinism' is a necessary presupposition for understanding the human genome project (on genetic determinism see Rehmann-Sutter 2008). Would research on the human genome project still be meaningful if 'genetic determinism' is rejected? If we have to answer this question in the negative, then we can indeed say that 'genetic determinism' is part of the conception of humankind of biomedical sciences. Or take the example of 'genetic reductionism': are assumptions of 'genetic reductionism' necessary presuppositions for biomedical research, without which this kind of research could not be understood coherently? If this question is answered affirmatively, then genetic reductionism would be part of biomedicine's conception of humankind.

Such an analysis of necessary presuppositions and implications is not only conceivable with regard to research, but also with regard to particular implementations. In this context, we could also distinguish between *necessary* and (more or less) *likely* implications. It could be investigated, for instance, whether there exist arguments for thinking that organ transplantation is necessarily connected with a mechanistic understanding of the human body – an understanding, that is, in which the human body is conceived of as standing in a purely instrumental relation to the human person. Or we could ask: is it possible to prove that in a society where organ transplantation belongs to the set of medical procedures that are standardly available, people are more likely to have mechanistic conceptions of the human body? If this could be argued, then it could be said that a mechanistic conception of the human body is a necessary or likely implication of the practice of organ transplantation. If, however, it turns out that such a conception of human beings is only associated with this practice if medical professionals are in the habit of expressing themselves in corresponding metaphors, or if campaigns for organ transplantation divulge such an image of human beings, then this conception of humankind would be only *contingently connected to this practice*. In any case it is a task to test to what extent certain conceptions of human beings do in fact influence the research and practice of new biotechnologies. This task has an empirical element, but for an ethical discussion it is initially more important to gain clarity about the question in which ways certain images of humankind are necessarily connected with research and practice.

In addition, however, a similar *disclosure of assumptions about images of humankind is also essential for bioethics itself*. It must be made clear what premises about human beings underlie our moral judgments. Something similar to what is true of research in the life sciences holds here. What is vital is not what particular assumptions some individual bioethicist makes, but the necessity or contingency of the connection of these assumptions with any given moral principle or ethical theory. It could be, for instance, that a theologian considers reproductive medicine problematic and that this opinion coincides with certain views he holds of humans as created by God. However, the grounds for his critical assessment of reproductive medicine could lie in doubts that this technology (for instance in light of its medical shortcomings and risks) is an appropriate solution for realising a couple's wish for having children of their own. His specifically Christian conception of humankind is not necessarily connected with his assessment of this technology. For the ethical discussion, however, it is only relevant to analyse to what extent certain conceptions of humankind are of constitutive significance for certain moral principles and judgments.

3.3.1.2 Is there such a thing as a 'correct' conception of humankind?

However, the point is not normally to disclose conceptions of humankind, but also to relate to them in a critical manner. Every criticism of a particular image of human beings is based on the critic having a notion of what would be a correct or appropriate image of human beings. Someone who holds that new biotechnologies have disregarded human finitude assumes that a fitting conception of human beings must place a certain significance on the finitude of human beings. Someone who thinks that the Christian conception of humanity hinders people in overcoming their suffering assumes that a fitting conception of humankind understands the endeavour to overcome suffering as characteristic for human beings. While my first question only enquired how it could be ascertained whether certain images of humankind are in fact present and influential for our judgments, the current question has to do with identifying the justification of a fitting, appropriate or correct conception of humankind. Without such disclosure, the critique of conceptions of humankind is entirely ungrounded.

There is an incredible tension, however, between the resoluteness with which conceptions of humankind are factically criticised and the relativism that most people advance in this regard. We know in the back of our minds that our conceptions of humanity depend on our culture and that in, for instance, Asian cultures, different images of human beings exist from those in occidental cultures. Nevertheless, collectivist conceptions of humanity, eugenic notions and religiously shaped worldviews are criticised. Insofar as these critiques are simply expressions of our own conceptions of humankind, there are no grounds for claiming any superiority for them. Some people view humans as footloose individualists, made for the uninhibited use of their bodies, while others conceive of them as fundamentally part of the chain of reincarnations, linked into a network of cosmic references. So why should one conception of humankind have normative priority? In political discourses, this seems to be only a matter of power relations. That, in any case, is the only way in which it could possibly be explained how unscrupulously the reference to a 'Christian image of humankind' is employed in political discourse, or how cavalierly the conception of humankind of the 'free West' is pulled up in order to legitimate wars. Yet right behind this appeal to an image of human beings lies a radical relativism, as long as it is not shown that we have reasons to consider this conception of humankind valid for others as well. The mere fact that a certain conception of humankind is *my* or *our* conception is not yet a reason for assuming that it is the better one.

It must be noted that the vehemence with which images of humankind are criticised and repudiated in no way corresponds to the philosophical discourse on such images. It seems exactly the task of philosophy to analyse to what extent certain aspects of human existence are nonarbitrary assumptions, that is, assumptions that we cannot controvert (Illies 2006). Yet the attempts at such an understanding of human nature (humankind) are relatively ill-represented in the current philosophical discourse. That is not only as a result of doubts about the justification of any conception of human nature, but even much more radically with fundamental suspicions that statements regarding the nature of humans are always inappropriate specifications in which historically grown images of humankind are simply conventionalised into universal constants. At the same time, there is no basis for criticising certain images of humankind without a philosophical account that can show that certain elements of a conception of humankind can only be given up at the cost of a fundamental internal contradiction. Why should the current perspective on humanity be better than that of earlier generations? Or what grounds would we have to suppose that people had a better perspective in the past? Why should the worldview of the West be better than that of the oriental world, or why would holistic worldviews have to be preferred to individualistic views as a matter of principle? Either critical philosophical treatment of such questions is possible, or the critique and normative employment of conceptions of humankind remain rhetoric and ideology.

Elements of an account that strives for a philosophically nonarbitrary view of human beings can be found, for instance, in Helmut Plessner, a biologist, philosopher and social scientist from the first half of the 20th century, whose work still plays a role in sociology. The core of Plessner's account is expressed by the notion, coined by him, of the 'eccentricity' of the human person. With this expression, Plessner refers to a 'double aspect of his existence as a material body and a lived body [als Körper und Leib]' (Plessner 1975: 294). A human being is 'a thing amongst things' (ibid.) that lives from the 'centre of its positionality' (ibid. 289), yet is capable of 'distancing itself from itself'. In this constellation, the 'way in which the subject is given to itself must not be explained by a multiplication of the core of the subject (which in itself is absurd)' (ibid.). On the basis of its capacity to distance itself, the individual is the 'subject of its experiences, its perceptions and his actions, its initiatives. It knows and it wants' (ibid. 293). Plessner manages to conceive of human beings as creatures whose mental and reflexive faculties and capacities constitutive for morality are compatible with their existence as biological creatures. He can conceive of humans as not predetermined to particular ways of acting, as having at least the leeway that allows them to ask about the goals of their actions. Similar attempts exist in the context of analytic philosophy of mind. Without going into too much detail concerning Plessner, it should become clear that this is a potential way in which a basis for ethics could be developed; a way that does not provide a fixed substantial image of human beings or a fixation on a contingent conception of humankind. Rather, Plessner and similar approaches try to offer elements of a philosophical account of human nature that presents us with starting points that are fundamentally necessary for our self-understanding as human beings.

We must assume, in this context, that this form of philosophy as concerned with human nature is capable of integrating the state of knowledge of contemporary biology (neuroscience, genetics and evolutionary biology). At any rate, it would be impossible to conceive without contradiction of a conception of humankind that fails to heed the biological possibilities of humans. It is also crucial for bioethics that human beings are aware of the spectrum of possibilities they have as biological creatures. Moral claims can only operate in the space that humans as biological creatures have at their disposal. Nevertheless, philosophy ought not to be uncritical in employing information regarding humans provided by biological sciences, for it does happen that philosophically uncritical assumptions creep into the theory formation of biology. And it is even less the case that the role of the philosopher ought to be to simply translate, say, biological theories concerning human behaviour (from ethology and evolutionary theory) into moral norms. What she must do is develop an awareness of the scope of human possibilities for action, in order to be able to discuss the legitimacy of moral norms.

3.3.1.3 Conceptions of humankind and ethics

In dealing with assumptions regarding human beings, then, one is confronted on the one hand with the question of how assertions on the factual authority of such assumptions can be verified, and on the other with the question of how it can be shown in a normative sense that certain assumptions hold true independently of culture. This does not yet determine the significance of conceptions of humankind for ethics.

According to an exceptionally popular standpoint, cases of moral dissent are caused by differences in conceptions of human beings. The frequent appeals to a 'Christian image of humankind' in the context of the euthanasia debate, for instance, seem to presume such a causal relation. According to such an appeal, proponents of a liberal image of human beings want to allow for as many life science technologies as possible, as long as these technologies do not thwart people's freedom, while proponents of a Christian conception of humankind tend to emphasise human finitude with respect to the development of such technologies. This could of course be qualified but, as a rule, cases of moral dissent can be traced back to differences in conceptions of humankind. If this idea were correct, then ethical discourses would be no more than intellectual battles between representatives of the worldviews of different groups in society. The conceptions of humankind would then be the results of pre-theoretical convictions and value judgments that one can become aware of, but that cannot really be justified. The idea that moral dissent lies in differences between conceptions of human beings also means that while it can be hoped that there will prove to be convergences amongst such conceptions, or that they will turn out to be at least somewhat tolerant of one another, it is not possible to argue for their plausibility. Moral learning processes would generally presume a modification of one's own worldview that would be so massive that it would almost amount to a conversion.

If for no other reason, this notion is questionable because conceptions of humankind can range from morally quite open to very substantive. A conception can simply amount to the interpretation of humans as free, as created by God or as finite, expressing only basic convictions about human beings that are still compatible with very diverse criteria for morally right conduct. On the other hand, images of humankind can be much richer; they can span the entirety of human existence and include beliefs about morally right conduct only as part of a larger whole. In both respects, the notion of a 'conception of humankind' is not specific enough to determine the moral domain. However, it is not a foregone conclusion that concrete moral judgments are necessarily the results of presuppositions about the 'nature of human beings' in a way that encompasses all aspects of human existence. Otherwise, moral communication would really only be conceivable either as an attempt at convincing others of one's own conception of humanity *in toto*, or as grounded in a willingness to divorce oneself from one's own conception entirely. If moral debates were nothing but ideological skirmishes in which different images of humankind clash irreconcilably, then there would be no hope of philosophical argumentation initiating a moral learning process in which the individual assumptions of our own moral judgments are up for debate.

This conception of moral debates as conflicts between different conceptions of humankind relinquishes familiar distinctions between ethical discourse and discourse regarding human nature. Ethical debates concern principles, rules and norms that are not nearly as comprehensive as conceptions of humankind, but represent mere criteria for morally binding conduct, in part even specific rules for concrete domains. These principles and their justification draw on individual concepts of human nature (such as assumptions regarding freedom of the will or the vulnerability of people), but all of these elements are up for concrete discussion and verification. Moral learning processes do not presuppose road-to-Damascus conversions that upset entire worldviews. Instead, moral learning processes can be thought of as modifications of individual aspects of our presuppositions for moral judgments, and cases of consensus can be understood as agreements on individual aspects of these presuppositions. It is also possible to share a moral conviction with someone despite disagreeing in many respects about the way one thinks of human beings. It is neither *eo ipso* clear that the justification of a moral principle requires assumptions regarding all aspects of human existence, nor is it plausible that those assumptions are by their very definition inaccessible to rational comprehension. The idea that moral discourses should be understood as the results of diverging conceptions of humankind thus relies on a number of presuppositions that are hardly self-evident. If it is assumed that moral differences are mere expressions of diverging conceptions of human beings *as a matter of principle*, then this comes down to revoking the willingness to argue with diverging presuppositions of moral judgments. An arbitrary appeal to a Christian, liberal, Islamic (or whatever other) conception of humankind in order to justify one's own moral judgment would be a form of relativism from which bioethical discourse must distance itself as ideology. On such an interpretation, the question of which conception of humankind prevails and whether several images of humanity coexist peacefully would be nothing but a matter of power relations and political willingness to compromise.

3.3.1.4 (Bio)ethics and concepts of human nature

It is still unclear how ethics and philosophical concepts of human nature relate to each other. It seems evident that moral judgments and the development of ethical theories are not independent from assumptions concerning human nature. At the same time, however, these judgments do not simply follow from an account of human nature as if ethics were a kind of applied philosophy of human nature and bioethics a domain-specific instantiation. It may be expected that a branch of philosophy that concerns itself with human nature – if such a discipline turns out to be possible at all – will only be able to sketch a philosophically binding image of human beings in a very rough manner, consisting of no more than basic abilities and aspects of human existence. Such a sketch would not suffice as a basis for justifying principles of right conduct. That means that we ought to conceive the link between ethics and our concept of human nature as a more complex relation.

Now the more recent debates are characterised on the one hand by doubts about the possibility of a philosophy of human nature, while on the other hand modern ethics tries, as a matter of principle, not to bind itself to specific images of humankind. If it is in the nature of human beings not to be bound to a specific image of humanity, then neither should they pin ethics down to a particular image. After all, modern, broadly liberal notions within ethics and political philosophy usually assume that universally binding norms cannot simply be expressions of a certain ideal conception of humankind. At the same time, modern liberalism is continually exposed to critiques of its untransparent concepts of human nature (Taylor 1985). Charles Taylor and many others have argued, for instance, that while Rawls's *A Theory of Justice* claims to have developed a procedure for identifying universal principles of justice that does not depend on specific conceptions of humans and society, his description of the procedure's starting points already smuggles in substantial assumptions about human beings, such as the image of rational persons who understand themselves as independent individuals. If such assumptions are indispensable for the development of theories, then they must be made explicit, and explicitly justified. This relevance of accounts of human nature for (bio)ethics can be located at *different levels*. I shall briefly discuss some of them.

At a very fundamental level, this whole issue revolves around the question of *whether we can understand humans as creatures that are capable of moral conduct and ethical reflection in the first place*. This understanding would mean, at least, that human beings are thought of as *free beings* in the sense that they can choose between different ways of acting, set themselves goals, and are capable of asking whether they want certain actions and whether they are morally obligated to do certain things. Furthermore, ethics must presuppose that people can *harm* others, that they are *needy creatures* and that they rely on the support of others. Without such assumptions, ethical discourse would lack an object. This is relevant, for instance, for bioethical positions that – in relation to brain research – question the freedom of the human will. Such positions should explain, before anything else, how they can support the possibility of a bioethical discourse in the first place.

The next question, however, is whether these considerations are sufficient for propagating an ethical concept of human nature, according to which what is morally right can be determined simply by reference to facts about human nature. Numerous philosophers, following Wittgenstein, Heidegger, Ricoeur and others, have proposed such a form of ethics. Reiner Wimmer asserts (1993: 157), for instance, that we are not even capable of understanding human beings as purely biological natural creatures; rather, we must assume for any conception of humans:

> ... that human beings always already seek to understand and grasp themselves and their existence, and relate, or can relate, to themselves and to the entirety of their existence. They cannot help but live with a view of the entirety of their existence, working out an understanding of their existence and taking a stand on themselves and their lives. Kant's formula of the end in itself of the categorical imperative, for example, is rooted, as Kant's analyses in the *Groundwork of the Metaphysics of Morals* show, in these anthropological facts, without which his (and any) ethics would be groundless.

With this interpretation of the fact that humans cannot be understood as mere natural beings, however, Wimmer comes to the following description (1995: 218ff) of the relation between ethics and concepts of human nature:

> If, however, the notion of a human being as a purely natural creature is an unacceptable abstraction, if we know humans only as endowed with practical reason, then the battle regarding the naturalistic fallacy can rightly be relocated to the question of the appropriate conception of human nature; the question concerning ethics then becomes the central question of anthropology.

It is true that ethics would be groundless if humans were not endowed with practical reason. Yet it is a different question of whether – as claimed here – even the question of human nature can only be developed on the basis of the central questions of ethics. Even if that were true, this consideration concerning humankind would still not predetermine ethics in terms of substance. Whether we are obliged on the basis of the fact that humans are endowed with practical reason to pay heed to the dignity of every person would require further justification. The utilitarian moral principle could be just as appropriate, as could a notion of prima facie duties that does not assume that human beings are 'ends in themselves'. We do not gain such a moral principle from a concept of human nature without drawing on the accomplishments of normative theories that hand us criteria for morally right conduct. One could of course try to consider the nature of humans at a deeper level, until one arrives at the conditions for rational self-understanding, which would then ground moral criteria. However, a further argumentative step would be required to show not simply which properties fundamentally characterise humans, but also how duties to act in particular ways, moral oughts and principles of right conduct are connected to these fundamental characteristics of human existence.

In order to show that the latter does not necessarily follow, we could take the property of *finitude* as an example – a quality often referred to in bioethical debates. Presume that it can be demonstrated that the finitude of human existence is not merely a biological fact, but also necessary for the development of a rational self-understanding (a matter that will not be decided here). From the emphasis on such a positive significance of finitude, we can still only conclude that people must be aware of their finitude. Moral questions concerning the extension and ending of life remain underdetermined. Even anti-aging remedies, the extension of life through organ transplantation or even the doubling of the average life expectancy would not annul human finitude. Only after the discovery of a 'herb against death' could we start to file complaints. Nor can the reference to the finitude of human existence provide a criterion for dealing with decisions about the end of life. Active euthanasia is just as compatible with human finitude as the denunciation of any form of assisted suicide. Moreover, the positive significance of finitude would be relevant only for our relation to ourselves, and not in itself a justification for duties in interpersonal relationships or on the part of the state.

A further example could be discussions about the *definition of brain death*, in which considerations concerning the nature of the human being have also played an important role. One possible question in this context could be what kind of meaning the brain or the loss of brain function has for the entirety of a human life. This question will be relevant for ethical assessments. However, if the result of corresponding deliberations would be that human beings have to understand themselves as organic wholes that have phases before and after brain activity too, then this does not yet mean that all of those phases are morally equally worthy of protection, or that they form the basis for other people's duties. If, conversely, it were to be the case that the control exercised by the brain is of constitutive for human beings, that does not yet mean that brain death is necessarily the appropriate criterion for the determination of the point in time at which it becomes morally legitimate to retrieve organs. Ethical assessment requires a criterion that shows in what respect we have moral obligations to people in particular phases of their lives. These obligations will look different depending on the ethical theory at hand. Assumptions regarding the nature of human beings of the kind described above, however, do not yet yield such an answer.

Nonetheless, the example shows that an ethical judgment does not get off the ground without argumentation concerning humanity. A different example could be the debate about personal identity (see for instance DeGrazia 2005a). Does the identity of a person extend over only those phases of her existence in which the brain is active in its integrating function? Or is personal identity to be thought of in such a way that a person's body is included in her identity even before and after these phases? Can it be claimed that personal identity is an achievement of the brain, or is it an achievement of the entire organism, dependent on performances that take place prior to all reflection (pre-reflexively)? This question plays a role in the bioethical debate, but a judgment on moral duties towards brain-dead persons can be arrived at only in light of justified criteria for morally right conduct.

In a different respect, accounts of human nature can be important for ethics when it comes to understanding the spectrum of *human possibilities for action*. Ethical considerations always rely on assumptions about what human beings can change through their actions, what limits restrict their conduct and which needs are indispensable for them. We will first have to understand the possibilities human beings have in terms of the ways they can act and the ways they can live their lives before we can determine what they are obliged to. *Ought implies can*. Humans cannot be morally obligated to do something that is outside their sphere of influence. For such determinations, biology is indispensable as well. Relevant here are neurobiologically identifiable limits to the domain of human action. A further element we will have to be acquainted with are the ways in which evolution limits human action. Christian Illies, moreover, proposed to involve the developmental tendencies of evolution in determining what is morally right (Illies 2006). That is, when we consider a criterion for morality according to which we are morally obliged to retain natural habitats and natural resources for future generations, it is important to know what strategies are most likely, in the light of evolutionary tendencies, to realise this goal. For the determination of concrete moral obligations in the domain of environmental protection, biological knowledge and facts about the nature of human beings (for example as social creatures) are relevant in a similar way.

In summary, one can say that assumptions regarding human nature are relevant for bioethics both with respect to understanding our possibilities for ethical reflection and for the concrete determination of moral norms, since these are always based on assumptions about humans and their possibilities for action. However, the philosophical identification of fundamental aspects of human existence must be distinguished from the specific justification of strict moral obligations. Reference to any number of basic facts regarding human existence cannot replace the justification of moral obligations. But both are to be distinguished from conceptions of humankind rooted in particular worldviews – of Christian, liberal, humanist, socialist, eugenic or other any provenance. Were bioethics to wish to support its normative foundations with such images of humanity, it would abandon the claim that its normative demands can be scrutinised in an intersubjectively reproducible manner. Bioethics would then merely rehash the conception of humankind of whatever social group it would be connected to, and would lose its status as an independent instance of critical reflection.

3.3.2 Gender

The lines that connect bioethics with feminist ethics and the gender discourse are manifold and complex. The life sciences have a special significance for the bodily self-understanding of women, and the development of biomedicine and biotechnology occurred parallel to the establishment of feminist positions in the public consciousness of the Western world. In addition, feminist ethics developed almost concurrently with the establishment of bioethics. I shall briefly address some concrete discussions and add some theoretical observations (for introductions to feminist ethics see Jagger 1992; Tronto 1993; Young 1990; for introductions to feminist bioethics see Wolf 1996; Tong 1997, 2001).

For the life sciences, the use of human embryos has been of central importance. Before the end of the 1970s, embryos were standardly understood to be part of the female body. In the context of reproductive medicine, researchers were interested in the development of the embryo and required eggs for their research. Of course sperm cells were required as well – but the production of eggs involves significant burden and risk, while the production of sperm cells is a procedure that many men experience as rather pleasant. Besides concrete risks and physical burdens, however, these developments launch culturally relevant shifts in the perception of the female body. The procedures surrounding birth are indeed textbook examples of the phenomenon of *medicalisation*, that is, that expansion of the medical domain into ever more areas of human life. In this context, 'medicalisation' is often used not only as a purely descriptive term, but also with a judgmental tone.

The embryo was long invisible. The discovery of ultrasound made embryonic phases visually accessible for the very first time. This visualisation, however, was not restricted to the mere visualisation of the embryo. Before anything else, it was a visualisation of the female body. This occurrence is part of a longer history. In her book *Disembodying women* (1993), Barbara Duden illuminates the history of the 'medicalisation' of birth and of the interest in researching embryos since the 19th century. Now it should not be overlooked that this 'medicalisation' resulted in plummeting mortality rates for newborns and pregnant women. The introductions of ultrasound technology and amniotic puncture, however, shifted the focus from care for the survival and health of mother and child to a search for deformities coupled with the option to terminate the pregnancy. In connection with the establishment of these technologies, shifts in the cultural perspectives on the female body can be observed. The visualisation not only makes the female body visible, but it also leads to the body no longer being experienced as the *woman's own body* – a phenomenon Duden describes with the term 'public space'.

Perhaps this situation can be illuminated through the debate on the so-called *Erlanger baby*, which received much attention in Germany. In 1992, a young woman was declared brain dead after a car accident. As she was pregnant, the Erlangen university hospital initially kept her alive with the intention of saving the foetus. No last will or testament was available. The question of whether the woman should be kept alive preoccupied public life for several days and led to a heated debate on brain death that lasted years. The loss of further vital functions, however, ended the situation after a few days. For our purposes, the topic of brain death per se is less interesting than the actual debate in the Erlangen case. The strong focus on the embryo in the German debate rendered the woman almost invisible. Indeed, the very expression 'Erlanger baby' diverted from the woman in ascribing the foetus a discrete existence independent from the pregnant woman. The term 'Erlanger baby', however, was inappropriate, at the very least because in the 15th week of pregnancy what is at stake is not a baby but a foetus. The additional fact that those who spoke up about the case as doctors, medical ethicists and clergymen were males, and mostly older gentlemen at that, amplified the impression that the case was one of male researchers wanting to find out how long a foetus can be kept alive. Furthermore, the local medical ethicist was a Catholic. The fact that biomedicine and Catholic embryo protection did not occur as opposing factors but in an intimate harmony, did not help to make the scenario any more attractive from a feminist perspective. The impression arose that the male exploratory urge in combination with considerations regarding the protection of life degrades the female body to a foetal environment: the brain-dead mother assigned the sole function of a birthing machine.

Notwithstanding all constitutional considerations, debates on brain death and deliberations regarding moral status, this situation is exemplary for configurations in which the experiential perspective of women is simply ignored. And in the experience of many women, the cultural history of gender relations repeats itself once more in the dominant separation of male researchers and women as research objects, or as the environment for embryos and foetuses. Furthermore, the fact that the female body is primarily affected is not restricted to biomedical research. Above and beyond this, what is altered by biomedicine in a very particular way are the contexts of life and decision-making that surround *pregnancy and birth*. The decisions and conflicts associated with these situations usually affect women first and foremost, for instance when social control of pregnancy peaks, or when pregnant women experience the range of medical possibilities as pressure to take decisions. However, reactions to the altered decision-making contexts are very diverse and often ambivalent. The desire to have children tends to be experienced strongly precisely by women and, correspondingly, fertility treatments are in high demand. The care for disabled children often falls to women as well, resulting in an end to one's professional life, which also is a relevant factor in prenatal genetic testing. At the same time, however, many women experience the establishment of prenatal diagnosis as part of the range of pregnancy tests as particularly ambivalent. Prenatal diagnosis does not primarily affect couples whose family histories provide reasons for expecting possible disabilities in their children. A majority of all pregnant women make use of special examinations aimed at precluding birth defects, while invasive methods are requested almost exclusively by pregnant women over 35 years of age.

Rather than as gender-specific, however, these kinds of experiences should be understood as typical for societies dominated by technology, in which technological developments change people's lives without those affected being asked whether they actually want all of these changes. Furthermore, even in the situations mentioned those affected are not only women, but couples. However, women tend to be more directly affected by these changes, and have fewer ways of avoiding the corresponding decisions than men. Moreover, biomedical research itself evidently has more implications for women's bodies than for men's.

In bioethics, the gender debate is present in a large variety of ways. In part, it is assumed, for instance, that the focus on the discussion of the *moral status* of embryos is the result of a gender-specific prejudice. By concentrating on the status of embryos, the debate systematically negates the role of the woman, and she is habitually reduced to a mere contextual feature. It is important, however, to distinguish between two aspects of this discussion: on the one hand, public and constitutional debates give the impression that the moral status of the embryo is the only relevant moral question, and all biomedical matters requiring moral assessment are settled when the question of status has been answered. This matter calls for ideology-critical observations. Yet in the light of the discussion of this topic (see above in this chapter) it is also clear that it is impossible to imagine moral judgments concerning embryos that do not answer the question of moral status. Any moral judgment that regards embryos presupposes a determination – either explicit or implicit – of the moral status of embryos. However, an answer to the question of status certainly does not settle every question that arises in the context of our engagement with embryos.

Life sciences are sometimes said to constitute an attempt to expand *reproductive autonomy*. In this context, reproductive medicine and prenatal genetic testing can be viewed as attempts to compensate and partially overcome traditional injustices in gender relations. In terms of the history of emancipation, biomedicine could then seamlessly be interpreted as being on the side of women. While women were traditionally at the mercy of threats of pregnancy, miscarriages, risks involved in giving birth, disabilities, infertility and the social consequences of all of these, they are now, thanks to medical science, increasingly independent of the accidents of fate. Contraceptives and medically relatively safe methods for terminating pregnancies allow women to decide for themselves when they want to get pregnant, disabilities in children and the need for a permanent carer become avertable and infertility can be overcome. In this way, medical science facilitates reproductive autonomy and, in the process, makes the factors that are instrumental in determining the social, professional and private situation of women fundamentally manageable. The notion of 'reproductive autonomy' does in several respects call for elucidation and legitimation (Buchanan et al. 2000). The horizon of this concept spans very diverse kinds of actions and moral entitlements. It can relate to the following aspects of 'reproduction':

1. A woman's right not to become pregnant against her will
2. A woman's right to terminate an existing pregnancy
3. The wish or right to be technologically supported in the course of a pregnancy
4. Having the opportunity to decide whether one is willing to give birth to a disabled child
5. Having the opportunity to exert further influence on the characteristics of the unborn child

These interpretations articulate very diverse moral entitlements, and the corresponding expectations of society, medical science and research are equally diverse. Whether such rights can (i) be considered morally legitimate and (ii) whether a society should consider itself obliged to assist in the realisation of such rights may be viewed quite differently in light of different ethical theories.

The desire to avoid a pregnancy or the corresponding medical dangers has to do with moral rights because (and insofar as) the pregnant woman protects herself against harm or adverse effects on her own person. Decisions about genetic configurations of possible children, on the other hand, determine their biological constitution and their possibilities in life. Similarly, moral expectations of medicine as well as of society and the state, which, by organising the corresponding research, create these medical possibilities in the first place, vary considerably. On the one hand, what is at stake is assistance in avoiding situations that are experienced as threatening (regardless of the question of when a pregnancy can justifiably be experienced as a danger or threat, which is viewed differently by different people). On the other hand, what is at stake is support for the realisation of desires that affect the life of the child that would come into existence. The emphasis on the difference does not indicate a hierarchy of moral entitlements. My point is to put the legitimacy and meaningfulness of the notion of 'reproductive autonomy' up for debate. Even if – rightly so, in my opinion – people assume that women are to be protected against unwanted pregnancies, this in no way justifies all of the other options mentioned. The notion of 'reproductive autonomy' obscures the structural differences between different moral rights and the necessity to legitimate each of the different possibilities individually. I therefore consider it desirable to avoid this concept.

Likewise, elaborate critiques of standard conceptions of normative ethics and political philosophy emerge from feminist quarters. In these critiques, it is the myopic emphasis on autonomy and the allegedly narrow conception of autonomy that are at issue. This debate is carried out primarily in the context of the 'ethics of care' (see Chapter 2). In this discussion, the allegation is raised that behind the conception of 'autonomy' as the central reference point of moral judgments stands an image of human beings as independent creatures, which does not do justice to the fundamental relationality of people (Sherwin 1992). Autonomy in this sense would be the tenet of a liberal subject, conceived along the lines of the market subject. Carol Gilligan has criticised Kohlberg's staged model, which is aimed at the moral subject who gains orientation from the universalisation of abstract moral principles. In the generalisation of this staged model – according to Gilligan's critique – gender-specific differences in the development of morality are ignored. The model conceives of the ascription of rights to negative freedom as the basis of moral relations. This, however, ignores the attitude of caring for others as the basis for moral relations. And since – according to traditional stereotypes – this basic attitude is taken up by women, morality and justice have a gender-specific bias. This analysis triggered extensive international debates on, for instance, the empirical evidence for the relevant assertions, but also their significance for ethics. Surely the preliminary attribution of the care perspective to women would lead to the consolidation, instead of a critique, of the traditional stereotypes, particularly in relation to the exclusion of women from the public domain? Much support, moreover, has been forthcoming with regard to proposals for connecting the perspectives of care and justice (see Chapter 2).

Nevertheless, this evokes the question of whether this emphasis on the point of view of care can form the basis for an independent *ethics of care*. Surely it is true that the basic attitude of care somehow forms the basis of the normative questions of justified demands and moral obligations without, however, having been normatively determined itself? It could be said, along these lines, that the very question of what our obligations towards others are emerge only when we 'care'. However, this does not tell us what obligations we have concretely. The opposition, in this context, of 'ethics of care' and 'ethics of autonomy' largely rests on presumptions that are nowhere near self-evident. It is assumed, for instance, that the moral focus on autonomy restricts itself to a moral admiration of the right to self-governance, while autonomy in the Kantian tradition refers to the vital significance of the capacity to base one's conduct on moral points of view (see Hill 1991: 43–51). The latter understanding certainly does not legitimate a restriction of the normative perspective to the protection of a freedom to choose. Moreover, even critics of the Kantian tradition seem to presume that underlying the emphasis on autonomy is a contractualist understanding of mutuality in the ascription of rights and duties (Nussbaum 2006). Finally, it is presumed that an 'ethics of justice and autonomy' entails a restriction of morality to negative freedom (see above). Against this, I have already shown in reference to Gewirth that there are conceptions of individual rights that assume exactly the opposite – that we have moral duties to support others by enabling them to develop their basic capabilities (see Chapter 2; Gewirth 1996: 31–70; a formulation in terms of duties to support is provided by Shue 1980). Such a theory of *positive rights*, however, is only valid as an ethical theory if the existence of corresponding obligations can in fact be justified. With regard to positive rights, this is all the more important since there is almost no consensus regarding their scope. In addition, such theory can only be translated into practice if a hierarchy of morally relevant points of view can be justified, since otherwise there would be an endless flood of duties to support. And finally, such a theory presupposes that it can be translated into a theory of political ethics since, in actuality, positive rights can only be realised by coordinated action of state institutions. Gewirth has endeavoured to find an answer to all three of these difficulties.

Without going into detail with respect to all of this, it is evident that a theory of justice must in no way be reduced to a protection of negative freedom, the protection of the right to self-determination and contractualist forms of moral philosophy. In that respect, criticisms from the side of the 'ethics of care' aimed at ethics of justice, principles or rights are only sound as criticisms of particular approaches. As soon as an 'ethics of care' were to try to show that there exist duties to care, that is, that the caring attitude should be understood not merely as a possible way of life, but as normatively binding, it would have to face the same questions as I have just formulated in relation to a theory of positive rights. As a rule, however, the 'ethics of care' fails to provide answers to such questions. A purely ideological turn against liberal views cannot replace the necessity to justify one's own normative conceptions.

So far, I have only highlighted a small number of discussions concerning the gender discourse along with their significance for bioethics. It should be pointed out that the relation between the 'ethics of care' and feminist ethics is exceptionally contentious. Other debates in this context have, for instance, considered the moral legitimacy of sex changes; indeed, the transgender debate played a vital role in the development of feminist theory. This debate is also interesting because it can function as an example for so-called 'wish-fulfilling medicine' – medical treatment that is provided in order to fulfil people's desires – a practice not justified within the traditional conceptions of health disease and medicine (see Chapter 4). Another example would be surgery on children whose genitalia are ambivalent. If the child's gender can be unambiguously determined, then this practice can certainly be backed up with reasons that have to do with saving children from future mental suffering. And yet such treatment involves profound (and sometimes risky) interventions, in order to avoid distress that is caused by the fact that most people are unwilling to accept the existence of more than two genders. It is important not to downplay the impact of these cases. However, it does not seem absurd to ask why technological alterations of the individual are viewed as the only viable option, instead of considering how public respect (beyond voyeuristic interests) for intersexuality could be encouraged.

None of these discussions answer the question of what a feminist bioethics is, anyway. Since the anti-ideological impulse of feminist bioethics accompanies very different intentions and concerns, it is impossible to simply identify this approach with the 'ethics of care' or with a paradigm of 'reproductive autonomy'. Nor can it be viewed as a form of moral philosophy (such as utilitarian ethics), since it also formulates fundamental criticisms of theories of normative ethics. I also wonder whether it might be the case that some authors are less concerned with constructively formulating a self-contained ethical approach than with the development of an ideology-critical perspective – which certainly does not need to be a weakness. In that case, the notion of gender would be rather like a perspective that plays a role in many bioethical discussions. However, this would also mean that a feminist bioethics would have to reference one of the existing normative-ethical theories when formulating normative statements, that is, that it would not be capable of legitimating normative assertions drawing on its own theoretical sources only.

The distinctive character of feminist bioethics could be seen to lie in the treatment of a series of core issues: the emphasis on the consequences of biomedical research on women's lives and opportunities, the role of the female body in biomedical research (for instance as egg donor) and the social effects of biomedical research on gender issues. How central a place these perspectives can have will depend on the overarching normative theory. In any case, a question of pivotal importance is whether ethical theories are able to view the long-term social effects of life science research as part of normative discourse in the first place. It is an empirical question, for instance, whether research in biomedicine leads to changes in our perception of the female body; whether perhaps we come to see it as purely instrumental. Yet at the same time it must be asked – insofar as this analysis is sound – whether this influences our moral assessment of the research. Different theories will answer this question differently. I personally would say: if it is essential for the moral justification of life science research that it enables people to live autonomous lives, then it must be part of the moral debate to ask whether we are establishing social perspectives on the female body that allow women to experience themselves as autonomous persons. Thus, whether analyses such as Barbara Duden's are connected with biomedical research as a matter of necessity or associated with contingent aspects of the way in which this research is carried out still seems an open question to me.

3.3.3 Disability[4]

The significance of the life sciences for people with disabilities has had a strong influence on the public conception of bioethics and on the 'biopolitical'

4 My reflections on this theme owe most to long-standing discussions with Sigrid Graumann and numerous suggestions from Andreas Kuhlmann.

discussion (Banks and Kaschak 2003; Boorse 2010; Brownlee and Cureton 2009; Charlton 1998; Edwards 1997; Goering 2008; Goffman 1963; Hacking 1990; Leach Scully 2006, 2008; Nordenfelt 1997; Oliver 1990; Scotch and Schriner 1997; Shakespeare 2006; UPIAS 1976). Those protesting the writings of Peter Singer were primarily advocates of the disability movement, and the debate on prenatal genetic diagnosis also predominantly homed in on the discrimination of people with disabilities (along with the question of the status of human embryos). For a long time, the relation between bioethics, biomedicine and the disability movement was characterised by a lack of any communication. That situation has changed drastically. Representatives of the disability movement are now much more likely to view the debates on bioethical questions as necessary and to consider bioethicists not just as a threat. Medical practitioners have generally appreciated the significance of a dialogue and, amongst bioethicists, people are starting to understand that bioethics has so far devoted very little attention to the perspective of people with disabilities.

The relation between the life sciences, bioethics and disability is in every way complex. Overcoming genetically determined disorders is a central motive of genetic research. While molecular genetics does expand our knowledge of the genetic basis of our bodies in other ways as well, its influence is almost nowhere as visible as in connection with disabilities. The implications of this research are very multifaceted and are experienced as ambivalent. First of all, genetically determined disabilities become biologically explicable. This eliminates part of their inescapability. For many disabilities, biomedicine carries a long-term promise of cures or clear improvements to the quality of life. For many people who are carriers of a hereditary disorder, even when they are not affected by the disease or disability themselves, genetic diagnosis can offer certainty about their own genetic situation for the purposes of family planning.

At the same time, people with disabilities experience these possibilities as threats, as signs of a lack of recognition and as symptoms of a decreasing willingness to show solidarity with disabled people. If disabilities can be prevented, that solution is thought to be more effective, cheaper and more humane than taking care of disabled people. But does such a thought not entail, either latently or openly, a profound judgment of the value of a life with disabilities? And isn't this value judgment an implicit *discrimination* of disabled people? If we consider the presence of a disability in an embryo to be a ground for terminating the pregnancy, this is criticised as prenatal selection. Does this not put the right to life of people with disabilities up for discussion? Perhaps we should then also consider whether there might be historical-ideological connections between the eugenics of the late 19th and early 20th centuries, the National-Socialist *praxis* of euthanasia and the later discipline of biomedicine.

As an introductory remark, it should be noted that discussions of the disability model have been taking place for a long time, especially within the discipline of 'disability studies'. As a rule, it is assumed that the so-called *medical model of disability* is aimed at tracing disability back to physical or mental forms of impairments and to equate disability with pain and suffering. This makes disability into an individual problem that is to be tackled by medical means. Within the discipline of disability studies, in contrast, a *social model of disability* tends to be preferred. This model makes a fundamental distinction between 'impairment' and 'disability'. According to this distinction, people are 'impaired' by physical or mental factors, but 'disabled' by societal barriers, lack of support and negative attitudes in their environment (Altman 2001; Amundson 2000; Shakespeare 2008; Wasserman 2001; World Health Organization 1980, 2001; Wright 1983). Perhaps this blunt opposition could be criticised for being too indiscriminate. However, the distinction between 'impairment' and 'disability' will have to be viewed as broadly necessary, even if one may disagree about terminology.

These days, the analysis of *genetic discrimination* is generally and resolutely rejected. Wolfgang van den Daele, for instance, concluded in a research project that there is no empirical evidence that the practice of genetic testing has any adverse effects on the lives of people with disabilities (van den Daele 2005). But what exactly constitutes genetic discrimination? Who is being discriminated, and on what basis, or by whom? What kind of assertion is it that is being defended or rejected here? It is difficult to evaluate the assertion of discrimination, since it has been brought up in very different political and social contexts and not as an academic claim. Yet it can be expected that academics, before assessing and rejecting the claim, first make the effort to reconstruct its meaning. The formulation of the discrimination thesis is based on statements of people with disabilities, who might say: if prenatal diagnosis involves a test for the disability that I have, and if the presence of the corresponding disposition forms a reason for terminating the pregnancy, then life with this disability is considered not worth living. In this context, Parens and Asch (2000) speak of an 'expressivist argument'. How exactly can this be understood?

A *first* interpretation could be that there is actual *discrimination of the embryo/foetus* examined in prenatal diagnosis (PND) (or the egg in vitro in the case of pre-implantation diagnosis). This interpretation extends the demand for solidarity with disabled people to embryos who will develop into disabled people. Such an interpretation is plausible for those who assert that all stages of life from fertilisation onwards are equal in terms of moral status. In that case, there is indeed no difference between killing an embryo with a disposition to a disability and killing a human being with this disability after birth. Yet this would also mean that the discussion loses its particular significance with regard to disability. For proponents of this interpretation of moral status, any termination of pregnancy is identical to killing a human being after birth, disabled or not. Moreover, this would render disabled people's assertions that these practices involve a value judgment of their own existence unintelligible. If the issue is the discrimination of the concrete embryo, then this has nothing to do with the specific concern of disabled persons.

A *second* interpretation would be that the claim is a *social-empirical claim* in van den Daele's sense. He seems to presume that the genetic discrimination thesis expresses the empirical claim that opportunities for genetic testing have direct or long-term consequences for the concrete living conditions of disabled people, for social willingness to show solidarity, etc. The point of the proponents of the discrimination thesis, then, would be to express their expectation of social effects, and to value these expected negative effects as discriminatory. Van den Daele shows that these consequences are not at all present. Yet he presumes that the claim is an empirical thesis about the influence on concrete living conditions, which consequently would have to allow for some sort of empirical verification. Even if empirical speculations may sometimes be connected with the discrimination thesis, it is not very likely that it should in essence be interpreted as van den Daele does.

A *third* interpretation could be *psychological*. According to this interpretation, the thesis would claim that the praxis of rejecting embryos with the genetic disposition for a particular disability has the consequence that people who have this disability do in fact feel hurt. The ethical debate would then have to focus on the following question: do disabled people in fact feel hurt? That would be an *empirical question* that could be answered by asking disabled people. In that way, it could be established what exactly the hurt consists of. Finally, it would have to be discussed whether this hurt is so important that it should be a major factor in the moral assessment of prenatal genetic testing. None of this, of course, means that all disabled people would experience such hurt in the same way. It is conceivable that it would become clear that not the praxis of genetic testing as such is hurtful, but the social discourse on this praxis (that is, more or less what the expression 'social consensus on selection' is supposed to refer to). It is also imaginable that the psychological hurt could be compensated by changes in the debate or in the political climate of disability policies. Genetic discrimination would then merely be a possible consequence of prenatal genetic diagnosis and not a necessary corollary.

A *fourth psychological interpretation* along similar lines would view the genetic discrimination thesis as a claim about the possible motives of couples who expect a baby and opt for genetic testing. On this interpretation, such a choice could mean that this couple intentionally discriminates against disabled people. In this case, too, the pertinent motivations would have to be verified. Now it may well be the case that a couple are in the first instance concerned with their *own* lives. They could make their decision purely on the basis that they personally do not want to lead a life with a disabled child, or that they do not deem themselves capable of it. So it is possible that a choice for prenatal diagnosis expresses a broad, universal value judgment about the value of life of disabled people, but it could also be the case that such a decision reflects merely on the desires and life choices of concrete individuals. This too is an empirical question.

The *fifth* interpretation is aimed at an *implicit, generalised value judgment*. The accusation of genetic discrimination would then mean that the *praxis* of prenatal genetic diagnosis as such expresses an implicit value judgment of the lives of people with the corresponding disabilities. Such a line of argument might look as follows: while in the case of an abortion without PND the decision is 'I don't want a child', the decision after PND is 'I don't want that kind of child'. Now this could – as indicated – be interpreted as the expression of a particular decision about one's life: 'I don't want a life with a disabled child', 'I don't trust myself to take care of a disabled child', etc. But it can also be the expression of a value judgment: an individual with such a disability should not exist, it is not a life worth living. If in the *praxis* of prenatal diagnosis such a value judgment is expressed, I am not surprised that disabled people feel discriminated against. Such a value judgment would indeed be a generalised appraisal of the value of their lives. Of course, it is not easy to decide in individual cases which motives have played a role in a couple's decision. Indeed, it would be morally very problematic to try to investigate such motives in the first place, since such decisions concern very intimate areas of life. But this may not be the most important question in the first place. The point is not what individual couples may or may not want. Rather, the question should be whether there are reasons to conclude that the establishment of the *praxis* of PND involves a negative judgment regarding the lives of people with particular disabilities. This is not the same as van den Daele's question of whether the living conditions of disabled people have declined or improved. Rather, the question is whether the practice of PND itself involves the expression of such a value judgment.

Now the establishment of prenatal genetic diagnosis does not simply reflect individual choices, but is a practice that requires significant organisational measures. These include not only the creation of institutions that offer PND, but also numerous costly provisions in research and education. It is exactly this organisational character that leads to the impression of a value judgment supported across society. In addition, this practice is connected with the establishment of certain norms, such as the standard recommendation of gynaecologists to take up the offer of PND. Whether the practice of prenatal genetic diagnosis does indeed convey such a value judgment depends in crucial respects on the way in which it is organised. The fact that biomedical research broadly seeks to prevent the occurrence of disabilities can hardly be denied. Whether such aims are defensible depends not only on the question of which value judgment they imply with respect to life with certain disabilities. It also matters what obligations we have towards the freedom of choice of future parents and what obligations we have towards the children that would be born (see Chapter 4). But it does not strike me as absurd to think that the establishment of such a practice in society expresses an implicit value judgment about life with certain disabilities. How this should be weighed in relation to other moral considerations is a different question. What matters to me first and foremost is to understand what exactly is at stake in this debate on genetic discrimination in the first place.

The reason I have discussed this matter in so much detail is that it has played a central role in the debate on bioethics and disability (also see Parens and Asch 2000). In a nutshell, the predominant impression in this debate is that, these days, the aim of biomedicine is essentially to prevent the occurrence of disabilities. A different, more specific discussion has centred on the question of *infanticide*, that is, whether there might be cases in which actively killing a newborn child should be considered (Kuhse and Singer 1985; Tooley 1983). As a rule, this concerns newborns who have a life expectancy of mere days and for whom it can be assumed that these days would be extremely painful. I will not discuss this debate in too much detail here (see Chapter 4). Yet this does raise the theoretically important question of whether a life that consists of nothing but suffering is imaginable at all. Do we have a moral obligation to end such a life, and why exactly? (See Tooley 1983.)

First of all, however, it should be noted that the bioethical focus on topics such as early euthanasia has introduced a somewhat peculiar imbalance to the discussion. The impression has been created that ethical questions regarding disability arise only as questions of life and death, and that these always concern straightforward cases of life with permanent suffering. Yet this is not at all the case. The predominant use of PND is still to test for Down's syndrome, which obviously has nothing whatsoever to do with the situation of a life that consists of 'nothing but suffering'. That is not to deny the existence of awful cases of extreme pain and suffering. The practice of PND, however, is normally concerned with other kinds of cases.

When we do consider the extreme case of a *life that consists only of suffering*, however, the question arises what kind of basis this would leave for any moral obligations. Can we imagine a creature having an exclusively painful existence? Surely the experience of pain or even suffering presupposes a certain distance from one's own experience, which makes the experience of pain possible in the first place? In addition, there is the question of whether a creature like this, even if it did possess such minimal reflexive distance, would be capable of having interests at all. For the question of whether there exist moral obligations towards a child, it is decisive, according to some ethical theories, whether this child can experience pain or develop interests. This question has a stronger presence in the context of early euthanasia than in relation to PND, mostly because the conditions for moral consideration are different. In general, an abortion after PND is still defended on the basis that a pregnant woman should be allowed to decide freely on a fundamental aspect of the way she wants to live her life. In this argument, a judgment on the objective value of life with a disability is evaded. In the case of early euthanasia, in contrast, the couple's decisions regarding their own lives do not play a central role. The only relevant perspective is that of the newborn. Even if it is unclear whether we have here a creature that has interests, surely the idea that we may be obliged to curtail suffering entails an objective judgment of the value of this life? The only alternative would be to say that the decision is made, as it were, on behalf of the newborn child; that it follows her own decision, which is assumed to be negative. Yet since in this case we have no way of imagining the individual wishes of the newborn child, for all intents and purposes this perspective coincides with the objective value judgment.

Yet if early euthanasia cannot be justified on the basis of the parents' freedom of choice, the only remaining possibility is an objective assessment of the child's quality of life. It is exactly this aspect that raises the fundamental question of how such an 'objective' assessment could be legitimated. At the very least, this calls into question the basic liberal conviction that the way in which people live together in society should be regulated without collectively predetermined value judgments. Whether the new technologies necessarily give rise to a denial of disabled people's right to life depends on the question of whether these technologies entail a generalised assessment of certain lives as (not) worth living, and what criteria are proposed to justify such assessments. In this context, the debate on 'wrongful life' is relevant too. This debate is initiated by legal disputes in which disabled children or adolescents have claimed damages on the basis that they exist only because physicians failed to diagnose their disability. This line of argument, however, appears to presuppose that the very existence of these young disabled people is itself a form of harm.

There is no need to address the legal particularities of such claims. Relevant for our purposes is the question to what extent these discussions imply an objective value judgment about life with certain disabilities. The debate on the 'ethics of care', for instance, is fundamentally motivated by the assumption that ethics is supposed to be determined from the perspective of independent and rational persons (see for example Kittay 1999; Nussbaum 2006). The question, then, is whether such medical and legal practices may not divulge a categorical disrespect for disabled people which is fundamentally embedded in modern conceptions of society and morality. The debate on the 'ethics of care', however, also introduced a discrepancy to the discussion, since the 'ethics of care' approach is unable to justify our moral obligations towards dependent and needy people. It is utterly impossible to avoid valuing capacities for, say, self-determination and agency as positive if we want to justify why we would want to enable disabled people to live an autonomous life. Yet the latter is the core of all political stipulations concerning disability. Only when it is possible to show that leading an autonomous life is valuable does it make sense to insist that we should also make autonomous living possible in cases where realising such a life requires considerable effort.

This brings us to a discussion with very profound consequences: what obligations does society have towards its members who have certain impairments? The 'ethics of care' is unable to answer such a question, since it calls into question the entire intelligibility of ethical rights and duties (see Chapters 2). If we understand moral rights and duties as contractual relationships in which moral obligations are judged on the question of whether they are mutually advantageous or to the equal advantage of all, then any special efforts to support disabled people are only justified insofar as we could all be disabled one day. Disabilities caused by accidents or old age could befall anyone. But in the case of genetically determined disabilities, this is different. From the perspective of a social contract, which ultimately traces moral institutions back to the self-interest of agents, obligations towards disabled people remain limited. From a Kantian standpoint, the situation is different: the capacity for autonomy grounds our moral obligations towards any being with this capacity, regardless of whether we ourselves could at some point be in situations others are in. Yet even in the Kantian context it should be asked whether this obligation is conceived only as a negative duty – that is, a duty not to thwart other people's exercise of their freedom – or as a positive duty to enable anyone to realise their freedom. The UN Convention on the Rights of Persons with Disabilities, in any case, presumes very far-reaching obligations for supporting disabled persons to make sure they lead lives in which they participate in society and are socially valued. Whether and to what extent it is also part of our moral obligation to enable disabled persons to live lives in which they can realise their own goals and projects depends how we conceive the justification of moral rights and duties. In any case, however, such justification is only possible if the opportunity to live an autonomous life is valuable. It is clear that this universalisable basis of valuation raises questions for a number of disabilities, which do not merely limit, but altogether eliminate this capacity for before a self-determined life. Yet such ambivalences will be part of the debate.

It is impossible even to come close to a satisfying depiction of the ethical discussion concerning disability and bioethics in the context of this brief sketch. For one thing, the whole question to what extent those who cannot give consent may be used in studies that do not benefit them has been entirely bracketed out (see on this matter Chapter 4). Our concern here, however, is with the way in which the discussion of disability-specific topics in bioethics touches on fundamental questions. In the end, I have returned to disabled persons' moral entitlements to political and social recognition. To me, this does seem the relevant horizon for discussing the relevance of biomedicine for disabled people, or early euthanasia, or prenatal diagnosis. The requests from the disability movement are only taken seriously if they are discussed in this broader context of claims to moral recognition.

3.3.4 Intercultural bioethics

Bioethics emerged in the United States of the 1970s and was exported to Europe in the 1980s and 1990s. Bioethics emerged in the Western world, and the intellectual traditions of the West have left their mark on the discipline. All the same, at this point there are bioethics institutions and professional bioethicists in Asia, Africa and Latin America as well. The reasons for the establishment of bioethics are manifold. In the entire world, ethics committees were required for assessing research on human subjects. International institutions such as the World Health Organisation and UNESCO have bioethics departments with international representatives. The UNESCO declarations on bioethical topics were drafted with the participation of representatives from all over the world. Yet it was also the international activities of pharmaceutical companies and biomedical research that led to worldwide demands for ethics committees in a number of areas. In the course of the establishment of bioethical consultancy, the need for certain degrees of professionalism have also increased. Something similar holds for the development of legislation. On the basis of the worldwide necessity to formulate laws to regulate the life sciences and biomedicine, bioethical expertise was also required.

Initially, the establishment of bioethics was an adaptation of Western models. In the meantime, however, contributions have emerged that develop standpoints based on non-Western traditions (for an Islamic bioethics, see for instance Atighetchi 2007). In addition, questions of *international justice* are not unimportant in bioethics. A question in that domain is whether it is morally defensible to conduct human-subject research on persons in developing countries which would not be permitted in developed countries because of stricter bureaucratic requirements and safety checks. In light of the global operations of certain pharmaceutical companies, this is an increasingly likely scenario. The beneficiaries of these studies are, both in the case of pharmaceutical research and for the human genome project, mostly inhabitants of developed countries. Conducting such studies in less prosperous countries seems questionable because the health care systems of those countries are generally so poorly developed that to people in those countries the progress gained from the studies is quite irrelevant, as the establishment of a decent health care system is much more pressing. Things would be different if the studies at issue were concerned with fighting diseases that put particular strain on people in poorer countries. This distinction, however, presupposes a well-developed debate on research goals and their realisation and legitimation. Besides research questions, deficits of local health systems are themselves a matter for bioethics, as are access to basic health care, vaccinations and HIV/AIDS prophylaxis and treatment. Moreover, a significant part of the bioethical debate that is concerned with biotechnology in agriculture, patenting and food ethics has to do with the developing world (see Chapter 4). The greater efficiency of genetically modified food products and the possibility of a better food situation in developing countries is ultimately one of the ways in which research is legitimated. At the same time, it is feared that the possibility of patenting research outcomes will in fact increase global inequality.

Besides these highly politically loaded questions, it is asked ever more often how different cultural backgrounds impact people's interaction with new technologies; how different relations to the human body, to nature and to the environment influence perceptions of, and discourse on, new technologies.

These questions are important to bioethics because traditional ethics is burdened with the charge of Eurocentrism, and it must be asked how our moral judgments can be defended beyond communities that share certain cultural convictions. This issue gains in importance since, first of all, within the Western world itself ever more people from non-Western cultures are present, and show up in medical contexts as patients and, second of all, because in international technology development there is a rapid increase in involvement of Asian countries in particular. The question of how such cultures deal with biotechnologies is no longer a matter that may interest some cultural researchers as a hobby, but is one that will fundamentally shape the implementation of these technologies in the future. For debates on cloning and stem cell research, livestock breeding and environmental biotechnology, the cultural perceptions of such issues predominant in Eastern cultures at the time will be crucial (Döring 2008; Qiu 2004).

This intercultural discussion manifests itself in many bioethically relevant domains. The relation to animals could serve as an example. Another example would be the ways of interpreting Western technologies. It is not self-evident that complex notions shaped by many implicit presuppositions, such as the notion of genes, can be captured within non-Western conceptions of nature. This raises the question of how informed decisions on the use of technologies in which genes are involved would be possible in such contexts. I shall proceed to discuss these two themes in a little more detail.

One domain that is relevant in this context relates to *conceptions of the human body* (see for example Douglas 2002; Hauser-Schäublin 2007). It has already been noted several times that the effects of new technologies on people's understanding of their own bodies can be relevant to their moral validation. If we assume that it is legitimate for people to expect that new technologies will not impede their possibilities, or that they are compatible with the conditions of a successful life, such a moral principle can mean something very different to people from different cultures. An example can be found in a report by Hauser-Schäublin (2007: 20ff) on Balinese conceptions of the body:

> Humans are not born as individuals, but as a human being that sees the light of the day together with four siblings. These are birth siblings that were vital for the becoming of the human inside the mother's body: amniotic fluid, blood, egg membrane and placenta. These four are regarded as the older siblings – the human is the youngest. [...] After birth, the four birth siblings are immediately ritually buried near the dwelling (kitchen or sleeping area). Every human is thus one of a total of five beings, which remain intimately connected with each other for the entire life. During birth, the power inherent in the birth siblings transforms into invisible beings. [...] During every ritual marking a life cycle of the child, small offerings are brought to these birth siblings. [...] These invisible beings, in turn, are not unchanging in the way in which

> they manifest; they resemble gods and demons at the same time. They impact on the human body and the entire world. [...] The four siblings permeate the human being, are 'elements' of him. They are omnipresent and influence or even determine his character, his talents, strengths and weaknesses.

According to this conception of the body, then, all interventions in the human body and body parts also affect the four birth siblings. This notion influences any medical treatment and, to an extent, the influence on the birth siblings provides the evaluative matrix for assessing the effects of modern technologies on a person's well-being. Apparently, these traditional ideas are still held by Balinese people who live in the context of modern urban culture. Presumably, for people in this culture this interconnection being respected is vital for the possibility to live a successful life and to develop one's capacity for agency.

However, this leads to a very serious problem for moral philosophy. This view of the human body seems to put the liberal idea that moral obligations are to be conceived independently from facts about the nature of humankind in a difficult position. If the conception detailed above is respected without qualification, then the implementation of new technologies becomes largely impossible. If, on the other hand, one were to ignore it, one acts on the assumption that one's own views of human nature are superior; the employment of one's own liberal ethos then leads to the very impact of such assumptions that was to be avoided. And why should we take the Western notions of individuality and corporeity to be necessarily superior in the first place? This question is of central importance for moral philosophy. When life science technologies collide with corresponding conceptions of human beings and the human body, their employment will have a profound impact on people's possibilities to live their lives well. If, on the other hand, the protection of the way people live and what they can do, including their ability to shape their own lives, gives rise to moral obligations, then bioethics cannot ignore this problem. The moral legitimacy of the introduction of new technologies in non-Western cultures will depend on the extent to which this problem can be solved. It should be noted that this problem does not only arise in relation to developing countries. In the light of reports that half the residents of the USA do not accept the theory of evolution, which is necessary for understanding genetics, we can conclude that here too certain natural-philosophical conceptions are culturally dominant, which makes it fundamentally unlikely that the life sciences could be understood, not to mention dealt with in a competent and autonomous manner.

Another example is the question of *family values and individual life decisions* (Becker 2008). Most international bioethics regulations prescribe that for the use of technologies or medical treatment an individual must be able to make a free and informed decision on what is done to him in light of his own interests and values. However it is reported that decisions in Eastern cultures are usually not made by the individual, but by families, and that not only consequences for the well-being of the individual are taken into consideration, but also the effects on the family. Similar practices are reported from Eastern European and African countries. That means that in the case of fertility treatment or prenatal diagnosis, it is not in the first instance the woman potentially undergoing the treatment who makes the decision, but the family. This is not changed by the fact that the person who undergoes the treatment is formally required to sign a permission form. The formal declaration of her decision can be the outward expression of deliberation within the family, or simply the ruling of the head of the family.

We must, then, imagine for many non-Western contexts that the persons involved do not in fact understand themselves as the decision-making subjects, and that their social environments do not expect them to make their own decisions. Moreover, it will be the case that their personal preferences do not play a guiding role in the decision-making process, and might not be at issue at all. It may not even cross their minds that the development of their own preferences and values, which can be understood as their own standpoint on the predominant opinion of the social environment, exists as a possibility at all. Perhaps one's relation to one's family and the fact that one shares one's values with family belong to the core of understanding oneself. Of course, in Western societies it is not uncommon for a woman considering prenatal diagnosis to consult her partner, family, a friend, priest or psychotherapist. As a rule, some such conversations will take place. Yet that does not change the fact that from a legal point of view and in the way she sees herself she is the decision-maker. Even if this may not always be the case, this description is an idealisation that is not inappropriate for Western societies. The moral conflict, then, does come out in a different way than we might suppose of non-Western countries.

Whether or not a woman can consider herself the subject of a decision, however, is a question that in many bioethical debates is treated not merely as a question about the decision-maker, but also about the description of the moral conflict. Take the example of PND and the possible sebsequent of whether or not to abort. If we are proponents of the moral standpoint that the embryo deserves moral protection but does not have the same moral status as the pregnant woman, then we can describe the moral problem as a conflict between duties of protection towards the embryo on the one hand, and the individual rights of the woman on the other. If, in contrast, individual rights to autonomy over one's own body play no role whatsoever in the decision-making process, then the conflict of values is different. As soon as, for instance, the patriarch, partner or husband decides whether the woman is in principle permitted to allow for the embryo to be tested, the use of PND can no longer be justified on the basis that the woman has the right to gain information on the genetic conditions of the embryo that is growing inside her. Or if the family decides whether or not a disabled child should be born, this is not a decision that can be described as a conflict between the embryo's entitlement to protection and the values and self-understanding of the pregnant woman alone. This discrepancy is intensified if PND is employed for reasons of gender selection in societies in which it is socially desirable to have male offspring.

The question here is not whether we can conceive of one moral principle as universal, but the description of the moral conflict at issue. If the ground for legitimising abortion after PND is that the pregnant woman has certain rights in relation to her body, then it should be asked how these rights can serve as a justificatory basis in a cultural situation in which the woman cannot understand the decision as hers alone. The situation looks very different if one were to argue that abortion is morally compulsory if a particular disability is detected during PND since we have a moral obligation to prevent people from having to live with this disability. For this standpoint it would be irrelevant whether the pregnant woman herself considers this a conflict, for even forced abortions could be a legitimate option. We need not develop the implications of such a position any further at this point. What is relevant is that culturally varying perceptions of one's own body and the self-understanding of those who make a decision are of central importance for the description of moral conflicts. This line of reasoning does not lead to moral relativism, for the assessment of the moral defensibility of the different ideological conceptions is distinct from the description of the value conflicts from the standpoint of the decision-maker. More concretely: if we can defend the principle that we are morally obliged to enable each person to develop certain capacities, or that we are to respect an individual's decision, then all of this may be universalisable, yet the significance of this moral principle for a concrete situation cannot be determined independently from the self-perception of those affected.

Certainly, one could also question the independence of women's decisions in Western decision-making contexts, and correspondingly view the practice of 'informed consent' as the sole method of protection as problematic in general. However, it should be assumed that the culturally dominant self-image allows women to understand themselves as independent decision-makers, both in medical contexts and in making decisions with regard to their profession, politics, etc. In cultural contexts in which this assumption cannot be made, in contrast, it is a valid question of whether informed consent constitutes an appropriate protective measure at all. This issue impacts the introduction of numerous new technologies – all those that are justified by pointing out that the protection of the individual is guaranteed through informed consent. However, in most international declarations and conventions informed consent is allocated a central place. The basic concept of most life science regulation is that biomedicine and the life sciences are able to develop cures and therapies due to the fact that they can generate knowledge that is important for people. At the same time, abuse of these technologies, such as genetic discrimination, the use of genetic knowledge for state control or unequal treatment of individuals, is possible, and ought not to be ignored. Since it is also not desirable to deny people the advantages these technologies bring, measures against possible threats to the individual are required. Informed consent is considered a suitable protective measure. Yet if the protective potency of informed consent is bound to particular cultural conditions, then it cannot have its protective power in cultures that do not have the conception of individual decision-making. If, then, the introduction of new technologies is considered legitimate on the condition that the individual is protected by informed consent, the introduction would not be legitimate in cultures in which this is not ensured.

The intercultural dimension of the life sciences was only recently discovered as a bioethical topic. The task for bioethics is not so much to work out the similarities between different cultures. A much more pressing task is to understand the social, cultural and political preconditions necessary for the realisation of moral protection. The international body of regulations for the life sciences presupposes an ethos that starts from the dignity of the individual and her fundamental rights. This ethos has evolved historically under cultural conditions. Nevertheless, in practice we assume its cross-cultural bindingness, and we have good reasons for doing so. For bioethics, it is vital to understand the tensions and dangers that are associated with the introduction of the life sciences in non-Western cultures, and to consider the cultural conditions of effective moral protection.

3.3.5 *Bioethics, religion, theology*[5]

Theology has played a profound role in the development of bioethics. Many bioethicists started their careers as theologians.[6] Numerous bioethics institutes were founded at theological departments. In addition, religious traditions, religious authorities and academic theology are very important factors in the determination of ethical themes, as well as in the dynamics of the discussion. I am only able to address a few relevant aspects here. I shall briefly discuss the role of official religion and the significance of academic theology.

Bioethics is concerned with several matters on which religious traditions and authorities tend to have very explicit standpoints. The regulation of sexuality, reproduction and death, for instance, plays a central role in the

5 What I have to contribute on this topic owes a great deal to stimulating conversations with Dietmar Mieth.

6 As an aside, it should be noted that in the USA the largest and oldest bioethics institute at Georgetown University in Washington DC was founded on a clearly Roman Catholic tradition. One of the first books on the topic was written in 1954 by the Protestant theologian Josef F. Fletcher (Fletcher 1954). Well known bioethicists such as Warren T. Reich and Albert Jonsen started their careers in theological contexts. The largest German ethics institutes in Tübingen and Bonn came into being with considerable input from Catholic theologians, the Bavarian Protestant church founded an ethics institute in München and, until recently, almost every ethicist in the Netherlands also had a theological background.

Christian tradition. Especially in the 1960s, the Catholic Church made the attitude towards abortion and contraception a central element of Catholic identity. In particular, the 1968 encyclical 'Humanae Vitae' expressed the negative attitude of the Roman Catholic Church towards the contraceptive pill and other forms of artificial contraception and in doing so caused quite a stir within and beyond the Christian community. This discussion is relevant in several ways. At that time, the Catholic Church had considerable authority in society as a moral institution. Even if secular people found the Church unworldly, it was still an important moral institution. The 'pill-encyclical', however, revealed the distance of the Catholic Church from the sexual liberation of the 1960s. Moreover, questions of reproduction became identity questions for Catholics, and the Church risked a grave conflict with theological ethics, which will be further discussed in due course.

For the debate on artificial insemination, prenatal diagnosis and all matters concerning research on and treatment of human embryos, the pressure from society on the Church and the fact that the identity of Catholicism was at stake were of crucial importance. The back-and-forth within the Catholic Church over a standpoint on brain death influenced the social acceptance in Catholic countries as much as the rejection of active euthanasia. Even in a denominationally diverse country such as Germany, the opinion of the Catholic Church was politically important in the development of the transplantation act of 1997. In all of these cases, both the introduction of the topics and the tone of the debate were influenced by the attitude of the Catholic Church.

However, the dynamics of the debate are not solely – perhaps not even principally – defined by the explicit statements of representatives of Catholicism, but also by their opponents' efforts to establish boundaries. In explicitly Catholic countries such as Italy, one can find a particularly strong secular ethics, the liberal character of which broadly coincides with anti-Catholicism. Something similar can be seen in the USA, where the strong connection between Christian fundamentalism and the anti-abortion movement has strongly polarised the debate on all matters regarding human embryos. This leads, for instance, to all matters of reproductive medicine, stem cell research and prenatal genetic diagnosis being reduced to the question of the status of embryos, while all questions of implementing and using these technologies are completely overlooked. Similarly, the debate on the doctrine of the 'sanctity of life' can only be understood as a reaction to a certain interpretation of Christian ethics. While it is the case that this doctrine is actually put forward by some religious authorities, it is equally astounding that there are secular ethicists who think that the question of whether one is in favour of the 'sanctity of life' or against it is *the* issue that divides bioethicists (Dworkin 1994; Singer 2002). With regard to reproductive medicine, for instance, there have been bioethical discussions on the success rate of *in vitro* fertilisation (IVF), which couples should be allowed IVF, on the psychological burden of IVF, on couples who harbour illusions with regard to this technology, couples that are helped by it, of whether IVF children develop differently from other children, of what further technological perspectives this technology offers, and all associated opportunities and problems. The 'sanctity of life' levels all of these distinctions. In the public debate, the impression arose that the central opposition was Catholic protection of life versus the liberal wish to help childless couples. This can only be described as a distortion of a complex debate that makes it seem as if bioethical questions are simply matters of following or criticising the Church. With reference to the Italian author Giovannino Guareschi, who caricaturised in his novels the quarrel between the Catholic Church and the communist party in mid-20th-century Italy, we might call this phenomenon the 'Don Camillo and Peppone syndrome' of bioethics. Many contributed to the emergence of this myth. Peter Singer, George W. Bush and Josef Ratzinger can be mentioned as a few out of many. The motives for cutting the discussion short in this way are equally diverse. The Catholic authorities propose that the entire discussion is only a matter of being 'for or against life'. Perhaps this is motivated by the cynical observation that only such simplification is capable of setting the political mood. For many supporters of reproductive medicine, too, the use of similarly straightforward oppositions might be an effective method for not having to engage in more complicated discussions. In any case, suspicion is called for whenever it is said that the ethical questions of reproductive medicine boil down to an acceptance or rejection of the doctrine of the 'sanctity of life'.

The influence of religion on bioethical debates can also be far less direct. Take the Dutch debate on euthanasia (Kennedy 2002). On the one hand, Dutch culture is strongly influenced by Calvinism; on the other, it is determined by the coexistence of communities with different worldviews and religions on a piece of land that is very small indeed (and threatened by the surrounding nature). From the second half of the 19th century until the 1960s, there was, for this reason, a system of 'pillarisation' (in Dutch 'verzuiling') that was characterised by the fact that the different communities (Catholics, Calvinists, liberals, socialists and a number of smaller subdivisions) organised political and social life separately from each other. There were ideologically specific schools, social institutions, sports clubs and political parties. The task of the state was to fund the 'pillars' for all these expenses (according to the principle of a just distribution of means) and to ensure peace between the groups. In this way, a two-stage model of morality emerged: on the one hand, as a member of a particular pillar one was bound to an internal morality; on the other hand, one was compelled to support a sort of national community morality that was characterised by tolerance between the different groups. It should further be noted that the culturally most influential group (although not nearly the largest in terms of numbers), the Calvinists, had a basic standard of exceptional loyalty to the state. This meant that even the groups that argued for some very strict standpoints in their religious principles were invariably willing to work towards compromises. This tolerance, however, was a tolerance between social groups, not between individuals. This led to the situation that the social consensus came across to outsiders as very liberal, while within individual religious groups some particularly restrictive beliefs prevailed. The bindingness of the moral norms of society thus always requires a form of tolerance that clashes with the moral norms of one's own ideological community. After the end of the pillarisation system in the 1970s, the strict separation of pillars was annulled, mostly because the religious groups became less significant. At the same time, however, it may well be said that the central mechanisms of the pillarisation system remained intact and produced, with the so-called 'polder model', a consensus culture which, for instance, was the first to establish freedom of prosecution for active euthanasia, even if religious groups maintained strong reservations.

What is relevant about this example is mostly the fact that this arrangement cannot primarily be understood as an expression of secularisation, or as the expulsion of religion from the bioethical debate. The discussion between religious and ideological groups is rather the driving force behind the debates, even if they seldom touch on religion explicitly. The model at hand pacifies cases of social dissent in which the relation between different religions is the motor of the entire discussion. That means that religion plays an indirect role even in efforts to establish liberal regulations, and that it is always present as a factor. More recent discussions with representatives of Islamic communities are often drafted on the model of such pacification strategies.

The influence of religion on the content and form of bioethical discussion can hardly be doubted. However, this does raise the question of what this (implicit or explicit) relevance of religion for ethics means, and what exactly the role of *theological ethics* can be. It might be clear, to begin with, that it would be an insufficiently complex conception of theological ethics if one were to think of it as the representation of the ethics of the faithful, and philosophical ethics as the counterpart for atheists and agnostics. In the light of the formative meaning of religion for the Western world, it would be naïve to think that a simple secularisation exercise could cancel out the influence of Christianity. Moreover, such a division of labour would also reduce the normative results of philosophical ethics to a mirror of the worldview of a liberal society. Philosophical ethics, on such a view, would not provide neutral ground, but simply develop a particular ideological counterpoint, just with a different worldview.

Quite a few 'secular' ethicists, however, appear to understand themselves as opposing forces to the power of the Church and academic theology. This certainly does not yield a concept for the academic discipline 'bioethics', nor is it a contribution to the sophistication of the public debate. Under such a conception, bioethics would also be forced into the role of a negotiator between the academic representatives of different groups in society. If liberal and religious bioethicists negotiate possible compromises for bioethical regulations, then ethics becomes a kind of political search for consensus amongst academics. Bioethicists may have an advisory role in political processes, yet a profile of an academic discipline is not gained by considering its task to consist in simply seconding different ideological communities. The discipline needs to legitimise its own claim to knowledge and its methodology, not any political assignments.

This does evoke the question, however, what the self-conception of the academic discipline 'theological ethics' or 'moral theology' is, exactly. The denominations do change sometimes, and within Protestant theology it happens frequently that ethics is not conceived of as an individual subdiscipline, but sorted with 'systematic theology'. These organisational allocations should be of less interest here, however, than the questions of what kind of self-conception is connected to them, and what the consequences of all this for the profile of bioethics are.

There are a number of indications that theology has trouble giving academic relief to its own normative propositions. The efforts from different sides are not very hopeful. For Catholic theology, there is Alasdair MacIntyre's proposal to look for a normative foothold in contemplating the tradition of one's own community of values. In his 1981 book *After Virtue*, MacIntyre suggests that through contemplating the shared values in individual traditions we may escape the aporia bestowed on us by the demands of universality and rationality in modern ethics. His book ends with a reference to communities of values such as the one of Saint Benedict; the only places from which we can still gain moral orientation. Now theology could justify itself by stating that it feels obliged to the explication of the tradition of Christian values and by pointing out that this tradition largely coincides with the development of Europe, but the incantation of the 'Christian Occident' is just about the least helpful basis for academic bioethics.

The discussion on a possible reference to God in the European constitution has an almost haunting character. Such a radical communitarianism would inevitably divide bioethics into communities of value that could no longer even claim to have a shared basis for conversation. Bioethicists of different worldviews would have to do no more than probe their own tradition to see what it might have to say on embryos, euthanasia and more such matters. The reference to the Christian Occident would also immediately make clear that a conflict with the rest of the world is anticipated. The debate on, say, embryos in Judaism, Islam and Christianity becomes an exegetical exercise in which the traditions of the larger religions are sounded out as to their contributions to the discussion in the life sciences. Relevant passages of the sacred texts of these religions and other elements from their traditions would be consulted regarding their answers to certain problems that are entirely beyond the experiential horizon of the eras from which the texts originate. Yet even if a consensus between religions could be established, this only says something about the legitimacy of the corresponding moral statements if one feels bound to the truth of one of the religions. For someone who considers neither the Torah, nor the Bible, nor the Koran as the basis of her moral convictions, it is not very helpful to learn that all these religions agree or diverge on the question of euthanasia. Moreover, the inferior position of women or the denunciation of homosexuality do not become morally legitimate simply because the three Abrahamic religions shared the core of these conceptions. Bioethics would be abandoning its claim to test the justification of moral assertions by means of arguments, and would instead merely describe what positions are taken by certain traditions on certain normative questions.

A radical approach to the theological answers to ethical questions of justification is the *divine command theory* (Quinn 1978; Beld 2006). According to this theory, moral statements can only be justified if they are based on God's command; that is to say, only on the basis of the divine command does moral obligation arise in the first place. This immediately raises the question of how exactly we are to recognise such a divine command. Yet even if we leave that problem for what it is, this theory has the potential to nip any effort of academic bioethics in the bud. If this theory is right, then there is no other form of legitimation for moral assertions than the fact that they are commanded by God. It makes no difference, then, whether any other pros or cons could be identified with regard to particular normative injunctions. The only relevant question is whether God commands them. Such a theory would thus have to reject any attempt to consider ethical questions on the basis of arguments, unless the arguments referred solely to God's will. The divine command theory, then, is the radical form of an ethical voluntarism, which reduces moral questions to acts of will – in this case the will of God (however we might know what he deigned to decide). An alternative interpretation could presume that while sensible human deliberations can reveal God's commands, these have their morally binding character only due to being commanded by God. In the former variant, ethical discourse would be restricted to an exegesis of the divine will; in the latter case, the theological foundation of our knowledge of what is morally right would be unhelpful.

Incidentally, in recent years it has been bioethical topics that have forced theological ethics to sharpen its academic profile. In Catholic theological ethics, the encyclical 'Humanae Vitae' provided the occasion for discussing whether the papal authority of the Church extends to dogmatic statements only, or to questions of moral law as well. The question, then, was whether the Pope should be allowed to make statements on contraception that would be binding for the entire Catholic Church, or whether these were questions that each would have to decide on the basis of his own conscience. The debaters drew on Thomas Aquinas's doctrine of natural law, which states that humans are capable, on the basis of their rationality, to comprehend what is morally right. That would be the exact opposite of an ethical relativism, and Aquinas did indeed not believe that he was merely articulating the value tradition of Europe.

In the wake of this discussion about the possibility of an 'autonomous morality', many Catholic theological ethicists argued that a Christian really should follow rational insights when it comes to moral questions, and that theological ethicists should engage with philosophical arguments. This rediscovery of the Catholic doctrine of natural law, however, does not lead to an independent profile for normative ethics, but to a situation in which theology represents the same range of standpoints that can be found in philosophical ethics as well. In an academically valid form of 'autonomous morality', the justification of moral norms would be a philosophical task, while the genuinely theological aspect becomes relevant with the question of how to integrate these moral insights into a Christian way of leading one's life. Yet if the task of critical reflection on the rightness of moral claims would need to restrict itself to purely philosophical means, it would have to be expected that references to a 'Christian conception of humankind' are omitted. Theological ethicists would not have any more sources of knowledge at their disposal than any other philosopher. Many theologians appear to have been guided by the expectation of a considerable continuity in the content of moral demands as expressed in the tradition of natural law. It may well be doubted that those theologians seriously took into consideration that there might be cases of great dissent, such as presented, nowadays, by animal ethics or cloning.

While Catholic theologians were remarkably present in bioethics, their Protestant colleagues had more difficulties with public normative statements. In part, this had to do with the Lutheran emphasis on freedom of conscience; in part with the transcendence of God, emphasised by Karl Barth in particular. The inscrutability of God's will makes any attempt at natural knowledge of morality a hopeless endeavour. Moreover, the fact that the Protestant Church is structured in a much more fragmented way makes it significantly more difficult to develop definite statements on bioethical questions than in the case of the central magisterium at the Catholic side. Protestant theology therefore often stresses that it is legitimate to have mixed convictions about moral questions. Instead of presenting a disadvantage, the institutional difficulties in taking a stand thus become a hallmark of Protestantism. Often then reference to the plurality of moral convictions within Protestantism is used to defend a more liberal position with regard to research on embryos. Now the standpoint that only research on excess embryos is morally defensible is one possible standpoint that is being argued for in bioethics. Yet this standpoint is by no means an expression of the plurality of evangelical traditions – it is a very specific position. Within the diverse range of bioethical positions one finds demands to allow for research on embryos, not to permit research on embryos at all, only to allow research on excess embryos, etc. All of these are standpoints that are advanced within bioethics. The appeal to plurality is, then, no more than a rhetorical trick that is supposed to save the trouble of motivating the specific position. For the bioethical debate, such a move is rather unhelpful. If theology is of the opinion that there are no theological arguments for some position, it can simply leave the debate to others. But if one argues for a bioethical position, and if one does so not as a private person but with the authority of a representative of an academic discipline (as is the case here), then one must be able to justify this particular position in a correspondingly academic manner. Anything else is a misdirection of the public.

This short overview of some aspects of the significance of religion and theology clearly shows that it is of fundamental importance for the future of bioethics that the relevance of religious traditions and the academic self-understanding of theology are discussed. For 'secular' ethics it is important to reflect systematically on its relation to religion and theology as well, since otherwise unrecognised oppositions, resentments and prejudices distort the discourse. Perhaps one should be careful in any case to overestimate the significance of religion for morality. Dostoyevsky's statement according to which if God does not exist, everything is permitted, probably is simply a grandiose misjudgment. Referring to God does not guarantee that one has the right moral belief and, vice versa, it is not obvious that renouncing religion destroys the capacity for acting morally or that it heightens moral sensitivity. If one were to describe the current role of religion and theology in bioethics, one image that suggests itself is that of a ghost that some summon and some fear, but about whose existence nobody can quite be sure any more.

3.4 New technologies and the scope of responsibility

3.4.1 Concepts of responsibility

In the context of bioethics and the debates on new technologies, the notion of responsibility became an issue in several different contexts (in relation to what follows see Austin 1979; Baier 1991; Feinberg 1970; Fingarette 1967; Fischer 1986, 1999; Fischer and Ravizza 1993, 1998; Frankfurt 1969; van Inwagen 1978; Strawson 1962/1993; Watson 1996; Zimmerman 1988). In Hans Jonas's book *The Imperative of Responsibility*, human responsibility appears to be metaphysically heavy and comprehensive, so comprehensive, indeed, that nobody can indicate who exactly is concretely responsible for what (see previously in this chapter). If people, after the ecological crisis of the 1970s, are starting to get an ever better grasp of the fact that human conduct and human technology form a threat to our natural environment, the *scope of responsibility seems to be very broad.* While morality traditionally was concerned mostly with the conduct of people in their direct environment, the question now is how far our moral *responsibility in dealing with nature* and natural resources extends. Moreover, this context makes clear in what way questions of international justice and *globalisation* remove the spatial boundaries of responsibility. At the same time, *temporal boundaries disappear* as well: our current conduct irreversibly exhausts resources, and in the process of using these, for instance by generating nuclear energy and the corresponding waste, we create subsequent problems for future generations. Yet who is to be made responsible for all of these developments? There are, then, numerous reasons why the notion of responsibility became a challenge for bioethics. In what follows, some conceptual problems of the notion of responsibility shall be briefly addressed. Subsequently, I shall try to give a systematic overview of the dimensions of responsibility mentioned above. The aim of this section is not to answer the questions regarding the ascription of responsibility, but to gain a clear understanding of the questions.

First, however, it should be pointed out that the significance of the notion of responsibility *in relation to other central ethical notions* is a matter of controversy. Attempts to position responsibility as an *alternative to the notions of duty and justice both* are quite common. In comparison with an ethics of duty, the notion of responsibility seems to emphasise the aspects of care and solicitude; compared with the concept of justice, the notion of responsibility appears not to be restricted to symmetrical relationships. While the notion of duty starts from rather strict oppositions of possible actions, and prescribes what should be done and what should not be done, the notion 'responsibility' strikes many as more open, both in scope and in terms of the kinds of responsibility. Responsibility can be gradated; one can be responsible to different degrees, and responsibility can be fundamentally shared. For this reason, it often seems as if the notion of responsibility belongs more to the domain of solicitude, while the *ethics of care* deals with the strict idea of a moral duty. In comparison with the notion of *justice*, responsibility seems exactly not restricted to relationships between equals: we can also be responsible for the garden, the dog, the children or the car. Indeed, responsibility seems to be called for more urgently if the other person or thing is weak or needy. While the notion of justice carries strong associations with the contractualist tradition, the concept of responsibility seems to stand for those aspects of morality that elude the rational equilibrium between equals. It is hardly astounding, then, that the notion of responsibility has made quite a career within bioethics. Hans Jonas's book is no more than a prominent example.

Nevertheless, the attractiveness of the notion of responsibility should not hide the fact that in ethical terms, the concept is a largely *empty notion* that leaves the exact content of the responsibility undetermined. Establishing who is responsible for what would require a theoretical framework, which cannot be developed from the notion of responsibility itself. The concept does not even denote merely moral responsibility, but also the responsibility inherent in legally or socially allocated functions. In order to arrive at a specifically 'moral' responsibility, the notion would first have to be elucidated, a task for which concepts such as 'duty', 'right' and 'justice' are essential. The very openness of the concept of responsibility does make it vulnerable to purely rhetorical usage or ideological manipulation. It makes sense, then, to use responsibility as a concept that raises, rather than answers, questions about the orientation of our conduct. In this function, however, the notion does prove exceptionally helpful. For the indeterminacy of the notion of responsibility makes it possible to keep different dimensions of our actions apart, exactly in opaque situations.

A number of ethicists have proposed a *formal notion of responsibility*, which should allow a closer look at the dimensions of responsibility. The conceptualisations differ in the details. The structure of the notion varies and can be expanded, and the concept can bear on different forms of responsibility. The basic structure of such a notion of responsibility, however, looks roughly as follows:

> A *subject* is responsible for an *object*, towards an *instance*, on the basis of a *normative criterion*.

The *subject of responsibility* can be persons. With respect to persons as subjects of responsibility, there are questions of freedom of the will, determinism and the conditions under which persons can be treated as responsible subjects. But it is also discussed to what extent institutions can be subjects of responsibility. In legal contexts, at least, this is possible. The *object of responsibility* will normally be an action. Responsibility can apply to the action itself (or its omission), or to its direct and incidental consequences. The *entity* towards which one is responsible can be a social or political institution, one's wife or one's own conscience – whomever one can be answerable to. The *criterion of responsibility* or the normative standard is decided on the basis of the kind of responsibility at issue. A criterion for medical conduct, for instance, will be the duty to preserve life. This criterion is included in relevant legal regulations and professional codes of conduct. Depending on the standard, the responsibility will be of a moral, legal, religious or political nature. In principle, one could draw on this formal notion of responsibility to analyse the responsibility of a mafia killer who is answerable to his godfather for the fact that he has not yet liquidated a member of a rival clan – the concrete threat of the competition and revenge for their violent deeds being the criteria for a successful completion of one's task according to the informal mafia code of conduct. One further significant point is that responsibility can be conceived broadly or narrowly, both spatially and temporally. And it is possible to ascribe responsibility *prospectively* (for future actions) and *retrospectively* (for past actions).

This formal notion of responsibility is useful because in the *bioethical discourse*, responsibility is demanded and ascribed. Particular actors accuse others of irresponsible conduct, who in response might claim to have acted responsibly. The basis on which responsibility is ascribed, however, is unclear and controversial. Before it is possible to verify the justification of such claims, the first concern should be to understand what kind of assertions and claims are at stake in the ascription of responsibility in the first place. On the basis of the distinctions detailed above, the *dimensions of responsibility* in bioethical discourses can be sketched as follows.

First, bioethics discusses a *normative standard of a moral nature*. Bioethical discourses are concerned with the question of moral responsibility in relation to new technologies. This moral responsibility is distinct from legal responsibility and the professional responsibility of particular professions and institutions. As a rule, the point is to develop a moral assessment of legal regulations and codes of conduct. Yet this moral claim is also invoked in the biopolitical debate, as individual states, concrete institutions or individuals rely on the idea of moral responsibility when legitimating their actions. In other words, they claim to be morally responsible, critically, in justifying themselves, etc. Now if a moral claim is raised, then this claim presumes to be binding in a way that must in principle hold independently of the concrete subject of responsibility. In that way, the determination of the moral standard has priority over the determination of the concrete responsible subject. The question of the concrete subject of responsibility, then, is initially bracketed, but for the concrete ascription of responsibility it is of course relevant. If we were to come to the conclusion that unlimited consumption of natural resources is not morally defensible, that does not yet mean that every individual actor is now banned from using any resources. Equally undetermined is what the appropriate body would be for regulating the use of resources, and what measures are best taken. Before the ascription of individual responsibility can be discussed, the use of these resources must first be morally assessed, and that issue is exactly what the moral criterion is about.

Secondly, depending on the criterion of moral responsibility, the *object of responsibility* can be determined. The relevant question here is which *entities* are to be taken into consideration, and in what *regard* we are responsible. Yet it is also relevant whether we are responsible only for the actions themselves, or also for their consequences. Since any action has further consequences, direct and indirect, the chain of effects could extend very far. The next section addresses this in more detail.

Thirdly, depending on the normative standard, the question of the *responsible subjects* inevitably returns. This is particularly tricky in the context of technologies, for the actions in that domain are collective activities. If in the context of the question of moral responsibility for considerate use of resources we were unable to identify criteria for the ascription of responsibilities to concrete actors, then we would get stuck with mostly indeterminate moral appeals. Since the evaluation of technology is an evaluation of collective activities, the first question that must be asked is whether there is such a thing as *collective responsibility*. For many debates on new technologies this will have to be assumed, since otherwise, the ascription of responsibility would be unfounded. Thalidomide – the active ingredient in a drug responsible for over 10,000 birth malformations in the late 1950s and early 1960s – was developed and launched by the German company Grünenthal. In that respect, the company is responsible. Nevertheless, this ascription of responsibility must be distinguished from the responsibility of the individual manager who acted irresponsibly. In this context, we must also ask whether there are boundaries to moral responsibility, as discussed in the debate on moral over-demandingness. If we were to claim, for instance, that every individual person must do everything in her power to reduce world poverty, then this would have ruinous consequences for individuals themselves. Peter Singer's demand that the interests of all people (and animals) be given equal consideration and his call on people in wealthy countries to part with substantial percentages of their income are often criticised as 'too much' along these lines (Kagan 1989). The question, of course, is what criteria for the determination of reasonable boundaries can be justified. Can we simply say: Peter Singer asks too much when he asks us to support the people in poor countries to such a profound extent? If we say that, we would have to answer the question of why it is not asking too much from people in the slums of Rio de Janeiro to respect the private property of the rich. We can refer to overdemandingness from various perspectives. It seems to me that our moral obligations should be seen as limited by the same criterion by which they are justified. If, for example, we demand that we must do everything we can to enable every person to lead a decent or successful life, this would imply that all addressees of this demand are entitled to such a decent or successful life as well. This shows: if our normative obligations towards others are consequences of their legitimate claim on some standards of living, this standard of living applies for us as well, and limits the possible scope of moral obligations on us. The reason that justifies our moral obligations at the same time limits it.

Finally, in morality the *instance* towards which we are answerable is our personal conscience. However, since in a domain of collective actions moral assessment is connected to the intersubjective ascription of responsibility, which often has political and legal consequences, there must at least be a correspondingly intersubjective justification of this standard.

3.4.2 The scope of responsibility: space, time, uncertainty

If we keep the numerous dimensions of the ascription of responsibility in mind, it may well be doubted it is even possible to claim moral responsibility in the first place. It seems far too ambitious to attempt to answer all questions regarding the dimensions of responsibility for it to be possible to ever come to satisfactory results. And yet the notion of responsibility is fundamental for our moral conduct and for moral discourses. It is simply essential for an understanding of morality and people's interrelations that we ascribe responsibility, and that we can expect from others that they will act responsibly. Even if in practice this expectation is often frustrated, the corresponding disappointment can only be understood if we are in a position to expect moral conduct in the first place.

While in everyday life expectations and ascriptions of responsibility are formed relatively naturally, ascriptions of responsibility in controversial domains such as bioethics presuppose that we explicate what exactly we expect when we demand responsible conduct, or in what respect we deem ourselves to have acted responsibly. Countless aspects of the ascription of responsibility within bioethics are contentious. I shall address three perspectives: questions of the possibility and boundaries of perceiving responsibility in *spatial* and *temporal* regards, and with respect to the *boundaries of our knowledge*.

3.4.2.1 *The scope of responsibility: spatial*

Calls for responsible conduct assume that we can determine the *scope of responsibility*. In our everyday communication about responsibility, we tend to be concerned with the direct environment of our actions. If I am in the possession of a lighter, I ought to take care not to burn down the house and also to make sure small children do not get their hands on it. Yet if someone steals the lighter from me and uses it to set a house on fire, I am not responsible for the fire. In jurisprudence there are sophisticated deliberations regarding this kind of situation. According to those deliberations, responsibility extends to the space on which the agent can have a grasp, and to consequences of an action that can be expected. With regard to moral and political responsibility, however, things are more complicated. If biotechnologists claim to deal with the opportunities offered by these technologies responsibly, or if their critics accuse them of not doing so, it needs to be asked what conditions must be fulfilled for an action to be responsible. Something similar holds when someone claims to deal with the environment responsibly, or if Greenpeace accuses many actors of being irresponsible.

In the light of the global context of our actions, it is very tricky to delimit the scope of responsibility *spatially*. Someone who genetically modifies seeds must assume that the product will be used all over the world. Yet our consumption of natural resources is a matter of global importance too. Should we demand that people take a global perspective on this? Should we make arrangements for the development of new technologies to ensure that they do not lead to massive injustice internationally? When the patents of genetically modified crops are registered, for instance, it is possible to lay down ownership structures. This practice consolidates global inequality. Energy resources too are currently unequally distributed in favour of the wealthy countries. If *per capita* energy consumption in the West were to be matched by all other countries, this would have ecologically catastrophic consequences.

Now the question is whether this *global perspective* is a possible or relevant perspective in the first place. Surely our moral communication inevitably becomes overstrained if we demand responsibility in such a global perspective? At the moment, this question is debated with regard to the fight against world poverty (Pogge 2001, 2002; Chatterjee 2004). While it seems clear that individuals would be overtaxed if they were to be held responsible for world hunger and its elimination, governmental and supranational institutions would certainly be possible subjects of responsibility. May we not expect from them that they will act in such a way that the interests of the poorest people are taken into consideration? Singer, for instance, demands the equal treatment of all sentient beings everywhere. Thomas Pogge (2002) argues that we have global responsibility purely on the basis of negative rights. He points out that the Western world is historically responsible for the situation of international injustice and that due to international interconnections in a global world, our political and economic actions effectively cause, or at least stabilise the poverty situation. In that sense, the very respect for poor people's rights to freedom and their right not to be harmed requires that we consider the moral consequences of our actions. If we assume, in contrast, that there are both positive and negative rights (see Chapter 2), then legitimate moral entitlements can extend even further. What is at stake here is not simply an irreconcilable opposition of utilitarian calls for equal consideration of all against liberal demands for restricted global responsibility. Rather, global consideration is called for from different theoretical perspectives. Criticisms of such a notion of global justice can be expected predominantly from standpoints that derive their idea of what is morally right entirely from the notion of a social contract. From the perspective of long-term self-interest, international justice will be fundamentally justified by the prevention of international conflict and will thus have a merely instrumental meaning.

If we do acknowledge, however, that in principle we owe needy people in far away countries the same respect as people near us, there are consequences for the assessment of the effects of technology, the limits on energy consumption, access to medicines (AIDS drugs) and for the question of priorities in research and health care, to single out but a few topics. It is an open question, however, how this moral responsibility relates to the kind of responsibility that can be concretely attributed in political and legal contexts. This reveals a fundamental tension. On the one hand, there are moral claims to a universal evaluative perspective while, on the other hand, concrete state institutions are first and foremost obligated to ensure the well-being of their citizens. It is easy to imagine situations where serious weighing conflicts arise. The question is, however, who the *addressees of moral obligations to global non-discrimination* are. While the effective realisation of political responsibility requires national institutions that have the power to act, the consideration required by a perspective of international responsibility clearly extends these national institutions. The power of individual states will be weakened by the increase in internationalisation and the establishment of supranational institutions, while on an international level comparable effective power to act may not emerge. These tensions may not be solvable in the short term. However, starting from the perspective that there is no responsibility towards people in poor countries would not just have consequences for our conduct towards people in developing countries, but should also be an occasion for questioning basic moral assumptions regarding human dignity and human rights.

3.4.2.2 The scope of responsibility: temporal

A similar question regarding the *scope of responsibility* arises in a *temporal* respect. The question of our responsibility towards future generations has arisen particularly in the current situation of ecological crisis and long-term responsibility for new technologies (Birnbacher 2006; Unnerstall 1999; Meyer 2010). Does moral responsibility extend to future generations? How far into the future should we look when considering *future generations*? To what extent can the interests of future generations justify the – potentially severe – restriction of opportunities for present generations? Another question that is being asked is whether we can *actually know the needs of future generations*. This problem is mitigated somewhat if what is at stake are fundamental goods and resources. Even if we do not know the needs of future generations in detail, we can still assume that they will need potable water, oxygen to breathe, natural resources, arable farm land, etc. We can also assume that they will want at least some uncultivated nature and that they desire living space that allows for mobility and privacy.

An entirely different question is how this *broad scope of responsibility* can be justified. In *A Theory of Justice* (see Chapter 2), John Rawls proposed to subject our principles of justice to a test in which we imagine not knowing our concrete position in society – that is, not knowing our gender, skin colour and social and economic status. Would it matter, for such a thought experiment, whether I know in what era I will live? Should not the generation of which I am part remain behind the 'veil of ignorance' as well? There does seem to be a very broad consensus on the idea that we ought to use environmental resources and devise technologies in a 'sustainable' way, which only makes sense if we do owe something to future generations. How exactly such responsibility is to be conceived of, however, seems to be unclear. Those taking the notion of justice as their starting point will always attempt to negotiate competing entitlements. But can we even consider future persons rights holders? After all, they do not even exist. Similarly, the utilitarian approach of balancing interests is confronted with a difficulty in the fact that the interested subjects do not yet exist. Now one could attempt to avoid speaking of 'rights of future generations' altogether, since what causes the problem is that we must assume nonexistent rights holders. But even if we simply talk of 'responsibility for future generations' we still assume that there is something about these 'future generations' that makes us accountable to them. This would merely mean, however, that there are obligations as far as there are (or will be) future generations. Yet if we do not also assume that we have a duty to beget future generations, it depends on us whether those generations will ever exist in the first place. If the argument depends on a duty to beget future generations in this way, then the responsibility for future generations would, of course, be up in the air.

Now the strong assertion that we are morally obligated to beget future generations is not necessary for justifying an obligation to leave these generations with a liveable world. Most utilitarian would probably take the interests of future persons into consideration in their calculus, despite the difficulties associated with doing so. In the case of contract theories, however, the enlightened self-interest does not necessarily demand such a step, since from the perspective of self-interest it suffices to be considerate of one's own generation. Nevertheless, one could point out that everybody has an interest in the well-being of their children and that generations tend to overlap. In this case, there would be an interest that could be generalised, although this interest is not necessarily shared by those without children. For conceptions of human dignity it is not necessarily a problem that future generations do not yet exist. If we take ourselves to have moral obligations to protect and preserve the conditions that are required by agents in order to live and flourish, then it suffices for making such duties plausible that we can assume that such creatures will also exist in the future (Unnerstall 1999). In the context of this entire debate, one should keep in mind that the protection of nature and environment effective enough to safeguard these necessary conditions for future generations, is only achievable with clear restrictions on actually existent freedoms. This is considered more or less justified in different ethical theories.

3.4.2.3 *Risk and uncertainty*

A final aspect of responsibility regards the boundaries of our knowledge regarding the possible consequences of an action. This debate has been conducted in relation to genetic and biotechnology in terms of 'risk' and 'uncertainty' (about the whole debate see Giddens 1999; Gigerenzer 2002; McCarthy 1997; McKerlie 1986; O'Mahony 1999; Roth 2010; Shrader-Frechette 1991; Otway and von Winterfeldt 1982; Schwing and Albers 1980; Slovic 1987; Teuber 1990; Thomson 1985; Tversky and Kahneman 1986; Zimmerman 2006). In addition, there are elaborate discussions of the conceptualisation of risk management in game and decision theory and sociology (Luhmann 1991/2002). Particularly in the context of the life sciences, long-term effects are in many ways unknown. This problem has been discussed mostly in relation to the use of genetic engineering in agriculture and with respect to environmental biotechnology. We gain knowledge of genetic engineering under laboratory conditions. In the conversion to outdoor situations, it is very difficult to limit the effects to the specific open-air experiment. Yet in numerous medical applications of genetic therapy, in pharmaceutical use or in, say, xenotransplantation, we only have limited knowledge of the effects. Many biologists doubt that these limits to our knowledge are fundamentally different from earlier agricultural experiments or other forms of medical therapy. Others, however, take the extent of uncertainty to be fundamentally more profound. Another question is whether some effects may only show themselves in the long term. This has led to the introduction of the notion 'acting under uncertainty'. This is distinguished from 'acting under risk', which is employed mostly in debates on nuclear energy.

This area relies on risk calculations in which the magnitude of potential damage and the probability of its occurrence are the basic factors taken into consideration. Of genetic and biotechnology, in contrast, it is said that the type and scale of potential adversities cannot be determined at the outset. Yet if the potential harm is not identified, it is also not possible to calculate the risk.

Now this debate is very technical and is concerned largely with diverging estimations of biological states of affairs. The ethical question, however, is to what extent a cautious attitude towards risks and uncertainties must be part of a responsible way of dealing with the opportunities of the life sciences. When discussing Hans Jonas's *The Imperative of Responsibility* I pointed out the received criticism that an absolute demand always to assume the worst prognosis imaginable would lead to inaction, which is also morally problematic. The question is whether there are criteria for deciding what extent of uncertainty and ignorance is morally acceptable. This question is relevant to genetic engineering in agriculture, since unfavourable prognoses often involve serious harm, and since the decisions that need to be made are always ones that can only be made collectively. In the case of collective decisions, the question cannot merely be to what extent an individual is prepared to bear certain risks. Nor can the moral assessment of risks depend simply upon the question of what risks the majority is prepared to bear, since this would disregard the perspective of minorities that are particularly at risk. What we could do is identify several factors that should be taken into consideration when assessing the *reasonableness of risks or uncertainties*, or their *acceptability*. The following considerations could be of use in determining this reasonableness (Skorupinski 1999):

- Is an intervention reversible or irreversible? Irreversible actions would have to be justified on stronger grounds.
- Can the goal of the action be attained in any other way? Goals that can be accomplished in other ways should not be realised through risky technologies.
- How essential is the desired good for people's health or environment? (Although it should be noted that the importance of a good is not independent of underlying value theories.)
- How vast is our ignorance of the effects of the technology?

Irreversibility, a lack of alternatives, the relevance of the desired good and the degree of uncertainty are factors that can play a role in our assessment. This does not exhaust the list of possible angles. The point is simply to note that such a discussion on the limits of reasonableness could offer opportunities for a concretisation of the 'precautionary principle'.

3.4.2.4 Summary

This overview of the use of the notion of responsibility in bioethics is not complete. That is not to say that the complexity of this issue should deter us from considering the question of moral responsibility at all. And it is certainly not the case that the notion of responsibility as such has become obsolete. Rather, my aim has been to show that any employment of the concept of responsibility will have to elucidate a number of questions and that in the absence of answers to these questions, the notion will remain empty. These questions can be addressed in different ways, but they cannot be avoided. Even an extremely libertarian position that wishes to use the notion of responsibility in a strictly limited way will have to answer questions concerning the subject, object, criteria and scope of responsibility, and justify its corresponding decisions.

4 Domains and debates in bioethics

So far, this book has presented elaborate introductions to theoretical discussions and to problems that are of fundamental importance for an understanding of current debates in bioethics. Along the way, numerous topics have come up that will also be relevant to the discussions in the current chapter, in which selected backgrounds of bioethical issues are addressed. The first part of this chapter is concerned with medicine, and thus with the core issues that have shaped the public debate on bioethics. In the second part, I shall present domains of bioethics that relate to animal and environmental ethics, or 'green' bioethics. This chapter thus presumes a broad notion of bioethics but with a concentration of questions of biomedical ethics (see Chapter 1.3.3).

It is hardly necessary to point out that this chapter cannot claim to have treated its themes exhaustively. Rather, my aim is to present central exemplary topics of bioethics. This discussion, moreover, may also shed some light on certain methodological questions regarding the interrelations between fundamental ethical questions and applied ethics.

4.1 Bioethics and biomedicine

4.1.1 Informed consent, patient autonomy and medical research

4.1.1.1 Informed consent and patient autonomy

In a way, the regulation of experiments on humans constituted the starting point of bioethics after the Second World War. The foundation for this was laid with the Nuremberg Doctors' Trial of 1946–1947. The way in which physicians in the Third Reich concentration camps conducted experiments on human subjects created an awareness of the need to develop standards for medical conduct, in order to make sure nothing of the kind could ever happen again. The first point of concern in this context was to establish clear boundaries for what physicians were allowed to do. These boundaries hold for medical conduct in general, but particularly for medical research. The *boundaries on physicians' actions* are primarily formulated negatively. A doctor is not allowed to act contrary to the patient's will. The doctor's task of curing, however, is determinative of the purpose of medical interference. The physician is not bound to follow the patient's will in every respect; rather, he has a duty to cure, and the patient's will draws a boundary he may not cross. In this context, 'informed consent' is initially a kind of negative boundary. If the doctor has informed the patient of the goal and foreseeable consequences of a course of treatment, and the patient refuses to consent, then the doctor is not allowed to go through with the treatment. This clause is part of all bioethical declarations since the famous declarations of the World Medical Association in Helsinki and Tokyo (1964 and 1975). In the first instance, the point of these declarations in the wake of the Nuremberg Trials was to provide a description of a boundary which no doctor may cross. Since then, however, there has been a move from informed consent to *patient autonomy*. Patient autonomy increasingly turns into a basic principle of medical ethics that forms the central reference point for medical conduct. The boundary is no longer negative; patient autonomy becomes part of the *purpose of medical conduct*. The physician is no longer first and foremost the party with a duty to cure who is limited in her actions by the patient's informed consent. Rather, the autonomy of the patient determines in a much more comprehensive sense how a doctor is to act.

In the meantime, informed consent and patient autonomy have become fundamental reference points for the bioethical debate (see also Archard 2007; Beyleveld and Brownsword 2007; Bielby 2008; Dresser 2007; Manson and O'Neill 2007; Manson 2007; Oakley 2007). Almost all bioethical declarations and conventions assign these notions a prominent position. This is partly due to the fact that the regulation of informed consent is particularly appropriate for formulating a basic level of consensus in pluralistic societies (anyone can make use of medical opportunities, but nobody has to). The other reason is that the notion of patient autonomy sits well with the ethos of human rights. In the following sections, I shall briefly address some conceptual questions, and subsequently discuss some practical conflicts surrounding patient autonomy.

For ethics, the question arises what status patient autonomy and informed consent have in the bioethical debate as a whole. Many official declarations on bioethical topics (from UNESCO to the Council of Europe) take their start from declaring the protection of human dignity and human rights to be the evaluative basis, and introduce patient autonomy as a concretisation of these values for the domain of medicine, and informed consent as the main instrument employed to ensure the protection of these values. In specifying this, the declarations focus largely on the realisation of the protection offered by informed consent, and discuss borderline cases of situations in which people are not capable of giving informed consent themselves. Such a conception would probably understand patient autonomy as a 'mid-level principle' in the sense of Beauchamp and Childress. As noted in Chapter 2, their theory proposes to develop moral judgments in bioethics by operating with four principles that are neither comprehensive nor overly specific. These principles are autonomy, beneficence, non-maleficence and justice. In relation to concrete bioethical questions, these principles are to be applied to the specific situation in order to determine their relative importance in that context. Patient autonomy would have a relative weight, to be balanced against justice and beneficence. Informed consent, in turn, would serve to concretise patient autonomy. Such a conception is mostly negative. While the physician's duty to cure positively determines the purpose of medical actions, informed consent expresses a boundary that may not be transgressed in the realisation of this duty. A *positive notion* of patient autonomy could mean that a doctor must wholly base herself on the patient's *wishes*, so that these wishes form the basic reference point for medical treatment.

Both interpretations have certain problems. In relation to Beauchamp and Childress's concept, for a start, it is not at all clear what weight should be assigned to patient autonomy. It seems rather arbitrary for the weight of patient autonomy to be prioritised over the duty to cure or over issues of justice. Beauchamp and Childress do not offer any way to tackle this problem, since their four principles are not at all interpreted in relation to each other, but stand for different dimensions of medical conduct. It would also be relatively odd to make human dignity concrete only by referencing patient autonomy if the latter is understood merely as a negative protection against violation. This would mean, for instance, that a very minimal level of health care would not violate patient autonomy at all, as long as no direct violations of the patient's explicit consent occur.

Yet a *positive conception of patient autonomy* would also not be very convincing, at least as long as this was understood as a medical obligation to *fulfil all of a patient's wishes*. Why should we have moral reasons for developing and expanding medicine in such a situation, with no purpose but the fulfilment of individual preferences and desires? And it is even less comprehensible why the fulfilment of individual wishes should be able to make claims to communal funding. But even if we were to decide that medical treatment beyond basic care is no longer to be funded by the community, it would still be true that the high costs of the development of medical technology are tax-supported. That is, it would require justification if medicine were to be financially structured in a way that is unlike almost any other part of life, and it does not do to point out that medicine fulfils the wishes of autonomous patients. It would somehow have to be shown what it is about these wishes that is so different, making preferential treatment justified.

There is, however, yet another perspective on patient autonomy; one that has been addressed above in relation to the notion of dignity (see Chapter 2). This conception of autonomy becomes significant when we try to understand why autonomy is of such fundamental moral importance in the first place. This question reveals a fundamental interrelation between the special moral significance of the protection of the individual and the capacity for autonomous action. In the notion of dignity, the absolute worth of the capacity for agency is the ground on which people are considered rights holders. This special moral position, or dignity, of people obliges us to respect them as subjects who shape their own lives. This is relevant in relation to medicine – that is, to the autonomy of a patient – in a distinctive way, since people are particularly vulnerable when they are patients and therefore deserve special protection in that position. Yet patients are not merely vulnerable; they also have exceptional needs, as they are dependent upon medical support and help. Now this support of patients is not external to patient autonomy, but crucial to its realisation. We can only realise our autonomy if we are supported when we are ill. The ability to live a life that we can experience as worth living, and in which we can develop ourselves as self-determining creatures is, in a way, the value we wish to protect and realise with the esteem of autonomy. Beyleveld and Brownsword named the normative sense of human dignity 'empowerment' to an autonomous life (Beyleveld and Brownsword 2001: 9–28). Yet if autonomy in this sense is the fundamental moral value, the treatment of patients must be oriented accordingly. In that case, a doctor would not only have to obtain the patient's consent to medical treatment, but the facilitation of a self-governed life would become one of the purposes of medical treatment in a much broader sense. Patient autonomy would also no longer be a mid-level principle amongst beneficence, non-maleficence and justice; it would be internally connected to these. What would be morally required are non-maleficence and the facilitation of those capable of autonomy as well as a just balance between their fundamental interests. In terms of normative justification, autonomy would have to be located at a far more fundamental level than the other mid-level principles. Obviously, the patient's informed consent would still be a boundary that should not (or only in very limited circumstances) be crossed. Yet the position in the entirety of bioethical reflections would be much more complex. Instead of identifying the basic value of human dignity with an understanding of patient autonomy, whose concretisation and central protective instrument would be informed consent, the facilitation of an autonomous life would be the meaning of the protection of human dignity, while patient autonomy would merely be a further specification applicable to those who are ill. The special significance of medicine in the facilitation of an autonomous life would be legitimised on the basis of the fact that basic corporeal functioning is of central importance to all manners of autonomous life. In the absence of a fundamental assumption regarding the value of persons, it would be impossible to justify either a prioritisation of patient autonomy or the exceptional social position of medicine and the financial implications of this position. This also means, however, that the development of medical research would have to be determined by the essential contribution of the relevant research aims to the possibility of autonomous life.

4.1.1.2 Experiments on human subjects

In the context of informed consent, there are a number of particular questions and problems regarding medical research (Brody 1998). Traditionally, there has been a distinction between different medical situations: *therapeutic treatment*, *experimental treatment* and *human subject research*. *Therapeutic treatment* is legitimised by the therapeutic value for the patient. As a rule, the expected medical benefits, possible risks and probability of complications are known. In the case of *experimental treatment*, therapeutic benefit to the patient is probable, but the effects of the treatment are not yet sufficiently documented. In that sense, the treatment has an experimental character, but it is still conducted both for the benefit of the patient and with the purpose of gaining scientific knowledge. *Human subject research*, in contrast, is conducted purely for the sake of scientific progress. Therapeutic effects cannot be expected. For human subject research in particular, there are strict regulations, and clinical ethics committees are assigned with the task of ensuring that researchers comply with these. This research concerns the medical quality of the research aims, the lack of alternative ways to attain these aims and the assurance that the experiment is conducted according to medical standards. At the same time, the procedure must identify risks and ensure that the patient is informed and has consented voluntarily. The assessment of the quality of the research aims depends, of course, on a number of assumptions, some of which can be tested medically and some of which ethically.

Since informed consent is of vital importance for the participation in a medical experiment, there are moral difficulties if the research aim itself does not allow for full disclosure. In pharmaceutical experiments, for instance, the effect of drugs can often only be tested by running a control group in which subjects are given a placebo. Informing patients whether they receive a placebo could invalidate the experiment.

Another subject of heated discussion is the inclusion of people who are themselves *not capable of consenting or entering into a contract*. These people could be children, but also persons with mental disabilities or limitations. Now a demand to abstain from conducting experiments on such persons would virtually end all research in paediatrics. Yet such research is essential in order for tested therapies to be available. Many consider informed consent by a legal representative to be an inappropriate measure of protection. The difficulty of such representation has to do with the fact that consenting to human subject research is not just a matter of being informed about risks, but always involves an evaluative moment. In that sense, the consent fundamentally depends upon the values of the patient, and can never be fully represented by another person. In addition, for mentally disabled persons, who often live in institutions, it can be difficult to ensure appropriate individual protection. It may be clear that it would be morally problematic to ban this kind of research altogether. But, at the same time, the people affected are often part of particularly *vulnerable social groups*. Their protection, therefore, requires special institutional hurdles. It seems particularly important to prevent persons with disabilities from being drawn into research that could be done on non-disabled people, simply because they are not able to stand up for themselves. One possibility could be to restrict experiments for which disabled persons can legitimately be used to those research aims that are specifically connected to the disability at issue – in other words, to research that could by its very nature not be done on other subjects. Furthermore, however, there would have to be some special requirements for the consent process. It is particularly important that the values of the persons concerned, insofar as these can be identified, are taken into account.

4.1.1.3 Informed consent in the public debate

Several developments within medicine repeatedly make the central status of informed consent in biopolitical regulations a topic of widespread public discussion, especially when research and diagnoses of large patient populations are concerned. I shall briefly discuss two examples. The development of 'biobanks', first of all, is a very important area of development in bioethics (Capron 2008; Dierickx and Borry 2009; Nuffield Council on Bioethics 2011; Rothstein 2005; Solbakk, Holm and Hofmann 2009). The purpose of biobanks is to collect large amounts of genetic data. It is exactly the quantity of information that makes collection scientifically interesting. At the same time, these databases are not compiled for just one research project, but can be employed in different ones. This, however, makes informed consent essentially problematic, for consent generally presupposes that the patient knows for what purpose his data are collected. When creating a database, the aims of the research it will support can only be indicated ahead of time to a limited extent. In practice, it may very well be nearly impossible to ensure informed consent in the establishment of biobanks. It is possible that the relevant research does not have any consequences for the test subjects. Still, it is problematic to simply leave the requirement of consent behind and issue the researchers with an uncontrollable carte blanche.

A second example are so-called screenings (Baily and Murray 2009; Juth and Munthe 2011; Nijsingh 2007; Nuffield Council on Bioethics 1993, 2006). The purpose of screenings is to examine entire sections of the population for certain medical conditions or dispositions to such conditions. A relevant instance are neonatal screenings, which are carried out with the intention of taking preventive measures in the case of dispositions for diseases that can be detected early and treated well. These examinations do not take place because a particular disease is suspected in an individual patient. Rather, all newborns are examined for a number of dispositions to certain diseases. Because of the standardised character of these screenings, gaining informed consent is not very practicable. Moreover, of course, for some people this procedure may induce fear of diseases without there being any reason to assume that they would be personally affected. This inherent problem of screenings acquires a new dimension in the context of genetic testing. Diagnostic possibilities have increased massively. Moreover, genetic diagnosis offers the possibility of gaining information on dispositions for diseases whose clinical significance is contentious or for which treatment options are non-existent or very limited. Since knowledge of possible genetic dispositions expands rapidly and the question of what should be screened for is controversial, the institutionalisation of such screenings is questionable. Now it would be wrong simply to assume that every citizen wishes to be informed of all possible genetic dispositions. Yet, in this context, informed consent is only suitable as a protective measure for the interests of individuals to a very limited extent.

These two examples show that, while the role of informed consent appears in almost all relevant documents, its function, appropriateness and normative significance in biomedical regulations are by no means beyond debate.

4.1.2 Euthanasia and the termination of medical treatment

The emphasis on the moral significance of patient autonomy has led to heated debate particularly in connection with decisions regarding the end of life (for instance Appel 2009; Battin 1982, 1994; Birnbacher and Dahl 2008; Brody 1988; Cohen-Almagor 2010; Dworkin, Frey and Bok 1998; Kuhse 1999; Nuffield Council on Bioethics 2006; Rachels 1986; Velleman 1999). Since the end of the 1960s, there have been debates in several Western countries on the question of whether and in what form the termination of medical treatment or actively ending a patient's life should be considered morally acceptable or even required. This debate gained its dynamics on the one hand from the emphasis of the patient's right to self-governance and on the other hand from the increase in possibilities for keeping patients alive for whom there is no hope that their situation will improve. Sometimes it is even possible to keep comatose patients alive for years and decades without their situation changing in any significant respect. The discussion of euthanasia also shows an intense examination by physicians of their own professional ethics. Many physicians consider it an essential element of their professional self-understanding that a doctor is obliged to sustain life, and that she is not to end it. Especially active euthanasia strikes many as an assault on a central element of the self-image of the medical profession. In addition to this, the memory of the National-Socialist euthanasia programme overshadows the debate, particularly in Germany. In the following sections, I shall introduce first some conceptual distinctions, and then several important discussions and problems.

4.1.2.1 Definitions

Some standard terminological distinctions have been introduced in the domain of end of life decisions. Occasionally, moral value judgments are already associated with the concepts employed. The notion of 'life extension', for instance, suggests that there is such a thing as a natural life span that is now artificially exceeded. The distinction between 'active' and 'passive' euthanasia also seems to tend to carry a value distinction. It would serve the transparency of the debate if terminological choices were only employed to distinguish between different kinds of situations, and if the moral assessment of these situations were to be understood as a different task. Since the boundaries between different types of situations concerning the end of life are fluid, people often do not speak merely of euthanasia, but prefer the broader term '*end of life decisions*'. Furthermore, there are distinctions between 'active', 'passive' and 'indirect' euthanasia, as well as 'assisted suicide'. As a rule, *active euthanasia* indicates an action that knowingly and deliberately induces death in a patient, for instance by administering a lethal dose of a certain drug. *Passive euthanasia* means refraining from certain actions (for example food supply and artificial respiration) in such a way that there is a conscious and deliberate aim to end the life of the patient. *Indirect euthanasia* is used for medical treatment in which high doses of painkillers are administered and the fact that the patient will die sooner as a result is accepted. *Assisted suicide* includes situations in which a patient who is not capable of taking her own life is aided in doing so. A difficult boundary to draw is the one between euthanasia and *palliative sedation*, that is, drug-induced sedation of a patient that leads to a comatose condition from which the patient often does not awake again. The final essential distinction is between different conditions of the patient: can he still decide for himself what should be done to him, or is he no longer capable of this?

4.1.2.2 The ethics of the medical profession

Numerous debates are concerned with the question of whether (predominantly active) euthanasia is compatible with the professional ethics of medical practitioners. Surely the medical profession is obliged to support, save and sustain life? How can it be a doctor's task to shorten or end life? Does this not indicate a profound change in the self-understanding of the medical profession? One question that arises, however, is what the weight of this question is within the debate on an ethics of euthanasia. Surely, the professional ethos should legitimate itself on the basis of a general ethics, and not the other way around. That means that the first point of concern should be the entitlements of and corresponding duties towards the dying patient. The question of whether a dying patient may expect assistance in the process of dying will have to be answered first and foremost on the basis of a general ethics, and not on the basis of the professional ethics of medical practitioners. If, then, the only argument against assisted suicide is that it is medically inappropriate, this would always fall short, regardless of the way in which the professional ethics of physicians is otherwise specified. Still, if euthanasia is allowed, someone will have to perform it. It is sometimes proposed to disconnect euthanasia from the medical profession, as is the case in Switzerland. The question is, however, whether this would increase the transparency and controllability of the administration of euthanasia. As long as end of life decisions take place in the medical domain, it is much easier to guarantee institutional control of these decisions. This does, however, evoke the question of what kinds of acts can be expected from a physician. Can a doctor be expected to actively kill a person? It should be clear that this can be a very significant burden on the physician. And while it is always emphasised that no doctor can be forced to perform euthanasia, such a clause is only a relief for individual doctors in individual cases. It does not change the fact that an institutionalisation of euthanasia introduces an expectation into the medical profession that its practitioners will carry out such acts. However, it should be stressed once more that the question of whether this is reasonable for the medical profession is subordinate to the moral evaluation of euthanasia as such.

4.1.2.3 Basic normative questions

The first question relevant to this moral evaluation is what criteria would be suitable to carry out such an assessment. One issue that is often debated in this context is the legitimacy of the stipulation that *(human) life as such* should be understood as *inviolable*. Since we have already discussed this (see Chapters 2 and 3), I shall not specifically address this perspective here. There is no good reason why life – without any further qualifications – should be understood as inviolable. While life is undoubtedly of fundamental importance, simply because it is only possible for people to realise any conceivable moral good insofar as they are alive, this still does not justify the standpoint that even when someone has no more chances of being cured or recovering, this person's life should still be understood as inviolable. Yet what strikes me as particularly misguided is the idea that the question of accepting or rejecting different forms of euthanasia is first and foremost connected to the question of whether one shares or rejects the doctrine of the sanctity of life. In the bioethical literature, this conviction is prevalent (Dworkin 1994; Singer 2002), and has contributed to a very lopsided polarisation of the debate.

Two arguments tend to play a role in the discussion: *autonomy* and *compassion or mercy*. The reference to a patient's autonomy would be a sort of expression of the respect for a person in the particular situation of hopeless suffering. When the situation arises that a patient's condition can no longer be medically improved, respect for this person demands that we assist him in ending his life. The pertinent thought here can be the desire to allow the dying person to have a 'dignified' death, which he can experience as compatible with his self-respect.

The strong focus on the *self-determination of the dying person* poses several problems. Many patients, first of all, are no longer capable of making a decision for themselves. Can respect for their self-determination still be the primary motive if that is the case? Of course it would be possible to refer to *earlier directives* of the patient, or to the possibility of a representative making a decision. Yet these possibilities come with their own set of problems, which we will discuss shortly. In any case, respect for a patient's self-determination can justify euthanasia only if the patient has autonomously chosen this option, or if the desire for euthanasia is covered by advance directives. Furthermore, emphasising the patient's autonomy makes it necessary to explain why offering euthanasia should be restricted to dying people in medically hopeless situations. If the pertinent ground for access to euthanasia (including assisted suicide) consists in allowing the patient a self-determined death, then it is unclear why this shouldn't hold for people who wish to end their lives in medically less dramatic conditions. In the Netherlands, which can look back on the longest debate on this question, there now is a movement that wants to make a voluntary death possible for people who are simply 'done with life' ('klaar met leven'). It should be noted that, in the Netherlands reactions to this proposal display significant reservations. It could of course be argued that persons in this group are not directly dependent upon medical support, but can help themselves. Yet this is not so much a systematic as a pragmatic ground. In any case, it could be said that in those cases whatever is at issue is not a matter of assistance in dying, since the dying process has not yet begun in the first place.

Another argument would be the *argument from compassion*, or the appeal to *mercy*. Permitting the practice of euthanasia should allow the physician to make it possible for patients in hopeless medical situations to die with no protracted suffering, without being punished for this. This argument probably has an intuitive plausibility for many people. At the same time, it is very hard to say what the justification for this line of argument is. In the context of a utilitarian theory, the argument can be reconstructed. If the moral preference is for the act that implies less suffering, then shortening the process of suffering is morally better. Outside a utilitarian framework, however, this is much harder to justify – disregarding the occasional reference to Schopenhauer's ethics. The appeal to compassion is problematic first of all because the affected patients are made dependent on the chance encounter with a good Samaritan; a rather unattractive basis for institutional regulations. On the other hand, the question is on what grounds compassion can form the basis for a decision. Surely, end of life decisions should not depend on whatever the emotional state of the doctor happens to be. If, on the other hand, the idea is that there is such a thing as 'rational compassion', it seems inevitable that some sort of objective value theory is presupposed. Surely it should be possible to attribute a universalisable valuation to people's conditions? The crucial question is whether such a valuation is based on the patient's subjective assessment (or, if she is no longer capable of expressing this, on the presumed assessment), or on a supposedly objective or subject-independent valuation of human conditions.

4.1.2.4 Value assumptions

Truly subtle distinctions can play a role in answering this question. Most people, for instance, will find it hard to accept the idea that they may at some point become Alzheimer's patients and lose their memory. Most people will wish never to end up in such a situation. Yet the question is what follows from this in terms of euthanasia. One answer could be that we open up the possibility for persons who will develop Alzheimer's to decide whether they wish to receive assistance in dying. In that case, a value judgment of the situation of a person with Alzheimer's would indeed be implied, but this judgment would not be the normatively decisive ground for the assisted suicide. The normatively decisive factor would be the patient's wilful decision, which would, however, only be open to him in a hopeless situation. An entirely different approach would be to argue that compassion demands the killing of Alzheimer's patients, since their condition is objectively dire. For the former line of argument, the right to self-determination would be decisive, or at least the respect for earlier decisions of the patient, even if he is no longer capable of making decisions in his current condition. The latter argument, which appeals to compassion for his condition, ignores the patient's own judgment and takes the objective valuation of the condition as a basis for the decision.

As indicated above, the line drawn here can be subtle. Looking at the earliest Dutch text addressing the euthanasia debate, the 1969 book *Medische macht en medische ethiek* by physician J. H. van den Berg, it is striking that a plea for a liberal regulation for euthanasia is connected with a negative valuation of the condition of people with thalidomide birth defects. Van den Berg even deplores the practice of physicians and parents making efforts to allow children with thalidomide defects to have a good life, rather than killing them directly after birth. In this book, appeals to compassion and appeals to the right to self-determination coexist (van den Berg 1969).

A further example of the problem of unrecognised value judgments can be found in the book *Dying with dignity* (1998; original 1995). In the name of human dignity, Küng and Jens argue that anyone has the right to decide on the way in which one dies. However, their book is full of unspoken value judgments, which make it clear that Küng and Jens hold that certain people have lives not worth living. This is clear, for instance, when Walter Jens reduces the dying person to a 'packet of muscles', a 'string puppet' (100). Or in the way Hans Küng responds to critical comments on his remark that he does not want to become an Alzheimer's patient who is 'ridiculed by the survivors' (Jens and Küng 1995: 209. Translation by N.v. Steenbergen). Küng attempts to meet this critique by saying [ibid. 218] that his comment should be understood as a personal statement; that 'initially' (!) he meant to speak 'merely' of himself. He is unaware that this 'initially' allows that he is indeed interested in objective findings; that, in other words, he intends to judge the worthiness of the life of an Alzheimer's patient in general. In the process, he uses a medical case study of Alzheimer's disease to suggest the moral permissibility of active euthanasia. Only by paying attention to the way he proceeds does it become possible to see that he speaks of an objective condition of the patient, and that this condition strikes him as showing that there is no reason to prolong such a life. This has nothing to do with respect for the dignity and the individual rights of the person concerned. In Küng, the discussion of human dignity turns into a discussion of the value of a human life under extreme pressure. The allegedly liberal concern with the protection of autonomy in this case certainly does not have liberal consequences. The same lack of differentiation can be found in Küng's boundary between self-determination and 'arbitrariness' [ibid. 60]. According to Küng, a 'man in his prime' who 'begs for assisted suicide' because of a career slump is not a suitable candidate for euthanasia. Of course, one will have to agree on the conclusion. Yet if we read this statement in conjunction with the remarks on the Alzheimer's patients, it becomes clear that he is not taking up the cudgels for individual responsibility. Küng only assesses the 'man in his prime' differently than the Alzheimer's patient, the 'ridicule of the survivors', on the basis of his physical health. It most certainly is the case, then, that in this account particular (if prevalent) value judgments are supposed to ground the legitimacy of euthanasia.

Now the question is what the nature of a universal value theory could be. The comparison with the persons with thalidomide defects, whom van den Berg wanted killed, is of course very instructive in this regard. Unless one defends a crude theory in which only moments of happiness are offset against each other, it is unjustifiable to declare the lives of people with physical disabilities – even severe ones – not worth living. With respect to the basic capacity for autonomous judgment, however, the situation looks different. If this capacity is absent, then there is no ground for ascribing human dignity on its basis (Chapter 2). Yet the point of ascribing dignity is not to stipulate the objective value of a human being. Rather, we merely come to recognise that the capacity for self-determination is valuable for any agent, and this universalised human self-assessment forms the basis for our respect for others. If, however, the consequence of the ascription of dignity is respect, this gives us no reason to accept the argument from compassion. Rather, it would be a reason to demand respect for autonomy. Now it could be argued that in the case of Küng's Alzheimer's patient this capacity is absent, and therefore nothing could be done to counter Küng's assessment. Yet if the presence of the capacity for autonomous judgment is viewed as grounding an entitlement to respect, then in relation to Alzheimer's patients there are really only two possible viewpoints. Either, one makes respect for a person purely dependent upon the actual possession of the relevant capabilities. As the person concerned does not actually have this capacity in the advanced stages of Alzheimer's, there is also no ground for proposing mercy as the basis for securing euthanasia. This line of argument would only really leave the option of not considering him a morally relevant creature at all. Or, alternatively, the patient is considered on the basis of his personal history, and the ground of respect for him is the person who he once was. Yet along these lines, mercy killing is also not the consequence.

This discussion is also relevant for the question of *early euthanasia*, that is, for the moral problem of whether in the case of severely disabled newborns it can be morally defensible to kill them or to withhold basic care (see Chapter 3). If mercy killing can only be defended on utilitarian grounds, early euthanasia could also be justified merely on the basis of the avoidance of suffering. Patient autonomy certainly cannot form the basis of early euthanasia. Even a decision by a representative is of limited justificatory use. In any case, it would be entirely unclear why parents or legal guardians could know what such a child would want. The only possibility is that the parents project their own values onto the child. A special question certainly arises in the case of newborns who only have a very short life expectancy, and whose life will be dominated by suffering. This situation requires specific reflection, in which it will be important to determine whether these cases can be sufficiently delimited and univocally regulated.

A very different argument emerges from the stipulation to respect the patient's decisions regarding her dying process and to support her correspondingly. There are a number of relevant distinctions in relation to this demand. The first question is whether the moral relevance of the distinction between different forms of euthanasia can be legitimised. It could be argued that if respect for a patient demands allowing her to die in a self-determined manner, the only question left concerns the means by which the patient will die. It is not controversial that treatments against the patient's will may not be performed. Forcing treatment onto a patient that she does not wish to receive would signify a fundamental refusal to respect her.

4.1.2.5 Advance directives – assisted suicide – active euthanasia

Less clear is whether respect for a patient demands that treatment is withdrawn when the patient can no longer decide on this herself. This question presents itself differently depending on whether earlier decisions of the patient are available or not. In several countries, moreover, there are elaborate debates on the moral relevance of *advance directives.* Is a patient's advance directive binding on a doctor? Must certain formal legal requirements be fulfilled for it to be binding? One reason why this question is relevant is that in most countries there exists no standard form for such a directive, but numerous versions. For that reason, there can be numerous problems in ascertaining the unambiguousness of an advance directive. Another controversial question is whether the patient is really capable of adequately anticipating how he will feel when death is near. Is it really possible to imagine what one would want in such a situation? A further question concerns the scope of the advance directive. How far can the patient's wishes go in order to be part of an advance directive? Is it possible, in the absence of clear regulations concerning scope, to oblige the physician to respect the patient's wishes? Moreover, is it possible for substantial or procedural arrangements to be prescribed in an advance directive? The author can, for instance, instruct that certain things should or may be done to him – or that they may not. But it is also possible for persons to be appointed who can, in case of doubt or disagreement, be authorised to make certain decisions. In relation to the role of such representatives it should be noted, however, that the delegation of the decision is distinct from the general inclusion of relatives in the decision-making process. The decision by the representative would be morally legitimated on the basis that the representative makes decisions for the patient *on behalf of the patient*. Yet relatives do of course have their own wishes, hopes and fears, and they are present, therefore, as persons who articulate their own preferences. These could range from the desire to keep the patient alive as long as possible, in the hope that she will be cured after all, to fear of the finality of death, to inheritance-related interests. Whatever the case may be, it is morally relevant to distinguish the standpoint of the representative of the patient and the standpoints of the relatives. In short, the regulation, bindingness and scope of advance directives are contentious. To what extent advance directives can be understood as realisations of the patient's right to self-determination effectively depends on the possibility of legally settling the above questions.

But must *assisted suicide* or *active euthanasia* also be understood on the basis of respect for the patient's autonomy? Legally, most countries deny that it should, although in many Western societies this is a matter of debate. Now it is possible, of course, to imagine situations in which it seems morally right to help a dying person fulfil her desire for a self-determined death. This will be all the more likely if one's ethical perspective has a central place for respect for the wishes of the persons affected by an act. *Methodologically*, however, the question is how ethics should deal with such a problem. Surely it is the task of ethics to formulate strict boundaries only for what is morally wrong, leaving everything else up to practical wisdom? A common methodological procedure in the moral assessment of active euthanasia is to distinguish between *categorical* and *pragmatic arguments*. Categorical arguments, here, are arguments that fundamentally prohibit or allow active euthanasia, while pragmatic arguments are those that, even when there are no fundamental objections against active euthanasia, identify a number of concrete reservations. This distinction, however, is problematic in a number of ways. First of all, it is an open question of whether 'categorical' arguments exist in the first place – especially independently from one's normative theory. Within standard utilitarianism it is far from clear what categorical arguments are supposed to be. Recourse to categorical arguments, then, depends on the underlying normative-ethical theory. Moreover, the distinction suggests that it is possible to describe some *typical decision-making situation*, in relation to which it is asked whether it is categorically demanded or allowed to perform euthanasia, or categorically indefensible. The question, however, is what such a 'typical' situation has to do with the concrete situations that we are trying to regulate. The distinction also does not explore what the moral significance of pragmatic arguments might be. Their role in the light of the moral assessment of the concrete situation remains unclear. Instead, it seems advisable to presuppose as a rule – in the sense of the notion of 'mixed judgments' elaborated above – that in order to make any moral assessment we will have to describe the complexity of the relevant situations, and that we will have to evaluate this complexity in the light of a moral principle or multiple moral principles. In this approach, all arguments obtain their moral significance only from the pertinent principle of evaluation, but there is no fundamental dichotomy between categorical and pragmatic arguments as two different *kinds* of arguments.

Following on from this brief side note, we should now discuss the distinctions between the different forms of euthanasia and assisted suicide. What is the pertinent difference between passive and active forms of euthanasia? If respect for the individual can demand that we help him shorten his dying process and alleviate his suffering throughout this process, the question of what forms of assisted dying are allowed seems to be rather instrumental. Surely the distinction between active and passive euthanasia is essentially a distinction for the medical profession, and for the institutionalisation of an exemption from punishment for physicians who assist their patients in the dying process? Does this mean that there are no principled grounds against euthanasia, but merely consequences for the ethics of the profession? Birnbacher (1995) argues that moral philosophy cannot justify any fundamental evaluative distinction between acts and omissions, or make the burden of justification for actions heavier than for omissions. Nevertheless, he does conclude that, in the case of euthanasia, there are reasons to maintain a morally relevant distinction between different forms of assisted dying (Birnbacher 1995: 337–374). A difference that is often appealed to is that it is not clear how the body will react to a withdrawal of treatment, while active euthanasia is irreversible.

Yet what does this mean for 'active euthanasia' and 'assisted suicide'? The basic motivation for these practices is grounded in the fact that many dying people have to endure suffering, which can be very intense. Some patients feel unable to cope with this, and want to spare themselves and others this experience. At the same time, concrete situations vary drastically. This is true not only of the patient's judgment and ability to make decisions, but also of the reactions from their environment. Relatives may find the situation unbearable, nursing homes and hospitals have interests, inheritances are at issue. If – as explicated – the avoidance of suffering is not a goal in itself, it seems that only respect for the person can be the normative ground for euthanasia. Yet if respect for the decision of the other is the reason why we contemplate allowing active euthanasia, the first thing we should do is protect this person, and preserve her life where possible. That means that active euthanasia for reasons of simple wish fulfilment is out of the question. Situations in which active euthanasia is considered would be situations in which the dying process has irreversibly commenced, and in which only a painful final phase can be expected. Such an act of killing could only be legitimate if there is no suspicion of external pressures and that it is solely and exclusively the patient's wish that initiates the act. It is crucial, moreover, that everything is done to make this decision avoidable. In other words, the decision should not result from any miserable circumstances that could be prevented (such as poor care). Since the patient is to be understood in this situation as someone to whom we owe moral respect, an act of killing that is not voluntarily desired or enforced by external pressure would be a very grave moral misdeed. The central question, then, is whether 'active euthanasia' or 'assisted suicide' can be controlled in a manner that guarantees that the act is performed only in morally acceptable cases, and that all possible alternatives are considered.

4.1.2.6 The Dutch example

At this point, I shall briefly discuss the Dutch euthanasia laws. As is well known, the Netherlands introduced a law according to which a physician performing euthanasia is not liable to prosecution, provided he has followed elaborate guidelines and procedures. The relevant cases are those in which a patient who is terminal and experiences his suffering as unbearable asks his physician for active euthanasia. The legal construction is thus based on a prohibition of euthanasia, but allows for an exemption from punishment for physicians insofar as due care is exercised. That does mean, however, that the physician does not obtain permission from an authority in advance. Therefore, he can not be certain that the conditions for permissible euthanasia are in this case met. After having performed euthanasia, the physician is bound to submit the supporting documentation for inspection. Regional committees have been established for this purpose. If the conditions for legitimate euthanasia turn out not to have been present, the legal prosecutor must start an investigation. However, such investigations rarely occur. The entire procedure was first regulated by law in 2002, yet the law merely represents a formalisation of a long-standing medical code of conduct. Since the establishment of the law, however, there have been complaints that some cases of euthanasia are not reported. In addition, there are some cases in which euthanasia was performed in the absence of an explicit request by the patient. (Different reports about this law issued by the Ministry of Health can be found on the Ministry's website: see http://www.rijksoverheid.nl/ministeries/vws/.) Nowadays, it also appears to be the case that physicians are more likely to opt for the alternative of palliative sedation, which counts as a standard therapeutic measure and is not subject to further documentation. The doctors complain of the significant bureaucratic burden associated with the control procedure, and of course of the risk (even if slight) of prosecution. At the same time, however, it should be noted that the institutionalisation – that is, the establishment of regional inspection committees, a national board which in turn evaluates the functioning of the committees, and the creation of methods to record all data relevant to the law – has produced a very sophisticated information system. That means that a number of important conditions for a transparent implementation of the practice are in place.

The practice of euthanasia is internationally controversial; in the Netherlands itself, new criticisms of particular aspects continue to crop up, but there is a broad endorsement of the practice as such. It may be worth pointing out that the regulation that is now established is the *result of a debate* that had its start in the 1960s. The present law and its acceptance cannot be understood in isolation from this debate (Cohen-Almagor 2010; the excellent study about the history of the debate in Kennedy 2002 is unfortunately available only in Dutch). In many respects, moreover, the debate and the law both mirror the very particular Dutch consensus culture, which, for several reasons, can hardly come into question as an example for other countries.

Over the years, there have been countless Dutch debates on a number of implementation issues, such as the question to what extent children and persons incapable of consenting can be considered for euthanasia. Recently, euthanasia's demarcation from palliative sedation and its extension to early euthanasia have been a central concern. It seems evident that the inclusion of early euthanasia would far exceed the framework of the present law. A last point that should be made is that the moral legitimation of the law contains some unclarities. It is usually said that the point of the law is to strike a balance between the *respect for the right to autonomy* of a patient and the desire to allow doctors *acts of mercy*. Whether mercy provides a workable ground for a moral argument has already been discussed. For the future debate, however, I believe that this lack of clarity in the moral argumentation poses a difficulty, for it is to be expected that there will be further discussions of the expansion of the scope of the law. It will be crucial for public confidence and for the moral acceptability of future regulations that the normative evaluative basis is transparent.

Independently of the specific situation in the Netherlands it should be emphasised once more that moral evaluation cannot be understood in isolation from the possibilities for establishing *legal regulations* that can guarantee *effective legal protection*. In this respect, it is worth pointing once more to the elaborate Dutch system of committees and evaluative procedures, which certainly is a fundamental part of the Dutch regulations. Yet the assessment also depends on the relevant health care system, and on the situation encountered by dying persons. The poorer the care in a person's final phases, the harder it is to avoid that a patient will express the desire to die on the basis of external circumstances. That means that the entire debate on active euthanasia cannot be held without considering the pressure on the health care system, which at the moment is a fact in most Western countries. It must be assumed, moreover, that this pressure will heighten. In the coming years, the demographic developments of Western countries will put enormous pressures on the treatment of dying persons. Any regulation of euthanasia will thus have to be scrutinised to establish to what extent it is capable of dealing with this pressure, and whether there are alternatives in which the respect that is required can be guaranteed.

4.1.2.7 Abuse and 'slippery slope'

These latter deliberations touch on the debate of the so-called 'slippery slope arguments' (van der Burg 2001; Lamb 1988). The discussion of the validity of these kinds of arguments is of importance for bioethics generally, but has mostly been held in relation to the euthanasia debate. The term incorporates a number of quite distinct forms of arguments. One typical form of a slippery slope argument would look like this: Opening the door to assisted dying will eventually lead to a situation in which it is first allowed to kill critically ill people, then it will become permissible to euthanise disabled persons and, finally, the right to life of each and every one of us will be up for debate. Different versions of this argument can be distinguished. At the level of generality at which Spaemann presents things, however, the slippery slope concern is not so much an argument as the expression of a hollow prejudice and a symptom of a cynical attitude towards severely ill people. A version of this argument would be: act A is in itself morally unproblematic; yet were we to permit A, this would in the long run lead to the occurrence of act B, which is indeed morally problematic. This should be strictly distinguished from the kind of argument that goes: act A is morally problematic; moreover, there is the additional danger that act B will also occur, and B is morally even more problematic. In this case, the slippery slope argument would merely be an additional argument and not itself decisive for the moral judgment. In this sense, the argument cannot be considered a true slippery slope argument, since the killing of critically ill persons is already taken to be problematic, and not only the acts it allegedly leads to.

The question is, however, what the relation between act A and act B might be. Is the latter an inevitable consequence, or merely a probable one? Is there empirical evidence for this causal relation? Since the claim involves a prognosis of future developments, it is difficult to provide empirical evidence. Is the claim an estimation of political processes and their internal dynamics? In terms of our case: can the fear that allowing active euthanasia will lead to the killing of people against their will legitimate, prohibiting the allowance of active euthanasia if it were otherwise morally demanded?

In order to evaluate the validity of this argument, at least the following questions should be discussed: (i) Is the danger of a slippery slope the sole objection against active euthanasia? The more depends only on this argument, the stronger the evidence for a slippery slope must be; (ii) What kind of evidence is available? Does it come in the form of historical analogies? Is there evidence that relates to actual practices? Much of the validity of the argument will depend on this; (iii) How grave would it be if the morally undesirable act actually were to occur? The less the weight of the possible undesirable development, the higher the bar for the evidence; and

(iv) How important is it for those concerned that active euthanasia be permitted? The more important it is for them, the stronger the evidence for a slippery slope must be. The answers to these questions will vary with the underlying ethical theory of the person answering.

Slippery slope arguments should be clearly distinguished from concerns about abuse. Sometimes, the latter are addressed under the heading 'slippery slope arguments'. The argument regarding abuse is: act A is morally unproblematic, act B is morally problematic. Yet if we make act A permissible, then we also exempt people doing act B from prosecution. This argument does not state that act B is a consequence of act A. Rather, its point is that the regulation at issue is incapable of sufficiently distinguishing between the two. In complex legal contexts, this is a very common occurrence. In such a situation, the feasibility of the regulation depends on the available legal control mechanisms. The more problematic act B, the higher the demands on controllability that can justify exempting act A from punishment. In the light of the debate on euthanasia, this demand seems perfectly reasonable to me. The empirical evidence of the effectiveness of control mechanisms, however, can involve significant difficulties itself. Moreover, it holds for this argument too that it is essential to confirm which regulation is more fit to safeguard fundamental respect for dying persons.

Finally, we should address the problem of *indirect euthanasia*, that is, those cases in which the life-shortening effects of high doses of painkillers are accepted as a side-effect of their anaesthetic function. An extreme version of this is *palliative sedation*, in which sedatives induce a coma from which the patient does not wake up again. Palliative sedation has become an established alternative to active euthanasia and, sometimes, the boundaries between the two are not easily drawn. In the literature, these kinds of cases are often justified on the basis of the *doctrine* or *principle of double effect* (Timmons 2002: 77–101). This principle is formulated in a number of very different ways, but the basic idea is that there are acts that are connected to multiple goals, in this case pain relief and hastening death. It is important that the fact that the pain medication hastens death is not its intended effect – the intention is for the pain to be alleviated. Yet, at the same time, the doctor knows that it is very probable that her act will lead to a quicker death. This consequence, however, is not intended, but accepted as an unavoidable side-effect of the pain relief. This situation is not very unlikely, since dying patients often do require high doses of pain medication. At the same time, this argument sounds like a sleight of hand: the physician knows good and well that the patient will die sooner. Would it not be more honest to admit that the patient's life is being shortened, instead of putting this down to an unintended side-effect? And in fact, that argument has a rather bad reputation in the bioethical debate and is rejected by many authors. A clear disadvantage of allowing these kinds of arguments is that they threaten to decrease transparency. The administration of painkillers is a very common medical procedure. Therefore, no special justification seems to be required for it. While in, say, the Netherlands, active euthanasia is subject to very high requirements with respect to control and legitimation, the appeal to unintended side-effects seems to be an elegant way of shirking the burden of justifying oneself. However, it would not be right to dismiss the idea as a mere trick. In the case of terminally ill patients who can only be helped by high doses of pain medication anyway, it is not that easy to determine, at least in the final phase, what exactly the main effects are and which events are side-effects. It certainly would be problematic if the possibility of taking recourse to extreme pain management made it possible to avoid having to justify one's actions. That there are many cases of palliative care in which it is almost impossible to distinguish between effective pain management and shortening the patient's life span, however, can hardly be denied. It seems that the principle of double effect has a specific legitimacy in a limited domain.

4.1.3 Organ transplantation and organ procurement

The desire to find solutions to organ failure is certainly one of the central motives of biomedical research (Nuffield Council on Bioethics 1996, 2011; Price 2001; Radcliffe Richards 1996; Wilkinson 2012). At the same time, however, the therapeutic possibilities have evoked a number of debates on organ donation and organ procurement, as well as research projects concerned with organ creation and regulative problems associated with this practice. In terms of transplantation, the creation of organs is not only aimed at the replacement of larger organs such as the liver and kidneys, but also with the transplantation of tissue and parts of organs. Organ transplantation is a complex field of diverse medical activities with many social and legal implications.

There are many hopes connected with the possibility of organ transplantation. People who previously had no choice but to come to terms with their fate now have a chance of survival. This alters our relation to diseases that can result in organ failure, and it changes our expectations of medical possibilities. However, significant technical difficulties were associated with organ transplantation and, to a certain extent, they still are. Yet progress in this area has been so rapid that many patients can live with a transplanted organ for decades. As organ transplantation evolved into a serious possibility for patients, the question of how organs can be procured became more pressing. This has now been a matter of debate for several decades.

First, however, we should be aware that many of the problems occurring here are new. For organ transplantation, that is, for something that probably makes it possible to survive, a patient is dependent on other people's organs. While usual medical treatment involves a doctor doing something to a patient's body, in this case a third party enters the stage. Because of the possibilities of organ transplantation, people's bodies become medically interesting to others. Of course, before the days of organ donation people would make their bodies available to science. These new opportunities, however, have a different dimension. This means that organ transplantation can never be the kind of issue that is discussed only from the limited perspective of the doctor-patient relation, for it necessarily has a social and societal dimension.

4.1.3.1 Brain death

Shortly before organ transplantations could be performed, heart-lung machines made it possible to maintain the vital functions of patients whose brain function had been irreversibly lost. Thus, it became possible for a dying person's organs to be kept functional until they could be retrieved. This possibility, however, evokes questions about a person's moral status during different phases of dying, and about the conditions under which organ retrieval can legitimately occur.

These questions led to the so-called brain death debate, which flared up for the first time in the late 1950s and early 1960s. The main concern at the time was to establish whether brain-dead persons are to be regarded as dead. The underlying conviction was that removing organs from a living person would violate his fundamental rights, and that the removal of vital organs would even amount to murder. At the same time, the patients at issue will never regain consciousness. A committee at Harvard University first proposed the so-called brain death definition, according to which a person should be considered dead if all brain function has been irreversibly lost. This definition takes its start from the notion of *whole brain death*. Other relevant notions are the concept of *partial brain death*, in which brain death can be pronounced even after the irreversible loss of functions of the upper brain and the definition of *cardiac death*, according to which death can only be pronounced when the heart has stopped beating. Nowadays, a distinction is generally made between the *definition of death*, that is, the establishment of signs or symptoms that are relevant to the time of death; the *death criteria* that must be fulfilled in order to conclude that these signs or symptoms are present; and the *tests* that are necessary in order to identify the fulfilment of the criteria.

In this debate, legal, anthropological, ethical and political themes were entangled in many ways (Hauser-Schäublin et al. 2001). The point of the debate was the legal and moral status of persons who are in the final phase of their lives, in which they are irreversibly unconscious. The dynamics of the debate stemmed from the possibilities of organ transplantation. Yet, at the same time, these patients are persons who are still breathing and who are, in a common-sense understanding of the term, not dead. The suspicion was raised repeatedly that what was happening was a manipulation of the common sense of death, in order to justify taking people's organs. Surely the definition that makes a person's death dependent on the way his body can be used by medicine is ultimately a pragmatic one? Their most prominent critic was Hans Jonas (1974), who accused this definition of death of understanding the human body as a mere material object, forgetting that the human body should be understood as the organism of a living person. This line of criticism was widely endorsed. The brain death definition was seen as a result of mind-body dualism, the dualistic image of humans of modernity, associated with a repressive understanding of the body. A further criticism was that with the notion of brain death, moral and legal criteria become detached from the world as it is normally experienced by people. Relatives of the patient and those caring for her experience a breathing being and, against that experience, brain death seems a legal fiction.

Moreover, proponents of the notion of brain death were accused of losing sight of the *anthropological basis* for the ascription of moral and legal status. Human beings, with whom morality is concerned, are not, after all, abstract bodiless persons, but creatures of flesh and blood whose hearts beat and who we think of as living beings 'until the final heartbeat', dying in the end, although a dying person is not yet dead. Anthropologically it is also plausible not to conceive human personhood dualistically. Accordingly, the debate was characterised by critiques of John Locke's notion of the person, which was accused of implying such an instrumentalisation of the human body (Locke 1689/1960: 387f). In contrast, some participants proposed phenomenological approaches to the body, which were deemed capable of evading this dualism. As pointed out in the previous chapter, however, the phenomenological tradition does not have a developed theory of moral obligation. If one draws on the phenomenological tradition, one needs to specify how it can be justified, on the basis of a phenomenological notion of the body, that brain-dead persons are entitled to moral respect. Others see in Lévinas's theory of the face an alternative to dualism. For Lévinas, the face of the other immediately confronts us with our obligations. However, the question would be how exactly this obligation is to be understood, and why a brain-dead person has such a moral authority. Lévinas holds that we cannot attribute properties to others, but that the encounter with the other has an immediacy that eludes such ascriptions. Yet this also means that his account cannot decide whether and when exactly a 'face' we encounter has moral authority. Is this the case only when the other is conscious? Or is it true for comatose persons too? Or even for corpses? Any way in which one of these possible boundaries would be declared morally significant would require the ascription of certain properties or characteristics, which Lévinas's approach explicitly refuses to do.

This issue raises some fundamental questions to what extent ethics depends or should depend on a theory of human nature (see Chapter 3). Presumably, it is broadly agreed that moral deliberations are not independent from philosophical accounts of human beings. A very different question, however, is whether anthropological insights lead directly to moral principles. If from an anthropological perspective we consider human beings as essentially embodied creatures, this does not yet mean that humans are entitled to the same moral protection in every phase of their lives. However, many participants in the debate, from different backgrounds, take it to be a matter of course that the brain death debate evolves around an *anthropological picture of human beings*.

It is not clear, however, that the question 'When is a human being dead?' is really the pertinent issue here. To my mind, the question is rather: what moral obligations do we have towards brain-dead persons? Or, in other words: what is a person's moral status in different phases of dying, and what moral obligations do we have towards him? This question is not a pragmatic question in the sense of how a person or body can be used. Rather, it is a genuinely ethical question about the justification of our moral obligations in relation to dying.

4.1.3.2 Organ transplant regulations

Even if we assume that the status of a brain-dead person does not fundamentally prohibit the removal of his organs, this still does not answer the question of what the *requirements regarding the legitimacy of organ removal* should be. It may be clear that the body of a brain-dead person cannot simply be considered an object that can be freely used. If we respect a (previously formulated) will, even when using or distributing a deceased person's property, it should be clear that the use of his organs cannot take place against his will. Most Western countries therefore established a legal format for expressing one's willingness to donate organs in the case of brain death. Still, in most Western countries the willingness to donate does not match the need for donor organs. For that reason, people often ask whether an explicit confirmation that one is willing to donate is really necessary. The debate has a peculiar dynamic, since the lack of willingness to donate seems to stand in stark contrast with the prevalent conviction that organ donation is a good thing. It is assumed that people tend to not to fill out a donor form as long as they are healthy, simply because it does not cross their minds (or because they do not want to be confronted with death); yet, if asked, they usually declare themselves willing.

In general, the following conditions for legitimate organ removal are considered. The solution of narrowly interpreted *express consent*, or a *'hard' opt-in system* involves that organ removal is only legitimate if explicit consent of the person concerned is available (this will often be in written form). Broadly interpreted express consent, or a *'soft' opt-in system* means that in certain circumstances, the consent can be given by relatives as well. *Presumed consent*, or an *opt-out system* means that organ removal is legitimate as long as the person concerned has never explicitly expressed wishes to the contrary. The opt-out system has 'hard' and 'soft' versions too.

In order to evaluate these possible ways of regulating organ donation, it must first be asked how exactly we are to think of the moral value of post-mortem organ donation (Schweda and Schicktanz 2008 on public opinion on this matter). Is it an act of benevolence that people can choose to do or not? Or is organ donation a kind of solidarity that can be expected of everyone? There seems to be broad consensus that organ donation is a morally good act. While brain death is extremely controversial, the desirability of post-mortem organ donation seems to be fairly uncontentious. This broad consensus includes Christian churches, which consider it an act of charity. Therefore, in several Western countries, it is generally assumed that post-mortem organ donation is morally acceptable or even morally required. Therefore the discussions focus mainly on the modes of regulations and the possibilities to increase the number of organ donators.

The following models for the moral evaluation of organ donation tend to be considered as serious options (see for instance Ravelingien and Krom 2005). Organ donation must be thought of as a *voluntary act* that nobody can be obliged to do. Or: donation is arranged in contracts between people on the basis of a mutual willingness to donate organs if they will also profit from organ donation were they to need it, i.e. an organ donation contract. Such a *club system* has the consequence that only people who have declared a willingness to be a donor are eligible to receive organ transplants; a modification could be that the club is not exclusive but that members have a kind of priority on the waiting list. The motivation for signing up to be an organ donor is thus heightened by self-interest. This solution would not presume that everyone approves of organ donation, and would not assume anyone's implicit consent. Under such a system, the willingness to donate could be expected to increase. On the other hand, this system requires a very rigid implementation model. People who have not signed up to the contract would have to be strictly excluded from organ transplantation. It is important to keep in mind that people's opportunities for gathering information on medical matters vary greatly. It is very likely that some people – especially those who are socially disadvantaged and those whose level of education gives them fewer opportunities to take part in social life – would hardly be aware of the consequences of not being a donor. It could be argued that the club system completely voids organ donation of its moral aspect: it is not seen as morally required or at least praiseworthy but just a matter of a contractual agreement. For, in the club system, organ donation simply presupposes a free agreement between citizens that is not legally different from any other form of contract.

On the basis of a pure utilitarian balance of the avoidance of suffering and the gain in preference fulfilment, organ donation might appear morally obligatory. Such deliberations could be taken so far that one might observe that most people are perfectly capable of living with just one kidney, while others depend on kidney donation. In any case, only the perspective of the avoidance of suffering would really imply that every single person's organs should be removed post-mortem. Since deceased people can no longer suffer, we would almost be obliged to get as much use out of their organs as possible. It would not seem very plausible that someone's possible refusal to be an organ donor could still be operative after her death, since at that point, she can no longer be harmed. The only restrictions to post-mortem use of body parts could be motivated by uncertainties regarding the point at which a brain-dead person has truly lost all sensation, and by questions of legal certainty and confidence in the medical system. Unrestricted use of the bodies of deceased persons could lead people to be concerned that when their end is near it will in fact be determined that they are truly dead. The fears associated with such concerns are certainly not to be disregarded.

From the perspective of a theory of human dignity as 'empowerment' there also are reasons to consider post-mortem organ donation as morally good. After all, this allows some other person to survive or significantly improves their situation, while it does not result in any restrictions for oneself. Yet in the context of such a theory, the agreement of the potential donor would be absolutely crucial. The only open question is which forms of expressing a willingness to donate would be appropriate.

However, this assessment of post-mortem organ donation as essentially morally positive and the debate on its regulation do require some nuance. First of all, the issue of confidence in the medical system should not be underestimated. Many participants in the brain death debate have already argued that people's confidence in medicine was an important factor. People may have a feeling that for some physicians the research interests associated with organ transplantation are more important than the actual therapeutic significance for those affected. They can doubt that in critical situations everything is done to keep patients alive, and suspect that intensive care patients are viewed as potential organ donors above all else. For a constructive discussion of medical possibilities and for the sake of the social acceptability of the corresponding regulations, confidence in the medical system is of vital importance. An opt-in system is more capable of countering wariness. It would also help if medical associations would foster a culture of open debate, in which it would be clear that openness is not a matter of patronising instruction by the medical community. The question of whether organ transplants really do help people live autonomous lives depends to a significant extent on the success with which opportunities for therapy and medical perspectives are relayed to patients and to the public. While there are forms of organ transplantation in which successes can be frequently recorded, it must not be forgotten that numerous conditions must be fulfilled in order for an organ transplant to be successful. For many patients, a transplant will not be an option. The boundary between justified hopes and illusions is fluid, and the way in which the topic is addressed can awaken hopes and expectations that cannot be met.

4.1.3.3 Organ transplants and body image

One question in this context is what kind of body image results from the presence of organ donation as a possibility.[1] The replacement of organs is not

1 In the context of the European research project 'Challenges of Biomedicine', focus groups on organ transplantation were conducted in several European countries. The researchers also investigated the way people perceive their bodies in connection with organ transplantation (Schicktanz 2007; Schweda and Schicktanz 2008; and see http://www.univie.ac.at/virusss/cobpublication/).

just a mechanical procedure; the human body is the organism in which we live. It is reported that patients do not experience the transplant of a new organ simply as a change in their basic biological setup, but as an event that influences their awareness of their body and their self-understanding. Quite often, receiving an organ is also experienced as a social exchange with the other. All of these are aspects of organ transplantation that are relevant for our moral evaluation. If public communication profoundly influences people's body image, this too is a factor that must be morally assessed.

A final consideration that is important for the way in which organ transplantation is arranged and regulated is whether organ donation is experienced as voluntary, or if the impression is raised that patients are entitled to the bodies of others. The possibility to use others' organs creates a whole new kind of interest in the human body, especially in the bodies of dying persons. In the past, corpses were only interesting for medical research. Yet that interest was much more anonymous than the interests of an ill person. As indicated, it would be consistent for certain forms of utilitarianism to consider the body of a brain-dead person as an object that can be freely used. Theories that take human autonomy to be a fundamental value will, in contrast, consider a person's consent essential. The question is whether radical notions of a Cartesian mind–body dualism wouldn't mean that only the embodied autonomous creature is valued, that is, that the body has value only insofar as it is the material substance of an autonomous person. Would such a perspective mean that when the autonomous person no longer exists, the body has become public property? It seems only consistent to assume that the status of the body would indeed change. However, that does not yet mean that it becomes an object that can be used by just anyone or in any way. Descartes's thesis that the body should be understood as a mere automaton is shared by almost nobody, and what exactly this conception meant for Descartes need not be discussed here.[2] Without this form of dualism, however, it is very hard to justify that people are entitled to the bodies of others in a way that negates individuals' decisions on whether they want to donate parts of their bodies. Yet for the way in which organ donation is to be regulated, this question is of fundamental importance.

4.1.3.4 Living donation and organ trafficking

So far, post-mortem organ donation has been discussed in a fair amount of detail. Another possibility is of course living organ donation. Living donation has become established for regenerative body parts, especially for blood, and

2 An ontological or anthropological dualism, which says something about the status of the body as such, should be distinguished from an epistemological dualism, which asks whether mental functions can be reduced to biological events, or makes a statement on the significance of the body for our knowledge of the ethical.

living donation of, say, bone marrow is certainly possible. Furthermore, it is an option for organs that are not directly vital – it is quite possible to live with one kidney rather than two. Obviously, in some of these cases the organ removal itself is associated with risks. A person with one kidney does of course live with the risk that this one kidney will fail, yet this is not an entirely unbearable risk. Now in most Western countries, living donation is only permitted within some boundaries; sometimes it is for example restricted to close relatives. This raises a whole range of questions. While it is entirely conceivable that a close relative can have a strong desire not to want to live without the person who motivates such a decision, it is exactly among close relatives that complex emotional constellations are not improbable (expectations, organs as a proof of love, etc). The fact that women seem to donate more often than men also raises certain questions. For a moral assessment of living donation, a closer look at the motives and emotional consequences of living donation seems necessary.

It is likely that an expansion of living donation beyond the domain of close relatives could only be successful if living donors could expect financial compensation. While for close relatives it is assumed that the special significance of the loved one in need of an organ is the decisive motive for donating, such motives can hardly be assumed for other living donors, at least in the case of organs such as kidneys. Yet if living donation were to be arranged as a kind of club system, in which signing up as a living donor makes one eligible for transplants, human organs would become socialised, and compensation would be out of the question. Two issues are directly relevant to this point: the commercialisation of the human body and the debate on organ trafficking.

The *commercialisation of the human body* is not entirely foreign. In many countries it has long been the norm for compensation to be paid for blood donations (for discussions see Radin 1996; Cohen 1999; Beyleveld and Brownsword 2001: 171–94; Holland 2001). Remuneration is also not uncommon for donations of hair or regenerative tissue for medical research. And payments for other kinds of employment of the human body (elite sports, prostitution) are common as well. Ultimately, the boundary between physically intensive hired labour and remunerated organ donation cannot be drawn very precisely. Indeed, there are calls for the liberalisation of these possibilities, as long as people do not make their bodies available to others unreservedly and irrevocably (enslavement). The argument for such a liberalisation could only be that it is morally unjustifiable to keep people from selling parts of their own body if they are so inclined. Such arguments, however, overlook the social circumstances of the people who would in those circumstances donate their organs. It would be almost impossible to avoid poor people being forced to consider selling their organs.

Now *organ trafficking* is indeed a significant problem in developing countries. In some situations people sell almost everything that is not vital: kidneys, retinas, eyes, etc. There are reports of mothers parting with their organs in order to make it possible for their children to have vital surgery. Many people who sell their organs in Turkey, Latin America or India become severely disabled or die. The buyers are not infrequently from Western countries. The moral assessment of such cases seems relatively unequivocal. However, this is not in the first place a question of medical ethics, but rather a problem of the political and social structures in these countries, given an international dimension by the involvement of buyers from the Western world. For the question of the feasibility of commercialising living donation in Western countries, it is a crucial question of whether such consequences would be avoidable.

4.1.3.5 Xenotransplantation

Since organ scarcity has been a well recognised problem for many years, there are now numerous research projects concerned with finding alternatives to organ procurement. *Stem cell research* is hoped to result in prospects for using embryonic stem cells for the production of human organs. The debate on this possibility is concerned for an important part with the question of the use of human embryos for obtaining stem cells, and the use of women as embryo donors (see later in this chapter). While in the case of regenerative tissue expectations are very high, it is not yet possible to predict with confidence whether it will ever be possible to produce entire organs from stem cells. Certainly, however, the hope of growing organs from stem cells is an important motivation for medical research.

Another widely debated research area is *xenotransplantation*, that is, the transplantation of organs and tissue across species boundaries. This technique has been used in a few isolated cases, but has not been developed to such an extent that routine clinical implementation will be the order of the day any time soon. The ethical questions associated with this practice can be divided into questions concerning the donors and questions concerning the recipients. On the side of the *donors*, of course, the pertinent questions concern *animal protection* – not only in relation to the animals used for transplantation purposes, but also because there would be an *increase in animal experiments*. These questions, however, are not very specific for the domain of xenotransplantation. If xenotransplantation could be successfully implemented, the use of an animal organ for saving a human life would surely be of greater importance than most of the purposes for which we currently use animals. Whether the use of animals for researching xenotransplantation is morally justifiable depends, on the one hand, on our theory concerning the moral status of animals; that is, on our obligations towards animals. It should be kept in mind that the animals that would be used for xenotransplantation would be animals that are biologically relatively similar to humans. Yet if great apes are involved, most theories of moral status set rather high standards for legitimatising the corresponding experiments. On the other hand, the question would be whether we have reason to expect that xenotransplantation would be a feasible long-term form of organ transplantation. If there were to be decisive reasons to suspect that this technique could never be a success, then the research would also be morally questionable.

With regard to the *recipients*, the most pertinent problems are medical. In the debate, it is frequently pointed out that there are risks and uncertainties regarding the ways in which biological matter reacts to a foreign organism. Exactly how high the risk of xenoses (infection with endogenous animal viruses) is, is unknown. It cannot be ruled out that entirely new contagious viruses will develop when an animal organ is transplanted into a human body. None of those possibilities can be simulated in animal experiments, since the very question is how animal organs will react to the human organism. In order to eliminate all risks, it would be necessary to monitor patients over long periods of time in order to determine whether such viruses arise. Since all of this is largely unfamiliar, it is very difficult to say whether such experiments would expose any third parties to dangers. It could be argued that the patient has a right to decide whether she is prepared to take such risks, if she has no other options. Yet if third parties could be endangered, the only truly acceptable research method would involve long-term quarantines. However, this also raises the question of how long-term monitoring of patients can be realised. Schicktanz points out that, in normal situations, informed consent only concerns the treatment itself. Expecting a patient to subject herself to long-term monitoring under quarantine would introduce an entirely novel kind of agreement. Yet performing xenotransplantation without corresponding control mechanisms would imply a readiness to subject third parties to profound risks.

4.1.3.6 Organ distribution

So far, we have mostly discussed how transplant organs can be obtained. Yet there is also a heated debate over the question of how, given the scarcity of organs, organs should be *distributed*. This question has direct political implications as well. Since organ distribution is organised at both the national and the European level, the criteria for the distribution of available organs are continually being discussed. These criteria are in the first place medical, and concern the compatibility of donor organs and expected reactions of the immune system. Another factor is the likelihood that a particular organ can be transplanted successfully at all. Further considerations, however, have moral and political aspects. Possible criteria are the *urgency* of a transplant for the survival of the recipient, and the *waiting time* – the time the patient has already spent on the waiting list. But there are also questions that have to do with the patient's personal situation or lifestyle. How can doctors make a decision between giving a kidney to a 75-year-old patient who will probably not live very much longer with his new kidney, and giving it to a young person? If one were to decide against transplantations in elderly persons, one would in effect establish an age limit, after which people are no longer entitled to this kind of medical support. Another question is whether the patient's lifestyle should be taken into account. Should an alcoholic whose liver no longer functions receive a liver transplant, or should the liver instead go to someone who has lost his liver function through no fault of his own? Besides the possibility that the alcoholic would start drinking again, these are questions that touch people's sense of justice.

Given the demographic development in the Western world, it is likely that the number of transplantable, well-functioning organs will diminish, while the number of those in need of them will increase. It can be expected that the demand for organs from poorer countries will grow, and that the social disputes will become harsher. We will need to ask to what extent organ transplantation can live up to all the expectations people have of it. A very important challenge for the future is the question of whether we are entitled to the body parts of others; a question that emerges as a latent or explicit expectation in many debates. For an ethics that makes the value of autonomy and the protection of individual rights central, much will depend on the possibility of effectively protecting and safeguarding individuals' decisions. A slow dispossession and socialisation of the human body, and social imbalance in the access to human organs would, in this respect, be serious threats.

4.1.4 Reproductive medicine, cloning and stem cell research

Within biomedical research, infertility treatment plays a large role (Archard and Benatar 2011; Cohen 1996; Dworkin 1994; Hildt and Mieth 1998; Mills 2011; Ruse and Pynes 2006; Steinbock 2002; The President's Council on Bioethics 2002). The end of the 1970s saw the emergence of in vitro fertilisation (IVF) and this domain has since gained an entirely new dynamic. The possibility of creating human embryos in test tubes did not simply offer opportunities for infertility treatment, but it also opened up important perspectives for research on human embryos, which has become a very prominent aspect of the public debate on bioethics. Someone who stays informed about bioethics merely through the daily newspaper could easily gain the impression that bioethics is only concerned with cloning, stem cells and embryos.

In the following sections, the term 'embryos' will initially be used in the broad sense of the word. The exact meaning of this term is, however, a matter of discussion. The phase between fertilisation and nidation, for instance, is sometimes called the 'pre-embryonic stadium', in which cell divisions occur to form the placenta. In this stadium the cells can also still divide as to form further embryos. Once such cell divisions can no longer take place, the embryonic phase is said to begin. Some think that it does not make sense to speak of an individual creature in the pre-embryonic phase. This discussion can be important for the attribution of moral status, since some theories consider it morally significant that the phase of identity formation has been concluded. However, the ethical question cannot be answered solely on the basis of biological definitions. The fertilised egg, for instance, is not automatically entitled to protection just because it is defined as an embryo, nor is it any less entitled to protection on the basis of being defined as a pre-embryo (see Chapter 3). First, it is necessary to determine what kind of properties entitle creatures to moral protection. One problem with the definition of an embryo is that it involves biological assertions that are not uncontroversial, or whose implementation is problematic. It is contentious, for instance, how long fertilised eggs are totipotent, that is, how long they can divide into further eggs that in turn can develop into human beings.

4.1.4.1 Artificial insemination

In the following sections, I shall discuss some problems with the implementation of IVF, the way in which human embryos are used, and research and experiments in which human embryos are involved. IVF has clearly expanded the spectrum of infertility treatment. The treatment started out as a therapy for functional disorders of the fallopian tubes, but is now used for other forms of infertility as well. Yet IVF is only one of several infertility treatments subsumed under the collective term *assisted reproductive technology* (ART). IVF led to the birth of a child for the first time in 1978, and since then it has been an established form of infertility treatment in most Western countries. It is, however, a treatment that evokes a wide range of questions (Hildt and Mieth 1998). First of all, the technology still has a relatively low success rate. Statistics vary, but the ratio of procedures to live-born children (the live birth rate or 'baby take-home rate') usually lies below 30 per cent. The success rate of IVF is a matter of much debate, and there have been criticisms of the fact that women under treatment are not always informed of these statistics (Wiesing 1998). This means that most women either complete the therapy without result or have to go through several treatment cycles. The success rate is improved when several embryos are transferred, yet this also increases the risk of multiple pregnancies. The production of eggs requires hormone stimulation that is particularly burdensome, especially in the case of repeat treatments. Reports show that there may also be significant emotional burdens (Maier 1998: 65ff). The increased rate of multiple births is associated with risks as well. But over and above that, there seem to be signs of increased risks of malformations and impairments in children conceived through assisted reproductive technologies.

In part, the debate was concerned with the question in what cases IVF can be recommended. The first factor relevant for that decision is the strain the procedure puts on the woman. The probability of success depends on a number of factors, such as the age of the couple. It is not unimportant, however, that the burden of the procedure is not only physical. Deciding to undergo the therapy also has a strong impact on people's hopes, desires and plans for the future. A further question is which couples should be allowed to receive fertility treatment: only married, heterosexual couples? Would

ART not also be a way of helping homosexual couples have a child? In most countries, fertility treatment is available to heterosexual, married couples only, yet this is a matter of debate. Another question is whether it should be possible for a different woman – other than the egg donor to carry the pregnancy to delivery. So-called 'surrogacy' seems to be a possibility for women with the desire to have a child who can donate eggs but are incapable of carrying a pregnancy to term. A possible concern, however, is that the surrogate mother who carries a child to term will usually develop an emotional attachment to the child, which cannot simply be ignored. The reverse situation is also possible: a woman is able to carry a child, but has no eggs of her own. Should egg donation by a third party (or sperm donation, in case the male partner is infertile) be permitted in such cases? Moreover, there are isolated attempts at using ART on women who are already past child-bearing age. As a rule, gynaecologists are sceptical towards such endeavours, if only for medical reasons. The different possibilities of IVF, in particular the admittance of homosexual couples, egg and sperm donation and surrogacy, were the subjects of lively bioethical discussions in the 1980s. Since most countries established laws that restrict IVF to married couples and prohibit surrogacy, these issues are no longer widely discussed. Only the entitlement of homosexuals to IVF still plays a certain role. In several countries, there are debates on whether reproductive medicine should be publicly funded and, if so, how many procedures should be paid for. For a few years now the possibility of intracytoplasmatic sperm injections (ICSI) has been discussed. In this kind of fertility treatment, there is no detour through fertilisation *in vitro*; the sperm is injected directly into the egg. ICSI can achieve fertilisation in cases where IVF is ineffective because of low sperm quality. It is repeatedly argued, however, that this procedure is likely to result in a higher number of birth defects.

These debates are also concerned with risks for the embryo, although these can be very uncertain, particularly in relation to ICSI. The question of whether ART opportunities should be publicly funded in turn raises the question of whether infertility should be understood as a disease. Does reproductive medicine belong in the domain of medical treatment available as standard, or is it rather similar to cosmetic surgery? (On the notion of disease see 4.1.6). Defences of IVF against Catholic-conservative objections often appeal to the crude comparison between doctors who want to help couples conceive a child, and conservative critics who try to prohibit this. This presentation is a little unappreciative of the fact that IVF treatments are very burdensome procedures whose success is far from certain. However, it should be pointed out that it is up to couples themselves to decide what treatment they elect to undergo, as long as they are sufficiently informed. The success rate and burden of the procedure become relevant only in relation to the question of how much effort in developing this technology is reasonable. It would be too crude simply to respond to all objections by saying that the point is to help couples conceive a child.

4.1.4.2 Research on embryos

An entirely different discussion emerges from the question of the research perspectives gained from the creation of embryos in IVF procedures. It should be noted that it is possible to freeze eggs after they have been fertilised *in vitro* (cryopreservation) in order to save them for later use. In addition, IVF treatment often results in so-called spare embryos. Since it is common for multiple courses of IVF treatment to be necessary, and since harvesting eggs is a very burdensome procedure, it is not uncommon that more eggs are fertilised during the first treatment cycle than are required for that attempt itself. The excess embryos can be frozen and used for later attempts. This practice is common in several countries, though other countries have embryo protection laws that prohibit this. Even in those countries excess embryos may exist, however, for instance because couples decide not to go through with the treatment between the fertilisation *in vitro* and the transfer of the embryo.

This reveals the complex interrelation of IVF and research on and with human embryos. These opportunities for research on embryos only exist because of IVF. The development and improvement of IVF were also important reasons for such research, at least in the early days of IVF. In general, this research is considered in need of strict regulations. In a number of countries, research on embryos is entirely prohibited. In the UK, any research on human embryos must be submitted for approval by the Human Fertilisation and Embryology Authority (HFEA). This means that UK law still attributes a certain value to the embryo that creates the need for regulation. However, for many people the fact that embryos from IVF are redundant changes the situation. These embryos are not created especially for research purposes; they are already there. When they are no longer needed for IVF, they are destroyed. This means that, on the one hand, the creation of excess embryos is legitimated by reproductive technology yet, on the other hand, their existence is used to justify their appropriation for research purposes.

In light of our deliberations on moral status (see above), a number of aspects of this situation call for further discussion. I have tried to show that utilitarianism and contractualism provide very few grounds for taking embryos to have fundamental worth. The fact that almost all laws assume that research on embryos needs to be regulated seems to call for explanation. It is astonishing, for instance, that attempts to ground a moral status for embryos, such as the potentiality argument, are straightforwardly rejected while, at the same time, laws are demanded that restrict research on embryos. The British arrangement of compulsive authorisation by a legislator also assumes that the embryo does have some moral value. Alternatively, all regulations for embryo protection should be viewed as purely political compromises that only serve to pacify the conservative (with a small c) electorate.

An approach that takes a human being to be dignified from the moment of fertilisation may well find that both the creation of excess embryos and research on embryos should be outlawed. If, on the other hand, one assumes that only persons have moral status, then restrictions on such research would be fundamentally morally problematic. It is entirely unclear, then, why research should be limited to spare embryos. And if one takes a gradualist position and assumes that embryos have a lesser moral status than persons, a number of follow-up questions are necessary. From a gradualist perspective, research on embryos could in some cases be justified; yet this seems to depend more on the status of the research goals than on the question of whether or not the embryo was left over from IVF. Why should the way in which an embryo was conceived be relevant to a concept of tiered protection at all? One argument lies in the fact that the acquirement of eggs is a burdensome procedure and one that is also risky for the female donor. The only argument I can see for the use of excess embryos as opposed to newly created ones would be that it can avoid burdening a woman with further donation, since the donor would already have decided on donation, on the basis of her desire to have a child. For gradualism, which is the only context in which this entire consideration is an issue in the first place, respect for the female donor and the question of the research aim would be the two pertinent factors.

The notion of 'gradualism' envelops a number of different conceptions of embryo protection, divided by the way in which they justify the entitlement to protection and by the scope of the protection demanded. One important approach makes a distinction in moral status between pre-embryos and embryos (Buckle 1988; Steigleder 1998). This distinction presupposes that, as potential persons, embryos are entitled to protection; otherwise the distinction with the pre-embryonic stadium would not be decisive. However, according to this line of argument, it can potentially be relevant, but only if there is an identity relation between the embryo and the later person. Such an identity is present in a foetus (although not in a sperm cell), but it is also *not yet* present directly after fertilisation. The zygote, that is, the cell immediately after the fusion of the egg and sperm cell, can still divide into multiple embryos, and divisions will also occur between the embryo and extra-embryonic structures such as the placenta. This means that I can not say about myself: 'I have been a zygote'. Rather, I should say: 'there was a zygote that brought about an embryo that I have been' (Steigleder 1998). Yet if the embryo's entitlement to protection depends on the presence of an identity relation between the embryo and the later person, this means the embryo does not yet have this status immediately after fertilisation.

However, if we take there to be no grounds for protection in the pre-embryonic phase, it would be unclear why there should be any regulation governing the first days after fertilisation. On this account, regulations would only become relevant after nidation. Since embryos can only survive in a human womb after the first days, embryo protection laws regulating the period before implantation would be pointless, except perhaps for the prevention of certain specific ways in which embryos could be used. It is possible that one might want to prevent reproductive cloning and the creation of human-animal chimeras. Keeping tabs on the use of embryos in the first 14 days would then be required not because we attach a moral value to the embryo itself, but only to check that no experiments take place that will lead to usages we consider morally objectionable. The effort of a procedural regulation for this purpose would no doubt be in vain, however. The undesirable experiments and usages (such as reproductive cloning and the creation of chimeras) could after all be simply prohibited, and the entire domain left unregulated in other respects.

If, however, one takes a gradualist approach, on which an embryo is entitled to protection from the moment of conception even if it does not yet have full moral status, it would be relevant what the embryo was going to be used for. What is the good that is weighed against the embryo's entitlement to protection? In this context, abortion is often used as a parallel case. In the case of abortion, the moral goods at issue are connected to the moral entitlements of a pregnant woman, that is, to the goods of a person. If the embryo owes its entitlement to protection to its potential personhood, it does not seem implausible that the rights of an actual person outweigh this entitlement. In the situation of a desired abortion, however, there is a direct conflict. The embryo lives inside the pregnant woman and is part of her body. This is fundamentally different from the situation of research on embryos, where protection of the embryo is weighed against mostly non-personal research aims. It does seem reasonably clear, however, that in the context of gradualism the legitimacy of a particular research project can only be assessed on the basis of the legitimacy of its research aims.

4.1.4.3 Embryonic stem cells

Of the research areas in this context, research on embryonic stem cells and cloning have attracted particular public attention. Embryonic stem cells are won shortly after fertilisation from the blastocyst. Yet it is also possible to obtain stem cell lines from aborted embryos, whose behaviour is similar to that of embryonic stem cells. Stem cells are assumed to be no longer totipotent; it is no longer possible for them to develop into a human. They are, however, exceptionally plastic and can still develop into different organs and tissues. Moreover, stem cells can be obtained not only from blastocysts and embryos, but also from the cells of adults – so-called 'adult stem cells'. It is expected that stem cell research will discover means of replacing the neurons that are no longer produced by the bodies of those with neurodegenerative diseases such as Alzheimer's and Parkinson's. For the longer term, it is hoped that stem cells can be developed into more complex human organs that can then be used for transplants. At the moment, however, clinical implementations are still a long way off. An advantage of adult stem cells is that they can be gathered from the cells of the patient himself, which ensures optimal compatibility for the new organ or tissue. Embryonic stem cells, on the other hand, are particularly interesting because they are still plastic enough to allow being developed into different kinds of tissue. It is hard to say how realistic current research perspectives are. Since research on stem cells is still only in its very first phase, relatively few stem cells are needed. Some researchers do question, however, whether the current level of research requires the use of embryonic stem cells at all. If the purpose of the research is merely to study the basic mechanisms and behaviour of stem cells, research on animal or adult stem cells would suffice. A very different perspective emerges if stem cell lines can be patented (Schneider 2006; also, on ethical aspects of patenting Beyleveld and Brownsword 2001: 195–218). Since the possibility of patenting embryonic stem cells creates legally relevant conditions on the future use of research outcomes, it seems important for researchers that they start research on their own stem cell lines early. If research on embryonic stem cells (which could be performed with adult cells as well) were conducted only for the sake of patenting, this would be a reason for a moral critique of patent law for approaches that take a zygote to have some (even if only low-level) entitlement to protection. Such a criticism would also be called for on the basis of the risks to which egg donors are exposed.

4.1.4.4 Cloning

Heated debates are also held on *cloning* (Humber and Almeder 1998; Kitcher 1997; Pence 2002). The birth of a cloned sheep evoked a worldwide discussion. In Dolly's case, the fusion of the DNA of the egg and sperm cells that usually occurs during fertilisation was bypassed. Instead, the DNA of a somatic cell was inserted into an enucleated egg cell. This led to the birth of a new sheep that was genetically identical to the sheep whose DNA was used. Researchers had not expected this to be possible. Nonetheless, Dolly's birth required a large number of attempts. Fairly soon, this was followed by a debate on the possibility of using this technique for cloning a human being who would be genetically identical to his 'original'. This so-called 'reproductive' cloning met with popular outrage, and there were initiatives that tried to enforce a global ban on the practice. Scenarios of the cloning of particularly gifted persons or children that could replace a deceased child evoked widespread repudiation. Many noted that the discussion became permeated with a strange genetic reductionism: most people seemed to take for granted that the reproduction of a genetically identical human being would also reproduce the initial person's characteristics and qualities. Cloning Boris Becker would mean the creation of a new Wimbledon champion. In actuality, it is far from certain that a cloned Becker could play tennis. Irrespective of the unrealistic expectations of the possibility of cloning some more Einsteins, however, the existence of a clone carries a considerable burden. In cloning, a creature is tailored to the needs of others in its entire genetic make-up. Aside from medical risks – which could be substantial – the question is what could justify such an experiment on a human being. The creation of humans as organ repositories for others (as depicted in the film *The Island*) would violate the clone's rights to a life of her own, for instance – although this is not an option that is taken seriously by anybody in the first place. What is frequently brought up is the possibility of creating a clone for a person who needs regenerative tissue. A frequently cited example is a child who needs a bone marrow donor and for whom there is no suitable donor amongst relatives. A cloned sibling would be the perfect donor. Since what is required is regenerative tissue, the clone is unlikely to be harmed by the donation and, afterwards, it could simply grow up as a (younger) twin. No objections could be had against this, since twins occur naturally too. The fact that even identical twins exist naturally is supposed to prove the harmlessness of such a procedure. From a moral point of view, however, there certainly is a difference between naturally occurring twins and twins that are born on the basis of human decisions. Only the latter situation raises questions of responsibility in the first place. At least in the first few attempts, moreover, the entire operation would pose a considerable risk for the clone, since it is unclear whether we even have command of the technology. Furthermore, the very fact of the psychological burden on the person whose biological make-up is fully dependent on the intentions of others calls for legitimation. Habermas has argued that this would introduce a problematic dependency into the biological lottery, since the parent generation takes decisions on the genetic constitution of the generation of their children, which creates an irreversible bias in the relation between generations (Habermas 2001/2003). While Habermas's argument has a number of weaknesses (see Chapter 3), he certainly makes a relevant point regarding the possibility of a dependency relation between generations.

It is worth noting that – if we can go by the presence of the issue in films and literature – almost no area of recent technological research has triggered people's imagination as much as reproductive cloning. The debate on reproductive cloning that followed the birth of Dolly seems to have influenced people's imagination quite extensively, and the expectation of potential threats posed by biomedicine was also determined to an important degree by the possibilities of reproductive cloning. This has led to the emergence of a domain of imagined meanings, fears and expectations that forms a reference point for the public debate on the life sciences. In a way, debates on biomedicine are held against the background of conceptions that were shaped by the notion of cloning. A cover of the German newspaper *Der Spiegel* with cloned versions of Claudia Schiffer, Albert Einstein and Adolf Hitler certainly had a massive influence on the public debate. However, this also has the effect that these technologies will strike people as morally unobjectionable as soon as it is clear that the applications will be much more innocent than cloning Adolf Hitler. What is remarkable about this is not so much the fact that the public debate has focused on cloning to this extent, but even more that the academic community – philosophers first – has gone along with this hype. Especially philosophers who never had any interest in bioethical questions all of a sudden reckoned that they should proclaim their insights on cloning. As philosophy appears to the public, it has simply accepted that reproductive cloning is the decisive issue of bioethics, without making any effort to understand the broader context of these discussions.

For the rest of the debate, the introduction between 'reproductive' and 'therapeutic' cloning has been essential.[3] The expectation is that cloning techniques will at some point allow the reproduction of cells and tissue that people with certain diseases no longer produce themselves. In that way, cloning could make therapies for neurodegenerative diseases available. However, there are doubts whether the distinction between 'reproductive' and 'therapeutic' cloning is conceptually apt (Schneider 2006). On the one hand, the criticism is that the therapeutic possibility is still only a hope, and that the likelihood of its realisation is still uncertain. Moreover, since research is still in the very early fundamental stages it is very tricky to distinguish different applications of cloning. How far-reaching such criticisms are can be debated, yet in light of the current level of knowledge, it would be appropriate to speak of 'research clones'.

Apart from this, the relevant questions are the same as those that apply to research on embryonic stem cells. Does the current state of research legitimate research on embryos? Could the expected knowledge gain be realised with animal experiments or the use of adult cells? These questions are relevant for any approach that ascribes human embryos a modest moral status. For approaches that take embryos to be entitled to the same protection as persons, this kind of research would not be a morally legitimate option at all. And for those who take embryos to have no moral value at all the only relevant consideration would lie in the risks the embryo donors are exposed to. In the latter case, the use of spare embryos from IVF would indeed be a full and adequate solution.

For a gradualist conception, the goods against which the protection of the embryo is weighed would be relevant as well. A gradualist position does not take the value of the embryo to be principally inviolable. The question is what is on the other side of the balance. In the case of abortion, there are goods at issue that are connected to the pregnant person who carries the embryo. In the case of embryo research, these goods are abstract, and it is very difficult to make the conflict concrete. At stake are therapeutic research outlooks. Yet whether these will ever materialise is entirely unknown. Now it is a universal characteristic of research that it cannot be known where it will lead and whether it will result in anything at all. Yet it is clear that the deliberation is not: embryo protection versus the ethics of healing and helping. Rather, the other side involves *hopes and expectations regarding possible cures*.

3 This distinction was first introduced in Opinion no 9 'Ethical Aspects of Cloning Techniques' of the European Group of Advisors to the European Commission on the Ethical Implications of Biotechnology of 28 May 1997.

The very least such an approach will have to demand is a confirmation of the researchers that their aims cannot be realised in any other way. In this respect, another specific question arises. Animal protection committees routinely demand that animal experiments be replaced by alternative methods as much as possible. That means that researchers applying for animal experiments will *also* have to show that their particular research aim cannot be arrived at by any other method. The question is, then, how these two demands would have to be weighed against each other. Our deliberations so far (especially Chapter 3) should have already made it quite clear that every ethical theory will come up with a different answer to this question.

4.1.4.5 Chimeras and hybrids[4]

To conclude, I want to bring up the research on *human-animal chimeras*, which currently is a much-debated issue (Badura-Lotter and Düwell 2009; Fiester and Düwell 2009). Biologically, a distinction is made between hybrids – composite beings that develop from an egg cell, but combine properties of different species, such as mules – and chimeras, which are composite beings that have cells of different genotypes. For the ethical discussion, however, this distinction has only limited significance. In relation to this research area, one should not imagine the creation of centaurs or humans with pig heads. Rather, this research spans the full range of cases in which boundaries between animals and humans are crossed – from studies of individual cells to the level of entire organs and embryos. These projects usually take place under laboratory conditions, but they could in principle lead to the breeding of hybrids or chimeras. Studies on composite organisms are motivated by a wide variety of goals. Their aim could be to examine the functioning of human neurons in more detail. In this case, the creation of animals with human cells would be primarily motivated by the desire not to perform the research on humans or human tissues. Other types of research, however, explicitly study the interactions between human and animal cells and organs, for instance in order to gain knowledge relevant to the development of xenotransplantation. Further goals are of a directly therapeutic nature, such as the insertion of human cells into certain kinds of animals in order to trigger the production of therapeutically important chemicals (such as insulin) in these animals. It is also conceivable that animal tissue would be used in humans for the improvement of qualities that tend to be less developed in the species *Homo sapiens* than in certain other animal species.

4 My deliberations on this matter owe much to the research project *Chimbrids*, a European cooperation led by principal investigator Jochen Taupitz, which was concerned with biological, ethical and legal questions concerning the creation of human/animal chimeras and hybrids.

The debate on the regulation of the creation of such chimeras and hybrids is still very new. It seems immediately clear that the differences between normative theories will be directly relevant. Theories that start from animal rights or from the obligation to prevent animal suffering will take other questions to be pertinent rather than theories with different starting points. Some crucial questions are associated with risk and safety assessments. So far, we know very little about the way in which biological substances behave beyond the species boundary. In that sense, high standards of security should be observed. The discussion, however, does not differ significantly from the debate on xenotransplantation (see the 2003 statement on xenotransplantation of the Council of Europe). As soon as the creation of embryos is at stake, the range of arguments and standpoints that are generally relevant to research on embryos will apply here as well. Yet beyond these general considerations, any case of a composite embryo being carried to term will be an experiment of which the outcome is largely uncertain – a situation that raises its own set of fundamental questions. The use of animal tissue in humans for therapeutic purposes also evokes the question of whether there is a danger that the procedure will alter the mental characteristics or appearance of the test subject. But what are the essential properties of human beings which it would be morally irresponsible to change? The answer to that question does not seem so hard when it comes to the capacity for agency as a fundamental human faculty. But how about further characteristics of human beings, for instance those connected with our external appearance? If the creation of chimeras were to disclose therapeutic opportunities, would it be justified to use these treatments if they involved a risk of the patient's appearance changing? The question is whether the basic external appearance of people, which depends on contingent biological factors, may be changed. This question goes beyond concerns about the risks and safety of such procedures, even though the latter could at the moment be a decisive objection. Philosophically, it will be very hard to justify demands that the outward appearance of humans be 'unchangeable'. Still, one's appearance both influences the possibility of developing a stable personal identity and the formation of social relations. In this respect, a human being's outward appearance has moral significance as the externally manifest symbolic expression of that person, and cannot be considered philosophically neutral.

All in all, it is clear that there are very fundamental issues that still need to be discussed. This debate is not trivial. All legal regulations and moral convictions, first of all, presuppose a conceptual distinction between 'human' and 'animal'. All regulations we have apply either to humans or to animals. With regard to the creation of embryos from human or animal tissue, for instance, there is an immediate question of what kind of regulation applies to these embryos. Do the legal guidelines on embryo protection apply here at all? Should we turn to animal protection acts? This discussion challenges the majority of bioethical regulations. In particular, a need for further conceptual differentiation arises from the fact that the notions 'human' and 'animal' are used on the one hand as biological concepts that indicate the biological origin of biological matter and, on the other, as concepts that indicate and assess mental or phenotypical properties of certain beings. From the former perspective, the notions are 'biological' species concepts; from the latter, they express value judgments. Research on hybrids and chimeras creates the philosophical necessity to clarify the interrelation of these notions in more detail.

4.1.5 Genetic diagnosis and gene therapy

It has already been shown that developments in human genetics have played a very important role in formulating the questions with which bioethics has occupied itself in the last three decades (Chadwick 2009; Resnik, Steinkraus and Langer 1999; Scott 2007). In the following sections, I shall attempt to give an overview of some relevant discussions. I am keenly aware, however, that it is not even remotely possible to do justice to the variety of discussions and debates.

4.1.5.1 Early genetic diagnosis

The possibility of prenatal diagnosis has existed since the 1980s. A sample of amniotic fluid allows physicians to test whether the embryo has any genetic abnormalities. Particular diagnostic techniques have continuously developed since that time. Given that the sampling of amniotic fluid is not without risk for the embryo, however, prenatal diagnosis is only performed if there is a significant known risk. As a rule, testing is done when the mother is of relatively advanced age, since statistically the probability of Down's syndrome increases with the age of the couple, or when there is a family history of genetic disability. In principle, it would of course be possible to test for all known genetic abnormalities. In practice, the only test that is usually done is chromosome analysis. A chromosome abnormality can lead to disabilities, and most embryos with such abnormalities are not viable. Trisomy 21 (Down's syndrome) is one of few chromosome abnormalities that do not interfere with the viability of the embryo. Genetic diagnoses, that is, testing for very concrete defects of individual genes is only carried out if the family history provides reason to suspect a genetic abnormality.

The ethical debate on prenatal diagnosis (PND) is concerned both with the effects of the technological possibilities *on the pregnant woman* and with the *perspective of the embryo*, that is, the children that will or indeed will not be born (Buchanan, et al. 2000; Alpern 1992; Baruch 1988; Bayles 1984; Brock 1992; Glover 1977; Harris 1992; Holm 1992; Hildt 1992; Mieth 1998; Holmes 1992; Overall 1987; Purdy 1989; Robertson 1994; Shenfield and Sureau 2006; Spallone and Steinberg 1989). Judgments of the effects on the *pregnant woman* differ greatly. On the one hand, it is emphasised that the possibility of prenatal diagnosis can alleviate the fear of giving birth to a disabled child, which, particularly in the case of women who are aware of a genetic 'risk', can be an important factor in the decision to have a child at all. Others stress that these diagnostic possibilities lead to ever more pregnancies being considered risky, and observe a considerable discrepancy between the heightened awareness of risk and the number of actual positive diagnoses. Moreover, most genetic abnormalities cannot be treated. The only option for a pregnant woman, then, is abortion. If she does not want this, there is usually no ground for conducting prenatal diagnosis, especially given the fact that the procedure involves risks for the embryo.

These reservations with regard to the pregnant woman herself are, however, hardly sufficient as arguments against PND. What they do make clear is that a positive moral valuation depends on several basic conditions. Besides due information, the point stressed most is that it ought not to be automatically assumed that the technology should be used, but that, instead, the possible ways of going forward are clarified before the diagnostic procedure is carried out. If abortion is not an option, this should be clear from the start. Another reason why informing the pregnant woman is not trivial is that the very interpretation of the medical results requires a translation from a biological state of affairs into her very personal situation. Genetic diagnosis can often only determine probabilities, and these are interpreted within an emotionally delicate context.

Since abortion is normally the only option in case of a negative outcome, the moral assessment of PND is based on all the arguments that were also pertinent in the discussion of abortion and the moral status of embryos (see Chapter 3). For strong gradualist standpoints – which take it that an embryo does not have full moral status from the start, but that it does have some moral status, which increases as it develops (after nidation, after the development of the brain, etc) – it could be relevant that abortion after PND often takes place at a very late stage. This perspective is sharpened as neonatal medicine becomes more developed and newborns can be kept alive from an ever younger age.

Moreover, the termination of pregnancy after PND stands in fundamental contrast to other cases of abortion when it comes to the underlying value judgment. While the decision of a pregnant woman who wants an abortion without diagnosis expresses the desire not to have a child (at this moment), the decision of the pregnant woman after prenatal diagnosis implies that she does indeed want to have a child (otherwise she would not have had the diagnostic procedure performed), but that she – for whatever reason – does not want *such* a child. It has been argued, therefore, that what is at stake here is a kind of selective treatment of disabled persons; that this situation is one in which people with disabilities are discriminated against (I have discussed the discrimination argument in Chapter 3). If one considers abortion fundamentally morally illegitimate in the first place, this argument is not of central importance. If, however, one considers abortion potentially morally legitimate, it can be significant whether PND is viewed as genuine selection on the basis of undesired qualities or as a relevant stigmatisation of a vulnerable social group. The accusation of selection is not only questionable in light of the association it evokes with Third Reich practices, but is also only sound if the embryo is ascribed full moral status. However, if the embryo does have full moral status, abortion is problematic in the first place, regardless of the accusation that a kind of selection is taking place. Bringing up stigmatisation seems completely reasonable to me, but the possibility of stigmatisation is not yet an argument against PND, since it must be weighed against the rights of the pregnant woman or the embryo/child.

A competing standpoint could be that a future child has a right not to be born with a severe genetic disease (Parfit 1984; Steigleder 2000). This argument presupposes, however, that a bearer of rights who does not yet exist has morally legitimate rights. In the context of the debate on the rights of future generations, such an assumption is not actually that rare. Yet this particular standpoint also presupposes that the future rights holder has a right not to exist in the first place. One could say that this argument at least assumes that the existence of the child comprises nothing but suffering (and even then, a corresponding right must still be argued for). An existence which consists only of suffering is an empirical borderline case, however, and is also confronted with conceptual difficulties. In order to ground a corresponding right, we would at least have to assume reflexivity to the extent that the child would experience its own existence as suffering. If such reflexivity is part of the child's existence, however, the question is whether that existence can then be said to comprise only suffering.

Yet even if the unborn child has no relevant right, it could still be the case that there is morally legitimate room for manoeuvre on the part of the pregnant woman (or couple) in which they can opt for abortion. An argument along such lines presupposes two things: on the one hand, the embryo does not yet have full moral status; on the other hand, the abortion does not take place on the basis of a right of the embryo or future child not to be born (or to have been born), but because the pregnant woman makes use of her right to decide against carrying the pregnancy to term. The basis for the moral legitimacy of the decision, then, is not the principled negative value judgment concerning a life with a particular disability, but respect for the pregnant woman's right to take a decision on the matter. This, I would say, is indeed a moral good and one that is fundamentally worthy of protection, even if there remain some doubts with regard to PND, such as those detailed above. If respect for the decision of the pregnant woman is the only reason for performing PND, then it is all the more important for the moral legitimacy of PND that the decision is informed and free of external pressures. The possible stigmatisation of persons with disabilities does remain a serious moral problem, even if it must be given a lower priority than the direct right of a person to make decisions about her own body.

Even when abortion after prenatal diagnosis seems morally defensible in principle, however, the problem remains that, ultimately, abortion is a burden and that abortions with PND involved will usually take place very late in the pregnancy. Many people therefore see a desirable alternative in pre-implantation genetic diagnosis (PGD), a technique that makes it possible to perform genetic testing before the start of the pregnancy. In PGD genetic diagnosis is carried out after an artificial fertilisation and, depending on the outcome, the fertilised egg is implanted or discarded. This technology has been employed since the early 1990s, although there are countries in which it is banned. Now the question is whether PGD is morally different from PND. Surely PGD is essentially an early form of PND faced with the same moral conflicts? It could be countered that there is a fundamental difference in the sense that in the case of abortion after PND there is a conflict between the woman's right to decide about her own body and the rights of the embryo, whereas in the case of PGD such a conflict does not yet exist, but is merely anticipated. If the justification for abortion is that in the case of a conflict the right of the pregnant woman has priority, the question is whether that conflict has already occurred here. If one is of the opinion that a newly fertilised egg has a lesser moral status than a more advanced embryo, however, this would be a consideration in favour of PGD.

Another question is whether this new technology will also come to produce other applications. In any case, PND is performed during pregnancy, and late-term abortion is a difficult procedure. PGD, on the other hand, is a form of diagnosis that can happen after longer deliberation and at a point in time that can be more or less freely chosen. Moreover, many people will feel different knowing that they have allowed a fertilised egg to be destroyed than having gone through a late-term abortion. Reports that, say, deaf parents or people of short stature desire PGD in order to ensure that their children will also be deaf or short may give an indication of the kind of conflicts that could arise. If the ground for the legitimacy of abortion is the decision of the couple, then nothing could be argued against their wish. If someone were to challenge their decision on the basis of the gravity of the disability or the belief that this would be unacceptable for the future child, then this would indeed comprise a stamp of disapproval. These are not disabilities that lead to nothing but unbearable suffering, but conditions that certainly do allow for a fulfilling life. If we are to develop a systematic argument to determine the limits on PGD instead of relying solely on casuistry, however, we would either need to base our indications on an uncontentious notion of severe disability or disease, which is unavailable (see earlier in this chapter), or compile a list of diseases that are legitimate grounds for abortion. Exactly such a list, however, is likely to hurt persons who have the relevant disabilities. For a complete moral assessment of PGD, then, it would be important to have an idea of the possible future applications to which it could give rise.

4.1.5.2 Postnatal genetic diagnosis

Prenatal diagnosis has attracted considerable attention in bioethics. Yet there is also an ever-increasing list of genetic disorders that can be diagnosed after birth. The nature of the corresponding diagnoses varies, of course, depending on when the testing takes place and the nature of the disorder tested for. I will only be able to address a few points in a very schematic manner.

Genetic diagnosis differs from other kinds of diagnosis in that what is established is not the presence of a disease, but the *probability* that a disease will occur. Of course, it is also possible for genetic diagnosis to detect a disease that is already present, for example when it is used to clarify the outcome of some other test. The typical case, however, is the determination of the *risk* that a disease will occur. Relevant questions, then, are why one would want to have this knowledge, how the information is interpreted and what is done with the knowledge. These questions come to a head in the case of diagnoses on children or on people who already have disorders, or if the knowledge gained allows for conclusions about the genetic constitutions of their relatives.

The first distinction we can make in this context is between genetic disorders that are *treatable* and those that are *not treatable*. In the case of a disease that can be treated, or for which preventive measures are available that can stop or delay its onset or slow down its progress, the benefit of a diagnosis is that such medical interventions are made possible. If the disease tested for is not treatable, however, it is much more difficult to see what good a diagnosis does. Many genetic tests merely offer information on probability that a certain disease will occur (how am I helped by the knowledge that I have such-and-such a risk of developing breast cancer?). A different situation covers genetic disorders that are incurable, but that only present later in life, such as Huntington's disease. If someone undergoes testing because of a family history, a negative outcome can liberate him from profound anxieties. A positive outcome, in contrast, can allow him to plan his life and family matters accordingly, but it can also lead to profound changes. The person might come to view himself from the perspective of his future disease. What makes genetic tests unusual is the fact that they do not indicate the presence of a disease, but a disposition for it. This can lead the person affected to see himself as a potentially sick person. It is often emphasised that the particularity of this kind of diagnosis requires that the patient be provided with very thorough information and counselling. Correspondingly, the moral assessment of such technologies depends on the question of whether such information can be guaranteed.

Yet there are some aspects that cannot be evaluated solely in the light of informed consent. One result of the debate on genetic testing, for instance, is the notion of a '*right not to know*' (Chadwick, Levitt and Shickle 1998). Basically, this right entails that no patient be forced to receive information about her own genetic constitution that she does not wish to have. This can be a problem if someone wants to submit himself to tests that make it possible to draw conclusions about the genetic constitution of close relatives. Another problematic context concerns the *confidentiality of genetic data*. The diagnosis of a genetic disposition for Huntington's disease is likely to be of considerable interest to both potential employers and insurance companies. It is not hard to imagine insurance companies even demanding genetic testing in some cases. This would mean that a patient's genetic disposition would not only have a profound impact on her chances in life in a biological respect, but that knowledge of the genetic disposition would also lead to numerous social restrictions to her development. Ethically, it can of course be asked whether the community has a legitimate claim to the information that is, in principle, available. Does this situation entail a conflict between legitimate collective interests and the protection of the privacy of an individual? The widespread cynicism about human genetics could be due to the fact that technological possibilities are developed that invade people's privacy and result in deep public control over people's biological constitution. Michel Foucault's notion of 'biopower' seems apt in this context. An ethical critique of a display of genetic data that is so generally accessible presupposes a theory of individual rights that fundamentally protects the rights to this kind of information.

In practice, however, it is very hard to realise the protection of genetic data and the guarantee that only the individual herself can have access to the genetic information that applies to her. In the context of the discussion of informed consent, two concrete debates were highlighted (see the beginning of this chapter): the establishment of *genetic databases* for research purposes and the practice of *genetic screening*. In both situations, it is very hard to ensure informed consent. Data stored in genetic databases could be anonymised to a high degree – something that is obviously not an option for genetic screening. In the case of neonatal screening, there are dispositions that present strong reasons in favour of being informed early on. If we suppose for a moment that information is given only in uncontroversial cases (a condition that is not necessarily always met in practice), it is still clear that routine screening as such requires restraints on informed consent. It is practically impossible to carry out such screening in any other way. Even if there are many reasons to consider this practice morally acceptable or even required, the examples show how difficult it will become to arrange genetic testing in such a way that the relevant information is only disclosed to those directly affected, and that even they are informed only if they wish to be. The right not to know thus becomes central to the debate. The fact that the availability of genetic information makes the person concerned exceptionally vulnerable is beyond question.

4.1.5.3 Gene therapy

From the very beginning of the human genome project the hope has been that, in addition to diagnostic functions, gene therapies could also be developed. Such therapies would consist in the introduction of a gene into cells in order to compensate for an absent or malfunctioning gene of that cell. In general, two types are distinguished: somatic gene therapy and germ line gene therapy. While in somatic gene therapy the intervention is restricted to the body of the individual patient, germ line gene therapy aims to alter a human germ cell, which means that it can directly influence the genetic constitution of offspring and future generations. Somatic gene therapy has already claimed its first successes. The ethical debate is primarily concerned with questions of risk assessment and controllability. The question would be, however, to what extent successful application of somatic gene therapy necessarily presupposes *genetic determinism* – that is, the notion of a causal relation between the genetic and phenotypical level which biologists now generally consider too simple. However, if genes do not work in such a way that a specific intervention at the genetic level can establish a precise localisable effect at the phenotypical level, so that we need cybernetic and systematic models in order to understand the ways genes function, then it seems difficult to carry out targeted therapeutic interventions while eliminating corresponding risks. However, under certain restrictions this has been done successfully in the domain of somatic therapy.

Germ line gene therapy has been met with more deep-seated reservations. The very attempt to alter the human germ line seems fundamentally immoral. In the meantime, the debate has seen statements that assume the inviolability of germ cells. Yet even if such mystification of the germ cell is barely credible, strong reservations remain. On the one hand, this technology establishes extremely far-reaching possibilities for intervening in the genetic constitution of offspring. This dramatically heightens the standards for dealing with these opportunities responsibly. One could also wonder whether people should be allowed to make such profound decisions on the physical appearance of others at all. In addition, there are significant concerns regarding risk. Since it will only be possible to say something about the success of germ line interventions after a human being has been produced by this method, this therapy involves an experiment on human beings that cannot be justified by any of our current standards.

4.1.6 Disease, enhancement and the aims of medicine

By expanding the scope of traditional medicine, biomedicine not only creates new opportunities for diagnosis, prevention and therapy, but also sparks a re-evaluation of the very concept of disease (on enhancement see Agar 2002, 2004 and 2010; Fukuyama 2002; Harris 1992, 1998 and 2007; Miah 2004; Parens 2006). In the traditional self-understanding of medicine, it was taken for granted that the notion of disease was central. Quite a few people now consider that notion so weak that they propose jettisoning it altogether. What is at stake, however, is not a mere terminological detail. The real issue is that technological advances have allowed medicine to take up new tasks, some of which are even diametrically opposed to its classical self-image. This is the context of the debate on enhancement, touched on previously in the Introduction to this book. On the basis of these discussions, we can address in a nutshell some issues that clarify the interconnections between biomedical technology, medical practice, ethics and anthropology (Boorse 1977; Caplan, McCartney and Sisti 2004).

4.1.6.1 Notions of illness and disease

In the context of human genetics there is a distance between the possibility of *describing someone as 'sick'* and the *subjective experience of the person affected*. Genetic diagnosis makes it possible to diagnose people as '*sick*' even if they have no symptoms or complaints whatsoever. It is possible, for instance, to diagnose genetic constellations that either will lead to a manifest disease in the distant future, or express an increased probability that a particular disease will develop. Through early genetic diagnosis it is possible to diagnose a fertilised egg before it is even implanted, and say something about the disposition for disease of a person who will exist only if the egg is in fact implanted.

In addition, we can now diagnose or treat conditions that traditionally were not even understood as diseases, or whose *clinical significance* is at least contentious. Some people wonder to what extent infertility is a disease; and small breasts most certainly were not viewed as pathological throughout history. A sex change remedies a person's suffering caused by their gender, although this does not necessarily mean that being male or female is therefore declared a disease, even so genderdysforie is recognized as a disease. Yet if such treatments are part of the kind of thing that medicine is expected to do, then why should not the medical domain as a whole be justified on the basis of the fact that it fulfils people's wishes regarding their bodies? If this is what medicine is for, however, there might perhaps be reasons to permit the institutionalisation of this kind of wish-fulfilling practice, yet it is unclear why such a health care system and the research supporting it should be publicly funded. The considerable amount of public funds supporting medicine and compulsory health insurance could not be justified if what they funded were mere political priorities that were ultimately based on the personal preferences of individual persons.

Yet there have also been moral arguments that relativise the significance of the notion of disease. As discussed at the beginning of this chapter medical ethics instigated protection of the patient against undesired medical treatment, initially through informed consent and later through the notion of *patient autonomy*. These developments mitigated the legitimising function of the notion of disease. Medicine is still concerned with the treatment of disease, but when it comes to legitimatisation the patient's will has gained normative priority. Is it not sufficient, then, to ask the patient what treatment he desires, regardless of whether there is a disease or not?

However, these debates seem to relate predominantly to borderline cases in which it is unclear what 'disease' means (in the context of human genetics or wish-fulfilling medicine, say). In everyday life, we still seem to know exactly what diseases are. If I have a fever, a headache or a cold, there is no doubt that I am ill. Surely we should start from such 'clear' and 'unambiguous' cases in order to establish what disease is? In any case we have reasons to expect that a robust notion of disease is possible. The following models suggest themselves:

According to a *scientific model*, diseases must be described as *physical functional disorders*, explained and treated by scientific means. This model is usually thought to lack complexity, even if it is hard to shed the impression that, in practice, medicine does indeed understand itself as 'applied science'. It is in fact possible to describe and explain certain mechanisms of the human body in a scientific way and to predict the consequences of treatment. It could be pointed out, however, that the scientific model has not thereby justified describing a certain condition as disease. Calling something a disease always implies a value judgment. The causes of a rise in body temperature can be scientifically explained, but if this altered condition is called a disease, that is a value judgment. Similarly, the assertion that this condition should be changed – that diseases should be cured – is not the result of a scientific description, but a value-driven conclusion.

Instead of relying on the explanations of a scientific model, disease can be interpreted on the basis of the *subjective experiences of the person affected*. This kind of phenomenological or psychosocial conception considers the subjective experience of the individual the ultimate reference point for understanding disease. Either I am ill or, conversely, if I am perfectly capable of living with a certain aberrancy, I am not sick. There are plenty of noticeable physical irregularities or dysfunctions that need not interfere with one living one's life. A weak sense of smell, for instance, can prove to be a great advantage in many situations. Others can suffer under the lack of a sense of smell to such an extent that the disorder has a severe impact on their lives. A subject-centred notion of disease makes it possible to take the emotional and social causes of a disease into account, instead of reducing it to its biological causes. This would make 'disease' ultimately dependent on the subjective interpretation of the person affected, which is likely to be influenced by culturally dominant norms. One could argue, however, that such a conception of sickness is not very useful in the context of medicine and medical ethics, since it does not allow for a systematic interpretation of the connection between the subjective experience of illness and the doctor's diagnostic access, which is based on the patient's objective physical condition.

A particularly broad notion of disease can be found in the constitution of the World Health Organization, which defines 'health' as a 'state of complete physical, mental and social well-being' and 'sickness' as the absence of this state. On the one hand, this broad definition was appreciated as not simply reducing disease to physical disorders, and taking into account mental and social factors. At the same time, however, the notion is so broad that very few people could call themselves unreservedly healthy. And if the battle against diseases is the task of medicine, there would hardly be an area of life for which medicine would not be responsible. It would basically have to battle all ecological and social reasons for the lack of such well-being. The result would be a truly all-embracing medicalisation.

If we take it that disease cannot be biologically determined without presupposing value judgments, yet that crudely drawing on subjective and social factors makes the entire concept unworkable, the question arises whether the notion of disease is not simply replaceable or dispensable. A *terminological replacement* with the notion of the 'medically necessary' does not help, since the difficulties that arise in relation to the question of what is necessary are no different than those relevant to disease. The notion of 'medical usefulness' also only says something about whether certain medical actions are appropriate for the realisation of certain aims, but does not contribute to an assessment of the aims themselves. It seems that a terminological replacement cannot fill in the blank contained in the notion of disease regarding the legitimation of medical acts.

4.1.6.2 Medicine without a notion of disease?

Could *dispensing with the notion of disease altogether* be an appropriate alternative? Perhaps the legitimation of therapeutic treatments, the way health care is financed and political decisions concerning health could be discussed in a different way. A pragmatic legitimation for the concrete actions of a physician could be, for instance, that anything a doctor does must be related to physical disorders, since that is what she is competent to do, and that her actions are only legitimated by the wishes of her patients. Political decisions on health are legitimated by being taken by a majority or by parliamentary representatives, who also decide whether and to what extent health care should be publicly funded. In such a system, changing norms and values in society influence the organisation of the health care system. Restrictions to the way health care is arranged only arise from the general legal limits to what citizens are allowed to do: female circumcision, for instance, would have to be considered a great bodily harm, but this would be true because of general moral and legal protective measures, not specifically in the light of any restrictions that arise from the definition of the task of medicine.

Thinking along these lines would result in a profound demoralisation of the entire domain of medicine. There would be questions, however, about the role of minorities and the use of public funds. It seems rather unlikely, for instance, that a majority would decide in favour of public funding for therapies and medication for the treatment of rare diseases that they have no reason to fear for themselves. We all have to face up to the possibility that we will at some point be affected by cancer, Parkinson's or Alzheimer's disease. Regarding many hereditary diseases, however, there is no real reason to be concerned. If the only moral legitimation for the development of diagnostic and therapeutic instruments lies in the majority decision, nothing could be morally held against the majority deciding against developing such treatments. A much more basic question would be why, on such an approach, the state would be involved with medicine (educating doctors, maintaining public health care) at all. If medicine has no moral legitimation, the only thing left is an instrumental legitimation in the sense of a contractualism, for which the task of the state is to guarantee its citizens fundamental security and to facilitate the realisation of freely chosen goals. For the state, then, health care would be restricted to, say, the prevention of epidemics and the provision of basic medical care to citizens who are confronted with unexpected physical problems (heart attack, traffic accident). All further medical opportunities, however, are associated with so many decisions about balancing financial cost and improved security that it does not seem it should be the task of the state to take those decisions on behalf of its citizens. It would be much more logical for civil society to permit voluntary organisation of medicine. State funding of health care and medical research could then be significantly more economical. This proposal raises all the same questions that are inherently connected with contract theories (see Chapter 2). In this context, the only thing that should be added is that such a demoralisation of medicine on the basis of an instrumental contractualism would also remove the grounds for any international involvement in health matters.

This kind of extensive demoralisation of medicine is not plausible, however, since there are certain tasks of medicine that have to do with supporting people in a very fundamental way to lead independent, autonomous lives. One intuition along these lines could be: if a person suffers from a severe but treatable physical disorder, it is a moral obligation to offer him the kind of treatment that will allow him to lead a self-determined life. If it is not considered a moral task of society and the state to help people in this regard, the next question would be why the state would need to provide education. Of course even that could be challenged by a radical libertarian, but if that is the case, the reasons for a demoralisation of medicine are not specific to medicine, but are reflections of deep-seated moral convictions.

The notion of disease (or a terminological equivalent) also seems dispensable in many versions of utilitarianism. If the morally preferable option is the action or arrangement that maximises everybody's chances of realising a successful life, the most important question would be how we can establish equal international access to available resources. Much less important, however, is the question of how the associated state expenditure can be cut down. Also less important is whether what is at issue are treatments of disease or other ways of improving well-being. A question that would be central for utilitarian is how a health care system can balance different priorities. Relevant for the answer to that question is the influence of different treatments of a person's well-being, and not so much whether the treatment is a treatment of a disease.

4.1.6.3 Species-typical functioning

An important proposal for an alternative to the traditional notion of disease is provided by Norman Daniels. He defined health as the possibility of 'species-typical functioning' (also 'normal species functioning' and other variations; Daniels 1985: 19ff). In this approach, health is present when a person can realise those capacities that members of the human species normally have – the relevant 'norm' depending on factors such as age and geographical location. This notion has a scientific component, since the list of typical ways of functioning can be described from a biological standpoint. Yet the notion also leaves room for taking subjective interpretations into account. Physical abnormalities can influence individuals' functioning in any number of ways. Daniels's conception acknowledges that health and disease are value-laden notions but, at the same time, he tries to employ the idea that certain conditions can be typical for a species to show that these values are not arbitrary. His conception is also practical, since it does not identify people in an anthropologically comprehensive manner as healthy or sick, but provides a notion of disease that is directly relevant to the legitimation of a health care system. Health care should be provided to such an extent that a life typical for the human species is possible. This involves more than minimal funding for basic health care, and yet it does not open the floodgates to all kinds of wish-fulfilling medicine.

Nonetheless, the proposal has been criticised from several quarters. Representatives of the disability movement fear that the emphasis on species-typical functioning does not do justice to persons with disabilities, who, after all, function in atypical ways (Silvers 1998). Daniels's notion takes the anthropology of a physically healthy human being and turns it into a model for all. So-called 'transhumanists', in contrast, criticise the restriction to the typical biological possibilities of the species (Bostrom 2005; Buchanan 2011; Gordijn and Chadwick 2010; Savulescu and Bostrom 2011). Why shouldn't human beings take advantage of medical possibilities to broaden the range of ways to live and act? Do we not have a moral obligation to improve the opportunities of the human species?

So far, the transhumanists have not bothered to offer a developed moral-philosophical theory in support of their claims. Nor does a proper theoretical basis underlie the proposal to improve the collective performance of our species. In any case, neither of the two criticisms quite arrives at the heart of Daniels's theory. His point is not to establish a fixed anthropology. He proposes no comprehensive descriptions of human functioning and successful living. Rather, the point of his approach is to determine, in a situation of sparse resources, what kind of health care should be available to everyone in a just society. Along the lines of Rawls's theory of justice, this would be health care that we would make available from an impartial standpoint, and since in the light of our biological-physical constitution we have our species membership in common, this is the reference point for Daniels's identification. From the perspective of justice, it is fair to make this kind of functioning possible for everyone. This averts both radical negative forms of liberalism and utilitarian demands for maximisation.

The advantage of Daniels's restriction to a criterion for the just distribution of resources is that his approach will strike many as plausible, which explains the resonance of his book. Still, the moral relevance of his conception has not really been demonstrated. The libertarian proposal of restricting publicly funded health care has thus not been countered. And the objection that Daniels's approach is based on a latently discriminatory anthropology cannot be dismissed. The concept seems most fitting for answering questions that transcend the context of the distribution of available resources. The critiques of the transhumanists (and Silvers) make clear that what is at stake in the legitimation of the domain of medicine is not only the distribution of available resources, but the delineation of the domain itself, and the fact that many substantial moral-philosophical questions are associated with the development of new medical possibilities. These questions, however, clearly go beyond the matter of distributive justice.

4.1.6.4 A normative notion of disease

Now one could try to develop a notion of disease that has a stronger normative component in order to avoid some of the problems Daniels faces. Such a notion could acknowledge that disease is essentially a value-laden concept that cannot be identified with medical instruments only. Nevertheless, this kind of evaluative interpretation of disease would not necessarily result in a situation where any specifications could only be conceived as pragmatic moves in political negotiation processes. Rather, one could accept that normative claims will be part of the discourse on disease. Medicine would then not be primarily about the question of whether a patient is sick in an objective sense, but rather about the question of whether the patient shows that she is entitled to some kind of support. The patient's moral right concerns – insofar as she turns to medicine for support – physical dysfunctions, for this is the only thing for which she can expect to gain medical support. Yet the normative basis for granting her this support has to do with moral entitlements. Monika Bobbert has reconstructed these entitlements in the context of a conception of human dignity that was discussed in Chapter 2. According to this conception, the normative implications of human dignity are that we should ensure that every person has access to the goods that comprise the basic conditions of his ability to act and live autonomously. Society, to an extent, is obliged to provide this basic form of citizen empowerment. The consequence would be a notion that is very similar to Daniels's concept of species-typical functioning. The difference is that the former notion is not understood only as a pragmatic criterion of distributive justice, but as a much more fundamental right. Such a moral-normative conception of disease would necessarily interpret rights to medical treatments within a broader horizon. It is also important, here, to ask how the satisfaction of medical rights relates to other social rights – the aim should be to balance the rights to empowerment within and outside of medicine. In principle, however, such a notion of disease would not only be a pragmatic criterion that – like Norman Daniels's concept – must be understood in relation to conceptions of justice more broadly. Rather, what is formulated here are rights to support that every human being may expect to receive. For the justification of such a right no strong value-laden assumptions are required, nor must the notion of disease be scientifically objectified. It is enough to show that these are legitimate claims; and that is a normative form of discourse.

4.1.6.5 Enhancement

From this perspective, we shall now briefly return to the enhancement debate that was discussed in Chapter 1 (Elliott 1998; Harris and Holm 2002; Glannon 2002; Siep 2003; DeGrazia 2005). In the case of enhancement, citizens ask that they be allowed to use technologies that can alter their bodies in ways that are meaningful for them. The development of these technologies entails changes in the expectations people have of medicine – changes in people's relation to their own bodies and an almost boundless expansion of the medical domain. Some forms of wish-fulfilling medicine even have effects that would have been traditionally categorised as automutilation. Normative reactions to this development vary greatly. Some will point out that free disposal of one's own body would lead to people failing to appreciate fundamental aspects of being human (developing illusionary notions of identity or happiness, for instance). Transhumanists, in contrast, will demand that all opportunities of human self-improvement be used. Liberals, finally, will base their reaction on the conviction that citizens should in principle be allowed to have things done to themselves that others cannot understand or appreciate, and that there must only be limits where third parties are threatened with harm, or when children display automutilative behaviour.

A normative notion of disease in the sense indicated would have to point out, first of all, that society has obligations to provide individuals with the means necessary for them to live their own lives. Since the goal would be to enable people to live independently, however, it would seem necessary also to accept decisions that would lead to the irreversible loss of certain ways of living one's life. Yet this basic liberal attitude must be subject to certain restrictions. Since medicine is necessary for the realisation of these goals and since it is legitimised by the fact that it facilitates people's independence, medicine is allowed – to an extent – to refuse to be involved in certain acts. It would be very difficult, however, to determine the scope of medically reasonable treatment on the level of principle. Further determination of such boundaries would require concrete rules. I would propose the following:

1. The less we know about the risks and dangers of an action or intervention, the greater its significance must be for the preservation or restoration of the capacity for agency.

2. The more irreversible an intervention is, the higher the demands on the reasons for going through with it.
3. The stronger the reasonable doubt that a patient does not fully appreciate the consequences of the treatment, the more stringent the decision procedure must be (in the case of very young persons, for instance, there are reasons for a more thorough ascertainment of their motives).
4. The more profoundly an intervention alters the nature of a person, her capacity for agency or the way she can live her life, the stronger the reasons for undertaking the operation must be.

I realise that these proposals raise a whole host of questions that cannot be addressed here. In more elaborate discussions these proposed rules would most likely have to be tweaked. However, what is crucial are the underlying methodological considerations. If it is morally decisive that the conditions for living an autonomous life are protected, the moral assessment of these technologies cannot ignore decisions of individuals. At the same time, any moral assessment should ensure that the implementation of these technologies does not threaten to destruct the very value that the positive evaluation of human freedom sought to protect in the first place. If there is a danger, then, that the capacity for agency will be critically threatened, the implementation of such an intervention cannot be demanded in the name of individuals' freedom of choice (informed consent).

It should be added that these considerations have only targeted the level of individual ethics. In light of the fact that in some countries (especially the USA and Brazil) cosmetic surgery is starting to become almost normal amongst middle-class youth, it would also need to be asked what effects these technologies have on the developmental possibilities of young people. The latter could be a reason to view the use of some of these technologies as even more deeply morally questionable.

4.2 'Green' bioethics

The final part of this chapter will be concerned with bioethical questions outside the context of human medicine. The label 'green bioethics' is not a technical term, but merely a very tentative description of a number of bioethical themes related to animals and the environment. So far, no truly suitable term has been established. These debates interweave ethical, political, sociological and legal discussions even more strongly than is the case in biomedical ethics. Therefore, it is somewhat difficult to isolate the specifically ethical discussions. So far, moreover, these topics have been considered genuine questions of philosophical ethics only to a very limited extent, although by now there is a small body of literature, as well as some relevant journals. At least four core areas of debate can be identified: *animal ethics*, *ethics of biotechnology*, *environmental ethics* and *food ethics*. The boundaries between these are fluid and in flux. The purpose of the following sections is simply to indicate key areas, and to sketch some methodological considerations concerning future research.

4.2.1 Animal ethics[5]

If we were to ask what has called traditional moral convictions into question most profoundly, we could point to radically sceptical and relativistic notions of morality, or to, say, Nietzsche's critique of altruism-based morality. Yet many standpoints being discussed in contemporary animal ethics pose an equally significant challenge, at least for Western conceptions of morality, which do not find cultural examples or guidelines in their history. In Eastern cultures, for instance, animals are considered part of the social world to a much greater extent than in the West. While in the Western tradition animals are not viewed as mere objects either (Sorabji 1993), it was only in the 20th century that the idea of 'animal liberation' became a movement with political influence. Global protest movements stand up for the protection of endangered animal species or demand equality for great apes, the 'Party for the Animals' (Partij voor de Dieren) enters the Dutch Parliament, and vegetarian and vegan eating habits become established all over the world. In Eastern religions or for Saint Francis of Assisi, devoting oneself to animals is part of a spiritual and religious practice. Modern movements, in contrast, attempt to enforce animal rights by legal action, and demand that our moral framework be reworked. This new sensibility for animals occurs in a context of clear threats to animal habitats and tougher living conditions for many animals. Mechanisation and economic competition pressure in agriculture result in harsher conditions for livestock and, for wild animals, adapting to the current ecological changes is often nigh on impossible. While current animal protection efforts aim at an expansion and revision of traditional morality, they can also be understood as a reaction to the altered situation of animals.

4.2.1.1 Basic questions of animal ethics

The context of the renewed interest in animals also means that several academic disciplines now discuss animals' mental capacities and social behaviour. Animals' cognitive and emotional abilities, their capacity for language and patterns of social interaction are the subject of academic debates (see for instance Beauchamp and Frey 2012; Bermudez 2007; DeGrazia 1996; Rollin 2011; De Waal 2006). This also, once more, raises the issue of the moral and legal status of animals. In Chapter 3 I discussed part of this set of questions (in relation to what follows see Armstrong and Botzler 2008; Baranzke 2002;

5 I owe many of my thoughts on this topic to collaborations with Robert Heeger, Frans Brom and Frederike Kaldewaij.

Adams and Donovan 1995; Garner 2005; Garrett 2012; Holland and Johnson 1997; Midgley 1983; Regan 1983; Rollin 1990; Sandøe and Christiansen 2008; Singer 1974; Steiner 2010; Twine 2010; Sunstein and Nussbaum 2004). The first pertinent question is what overarching theory is used in order to determine the *moral status* of animals. Certain authors attempt to ground an animal ethics by either drawing on Albert Schweitzer's 'ethics of reverence for life' or on the notion of 'pity'. In the context of *classical utilitarianism*, the question is how pain and suffering can be reduced for all sentient creatures and how their well-being can be improved (see Chapter 2). That means that, for utilitarianism, it is sufficient to know that animals are capable of experiencing pain, and that it makes sense to think of them as having certain preferences with respect to their well-being. For utilitarian, these facts are enough to demand that the well-being of animals be taken into consideration. The question of whether animals have further mental capacities is not initially of importance. It can become pertinent, however, if Singer is right in claiming that killing is only morally problematic in the case of creatures that have a notion of the future, which is frustrated if they are killed. Creatures that lack any expectation for the future are in no way harmed by being killed (for a critical perspective see Kaldewaij 2008). According to Singer, those who are harmed by being killed are only beings with certain self-reflexive capacities. In the context of utilitarianism, evidence that many animal species are more cognitively capable than was previously thought could be a ground for demanding an expansion of the prohibition to kill.

The debate on animal ethics was initially strongly focused on establishing guidelines according to which animals are *not allowed to be harmed* or in which harming animals requires special justification (such as in the case of animal experiments). Nowadays, in contrast, there are debates on both the possible expansion of the prohibition to kill and on the living conditions of animals more broadly (Rutgers and Heeger 1998; Dol, Fentener van Vlissingen, Kasanmoentalib, Visser and Zwart 1997; Brom 1997; Bovenkerk, Brom and van den Bergh 2002). These debates are not only concerned with the demand that animals are not to be harmed, but also with efforts to care about animal *well-being* in a broader sense, and to establish, for instance, *species-appropriate animal husbandry*. This also includes securing freedom of movement and other conditions necessary for animals to develop according to the possibilities they have as a species. But even the notion of the 'well-being' of animals is connected to their interests or preferences, reconstructed by us from the behaviour typically displayed by the species. Some participants in the debate, however, try to go one step further, making the *integrity of animals* into a moral benchmark. Integrity of animals, here, means the 'wholeness and intactness of the animal and its species-specific balance, as well as the capacity to sustain itself in an environment suitable to the species' (Rutgers and Heeger 1998). This normative demand clearly goes beyond the demand for avoiding pain and securing animal well-being, as can be shown by way of an example. If it were possible to sedate chickens in such a way that they do not move, live in a very small space, accept food and do not deploy any activity whatsoever, they could be reduced to egg-producing organisms without experiencing pain. We need not necessarily assume that these chickens would feel unwell; it is imaginable, after all, that their sentience is reduced to such an extent that no feeling of malaise emerges. Nevertheless, most people have the intuition that something is not quite right here. 'Animal integrity', then, is the expression of a certain limit to the instrumentalisation of animals that can be described by the notion of 'species-appropriate' ways of dealing with them. There may be empirical questions as to what 'species-appropriate' is in particular cases, yet it can be assumed that it will be possible to develop an understanding that is sufficiently plausible and that can be put into practice. The normative question, however, is why we should be morally obliged to respect 'animal integrity'. That this term coincides with a widespread intuition seems plausible, yet that is not a very strong argument. What justifications, then, are imaginable?

If we take morality to be a *system of contracts* in which rules are established that are in the *equal interest of all*, and that are aimed at securing fundamental opportunities for all parties and at all parties allowing each other certain benefits and security, then the interests of animals would, as a matter of principle, not be relevant, since animals cannot be held to their part of the bargain (see in this context Donaldson and Kymlicka 2011; Rowlands 2002). We may very well use animals to our benefit, but the ways in which we do so are not based on mutual agreements with them. Nonetheless, it could be said metaphorically of livestock that people enter into a contract with them in which the animals provide a service, and the owner in turn provides a certain measure of protection. This idea would push the boundaries of the notion of a contract, however, since ultimately the reason why the owner provides protection is that he considers it right or desirable to take the interests of the animals into account, without the idea of a contract playing any role whatsoever. Even if animals are able to experience pain or have reflexive capabilities, they are not automatically also capable of meeting demands regarding considerateness or behaviour that we may wish to subject them to. For this theoretical context, then, it is not necessarily pertinent what science may find out about the experience and behaviour of animals, as long as we cannot presume animals to be capable of taking our interests into account. The reciprocity of consideration is fundamentally precluded. Now if this is the case, there could be two reasons within contract-based morality for the consideration of the interests of animals: on the one hand, we could say that animals are valuable only as long as humans have an interest in their continued existence (for food or as part of an environment that is worth living in); on the other hand, uncertainty about the possible relevance of animals in our ecosystem could be a precautionary reason to pursue active animal protection. Neither of these reasons may suffice, however, for demanding the protection of all animals.

In the context of *Kantian forms of ethics*, moral obligations are related to persons as creatures capable of agency and morality (see Chapter 2; Anderson 2004; Korsgaard 2005; Nussbaum 2006). In contrast to contractualism, the pertinent fact here is not that these creatures provide us with some sort of benefit in return for something we do for them. For Kantians, respect does not depend on expected advantages, but stems from certain morally relevant capacities. For this theoretical context, it is indeed a crucial question what mental, cognitive and moral capacities animals have. Tom Regan (1983) has attempted to interpret concepts relevant to Kantian ethics such as 'autonomy', 'agency' and 'goals' in such a way that animals become agents as well. All creatures that set themselves goals as 'subjects of a life' ought to be viewed as creatures who have inherent worth or dignity, and who must in that regard be viewed as rights holders too. While utilitarian theories generally aim to do without the notion of individual rights, theorists such as Regan seek to avoid the philosophical weaknesses of utilitarianism, and to expand the notions of dignity and rights (see 2.2.2., regarding the weaknesses of utilitarianism). It could be doubted that these authors have indeed interpreted concepts such as 'autonomy' and 'rights' in a way that legitimates an expansion of the Kantian formula of *the end in itself* to animals.

In the context of a Kantian-inspired ethics it would also need to be discussed whether uncertainty with regard to the extent to which animals are capable of agency could be a reason to treat them, for the sake of *precaution*, as if they were capable of agency. At least for great apes this seems a plausible line of reasoning. Another proposal is to consider at least some animals, those whose capacities are comparable to the capacities of severely mentally disabled humans, as *marginal agents* (Dombrowski 1997). As they possess some of the qualities that in humans are considered essential for the ascription of rights, they would be entitled to those rights at least to the extent that they possess the relevant capacities (Gewirth 1978: 121 ff; Hill 1984). This proposal entails a number of problems, which have been discussed before (see Chapters 2 and 3). For all theories that demand consideration for animals it is a relevant question of whether they demand equal treatment of animals (*egalitarian standpoints*) or whether human beings have priority in case of conflict. In theories that justify animal protection through the precautionary principle, or that seek to protect animals as 'marginal agents', persons whose capacity for agency is beyond reasonable doubt could always be granted priority. Approaches such as Tom Regan's, however, which consider both animals and human beings as full rights holders, would have to demand *strictly equal treatment*.

If we assume that we have obligations towards animals, we have to abandon, in a sense, the internal interrelation between rights and duties. That is to say, we would have to assume that there are creatures that are the beneficiaries of moral acts (*moral patients*) without being *moral agents* themselves. Now this is true with respect to certain humans as well, yet those situations could be understood as borderline cases of a moral community in which people are fundamentally obliged to mutual moral respect. In the case of animals, this is essentially different. It should be noted, however, that the morally relevant properties of humans are their capacity for agency and their vulnerability. Only because we are capable of exercising our agency are we able to ask about the goals of our actions, relate to moral norms and take the interests and needs of others into consideration. Yet only insofar as we are vulnerable and needy creatures does the necessity for moral rules and guidelines arise in the first place, since only then can we be harmed by the actions of others and because we are dependent on how others act. Now we do not share our capacity for agency with animals, but we do share the vulnerability and neediness. Since we are capable of putting ourselves in the place of others, we are at least in principle capable of grasping the interests of animals. Certain circumstances mean something different for an animal than for a human (if a pig spends the entire day lying in the mud, this reputedly has a different influence on its well-being than it would have on a human), but we are capable of understanding that pain and severe austerity are bad circumstances for an animal. Because of this ability, it could be argued, we owe it to ourselves to be considerate of the vulnerability of animals. While it seems complicated to grant animals rights, the fact that we are (to some extent) capable of grasping and acknowledging their suffering evokes the question of whether we owe it to *our own self-respect* to protect animals. From a Kantian perspective, the esteem for other people is connected with our self-esteem, or is a form of respect for 'humanity' that we share with others. One could ask whether there might be reasons to expand self-esteem to creatures who share our vulnerability, and of which we may wonder to what extent they have the mental capacities essential for agents. At the very least, it would have to be asked whether this line of reasoning might ground a moral status – even if that status would hardly be dignity proper. Kant's argument that humans deaden their sense of sympathy if they treat animals poorly, so that they will in the long run treat their fellow human beings badly too, however, is weak, at least if it is understood as an *empirical* argument. When one reads about the care with which Rudolf Höss (the first commandant of Auschwitz, Höss 1963/1992) treats his horses, anyway, one gains the impression that the relation between affection for animals and the way one treats human beings is far more complicated.

Why are we morally obliged to respect the integrity of animals? Notions such as the 'dignity of living beings' are merely metaphorical expressions that do not ground any moral obligations. The term 'intrinsic worth', too, only indicates the intuition that one cannot just treat animals in whatever way one likes. If it turns out that the utilitarian foundation of animal ethics (see Chapter 2) is insufficiently grounded; that Nussbaum's expansion of the capabilities approach still ought to be justified (see Chapter 3); that the crude extension of the basic principles of deontological ethics (autonomy, freedom of action) to animals, as proposed by Regan, is out of line with the normative content of these concepts; and if the contractualist perspective fails to provide a solid foundation as well, then the justification of moral duties towards animals is still very much in the early stages.

We can observe, however, that many countries have animal protection acts, and thus that a certain moral commitment with respect to animals is present. The demand for the *avoidance of pain*, consideration for the *well-being of animals* and respect for the *integrity of animals* can be thought of as competing concepts of the substantive constitution of animal protection ethics. There seems to be a widespread intuition that while the avoidance of pain certainly can be called for, any further demands would be difficult to justify. However, this conclusion does not seem necessary to me. If we have reasons for demanding animal protection, then this would not be on prudential grounds, nor because animals have the same status as humans. The avoidance of pain alone could only be justified from a negative utilitarianism, which as a whole suffers from justificatory deficits. If a justification of animal protection is possible, it would have to be connected to some property of animals that constitutes a self-standing moral value. In that case, however, the notion of the 'integrity of the species' would suggest itself over the demand for the avoidance of pain. But, as mentioned above, a justification for corresponding moral obligations is, in my judgment, yet to be established.

4.2.1.2 Animal experiments

While for the idea of human dignity and in the case of individual rights we presume that at least the fundamental rights of rights holders cannot be subject to a *weighing* process, this is not a widespread presupposition with regard to animals. But what perspectives can play a role in a morally legitimate form of weighing? The legitimation of animal experiments generally refers to its contribution to essential human needs. It is a starting point of many experiments that animals will be systematically hurt.

In general, it is assumed that animal experiments are only legitimate when they are indispensable for research. Many countries have established committees that have the task of assessing proposed animal experiments. Three concepts have become familiar as guidelines for such committees: reduction, refinement and replacement (Balls 2000; Nuffield Council on Bioethics 2005; Vorstenbosch 2000). Animal experiments should be, where possible, reduced; they should be conducted in a manner that causes as little harm and pain as possible (refined); and, where possible, they should be replaced by alternatives. Several ethical approaches consider the differences between different species of mammals to be morally significant. For some higher mammals, for instance, it is certainly possible that morally relevant properties and capacities are present; at the very least we cannot rule out the possibility that they are. This would be a reason to treat them similarly to humans, both from a utilitarian perspective, since the quality of their experience of pain might well be similar to the human experience of pain, and for theories that have a central place for the dignity of persons, because we cannot be certain about the extent to which qualities of personhood are present in animals.

The demand for replacement, incidentally, also is a reason for moral demands for research on alternatives to animal experiments. Sometimes distinctions are made with respect to the kind of research and the research goals. It seems easier to legitimate animal experiments for research that will be of direct therapeutic use for people than experiments for fundamental research. In general, however, this distinction does not play a central role. In principle, fundamental research is also considered legitimate. Perhaps the distinction is hard to uphold in practice anyway.

The moral obligation that *only scientifically indispensable animal experiments be conducted* does lead to the ethical necessity to discuss the *feasibility and desirability of research perspectives*. If, for instance, the only benefit of a certain experiment is that it enhances opportunities for xenotransplantation (transplants of animal organs into human patients), then the defensibility of the experiment depends on the question of whether xenotransplantation can be considered a promising technological perspective in the first place (see earlier in this chapter). Of course this cannot be known fully before the research has even started, but the possible scenarios certainly can be outlined and discussed. The ethics of animal experiments presumes, in any case, that the pain, well-being or integrity of the animals is balanced against the importance of the research. Still, research is considered as societally valuable. That is to say, animal protection is presumed to be morally valuable, but it is still subjected to weighing. The other side of the trade-off, however, is no longer debated in any detail. Such a debate would indeed be difficult given the complicated subject matter and the freedom researchers require. Yet if the weighing process is to be substantially relevant, discussion of research aims, their desirability and the available alternatives is necessary.

4.2.1.3 Animal husbandry

A further traditional topic of debate is *animal husbandry*. This sector is under enormous pressure to be productive and efficient. For approaches that consider the killing of animals fundamentally morally problematic, the very notion of livestock breeding for food is objectionable. For approaches that consider the killing of animals morally acceptable, yet take the well-being or integrity of animals to be morally binding, animal husbandry as such is not morally problematic. However, from the latter perspective meat consumption can only be deemed morally acceptable if the conditions for species-appropriate treatment are present. This position too can be a ground for a vegetarian diet, if one finds that given the existent economic and political conditions appropriate treatment cannot be guaranteed, or that it is impossible for the consumer to verify whether circumstances are acceptable.

Comparing the moral aspects of animal husbandry with the questions regarding animal experiments, the following differences stand out: for animal husbandry, inflicting pain and curtailing the well-being of animals is not a goal; in fact, it can negatively influence the quality of the meat. Numerous animal experiments, in contrast, systematically attempt to test the behaviour of animals under certain stressful circumstances. On the other hand, animal experiments tend to be motivated by goods that have strong moral relevance to humans, while a meatless diet is perfectly feasible. Insofar as killing itself is not considered fundamentally objectionable, however, most ethical approaches would consider the central question to be whether changes in living conditions could be practically-politically enforced. Still, the epidemics emanating from the livestock industry have, in recent years, also given cause for including *safety for humans* as a morally relevant consideration for changes to the way animals are bred and kept.

We shall speak of the role of *wild animals* only briefly. While in the case of animal experiments and animal husbandry moral obligations stem from the specific role of the owner of the animals, who as such has a special responsibility, this is different in the case of wild animals. The direct infliction of pain by humans cannot be expected to be of central concern. All the same, human conduct directly and indirectly influences the well-being and integrity of wild animals too. While specific responsibilities towards these animals can apply to individual institutions (such as forestry authorities), a more profound responsibility arises from the fact that humans systematically threaten animal habitats through behaviour that damages the environment. While even in this respect some very specific obligations towards animals in particular, forests or habitats could be formulated, this question mostly applies to a more general context of environmental responsibilities, in which the living environment of both animals and humans is at stake.

4.2.1.4 Biotechnology in animals

In the past few decades, there have been debates focused on *biotechnology in animals* and the *breeding of transgenic animals*. In these contexts, the relevant moral perspectives are the same as those that played a role in the debate on animal experiments. The possibility of cloning animals and the creation of transgenic animals, however, opens up an entire range of applications in which animals can be altered in very selective ways. With regard to transgenic livestock, there are attempts to attain quantitative and qualitative improvements in tolerance of several aspects relevant to the livestock industry through targeted breeding. Of course, in a way this is only an intensification of a tendency that has existed in agriculture for a very long time. Yet selective alteration of single genes in order to optimise growth, milk production, etc is of a different quality. If the well-being and integrity of animals are considered morally binding, it must be demanded that any changes be species-appropriate and compatible with animal health. Moreover there are *questions of risk*. Since alterations of a gene in complex organisms often result in unexpected effects on the entire organism, risk assessment is not negligible. With respect to research, the risk to humans is probably of secondary importance as long as animals are kept under controlled conditions. Yet even if this is feasible in the lab, controllability becomes a different issue when large animal populations have been genetically altered. Moreover, it can of course be expected that a successful increase in productivity will make these transgenic animals the dominant phenomenon. In this respect it is morally relevant that animals kept for food are not only economic factors, but also form a part of our living environment. Cows are not only milk producers, but also part of rural life. The experience of the people who live with them may well be a moral consideration too.

Several debates have been concerned with the *possibility of patenting* genetically modified animals (Beyleveld and Brownsword 1993). While this debate can hardly be held without technical and legal details, I shall indicate some aspects. The first question is whether it is acceptable to issue a patent on a transgenic animal in the first place. This is not initially a moral question, but a legal question as to what kinds of things can be patented. Patents apply to inventions made by someone. A patent being issued does not constitute an acknowledgement that a given object is some person's property, but an entitlement to use certain inventions – or rather, the exclusion of third parties of such use. If I invent something and am granted a patent for it, then nobody else is allowed to use it without my permission. The question then is, first of all, whether transgenic animals are inventions, or whether they are, rather, discoveries. The researcher has not invented the transgenic mouse; she has altered its genetic basis. But is that an invention? What exactly is the novelty that justifies patenting? Is some genetic information being produced here, or is it the case that a gene is isolated, described and synthetically reproduced? To the latter interpretation, it is argued that the patent does not relate to the material substance of the animal, but to the process that was necessary for its creation. In other words, what is at stake is not a substance patent, but a utility patent – a patent protecting a specific use. One could ask, however, how far the possibility of patenting in fundamental research can go. There seems to be a distinction between, on the one hand, cases in which a patent is issued for a procedure for developing a certain pharmaceutical or, on the other, a procedure for synthesising a gene that leads to a mouse that is somehow genetically modified. Assessing a patent that should apply to the creation or reproduction of an animal as such involves a need for further discussion.

4.2.2 Agriculture, food, environment[6]

Besides animal ethics, two areas have been dominant in the debate on 'green' bioethics. Ever since the 1970s there have been questions of global responsibility for the future in the light of insights into the limits of natural resources and climate change; and applications of genetic engineering and biotechnology in agriculture and food production have also provoked debates.

6 I would like to thank Frans Brom, Uta Eser, Konrad Ott, Thomas Potthast and Barbara Skorupinski for many discussions in this area.

4.2.2.1 Environmental ethics

There are several ways in which environmental ethics has called our traditional moral convictions into question (Gardiner et al. 2010; Gardiner 2011; Keller 2010; Light and Rolston 2003). With the progressive ecological destruction, the 1970s saw the dawn of the realisation that humankind is destroying its own natural living environment – not because of the interference of a divine power nor as the result of extreme wartime devastation, but as the consequence of the use of technologies and the exploitation of nature for energy purposes. This seems to increase the *scope of human responsibility* in two respects. On the one hand, it does so in relation to the *spatial and temporal extension of the consequences* of our actions: energy consumption and environmental degradation are almost unbounded in their impact, and both the ecological destruction and (for instance) nuclear waste of our current energy use will burden many generations to come. On the other hand, there are ever more *kinds of actions* that raise moral questions: the effects and after-effects of the civil use of energy, especially nuclear energy, has been a central topic of moral outrage and reflection from as early as the 1970s. These debates also show that what is at stake is not merely a political matter, but ultimately a moral question concerning the *criteria for moral accountability*. How many risks and negative consequences of energy consumption should a majority of society be allowed to impose on a minority, and how much cleaning up do we get to put on the shoulders of future generations? Advocates of nuclear power appeal to its lower pollution, while critics point out that it would be altogether irresponsible to risk the impact of a potential accident and that, moreover, nuclear waste will be a strain on the planet for an almost inestimable period of time (on the notion of responsibility also see Chapter 3).

The debates on *criteria for moral conduct* in relation to nature quickly led beyond the problem how the available natural resources could be distributed justly, to the question of whether nature may not have its *own proper* worth. This debate has already been referred to multiple times (see in particular Chapter 3), but it is still an open question which ought to be taken into consideration in our moral decisions. Traditionally, a distinction has been made between *anthropocentric*, *pathocentric*, *biocentric* and *ecocentric approaches* (see for instance Midgley 1994; Naess 1995; Rolston 1988). According to a prevalent interpretation, anthropocentric approaches presume that all decisions concerning the environment must take their start from human interests and needs (however these are to be interpreted), whereas pathocentric approaches include all creatures that can suffer in their moral considerations, biocentric approaches include all living beings, and ecocentric approaches include even ecosystems. What is meant is usually that within the respective approaches all humans, sentient creatures, living creatures and ecosystems are accorded a moral significance of their own; in other words, that they have their own proper moral worth. Another common distinction is between *egalitarian* and *non-egalitarian bio-* and *pathocentrism*, which indicates whether all living or sentient creatures are considered equal. An egalitarian patho- or biocentric position would result in a profound revision of our traditional moral convictions. The moral belief that there are fundamental boundaries to legitimate moral considerations, boundaries that are expressed in the set of human rights, is particularly difficult to square with these approaches. For these positions, the interests and needs of humans would be exactly as important as the interests of animals and, possibly, plants.

The notions that have been mentioned as identifying marks of very common environmental positions are, however, entirely unclear in their moral-philosophical conception of environmental protection. Is the point to ascribe animals and perhaps plants *dignity and rights*? In that case, we should not only take nature into account, but we would owe it respect as well (Taylor 1986). Besides the question of whether the notion of rights would even be intelligible when applied to plants, there is the issue of the justification of such respect outside of religious foundations (see Chapter 3). Or is the point that *interests and needs* of humans, plants and animals ought to be strictly balanced against each other? In that case, the egalitarian version would indeed make jettisoning human rights and liberal rights to freedom all but inevitable. Such a balance is rather foreign to utilitarianism, however, for the presence of interests and needs presupposes some form of capacity for experiencing pain. As a rule, utilitarianism is a pathocentric form of ethics. The way in which 'interests' of plants are supposed to be taken into account is unclear. Yet it is possible to speak of damage. Plants, too, evidently develop in ways that are typical for the respective species. A plant that has withered from a lack of water has been hindered in its developmental potential. It is conceivable to assess and weigh such damage from an impartial perspective. How, then, should we compare and weigh different forms of damage? And why should we be morally obliged to take all such 'interests' into consideration in the first place?

The most likely candidate for developing the idea of a self-standing worth of nonhuman nature is a strong *value theory*. As a rule, such a theory will presume that there is a large variety of values, which exist independently of human life and which humans can grasp. People would then be morally obliged to protect, preserve or realise the values they recognise. However, such a form of ethics faces the difficulty that it needs to show why all values directly ground moral obligations. I might aesthetically value a work of art, or consider a friendship valuable, but why does this morally oblige me? Furthermore, such a notion of value recognition mostly presupposes an intuitionist epistemology, and is thus burdened with the corresponding challenge of showing why everyone should share such intuitions (on this problem, see Chapter 3). A value theory based on intuitionism, moreover, usually presumes a variety of values and will therefore have to show how priorities ought to be determined in case of conflicts between values. With respect to environmental ethics, the main question is how such a value theory considers the prioritisation of humans. An associated problem is how the demand for moral respect could be justified if this prioritisation does not apply. Recourse to value-laden conceptions of nature cannot serve as a substitute for such a justificatory burden. However, the criticism of the special position of humans, characteristic for the critique of anthropocentrism, undermines the possibility of justifying moral obligations in the first place. This is different when the significance of nature is justified on the basis of central aspects of human existence, as discussed in relation to the aesthetic experience of nature (see Chapter 3).

Because of the numerous problems of nonanthropocentric ethical theories, it is natural to ask whether it may not be possible to develop an environmental ethics on the basis of a prioritisation of humans, that is, an *anthropocentric* ethics. It must be noted that the notion 'anthropocentric' is used in different ways. The concept is most commonly used critically or polemically, as a condemnation of the boundless exploitation of nature by humans. From this perspective, 'anthropocentric' would be the name for an ethics that considers it morally acceptable for humans to use nature for their own purposes without any restriction. But 'anthropocentric' can also indicate forms of ethics that assume that moral demands for the protection of nature must, in the broadest sense, be *legitimised* on the basis of human values and interests. This flags a further unclarity in the distinction signified by the '-centrisms'. Do they delineate a *sphere of entities* that are to be taken into account in our moral decisions, or is the point to say something about the *grounds for moral consideration*? As a rule, the notions 'anthropocentric', 'biocentric', 'pathocentric', etc single out the sphere of entities that 'count' in a moral respect. Yet this does seem to suggest that these approaches are not far from an egalitarian perspective. If we focus on the grounds we have for demanding moral protection, in contrast, it could be the case that we call for the protection of ecosystems because they are aesthetically valuable to us. Along the same lines, we could argue on the basis of precautionary principles. Yet this distinction between the *sphere of those entitled to protection* and the *justification of protection* sits rather awkwardly with the distinction of the '-centrisms'. Because of the large number of ambiguities associated with these notions, it seems advisable to abstain from using them. Still, misgivings about the terminology do not change the fact that the questions and perspectives discussed in this context are of central importance for environmental ethics.

A *justification of environmental ethics* on the basis of the needs, interests and rights of humans can take a large variety of forms. First of all, questions of *distributive justice* in the use of natural resources can play a role. *Resources are then protected as sources of food and energy.* In the light of the scarcity of these resources, it would be morally demanded to exercise restraint in using them, in order to allow them to be shared by as many people as possible. This duty of restraint becomes all the more urgent if the *rights and interests of future generations* are taken into account (see Chapter 3). Since it is impossible to keep supplying the (ever growing) world population with currently existing energy sources, the perspective of future generations not only shows restraint to be crucial, but also the development of alternative energy sources.

In this context, one topic that is brought up often is the demand for *sustainability*. This notion is enigmatic, but basically aims at the protection of the chances of future generations. It is controversial to what extent we can actually know the needs and interests of future generations in the first place. But even if we can assume that their interests will differ from ours in many respects, it is almost certain that clean air, potable water and opportunities for the production of food and energy will be indispensable for future generations as well. Furthermore, the question is whether we do in fact have a duty to ensure sustainability. Such an obligation certainly does not consist in prudential considerations (since it is not to our own advantage), and would hardly exist if we assume that moral obligations are always based on mutual consideration of interests. Indeed, the ecological crisis appears to have advanced so much that a drastic reduction of carbon dioxide emissions is unlikely to benefit the current generations much; it will only have a positive effect on future generations. Corresponding protective measures could therefore only be justified on the basis of moral obligations towards future generations. If, however, as shown in Chapter 2, rights and dignity are connected with a fundamental value judgment of the capacity for agency, and if the goods required to achieve or maintain this capacity are worthy of moral protection, then this does in principle hold for future generations as well. It is easy to see that natural resources are indispensable for the preservation of the capacity for agency. If moral protection – that is, the object of what we are morally obliged to protect – would be limited to not interfering with people's freedom, then long-term protection of the environment would be hard to justify. Yet if moral protection relates to the fundamental human capacity for living an autonomous life; if, that is, the conditions of agency are the object of moral protection, then threats to essential chances in life establish a very urgent object of moral care, without the necessity of recourse to a self-standing worth of nature.

Beyond the aspect of the protection of resources, the genuinely anthropocentric perspective allows for the protection of nature and species to be justified in other respects as well. On the one hand, the *unpredictability* of interventions in ecosystems and the dependency of humans on certain ecological surroundings can form a ground to limit human intervention in nature. The demand for the preservation of *biodiversity* would be one of the ways to make this concrete. But nature is not only a resource that is necessary for human survival; it is also a space in which we live and which, in several respects, allows us quality of life. In that sense, there are reasons to protect landscapes as the *living environment of humans* and as the *basis of aesthetic experience*. Such grounds for the protection of nature and landscapes do not depend on speculations on nature as teleological, but simply rest on the insight that it is important for humans to have nature as a space for aesthetic experience (as discussed above and see Chapter 3).

Yet even if sustainable use of nature is considered morally required, we have to ask how much abstinence those who are currently alive can tolerate, and how such protection of future possibilities for life and agency relates to basic rights to freedom of the current generation. In light of the dramatic proportions of current energy consumption, very profound restrictions might be necessary in order to have any chances at all of leaving behind acceptable living conditions for future generations. Furthermore, the growing world population will also play a key role in considerations on energy consumption. At the moment, it is hard to imagine what the expansion of the world population to nine billion people in 40 years' time will mean for the question of natural resources. Does this mean that it is morally demanded to restrict people's rights to freedom, including the right to reproduction, in order to sustain life chances for future persons? I would not want to argue for this specifically, but it seems to me that in the light of climate change, the central challenges of environmental ethics are in this area. If the moral worth of our right to freedom is based on the fact that the possibility of leading a free and self-determined life is essentially valuable, then it cannot be morally neutral whether this possibility will continue to exist in the future. At the same time, the moral quality of measures to preserve these fundamental possibilities will have to be measured by their compatibility with basic human rights. In this respect, however, serious conflicts can be expected.

This brief sketch on environmental ethics is very rough and superficial. There are many detailed conflicts that have, so far, been in sufficiently addressed in ethics and in the discourse on human rights or rights to freedom. Besides the conflict on consumer interests between current and future generations, there are central conflicts between sustainable treatment of the environment and the legitimate expectations with regard to developmental opportunities of people in developing countries. Yet the repercussions of climate change are likely to be such that environmental catastrophes will be more prevalent in the poorer parts of the world, and that some parts of the world will become barely inhabitable. It is not improbable that this will result in mass migrations. To ensure appropriate ways of reacting to these developments, a dense network of relevant regulations, international treaties and institutions is already starting to take shape. It is not unlikely that in the future new forms of international cooperation will be necessary. Some of these regulations and institutions have a profound impact on commercial activities and individuals' lives. At times, they require downright drastic changes of traditional cultural ways of life.

So far, ethics has barely risen to this challenge. Its task here could be to develop critiques that identify moral urgencies within these conflicts. In so doing, it would be necessary – along the lines of the theory of mixed judgments sketched above – to start by predicting, as accurately as possible, the different foreseeable scenarios and possible implications for different social, political and economic domains. The resulting possible courses of action would then have to be assessed in the light of the ethical theories at our disposal. Considerations of the following form could play a role: the more indispensable certain natural goods are for the production of food and energy, and the more irreversible the disturbance of nature, the stronger our grounds for a cautious attitude. Even forms of ethics that find their motivation in rights to freedom will have to demand restrictions on freedom in order to be able to ensure the preservation of human possibilities for agency in the long term. Through considerations of this kind, the number of moral discourses can probably be significantly reduced.

However, the moral demands in the domain of environmental ethics will not only consist of the restriction of freedom and sustainable treatment of nature. In the long run, it will be the case that climate change cannot be arrested by any amount of caution and abstinence by individuals, but only through a science and technology policy that makes more sustainable energy sources available. If it is true that we are morally obliged to protect the conditions of human agency, and if it is true that this is only possible with new forms of energy production, then a corresponding research policy, urgently implemented, seems to be morally demanded. The foreseeable implications of the ecological crisis on all areas of human life are enormous, and the possible interventions in human freedom considerable. At the same time, there are almost no established moral insights that can be drawn on in this area. In that sense, a systematic ethical legitimation of our actions would be particularly urgent. The ethical debate in this domain, however, is largely in the very early stages.

4.2.2.2 Food and agriculture

Within bioethics, debates on questions of food and agriculture in the context of 'green' genetic engineering and biotechnology have been held since the 1980s (Nuffield Council on Bioethics 1999, 2011). Initially, the dominant questions were fundamental ones, most notably whether changing nature in such profound ways is morally defensible, and how the uncertainties associated with these technologies should be dealt with (see Chapter 3). It is a matter of controversy to what extent the agricultural implementation of biotechnology is qualitatively distinct from previous growing methods. Is not biotechnology merely a somewhat more intensive form of plant breeding? The resistance of plants against pests seems to be substantially heightened by genetic and biotechnology (on this debate see in particular Skorupinski 1999). The ethical debate is mostly concerned with the question of how we should assess the ecological and economic effects. The fear is for an even more intensive agriculture with corresponding consequences. Moreover, there is the question of how such developments will work out in terms of national and international justice. On the one hand, the increase in productivity promises to be essential in battling world hunger. On the other hand, the possibility of patenting genetic modifications entails the danger that very high-yield forms of food production are permanently concentrated in the hands of a small number of Western companies, further increasing the dependency of poor countries.

In addition, questions of risk are being discussed. Both in relation to the use of genetically modified microorganisms (such as pesticides) and in the creation of transgenic plants it is contentious how the associated risks should be handled. However, risk assessment in this context differs from that in familiar debates on risk. In the risk discourse regarding nuclear energy, the dangers of an accident are perfectly evident, and the debate is concerned with the question of whether the corresponding risk is acceptable or not. Risk in that context is understood as the mathematical result of the multiplication of damage and the probability of such an accident occurring. In the case of nuclear energy, the probability of occurrence is supposedly remote, yet the damage in case of an accident is so enormous that many find even a small risk unacceptable. In the context of 'green' genetic technologies, in contrast, the risks are often unknown. This could simply mean that we do not know what damage might occur. Correspondingly, people often do not speak of 'acting under risk', but of 'acting under uncertainty'. We cannot calculate the probability of a certain form of damage occurring if we do not know what damage is possible.

Yet what is an acceptable risk? Does it suffice if laboratory conditions do not show the incidence of any damage? An argument against that line of reasoning is that an undetectable risk in the lab does not yet mean that no harm can possibly occur when modified plants and microorganisms are set free in nature. It could not be predicted, for instance, how substantial the risk of gene transfers would be. And once they are in the open air, it is difficult to permanently separate modified plants and microorganisms from genetically unmodified specimens.

This debate on the uncertainties associated with *open air tests* evokes a wide range of questions. Some of these questions are *empirical*, some are conceptual, such as what a risk is in the first place. But it is also contested how significant biological knowledge gained under the isolated conditions of lab experiments is for predicting how the same biological entities will fare in nature. Moreover, in the light of the persistent disagreements on this matter, the way in which decisions are being made is controversial too, as is the question of how we should morally deal with the differences in attitude between those who are willing to take risks and those who are risk-averse. In short, what is at stake here are collective *decision-making processes*. The morally relevant questions do not only concern the *risk assessment* and *expected success* of the relevant technologies; the appropriate *standards for risk assessment* are disputed as well. While some of these questions can be answered in reference to empirical data, this domain will remain one in which there are disagreements on how morally to assess such risks. Many people do not consider it a convincing solution to prescribe the lowest-risk option as compulsory for all, especially if the alternative promises significant increases in agricultural productivity. It is also problematic, however, crudely to impose a risk on the minority through a majority decision. Yet with regard to the employment of genetic engineering in agriculture itself, there are no convincing alternatives. One could try to isolate genetically modified plants and introduce special safety standards for the use of genetically modified pesticides. As soon as a principled decision has been made to go down this route, however, this also means that the existing uncertainties will remain.

In the case of food products, the situation is different. Here, a compromise would mean that the introduction of relevant products is subject to a *labelling obligation*. Products that have been genetically modified would have to be labelled as such in a way that would be sufficiently clear to the consumer. This solution means on the one hand that corresponding agricultural production and access to products are possible, and on the other that consumers have the opportunity to avoid such products. However, the details of such a labelling obligation are disputed: should only those products be labelled that have been produced from genetically modified crops? Or should the use of genetic technology in the manufacturing process be indicated as well? Given the widespread use of genetically modified substances in food manufacturing, it is very likely that such a broad option would lead to inflationary and therefore less meaningful labelling, while a more restrictive duty would hardly appease the worries of consumers.

Considering the extent to which biotechnology and genetic engineering play a role in agriculture and food production, one could wonder whether questions of morally acceptable employment of these technologies can be addressed merely by allowing consumers leeway in their decisions. Of course there are good reasons to consider the possibility of informed consent on the part of consumers as particularly morally valuable. Yet the possibilities of delegating all moral questions to consumer decisions are limited. It is difficult in practice to ensure sufficiently meaningful yet intelligible forms of consumer information. Furthermore, informed consent comes into play only when products are already being produced and sold. Many citizens fear these technologies. In this respect, it is also relevant how confidence in agriculture and food production is established. When it comes to their nutritional needs, people are particularly vulnerable, as scandals such as foot-and-mouth disease and mad cow disease have recently shown. At the same time, opportunities for monitoring are arguably limited. One kind of suspicion that seems not uncommon emerges from doubts regarding the honesty of relevant institutions. On the other hand, however, in the domain of genetic engineering there are very fundamental doubts whether it is possible at all to monitor technologies to such an extent that the available information truly does provide a sufficiently sound basis for decisions. It is possible that the uncertainty in this area is so extensive that such predictions are hardly feasible at all.

Confidence in the monitoring institutions, the state and industry becomes a central topic in the debates on how to deal with genetic engineering and food production in general (on this debate see Meijboom, Visak and

Brom 2006; O'Neill 2002).[7] One question, to start with, would be what the conditions of the emergence of confidence in this domain are, or how a lack of confidence comes about. Meijboom notes, for instance, that governments tend to react to a lack of confidence by dispensing large amounts of information on the relevant food products to their citizens. This strategy implicitly presupposes that the lack of confidence is due to a lack of information. Without wanting to detract from the significance of a transparent information policy, the question is whether the core of this discussion really is a lack of information. The divisive point could also lie in fundamental value differences, in disbelief in the integrity of institutions or doubts about the possibility of effective control. The availability of technical information, in contrast, is mostly relevant if there are divergences with respect to empirical questions, which is probably the case only in relatively few instances. In any case, the debate shows that the structures of decision-making and judgment formation should be addressed as part of the ethical discussion.

These days, the ethical debate on food and agriculture has separated into a number of more specialised discussions (Coff 2006; Korthals 2004; Mepham 1996, 2001; Singer and Mason 2007; Skorupinski 2003; Thompson 2010). On the one hand, the debate springs from scandals in the food industry; on the other, from the development of genetically modified 'novel food'. In addition, new opportunities in food production are debated under the heading 'functional food'. This term refers to attempts to manufacture food in such a way that it not only satisfies, but is also tailored to meet other specific needs of particular groups of consumers. Dietary wishes, allergies and intolerances of different kinds can thus be taken into account in the production of foods. At the moment, we can probably evaluate the feasibility of these opportunities to a limited degree. In some domains – such as hypoallergenic foods – there is apparently already a thriving market. This differentiation has numerous consequences, including social ones (how to invite a group of friends to dinner if besides vegetarian, vegan and meat options there also have to be three kinds of hypoallergenic foods?) Perhaps some reluctance also stems from the idea of reducing food to purely a matter of health and hygiene.

In any case, the debate spans a much wider range of topics than only questions of animal husbandry and risk assessments in genetic engineering. Eating as a social *praxis* and as an economically essential production process is at issue in many shapes and forms. At stake are both protection from risks and the preservation of culinary choice. In addition, however, the debate concerns far more rights and interests than only freedom of choice. Citizens' rights to be included in a shared decision-making process, to be governed by transparent institutions and not to be forced to eat simply what the industry delivers to the supermarket shelves are essential parts of this discourse.

7 With regard to this question, I am particularly grateful for helpful suggestions from Franck Meijboom, who recently finished a research project on this matter.

'Food ethics', too, will therefore have to be understood as part of a broader political ethics, which finds itself obliged to the protection of civil liberties and consumer rights. But even more pressing than the moral entitlements of people in prosperous countries is probably the question of how food supplies to developing countries can be ensured. Vital questions concern not only the quality of the relevant foods, but also ownership structures and economic dependencies. And if one considers rights to comprehensive information, freedom of choice and protection against the risks of new technologies to be morally demanded, then one would have to take these rights not to apply solely to citizens and consumers in wealthy parts of the world.

5 Conclusion

5.1 Bioethical perspectives

It is not easy to predict how bioethics will develop thematically and methodologically. In the past decade, the scope of the discipline has constantly expanded and shifted. The ethical debate on new biotechnologies has also been developed in the context of the ethics of technology and information ethics. The relation between bioethics and the social sciences has in the past decade increased in significance, both within bioethics and medical ethics and within the social sciences. There are now debates specifically focused on clinical ethics (Jonsen, Siegler and Winslade 2002). Furthermore, medical practitioners increasingly playing a role in bioethical debates, both because ethics has become established as part of nursing education, and because of the development of an ethics of nursing, focused on particular aspects of the *praxis* of nursing. Ethical discussions on neurosciences and on the relevance of nanotechnology for bioethics are maturing. Questions of public health ethics and the significance of biotechnology to developing countries can also be expected to be on the agenda in future debates.

The point of this book has not been to cover the entire thematic spectrum. What should have become clear is that bioethics operates on a certain *level of complexity*. Bioethics is concerned with questions that are fundamentally connected to the way in which the future will be shaped. Its scope does not just extend to the question of how individual conflicts in hospitals are solved, but also how technological attainments influence people's self-image, social relations and opportunities in life. How we can deal with these possibilities responsibly is, in many respects, an open question. We have neither a sufficiently secure empirical basis for maintaining an overview of the *consequences of changes* generated by the life sciences, nor do we have satisfactory models for *interpreting societies* that develop and are at the same changed by such technologies. In addition, there is some *serious disagreement on the normative foundations* for assessing these developments.

This book has attempted, where possible, to refrain from judgments about the tensions and uncertainties this situation entails at all levels. All moral answers that can be given in response to bioethical questions are disputed and will give rise to objections. Yet at the same time, proposing moral answers entails the claim that these answers should be generally acceptable. We expect that others will in principle agree with our judgment. The more complex and convoluted the questions, however, the less likely it is that such agreement will indeed occur unproblematically. There is too much room for conflict, too many levels of disagreement and too many ideological interests.

The temptation is strong, therefore, to temper expectations of understanding and consensus in bioethics, and instead only consider strategies for shaping a shared community that is fairly peaceful despite existing divergences. It is true, of course, that given the existence of moral disagreements we have no choice but to search for a *modus vivendi* if political institutions are to be capable of doing what they are there for. Yet, at the same time, we would fall drastically short of the demands of morality if we were to restrict ourselves to managing disagreements. Such fatalism is also questionable in the sense that it would altogether preclude the possibility of learning processes. The contribution of bioethics in dealing with the possibilities of the life sciences will certainly take shape differently depending on one's perspective. A range of approaches to this question has been discussed.

In this book, I have made a proposal. In a way, this proposal stands on two pillars. On the one hand, I believe it is important to *understand the life sciences as part of a broad social and cultural context* in which technologies shape, expand and limit what will be possible in the future. In my opinion, the *interdisciplinarity of bioethics* can only be justified as an attempt to understand this influence of bioethics on our lives and on future possibilities. Only when we have a sense of the possible consequences of these technologies and an insight into their meaning for culture and society will we be able to ask which possible ways of acting would have to be assessed and justified in the first place.

On the other hand, it should become clear that each and every moral assessment of responsibility in the life sciences will *depend on contested metaethical and normative presuppositions*. It is a matter of controversy how morality ought to be understood and there is no agreement on the way in which the accuracy of moral judgments and moral conduct should be measured. The fact of theoretical pluralism leads many philosophers to conclude that no practical answers can be expected from an engagement with normative theories. Instead, they propose we look for ways in which the plurality can be evaded. However, if one acknowledges the existence of pluralism such an evasion strategy is impossible from the start. Any normative bioethical proposal draws on assumptions that are not themselves indisputable. Yet that certainly does not mean that all ethical theories are false or ungrounded. It simply means that it is impossible to make a judgment in bioethics that cannot be disputed – and thus that it can be expected of every single bioethicist that she will demonstrate the grounds of her own judgment.

All of this means that bioethics is not a straightforward task, but scientifically and academically challenging. Quick and easy consensus cannot be expected, either with respect to moral principles and theories or in relation to individual moral judgments. It is exactly for this reason that academic bioethics is a complex endeavour. Its merit should be to establish ways for grounding concrete moral judgments that take the level of complexity of the question at issue seriously. Such ways will not be fast or effortless, but the institutionalisation of bioethics is only legitimate if such an attempt is made. It should be clear in all this that the issue here is not first and foremost the future of academic bioethics, but the question is on what level of reflection we address questions that are of fundamental importance for the way the future will take shape. The life sciences, the technological possibilities of medicine and the willingness towards solidarity in health care will have a profound impact on society in the future. Whether we will be able to find adequate answers to the moral challenges associated with these developments will depend on the level at which we will be able to discuss such questions. Whether moral responsibility in all of these contexts is a mere rhetorical truism or genuinely meaningful will also depend on how much we care to identify what is morally right in the life sciences. The point of bioethics is not to demand and preach moral responsibility but to contemplate what acting responsibly in dealing with the living world around us would mean in the first place.

Bibliography

Introductions and reference works in ethics, applied ethics and bioethics

Alexander, L.; Moore, M. 'Deontological ethics', *The Stanford Encyclopedia of Philosophy (Fall 2008 Edition)*, Edward N. Z. (ed). http://plato.stanford.edu/archives/fall2008/entries/ethics-deontological/.

Arras, J. 'Theory and bioethics', *The Stanford Encyclopedia of Philosophy (Summer 2010 Edition)*, Edward N. Z. (ed). http://plato.stanford.edu/archives/sum2010/entries/theory-bioethics/.

Baron, M.W.; Pettit, P.; Slote, M. *Three Methods of Ethics: A Debate*. Blackwell 1997.

Beauchamp, T.L. *Philosophical Ethics: An Introduction to Moral Philosophy*. McGraw-Hill 2001.

Beauchamp, T.L.; Walters, L. (eds). *Contemporary Issues in Bioethics*. Wadsworth 1989.

Beauchamp, T.L, Frey, R.G. (eds). *The Oxford Handbook of Animal Ethics*. Oxford University Press 2012.

Becker, L.C.; Becker, C.B. (eds). *Encyclopedia of Ethics*, 2 vols. Routledge 1992.

Cahan, S.M.; Markie, P. (eds). *Ethics. History, Theory, and Contemporary Issues*. Oxford University Press 2002.

Chadwick, R. (ed). *Encyclopedia of Applied Ethics*. Academic Press 1998.

Chadwick, R. (ed). *The Concise Encyclopedia of the Ethics of New Technologies*. Academic Press 2001.

Crisp, R.; Slote, M. (eds). *Virtue Ethics*. Oxford University Press 1997.

Darwall, S. *Philosophical Ethics*. Westview Press 1998.

Darwall, S. (ed). *Deontology*. Blackwell 2007.

Düwell, M.; Hübenthal, C.; Werner, M.H. *Handbuch Ethik*. Metzler 2011.

Engelhardt, H.T. 'The philosophy of medicine and bioethics: An introduction to the framing of a field', in: H.T. Engelhardt (ed). *The Philosophy of Medicine*, vol 64, pp. 1–15. Kluwer 2000.

Engelhardt, H.T. *Global Bioethics: The Collapse of Consensus*. M&M Scrivener Press 2006.

Frankena, W.K. *Ethics*. Prentice-Hall 1973.

Frey, R.G.; Wellman, C.H. (eds). *A Companion to Applied Ethics*. Blackwell 2003.

Grodin, M.A. *Meta Medical Ethics: The Philosophical Foundations of Bioethics*. Springer 2001.

Harman, G. *The Nature of Morality: An Introduction to Ethics*. Oxford University Press 1977.
Holland, S. *Bioethics. A Philosophical Introduction*. Cambridge 2003.
Hottois, G.; Parizeau, M.-H. (eds). *Les mots de la bioéthique. Un vocabulaire encyclopédique*. De Boeck Université 1993.
Jardins, J.R. des. *Environmental Ethics. An Introduction to Environmental Philosophy*. Wadsworth 1997.
Jecker, N.; Pearlman, R.A.; Jonsen, A.R. *Bioethics: An Introduction to the History, Methods and Practice*. Jones & Bartlett Publishers 2011.
Kuhse, H.; Singer, P. *A Companion to Bioethics*. Blackwell 1998.
Kuhse, H.; Singer, P. *Bioethics. An Anthology*. Wiley-Blackwell 1999.
LaFollette, H. (ed). *The Blackwell Guide to Ethical Theory*. Blackwell 2000.
Mepham, B. *Bioethics. An Introduction for the Biosciences*. Oxford 2005.
Munson, R. *Intervention and Reflection: Basic Issues in Bioethics*. Wadsworth 2011.
Pattinson, S. *Medical Law and Ethics*. Sweet & Maxwell 2006.
Post, S.G. (ed). *Encyclopedia of Bioethics*, 5 vols. Macmillan 2004. Previous editions. Reich, Warren T. (ed). *Encyclopedia of Bioethics*, 5 vols. Macmillan 1978.
Rachels, J. *The Elements of Moral Philosophy*. McGraw-Hill 1993.
Sinnott-Amstrong, W.; Timmons, M. (eds). *Moral Knowledge? New Readings in Moral Epistemology*. Oxford University Press 1996.
Steinbock, B. (ed). *The Oxford Handbook of Bioethics*. Oxford University Press 2007.
Taylor, R. *Virtue Ethics*. Prometheus Books 2002.
Timmons, M. *Moral Theory. An Introduction*. Rowman & Littlefield 2002.
Veatch, R.M. *Medical Ethics*. Jones & Bartlett 1997.
Winkler, E.; Coombs, J.R. *Applied Ethics. A Reader*. Blackwell 1993.

Other works

Adams, C.; Donovan, J. (eds). *Animals and Women: Feminist Theoretical Explorations*. Duke University Press 1995.
Adorno, T.W. *Ästhetische Theorie*. Suhrkamp 1970. English translation: *Aesthetic Theory*, Gretel Adorno and Rolf Tiedeman (eds). trans. Robert Hullot-Kentor. Continuum 2001.
Agar, N. *Perfect Copy*. Icon 2002.
Agar, N. *Liberal Eugenics, In Defence of Human Enhancement*. Blackwell 2004.
Agar, N. *Humanity's End: Why We Should Reject Radical Enhancement*. MIT Press 2010.
Albert, H. *Traktat über Kritische Vernunft*. Tübingen 1980. English translation: *Treatise on Critical Reason*. Princeton University Press 1985.
Alpern, K.D. (ed). *The Ethics of Reproductive Technology*. Oxford University Press 1992.
Altman, B. 'Disability definitions, models, classification schemes, and applications', in: G.L. Albrecht; K.D. Seelman; M. Bury (eds). *Handbook of Disability Studies*, pp. 97–122. Sage Publications 2001.
Amundson, R. 'Against normal function', *Studies in History, Philosophy, Biology and Biomedical Science* 31:1 (2000), pp. 33–53.
Anderson, E. 'What is the point of equality?', *Ethics* 109 (1999), pp. 287–337.
Anderson, E. (2004). 'Animal rights and the values of nonhuman life', in: C.R. Sunstein; M.C. Nussbaum (eds). *Animal Rights, Current Debates and New Directions*, pp. 277–98. Oxford University Press 2004.

Andrews, L. *Between Strangers: Surrogate Mothers, Expectant Fathers, and Brave New Babies*. Harper & Row 1989.

Anscombe, G.E.M. 'Modern moral philosophy', *Philosophy* 33 (1958), pp. 1–19.

Apel, K.O. 'Das Apriori der Kommunikationsgemeinschaft und die Grundland der Ethik' in: Apel, K.O., *Transformation der Philosophie*, vol. 2, pp. 358–436, Suhrkamp 1973. English: 'The A Prior of the Communication community and the Foundations of Ethics', in: Apel K.O. Towards a *Transformation of Philosophy*, trans. G. Adey and D. Frishy, Roudledge and Kegan Paul, 1980, 225–360.

Appel, J.M. 'Neonatal euthanasia: Why require parental consent?', *Journal of Bioethical Inquiry*, 6:4 (2009), pp. 477–82.

Archard, D.W. 'Children's consent to medical treatment', in: R.E.Ashcroft.; A. Dawson.; H. Draper.; J.R. McMillan (eds). *Principles of Health Care Ethics: Second Edition*, pp. 311–17. John Wiley & Sons 2007.

Archard, D.; Benatar, D. *Procreation and Parenthood: The Ethics of Bearing and Rearing Children.* Clarendon Press 2011.

Arendt, H. *The Origins of Totalitarianism*. Harcourt Brace Jovanovich 1951.

Armstrong, S.J.; Botzler, R.G. *The Animal Ethics Reader*. Routledge 2008.

Arnold, R.M.; Forrow, L. 'Empirical research in medical ethics: An introduction', *Theoretical Medicine* 14:3 (1993), pp. 195–96.

Arras, J.D. 'A case approach', in: H. Kuhse; P. Singer (eds). *A Companion to Bioethics*, pp. 106–14. Blackwell 1999.

Ashcroft, R.E.; Dawson, A.; Draper, H.; McMillan, J.R. (eds). *Principles of Health Care Ethics: Second Edition*. John Wiley & Sons 2007.

Atighetchi, D. *Islamic Bioethics. Problems and Perspectives*. Springer 2007.

Audi, R. *The Good in the Right. A Theory of Intuition and Intrinsic Value*. Princeton University Press 2004.

Austin, J.L. 'A plea for excuses', in: *Philosophical Papers*, J.O. Urmson and G.J. Warnock (eds). Oxford University Press 1979.

Ayer, A. *Language, Truth and Logic*. Dover Publications 1936.

Badura-Lotter, G.; Düwell, M. 'Man-made chimeras, hybrids and mosaics – ethical perspectives', in: J. Taupitz; M. Weschka (eds). *CHIMBRIDS – Chimeras and Hybrids in Comparative European and International Research: Scientific, Ethical, Philosophical and Legal Aspects*, pp. 571–92. Springer 2009.

Baier, K. 'Types of responsibility', in: P. French (ed). *The Spectrum of Responsibility*. St. Martin's Press 1991.

Baily, M.A.; Murray, T.H. (eds). *Ethics and Newborn Genetic Screening: New Technologies, New Challenges*. The Johns Hopkins University Press 2009.

Balls, M. (ed). *Progress in the Reduction, Refinement and Replacement of Animal Experimentation.* Elsevier 2000.

Balzer, P.; Rippe, K.P.; Schaber, P. 'Two concepts of dignity for humans and non-human organisms in the context of genetic engineering', *Journal of Agricultural and Environmental Ethics* 13 (2000), pp. 7–27.

Banks, M.E.; Kaschak, E. (eds). *Women with Visible and Invisible Disabilities: Multiple Intersections, Multiple Issues, Multiple Therapies*. Haworth Press 2003.

Baranzke, H. *Würde der Kreatur? Die Idee der Würde im Kontext der Bioethik*. Würzburg 2002.

Baruch, E. *et al.* (eds). *Embryos, Ethics and Women's Rights: Exploring the New Reproductive Technologies*. Routledge 1988.

Basnett, I. 'Health care professionals and their attitudes toward decisions affecting disabled people', in: G.L. Albrecht, K. Seelman and M. Bury (eds). *Handbook of Disability Studies*, pp. 450–67. Sage Publications 2001.

Battin, M.P. *Ethical Issues in Suicide*. Prentice-Hall 1982.

Battin, M.P. *The Least Worst Death: Essays in Bioethics and the End of Life*. Oxford University Press 1994.

Bayertz, K. 'Human dignity. Philosophical origin and scientific erosion of an idea', in: K. Bayertz (ed). *Sanctity of Life and Human Dignity*, pp. 73–90. Kluwer 1996.

Bayles, M. *Reproductive Ethics*. Prentice-Hall 1984.

Beauchamp, T.L.; Childress, J.F. *Principles of Biomedical Ethics*. Oxford University Press 2008 [1979]; 5th edition 2001.

Becker, G.K. 'Normative relations. East Asian perspectives on biomedicine and bioethics', in: M. Düwell; C. Rehmannh-Sutter; D. Mieth (eds). *The Contingent Nature of Life. Bioethics and Limits of Human Existence*, pp. 277–92. Springer 2008.

Beld, A. van den. 'Human rights, moral obligations and divine commands', *Faith and Philosophy*, 23:2 (2006), pp. 119–36.

Benjamin, M. *Splitting the Difference. Compromise and Integrity in Ethics and Politics*. University Press of Kansas 1990.

Bentham, J. *An Introduction to the Principles of Morals and Legislation*, J.H. Burns and H.L.A. Hart (eds). Methuen 1982 [1780].

Berg, J. Hendrik van den. *Medische Macht en Medische Ethiek*. Callenbach 1969.

Berlin, I. *Four Essays on Liberty*. Oxford University Press 1969.

Bermudez, J.L. 'Thinking without words: An overview for animal ethics', *The Journal of Ethics* 11 (2007), pp. 319–35.

Beyleveld, D. *The Dialectical Necessity of Morality. An Analysis and Defense of Alan Gewirth's Argument to the Principle of Generic Consistency*. The University of Chicago Press 1991.

Beyleveld, D. 'The moral status of the human embryo and fetus', in: H. Haker; D. Beyleveld (eds). *The Ethics of Genetics in Human Procreation*, pp. 59–85. Ashgate 2000.

Beyleveld, D.; Brownsword, R. *Mice, Morality, and Patents. The Onco-mouse Application and Article 53(a) of the European Patent Convention*. Common Law Institute of Intellectual Property 1993.

Beyleveld, D.; Brownsword, R. *Human Dignity in Bioethics and Biolaw*. Oxford University Press 2001.

Beyleveld, D.; Brownsword, R. 'Principle, proceduralism, and precaution in a community of rights', *Ratio Juris* 19:2 (2006), pp. 141–68.

Beyleveld, D.; Brownsword, R. *Consent in the Law*. Hart 2007.

Bickenbach, J. *Physical Disability and Social Policy*. University of Toronto Press 1993.

Bielby, P. *Competence and Vulnerability in Biomedical Research*, International Library of Ethics, Law, and the New Medicine, vol. 40. Springer 2008.

Birnbacher, D. 'Welche Ethik ist also Bioethik tauglich? in: J.S. Ach/A. Gaidt (eds): Herausforderung der Bioethik, pp. 45–67. Fromann-Holzboog 1993.

Birnbacher, D. 'Two methods of doing bioethics', in: H. Pauer-Studer (ed). *Norms, Values, and Society*, pp. 173–85. Kluwer 1994.

Birnbacher, D. *Tun und Unterlassen*. Reclam 1995.

Birnbacher, D. 'Responsibility to future generations – scope and limits', in: J. Chet Tremmel (ed). *Handbook of Intergenerational Justice*, pp. 23–38. Cheltenham 2006; and in *Studia Ecologiae et Bioethicae* 7:1 (2009), pp. 75–106.

Birnbacher, D. 'Brain death – a pragmatic defence', in: A. Beckermann; H. Tetens; S. Walter (eds). *Philosophy. Foundations and Applications*, pp. 161–80. Mentis 2008.

Birnbacher, D.; Dahl, E. (eds). *Giving Death a Helping Hand: Physician-Assisted Suicide and Public Policy. An International Perspective*, International Library of Ethics, Law, and the New Medicine, vol. 38. Springer 2008.

Blackburn, S. *Essays in Quasi-Realism*. Oxford University Press 1993.

Boorse, C. 'Health as a theoretical concept', *Philosophy of Science* 44 (1977), pp. 542–62.

Boorse, C. 'Disability and medical theory', in: D.C. Ralston and J. Ho (eds). *Philosophical Reflections on Disability*, pp. 55–90. Dordrecht: Springer 2010.

Borry, P.; Schotsmans, P.; Dierickx, K. 'What is the role of empirical research in bioethical reflection and decision-making? An ethical analysis', *Medicine, Health Care and Philosophy*, 7:1 (2004), pp. 41–53.

Borry, P.; Schotsmans, P.; Dierickx, K. 'The birth of the empirical turn in bioethics', *Bioethics* 19:1 (2005), pp. 49–71.

Bostrom, N. 'In defense of posthuman dignity', *Bioethics* 19:3 (2005), pp. 202–14.

Bovenkerk, B.; Brom, F.W.A.; Bergh, B.J. van den. 'Brave new birds. The use of "animal integrity" in animal ethics', *Hastings Center Report* 32:1 (2002), pp. 16–22.

Boylan, M. (ed). *Gewirth. Critical Essays on Action, Rationality, and Community*. Rowman & Littlefield 1999.

Brock, D.J. *et al.* (eds). *Prenatal Diagnosis and Screening*. Churchill Livingstone 1992.

Brock, D.W. *Life and Death: Philosophical Essays in Biomedical Ethics*. Cambridge University Press 1993.

Brody, B.A. *Life and Death Decision Making*. Oxford University Press 1988.

Brody, B.A. *The Ethics of Biomedical Research. An International Perspective*. Oxford University Press 1998.

Brom, F.W.A. 'Animal welfare, public policy and ethics', in: M. Dol; S. Kasanmoentalib; S. Lijmbach; E. Rivas; R. van den Bos (eds). *Animal Consciousness and Animal Ethics. Perspectives from the Netherlands*, pp. 208–22. Van Gorcum 1997.

Brownlee, K.; Cureton, A. (eds). *Disability and Disadvantage*. Oxford University Press 2009.

Buchanan, A.E. *Beyond Humanity? The Ethics of Biomedical Enhancement*. Oxford University Press 2011.

Buchanan, A.; Brock, D.W.; Daniels, N.; Wikler, D. *From Chance to Choice. Genetics and Justice*. Cambridge University Press 2000.

Buckle, S. 'Arguing from potential', *Bioethics* 2 (1988), pp. 227–53.

Burg, W. van der. 'Slippery slope arguments', in: R. Chadwick (ed). *The Concise Encyclopedia of the Ethics of New Technologies*, pp. 384–96. Academic Press 2001.

Burg, W. van der; Willigenburg, T. van (eds). *Reflective Equilibrium. Essays in Honour of Robert Heeger*. Kluwer 1998.

Callahan, D. 'The social sciences and the task of bioethics', *Daedalus*, 128:4 (1999), pp. 275–94.

Caplan, A.L.; McCartney, J.J.; Sisti, D.A. (eds). *Health, Disease, and Illness: Concepts in Medicine*. Georgetown University Press 2004.

Capron, A.M. *et al.* (eds). *Ethical Issues in Governing Biobanks: Global Perspectives*. Ashgate 2008.

Chadwick, R.; Levitt, M.; Shickle, D. (eds). *The Right to Know and the Right not to Know*. Ashgate 1998.

Chadwick, R. 'Genetic screening', in: R. Chadwick (ed). *The Concise Encyclopedia of the Ethics of New Technologies*, pp. 193–99. Academic Press 2001.

Chadwick, R. 'Gene therapy', in: H. Kuhse; P. Singer (eds). *A Companion to Bioethics*, pp. 207–15. Wiley-Blackwell 2009.

Charlton, J. *Nothing About Us Without Us: Disability, Oppression and Empowerment*. University of California Press 1998.

Chatterjee, D.K. (ed). *The Ethics of Assistance. Morality and the Distant Needy*. Cambridge University Press 2004.

Childress, J. *Practical Reasoning in Bioethics*. Indiana University Press 1997.

Claassen, R.; Düwell, M. 'The foundation of capability theory. Nussbaum and Gewirth compared', in: *Ethical Theory and Moral Practice* (2012, DOI 10.1007 S10677-012-9361-8).

Clarke, S.R.L. *The Moral Status of Animals*. Oxford University Press 1977.

Coff, C. *The Taste for Ethics: An Ethic of Food Consumption*. Springer 2006.

Cohen, C.B. (ed). *New Ways of Making Babies: The Case of Egg Donation*. Indiana University Press 1996.

Cohen, C.B. 'Selling bits and pieces of humans to make babies. The gift of the Magi revisited', *Journal of Medicine and Philosophy*, 24:3 (1999), pp. 288–306.

Cohen-Almagor, R. *Euthanasia in the Netherlands: The Policy and Practice of Mercy Killing*, International Library of Ethics, Law, and the New Medicine, vol. 20. Springer 2010.

Council of Europe. *Recommendation REC (2003)10 of the Committee of Ministers to member states on Xenotransplantation*. Strasbourg 2003.

Daele, W. van den. 'Vorgeburtliche Selektion. Ist die Pränataldiagnostik behindertenfeindlich?', in: W. van den Daele, *Biopolitik*, pp. 97–122. Leviathan Sonderheft 23 (2005).

Dancy, J. *Ethics Without Principles*. Oxford University Press 2004.

Dancy, J. 'Moral particularism', *The Stanford Encyclopedia of Philosophy (Spring 2009 Edition)*, Edward N.Z. (ed). http://plato.stanford.edu/archives/spr2009/entries/moral-particularism/.

Daniels, N. *Just Health Care*. Cambridge University Press 1985.

Daniels, N. *Justice and Justification. Reflective Equilibrium in Theory and Practice*. Cambridge University Press 1996.

DeGrazia, D. *Taking Animals Seriously. Mental Life and Moral Status*. Cambridge University Press 1996.

DeGrazia, D. 'Common morality, coherence, and the principles of biomedical ethics', *Kennedy Institute of Ethics Journal* 13 (2003), pp. 219–30.

DeGrazia, D. 'Enhancement technologies and human identity', *Journal of Medicine and Philosophy* 30:3 (2005), pp. 261–83.

DeGrazia, D. *Human Identity and Bioethics*. Cambridge University Press 2005 (cit. DeGrazia 2005a).

Denier, Y. *Efficiency, Justice and Care. Philosophical Reflections on Scarcity in Health Care*. Springer 2007.

Dierickx, K.; Borry, P. (eds). *New Challenges for Biobanks: Ethics, Law and Governance*. Intersentia 2009.

Dol, M.; Fentener van v.M.; Kasanmoentalib, S.; Visser, T.; Zwart, H. (eds). *Recognizing the Intrinsic Value of Animals. Beyond Animal Welfare*. Van Gorcum 1999.

Dombrowski, D.A. *Babies and Beasts. The Argument from Marginal Cases*. University of Illinois Press 1997.

Donaldson, S.; Kymlicka, W. *Zoopolis. A Political Theory of Animal Rights*. Oxford University Press 2011.

Döring, O. 'Limits of human existence according to China's bioethics: Reproductive medicine and human embryo research', in: M. Düwell; C. Rehmann-Sutter; D. Mieth (eds). *The Contingent Nature of Life. Bioethics and Limits of Human Existence*, pp. 293–306. Springer 2008.

Douglas, M. *Purity and Danger. An Analysis of Concepts of Pollution and Taboo*. Routledge 2002 [1966]. Also as: *Mary Douglas: Collected Works*, vol. 2. Routledge 2003.

Dresser, R.S. 'Treatment decisions for incapacitated patients', in: Richard E.A.; A. Dawson; H. Draper; J.R. McMillan (eds). *Principles of Health Care Ethics: Second Edition*, pp. 305–10. John Wiley & Sons 2007.

Duden, B. *Disembodying Women: Perspectives on pregnancy and the unborn*. Harvard University Press 1993.

Dunstan, G.R.; Seller, M.J. (eds). *The Status of the Human Embryo: Perspectives from Moral Tradition*. King Edward's Hospital Fund for London 1988.

Düwell, M. *Ästhetische Erfahrung und Moral. Zur Relevanz des Ästhetischen für die Handlungsspiel-räume des Menschen*. Alber 1999.

Düwell, M. 'One moral principle or many?', in: C. Rehmann-Sutter; M. Düwell; D. Mieth (eds). *Bioethics in Cultural Contexts. Reflections on Methods and Finitude*, pp. 93–108. Springer 2006.

Düwell, M. 'Needs. capacities and morality. On problems of the liberal in dealing with the life sciences', in: M. Düwell; C. Rehmann-Sutter; D. Mieth (eds). *The Contingent Nature of Life. Bioethics and Limits of Human Existence*, pp. 119–30. Springer 2008.

Düwell, M. 'Equality, speciesism, and "sanctity of life". On some philosophical presuppositions of Peter Singer's practical ethics', in: J. Schaler (ed). *Singer under Fire: The Moral Iconoclast Faces His Critics*. Open Court 2008 (cit. Düwell 2008a).

Düwell, M.; Braarvig, J.; Brownsword, R.; Mieth, D. (eds). *The Cambridge Handbook of Human Dignity*. Cambridge University Press forth coming 2013.

Dworkin, R. 'Rights as Trumps', in: Waldnon, J. (ed.), *Theories of Rights*. pp. 153–167, Oxford University Press 1984.

Dworkin, G.; Frey, R.G.; Bok S. *Euthanasia and Physician-Assisted Suicide (For and Against)*. Cambridge University Press 1998.

Dworkin, R. *Life's Dominion. An Argument about Abortion, Euthanasia and Individual Freedom*. Vintage Books 1994.

Edwards, S. 'Dismantling the disability/handicap distinction', *Journal of Medicine and Philosophy* 22 (1997), pp. 589–606.

Elliott, C. 'The tyranny of happiness. Ethics and cosmetic psychopharmacology', in: Erik Parens (ed). *Enhancing Human Traits. Ethical and Social Implications*, pp. 177–88. Georgetown University Press 1998.

Elliott, C. *A Philosophical Disease: Bioethics, Culture and Identity*. Routledge 1999.

Engelhardt, H.T. 'Health care reform. A study in moral malfeasance', *The Journal of Medicine and Philosophy* 19 (1994) pp. 501–16.

Engelhardt, H. Tristram. *The Foundations of Bioethics*. Oxford University Press [1986].

Faden, R.R.; Tom L. Beauchamp. *A History and Theory of Informed Consent*. Oxford University Press 1986.

Feinberg, J. *Doing and Deserving: Essays in the Theory of Responsibility*. Princeton University Press 1970.

Feinberg, J. *Harm to Others*. Oxford University Press 1984.

Felt, U.; Fochler, M. *et al.* 'Visions and versions of governing biomedicine. Narratives on power structures, decision-making and public participation in the field of biomedical technology in the Austrian context', *Social Studies of Science* 38:2 (2008), pp. 233–55.

Fiester, A.; Düwell, M. 'Ethics', in: J. Taupitz; M. Weschka (eds). *CHIMBRIDS – Chimeras and Hybrids in Comparative European and International Research: Scientific, Ethical, Philosophical and Legal Aspects*, pp. 61–79. Springer 2009.

Fingarette, H. *On Responsibility*. Basic Books 1967.

Fischer, J.M. (ed). *Moral Responsibility*. Cornell University Press 1986.

Fischer, J.M. 'Recent work on moral responsibility', *Ethics* 110:1 (1999), pp. 93–139.

Fischer, J.M.; Ravizza, M. (eds). *Perspectives on Moral Responsibility*. Cornell University Press 1993.

Fischer, J.M.; Ravizza, M. *Responsibility and Control: A Theory of Moral Responsibility*. Cambridge University Press 1998.

Fletcher, J. *Morals and Medicine. The Moral Problems of the Patient's Right to Know the Truth, Contraception, Artificial Insemination, Sterilization, Euthanasia*. Beacon Press 1954.

Forst, R. 'Das grundlegende Recht auf Rechtfertigung. Zu einer konstruktivistischen Konzeption von Menschenrechten', in: H. Brunkhorst; W.R.Köhler.; M.L. Bachmann (eds). *Recht auf Menschenrechte. Menschenrechte, Demokratie und internationale Politik*, pp. 66–105. Suhrkamp 1999. English translation: *The Right to Justification. Elements of a Constructivist Theory of Justice*, trans. Jeff Flynn. Columbia University Press 2011.

Forst, R. 'Ethik und Moral', in: L. Wingett; K. Günther (eds). *Die Öffentlichkeit der Vernunft und die Vernunft der Öffentlichkeit. Festschrift für Jürgen Habermas*, pp. 344–72. Suhrkamp 2001. English translation: 'Ethics and morality', in: *The Right to Justification. Elements of a Constructivist Theory of Justice*, trans. Jeff Flynn. Columbia University Press 2011.

Foucault, M. *Histoire de la sexualité I. La volonté de savoir.* Gallimard 1976. English translation: *The History of Sexuality. Volume 1: The Will to Knowledge*, trans. Robert Hurley. Penguin 1998.

Foucault, M. *Il faut défendre la société.* Gallimard 1996. English translation: Mauro Bertani; Alessandro Fontana (eds). *Society Must be Defended: Lectures at the Collège de France, 1975–1976*, trans. David Macey. Picador 2003. Lecture course in French available at the IMEC Michel Foucault Archives: http://michel-foucault-archives.org/?Il-faut-defendre-la-societe and at the University of California Foucault Audio Archives: http://www.lib.berkeley.edu/MRC/foucault/ds.html.

Foucault, M. *Histoire de la gouvernementalité. Naissance de la biopolitique*. Gallimard 2004. English translation: Michel Senellart (ed). *The Birth of Biopolitics: Lectures at the Collège de France, 1978–1979*, trans. Graham Burchell. Picador 2010.

Frankena, W.K. 'The concept of morality', *The Journal of Philosophy* 63:21 (1966), pp. 688–96.

Frankfurt, H. 'Alternate possibilities and moral responsibility', *The Journal of Philosophy* 66 (1969), pp. 828–39.

Fukuyama, F. *Our Posthuman Future: Consequences of the Biotechnological Revolution*. Picador 2002.

Gaard, G. (ed). *Ecofeminism: Women, Animals, Nature*. Temple University Press 1993.

Gardiner, S.M.; Caney, S.; Jamieson, D.; Shue, H. (eds). *Climate Ethics: Essential Readings*. Oxford University Press 2010.

Gardiner, S.M. *A Perfect Moral Storm. The Ethical Tragedy of Climate Change*. Oxford University Press 2011.

Garner, R. *Animal Ethics*. Polity Press 2005.

Garrett, J.R. (ed). *The Ethics of Animal Research: Exploring the Controversy*. The MIT Press 2012.

Gauthier, D. *Morals by Agreement*. Oxford University Press 1986.

Gehlen, A. *Der Mensch. Seine Natur und seine Stellung in der Welt*. AULA-Verlag 1986 [1940]. English translation: *Man: His Nature and Place in the World*, trans. Clare McMillan and Karl Pillemer. Columbia University Press 1988.

Gert, B. *Morality. Its Nature and Justification*. Oxford University Press 1998.

Gert, B. 'The definition of morality', *The Stanford Encyclopedia of Philosophy (Summer 2011 Edition)*, Edward N.Z. (ed). http://plato.stanford.edu/archives/sum2011/entries/morality-definition/.

Gert, B; Culver, C.M.; Clouser, K.D. *Bioethics. A Return to Fundamentals*. Oxford University Press 1997.

Gewirth, A. *Reason and Morality*. University of Chicago Press 1978.

Gewirth, A. 'Human dignity as basis of rights', in: Michael J.M.; William A.P. (eds). *The Constitution of Rights. Human Dignity and American Values*, pp. 10–28. Cornell University Press 1992.

Gewirth, A. *Community of Rights*. University of Chicago Press 1996.

Giddens, A. 'Risk and responsibility', *The Modern Law Review* 62:1 (1999), pp. 1–10.

Gigerenzer, G. *Calculated Risks: How to Know When Numbers Deceive You*. Simon & Schuster 2002.

Gilligan, C. *In a Different Voice. Psychological Theory and Women's Development*. Harvard University Press 1982.

Gillon, R.; Lloyd, A. (eds). *Principles of Health Care Ethics*. John Wiley & Sons 1994.

Glannon, W. 'Extending the human life span', *Journal of Medicine and Philosophy* 27:3 (2002), pp. 339–54.

Glover, J. *Causing death and saving lives*. Harmondsworth 1977.

Goering, S. '"You say you're happy, but ...": Contested quality of life judgments in bioethics and disability studies', *Journal of Bioethical Inquiry* 5 (2008), pp. 125–35.

Goffman, E. *Stigma: Notes on the Maintenance of Spoiled Identity*. Prentice-Hall 1963.

Gordijn, B. 'Das Klonen von Menschen. Eine alte Debatte – aber immer noch in den Kinderschuhen', *Ethik in der Medizin* 11:1 (1999), pp. 12–34.

Gordijn, B.; Chadwick, R. (eds). *Medical Enhancement and Posthumanity*, The International Library of Ethics, Law and Technology, vol. 2. Springer 2010.

Green, R.M. 'Method in bioethics: a troubled assessment', *Journal of Medicine and Philosophy* 15:2 (1990), pp. 179–97.

Griffin, J. *On Human Rights*. Oxford University Press 2008.

Gruen, L. *Ethics and Animals. An Introduction*. Cambridge University Press 2011.

Haakonssen, K. *Natural Law and Moral Philosophy. From Grotius to the Scottish Enlightenment*. Cambridge University Press 1996.

Habermas, J. 'Zum pragmatischen, ethischen und moralischen Gebrauch der praktischen Vernunft', in: *Erläuterungen zur Diskursethik*, pp. 100–18. Suhrkamp 1991. English translation: 'On the pragmatic, the ethical, and the moral employments of practical reason', in: *Justification and Application: Remarks on Discourse Ethics*, trans. Ciaran P. Cronin. The MIT Press 1994.

Habermas, J. 'Erläuterungen zur Diskursethik', in: *Erläuterungen zur Diskursethik*, pp. 119–226. Suhrkamp 1991 (cit. Habermas 1991a). English translation: 'Remarks on discourse ethics', in: *Justification and Application: Remarks on Discourse Ethics*, trans. Ciaran P. Cronin. The MIT Press 1994.
Habermas, J. 'Treffen Hegels Einwände gegen Kant auch auf die Diskursethik zu?', in: *Erläuterungen zur Diskursethik*, pp. 9–30. Suhrkamp 1991 (cit. Habermas 1991b). English translation: 'Morality and ethical life: Does Hegel's critique of Kant apply to discourse ethics?', in: *Moral Consciousness and Communicative Action*, trans. Christian Lenhardt; Shierry Weber Nicholsen, pp. 195–216. The MIT Press 1994.
Habermas, J. *Die Zukunft der menschlichen Natur. Auf dem Weg zu einer liberalen Eugenik?* Suhrkamp 2001. English translation: *The Future of Human Nature*, trans. Hella Beister; William Rehg. Polity Press 2003.
Hacking, I. 'The normal state', in: *The Taming of Chance*, pp. 161–88. Cambridge University Press 1990.
Haimes, E. 'What can the social sciences contribute to the study of ethics? Theoretical, empirical and substantive considerations', *Bioethics* 16:2 (2002), pp. 89–113.
Hampton, J. 'Should political philosophy be done without metaphysics?', *Ethics* 99 (1989), pp. 791–814.
Harris, J. *The Value of Life: An Introduction to Medical Ethics*. Routledge & Kegan Paul 1985.
Harris, J. *Wonderwoman and Superman: Ethics and Human Biotechnology*. Oxford University Press 1992.
Harris, J. *Clones, Genes and Immortality: Ethics and the Genetics Revolution*. Oxford University Press 1998.
Harris, J. *Enhancing Evolution: The Ethical Case for Making Better People*. Princeton University Press 2007.
Harris, J.; Holm, S. (eds). *The Future of Human Reproduction. Ethics, Choice, and Regulation*. Clarendon Press 1998.
Harris, J.; Holm Søren. 'Extending human lifespan and the precautionary paradox', *Journal of Medicine and Philosopy* 27:3 (2002), pp. 355–68.
Hauser-Schäublin, B.; Kalitzkus, V.; Petersen, I.; Schröder, I. *Der geteilte Leib. Die kulturelle Dimension von Organtransplantation und Reproduktionsmedizin in Deutschland*. Campus 2001.
Hauser-Schäublin, B. 'Was die Europäer uns gebracht haben, ist der Körper.' Von der Undenkbarkeit des Körpers als Objekt', in: Jochen T. (ed). *Kommerzialisierung des menschlichen Körpers*, pp. 16–25. Springer 2007.
Heeger, R. 'Genetic engineering and the dignity of creatures', *Journal of Agricultural and Environmental Ethics* 13 (2000), pp. 43–51.
Heeger, R.; Brom, F.W.A. 'Intrinsic value and direct duties. From animal ethics towards environmental ethics?', *Journal of Agricultural and Environmental Ethics* 14:2 (2001), pp. 241–52.
Hegselmann, R.; Merkel, R. (eds). *Zur Debatte über Euthanasie. Beiträge und Stellungnahmen*. Suhrkamp 1991.
Heidegger, M. *Sein und Zeit*. Max Niemeyer Verlag 1927. English translation: *Being and Time*, trans. Joan Stambaugh, revised by Dennis J. Schmidt. State University of New York Press 2010.
Heidegger, M. *Über den Humanismus*. Klostermann 1947. English translation: 'Letter on "Humanism"', trans. Frank. A. Capuzzi, in: William McNeill (ed). *Pathmarks*, pp. 239–76. Cambridge University Press 1998.

Heidegger, M. *Die Technik und die Kehre*. Neske 1962. English translation: 'The question concerning technology' and 'The turning', in: *The Question Concerning Technology and Other Essays*, trans. William Lovitt. Harper & Row 1977.

Herman, B. *The Practice of Moral Judgment*. Harvard University Press 1993.

Heyd, D. *Genethics: Moral Issues in the Creation of People*. University of California Press 1992.

Hildt, E.; Mieth, D. (eds). *In Vitro Fertilisation in the 1990s. Towards a Medical, Social and Ethical Evaluation*. Ashgate 1998.

Hill, J.F. 'Are marginal agents "our recipients"?', in: Edward Regis Jr. (ed). *Gewirth's Ethical Rationalism. Critical Essays with a Reply by Alan Gewirth*, pp. 180–91. University of Chicago Press 1984.

Hill, T. *Autonomy and Self-Respect*. Cambridge University Press 1991.

Hill, T. *Human Welfare and Moral Worth. Kantian Perspectives*. Oxford University Press 2002.

Hoedemakers, R. 'Geneticization', in: R. Chadwick (ed). *The Concise Encyclopedia of the Ethics of New Technologies*, pp. 158–66. Academic Press 2001.

Holland, A.J.; Johnson, A. (eds). *Animal Biotechnology and Ethics*. Chapman & Hall 1997.

Holland, S. 'Contested commodities at both ends of life. Buying and selling gametes, embryos, and body tissues', *Kennedy Institute of Ethics Journal* 11:3 (2001), pp. 263–84.

Holmes, H.B. *Issues in reproductive technology*. New York University Press 1992.

Holmes, R.L. 'The limited relevance of analytical ethics to the problems of bioethics', *Journal of Medicine and Philosophy* 15:2 (1990), pp. 143–59.

Honnefelder, L.; Lanzerath, D. *Cloning in Biomedical Research and Reproduction. Scientific Aspects – Ethical, Legal and Social Limits*. Deutsches Referenzzentrum für Ethik in den Biowissenschaften 2003.

Horkheimer, M.; Adorno, T.W. *Dialektik der Aufklärung. Philosophische Fragmente*. Fischer Verlag 1969. English translation: Gunzelin Schmid Noerr (ed). *Dialectic of Enlightenment*, trans. Edmund Jephcott. Stanford University Press 2002.

Höss, R. *Kommandant in Auschwitz: autobiografische Aufzeichnungen*. Deutscher Taschenbuch Verlag 1963. Two English translations: Steven Paskuly (ed). *Death Dealer: The Memoirs of the SS Kommandant at Auschwitz*, trans. Andrew Pollinger. Prometheus Books 1992. *Commandant of Auschwitz: The Autobiography of Rudolf Hoess*, trans. Constantine FitzGibbon. Phoenix Press 2000.

Humber, J.; Almeder, R. *Human Cloning*. Humana Press 1998.

Hurka, T. *Perfectionism*. Oxford University Press 1993.

Hursthouse, R. *On Virtue Ethics*. Oxford University Press 1999.

Hursthouse, R. *Ethics, Humans and Other Animals*. Routledge 2000.

Illies, C. *The Grounds of Ethical Judgement. New Transcendental Arguments in Moral Philosophy*. Oxford University Press 2003.

Illies, C. *Philosophische Anthropologie im biologischen Zeitalter*. Zur konvergenz von Moral und Natur. Suhrkamp. 2006.

Inwagen, P. *An Essay on Free Will*. Oxford University Press 1978.

Jagger, A.M. 'Feminist Ethics', in: Lawrence C.B.; Charlotte B.B. (eds). *Encyclopedia of Ethics*, pp. 364–67. Routledge 1992.

Jamieson, D. (ed). *Singer and His Critics*. Blackwell 1999.

Jamieson, D. *Morality's Progress: Essays on Humans, Other Animals, and the Rest of Nature*. Oxford University Press 2003.

Jonas, H. 'Against the stream: comments on the definition and redefinition of death', in: *Philosophical Essays: From Ancient Creed to Technological Man*. Prentice-Hall 1974.

Jonas, H. *Das Prinzip Verantwortung. Versuch einer Ethik für die technologische Zivilisation*. Suhrkamp 1979. English translation: *The Imperative of Responsibility: In Search of Ethics for the Technological Age*, trans. Hans Jonas; David Herr. Chicago University Press 1984.

Jones, A.H. 'Narrative in medical ethics', *BMJ* 318:7178 (1999), pp. 253–56.

Jonsen, A.; Toulmin, S. *The Abuse of Casuistry. A History of Moral Reasoning*. University of California Press 1988.

Jonsen, A.R. *The Birth of Bioethics*. Oxford University Press 1998.

Jonsen, A.R.; Siegler, M.; Winslade, W.J. *Clinical Ethics. A Practical Approach to Ethical Decisions in Clinical Medicine*. McGraw-Hill 2002.

Juth, N.; Munthe, C. *The Ethics of Screening in Health Care and Medicine: Serving Society or Serving the Patient?*, International Library of Ethics, Law, and the New Medicine, vol. 51. Springer 2011.

Kagan, S. *The Limits of Morality*. Oxford University Press 1989.

Kaldewaij, F. 'Animals and the harm of death', in: Susan J.A.; Richard G.B. (eds). *The Animal Ethics Reader*, pp. 59–62. Routledge 2008.

Kant, I. 'Grundlegung zur Metaphysik der Sitten', in: W. Weischedel (ed). *Werkausgabe*, vol. VII, pp. 11–102. Suhrkamp 1986 [1785]. English translation: 'Groundwork of the Metaphysics of Morals', trans. M.J. Gregor, in: Immanuel Kant: *Practical Philosophy*, pp. 37–108. Cambridge University Press 1996.

Kant, I. 'Metaphysik der Sitten', in: W. Weischedel (ed). *Werkausgabe*, vol. VIII. Suhrkamp 1986 [1797]. English translation: 'The Methaphysics of Morals' trans. M.J. Gregor, in: Immanuel Kant: *Practical Philosophy*, pp. 353–605. Cambridge University Press 1996.

Kant, I. 'Über ein vermeintes Recht aus Menschenliebe zu lügen', in: W. Weischedel (ed). *Werkausgabe*, vol. VIII, pp. 637–43. Suhrkamp 1968 [1797]. English translations: 'On a supposed right to lie from altruistic motives', trans. M.J. Gregor, in: Immanuel Kant: *Practical Philosophy*, pp. 605–616. Cambridge University Press 1996.

Kass, L. *Life, Liberty and the Defense of Dignity: The Challenge for Bioethics*. Encounter Books 2002.

Keller, D.R. (ed). *Environmental Ethics: The Big Questions*. Wiley-Blackwell 2010.

Kemp, P.; Rendtorff, J.; Johansen, N.M. (eds). *Bioethics and Biolaw, Vol. II. Four Ethical Principles*. International Science & Art Publishers 2000.

Kemper, A. *Unverfügbare Natur. Ästhetik, Anthropologie und Ethik des Umweltschutzes*. Campus 2000.

Kennedy, J. *Een weloverwogen dood. Euthanasie in Nederland*. Bert Bakker 2002.

Kerstein, S. 'Deriving the formula of humanity (GMS II, 427.437)', in: C. Horn; D. Schönecker; C. Mieth (eds). *Groundwork for the Metaphysics of Morals*, pp. 200–24. Walter de Gruyter 2006.

Kitcher, P. *The Lives to Come: The Genetic Revolution and Human Possibilities*. Simon & Schuster 1997.

Kittay, E. *Love's Labor. Essays on Women, Equality, and Dependency*. Routledge 1999.

Kleinman, A. *The Illness Narratives: Suffering, Healing, and the Human Condition*. Basic Books 1989.

Korsgaard, C.M. *Creating the Kingdom of Ends*. Cambridge University Press 1996.

Korsgaard, C.M. 'Fellow creatures: Kantian ethics and our duties to animals', *The Tanner Lectures on Human Values* 25 (2005), pp. 77–110.

Korthals, M. *Before Dinner. Philosophy and Ethics of Food*. Springer 2004.

Krämer, H. *Integrative Ethik*. Suhrkamp 1992.

Kuczewski, M.G. *Fragmentation and Consensus: Communitarian and Casuist Bioethics*. Georgetown University Press 1999.

Kuhse, H. 'Some reflections on the problem of advance directives, personhood, and personal identity', *Kennedy Institute of Ethics Journal* 9:4 (1999), pp. 347–64.

Kuhse, H.; Singer, P. *Should the Baby Live? The Problem of Handicapped Infants*. Oxford University Press 1985.

Kymlicka, W. 'Moral philosophy and public policy: The case of NRTs', *Bioethics* 7:1 (1993), pp. 1–26.

Lamb, D. *Down the Slippery Slope: Arguing in Applied Ethics*. Routledge 1988.

Latour, B. *Reassembling the Social. An Introduction to Actor-Network-Theory*. Oxford University Press 2005.

Leach Scully, J. 'Disabled embodiment and an ethic of care', in: C. Rehmann-Sutter; M. Düwell; D. Mieth (eds). *Bioethics in Cultural Contexts. Reflections on Methods and Finitude*, pp. 247–61. Springer 2006.

Leach Scully, J. *Disability Bioethics: Moral Bodies, Moral Differences*. Rowman & Littlefield 2008.

Lévinas, E. *Totalité et Infinit. Essai sur l'extériorité*. Nijhoff 1961. English translation: *Totality and Infinity: An Essay on Exteriority*, trans. Alphonso Lingis. Duquesne University Press 1969.

Light, A.; Rolston, H. III. *Environmental Ethics: An Anthology*. Blackwell 2003.

Little, M.O. 'On knowing the "why?": Particularism and moral theory', *Hastings Center Report* 31:4 (2001), pp. 32–40.

Lizza, J.P. (ed). *Defining the Beginning and End of Life: Readings on Personal Identity and Bioethics*. The Johns Hopkins University Press 2009.

Locke, J. *Two Treatises of Government*. Cambridge University Press 1960 [1689].

Luhmann, N. *Soziologie des Risikos*. Walter de Gruyter 1991. English translation: *Risk: A Sociological Theory*, trans. Rhodes Barrett. Aldine Transaction 2002.

Luhmann, N. 'Paradigm lost: On the ethical reflection of morality. Speech on the occasion of the award of the Hegel prize 1988', *Thesis Eleven* 29 (1991), pp. 82–94.

Maier, B. 'The effects of IVF on the women involved', in: E. Hildt; D. Meith (eds). *In vitro Fertilisation in the 1990ies. Towards a medical, social and ethical evaluation.*, Ashgate Publishing Company 1998: pp. 178–194.

MacIntyre, A. *After Virtue. A Study in Moral Theory*. University of Notre Dame Press 1981.

Maclean, A. *The Elimination of Morality. Reflections on Utilitarianism and Bioethics*. Routledge 1993.

Manson, N.C. 'Consent and informed consent', in: R.E. Ashcroft; A. Dawson; H. Draper; J.R. McMillan (eds). *Principles of Health Care Ethics: Second Edition*, pp. 297–303. John Wiley & Sons 2007.

Manson, N.C.; O'Neill, O. *Rethinking Informed Consent in Bioethics*. Cambridge University Press 2007.

McCarthy, D. 'Rights, explanation, and risks', *Ethics* 107:2 (1997), pp. 205–25.

McCormick, R. *How Brave a New World: Dilemmas in Bioethics*. Doubleday 1981.

McDowell, J. *Mind, Value, and Reality*. Harvard University Press 1998.

McKerlie, D. 'Rights and risk', *Canadian Journal of Philosophy* 16 (1986), pp. 239–52.
McKibben, B. *Enough: Staying Human in an Engineered Age*. Holt 2003.
McMahan, J. *The Ethics of Killing. Problems at the Margins of Life*. Oxford University Press 2002.
Meijboom, F; Visak, T; Brom, F. 'From trust to trustworthiness. Why information is not enough', *Journal of Agricultural and Environmental Ethics* 19:5 (2006), pp. 127–442.
Mepham, B. 'Novel foods', in: R. Chadwick (ed). *The Concise Encyclopedia of the Ethics of New Technologies*, pp. 300–15. Academic Press 2001.
Mepham, T.B. *Food Ethics*. Routledge 1996.
Merkel, R. *Forschungsobjekt Embryo. Verfassungsrechtliche und ethische Grundlagen der Forschung an menschlichen embryonalen Stammzellen*. Deutscher Taschenbuch Verlag 2002.
Merleau-Ponty, M. *Phénoménologie de la perception*. Gallimard 1945. English translations: *Phenomenology of Perception*, trans. Colin Smith. Humanities Press 1962. *Phenomenology of Perception*, trans. Forrest Williams. Routledge & Kegan Paul 2002.
Meyer, L. 'Intergenerational justice', *The Stanford Encyclopedia of Philosophy (Spring 2010 Edition)*, Edward N.Z. (ed). http://plato.stanford.edu/archives/spr2010/entries/justice-intergenerational/.
Miah, A. *Genetically Modified Athletes: Biomedical Ethics, Gene Doping and Sport*. Routledge 2004.
Midgley, M. *Animals and Why They Matter*. University of Georgia Press 1983.
Midgley, M. 'The end of anthropocentrism', in: R. Attfiled; A. Belsey (eds). *Philosophy and the Natural Environment*, pp. 103–12. Cambridge University Press 1994.
Mieth, D. *Dichtung, Glaube und Moral. Studien zur Begründung einer narrativen Ethik mit einer Interpretation zum Tristanroman Gottfried von Straßburg*. Matthias-Grünewald-Verlag 1976.
Mills, C. *Futures Of Reproduction: Bioethics And Biopolitics*, International Library of Ethics, Law, and the New Medicine, vol. 49. Springer 2011.
Molewijk, B.; Stiggelbout, A.M.; Otten, W.; Dupuis, H.M.; Kievit, J. 'Empirical data and moral theory. A plea for integrated empirical ethics', *Medicine, Health Care and Philosophy* 7 (2004), pp. 55–69.
Moore, G. Edward. *Principia Ethica*. Cambridge University Press 1903.
Murphy, D. 'Concepts of disease and health', *The Stanford Encyclopedia of Philosophy (Summer 2009 Edition)*, Edward N.Z. (ed). http://plato.stanford.edu/archives/sum2009/entries/health-disease/.
Musschenga, A.W.; Steen, W.J. van der (eds). *Reasoning in Ethics and Law: The Role of Theory, Principles and Facts*. Ashgate 1999.
Musschenga, A.W. 'Empirisch geïnformeerde ethiek', inaugural lecture. Vrije Universiteit 2004.
Musschenga, A.W. 'Empirical ethics, context-sensitivity, and contextualism', *Journal of Medicine and Philosophy* 30:5 (2005), pp. 467–90.
Naess, A. 'The deep ecology movement. Some philosophical aspects', in: George Sessions (ed). *Deep Ecology for the 21st Century. Readings on the Philosophy and Practice of the New Environmentalism*, pp. 64–84. Shambhala 1995.
Nelson, H.L. (ed). *Stories and Their Limits. Narrative Approaches to Bioethics*. Routledge 1997.

Nelson, H.L.; Verkerk, M.; Walker, M. (eds). *Bioethics Naturalized: Towards Responsible Knowing and Practice.* Cambridge University Press 2009.

Neumann-Held, E.-M.; Rehmann-Sutter, C. *Genes in Development. Re-Reading the Molecular Paradigm.* Duke University Press 2006.

Nijsingh, N. 'Informed consent and the expansion of newborn screening', in: A. Dawson; M. Verweij (eds). *Ethics, Prevention, and Public Health*, pp. 198–212. Oxford University Press 2007.

Nijsingh, N.; Düwell, M. 'Interdisciplinarity, Applied Ethics and Social Sciences', in: P. Sollie; M. Düwell (eds). *Evaluating New Technologies. Methodological Problems for the Ethical Assessment of Technological Developments*, pp. 79–92. Springer 2009.

Noddings, N. *Caring. A Feminine Approach to Ethics and Moral Education.* University of California Press 1984.

Nordenfelt, L. 'The importance of a disability/handicap distinction', *Journal of Medicine and Philosophy* 22 (1997), pp. 607–22.

Nuffield Council on Bioethics. *Genetic Screening: Ethical Issues.* 1993.

Nuffield Council on Bioethics. *Animal-to-Human Transplants: The Ethics of Xenotransplantation.* 1996.

Nuffield Council on Bioethics. *Genetically Modified Crops: The Ethical and Social Issues.* 1999.

Nuffield Council on Bioethics. *Ethical Issues Raised by Animal Research.* 2005.

Nuffield Council on Bioethics. *Genetic Screening: a Supplement to the 1993 Report by the Nuffield Council on Bioethics.* 2006.

Nuffield Council on Bioethics. 'Decision making: the ethical issues', in: *Critical Care Decisions in Fetal and Neonatal Medicine: Ethical Issues*, pp. 7–25. 2006.

Nuffield Council on Bioethics. *Biofuels: Ethical Issues.* 2011.

Nuffield Council on Bioethics. *Human Bodies: Donation for Medicine and Research.* 2011.

Nussbaum, M.C. *Frontiers of Justice. Disability, Nationality, Species Membership.* Harvard University Press 2006.

Oakley, J. 'Patients and disclosure of surgical risk', in: Richard E.A.; A. Dawson; H. Draper; J.R. McMillan (eds). *Principles of Health Care Ethics: Second Edition*, pp. 319–24. John Wiley & Sons 2007.

O'Hear, A. (ed). *Modern Moral Philosophy.* Cambridge University Press 2004.

Oliver, M. *The Politics of Disablement.* Macmillan 1990.

O'Mahony, P. *Nature, risk, and responsibility. Discourses of biotechnology.* Macmillan 1999.

O'Neill, O. *Towards Justice and Virtue: A Constructive Account of Practical Reasoning.* Cambridge University Press 1996.

O'Neill, O. *Autonomy and Trust in Bioethics.* Cambridge University Press 2002.

Otway, H.J.; Winterfeldt, D. von. 'Beyond acceptable risk: On the social acceptability of technologies', *Policy Sciences* 14 (1982), pp. 247–55.

Overall, C. *Ethics and Human Reproduction. A Feminist Analysis.* Allen & Unwin 1987.

Parens, E. (ed). *Enhancing Human Traits. Ethical and Social Implications.* Georgetown University Press 1998.

Parens, E. (ed). *Surgically Shaping Children.* The Johns Hopkins University Press 2006.

Parens, E.; Asch, A. *Prenatal Testing and Disability Rights.* Georgetown University Press 2000.

Parfit, D. *Reasons and Persons.* Oxford University Press 1984.

Pellegrino, E.D. 'Toward a virtue-based normative ethics for the health professions', *Kennedy Institute of Ethics Journal* 5:3 (1995), pp. 253–77.

Pellegrino, E.D. 'Bioethics at century's turn: Can normative ethics be retrieved?', *Journal of Medicine and Philosophy* 25:6 (2000), pp. 655–75.
Pellegrino, E.D. 'Bioethics as an interdisciplinary enterprise: Where does ethics fit in the mosaic of disciplines?', in: R.A. Carson; C.R. Burns (eds). *Philosophy of Medicine and Bioethics*, pp. 1–23. Springer 2002.
Pence, G. *Brave New Bioethics*. Rowman & Littlefield 2002.
Peters, T. *Playing God: Genetic Determinism and Human Freedom*. Routledge 1997.
Pettit, P. 'The consequentialist perspective', in: Marcia W.B.; P. Pettit; M. Slote (eds). *Three Methods of Ethics: A Debate*, pp. 92–174. Blackwell 1997.
Pico della Mirandola, G. *Oratio de hominis dignitate*. 1486. English translation in: *On the Dignity of Man*, trans. Charles Glenn Wallis. Hackett 1998.
Plessner, H. *Die Stufen des Organischen und der Mensch. Einleitung in die philosophische Anthropologie*. De Gruyter 1975.
Pogge, T. (ed). *Global Justice*. Blackwell 2001.
Pogge, T. *World Poverty and Human Rights*. Polity Press 2002.
Potter, V.R. *Bioethics. Bridge to the Future*. Prentice-Hall 1971.
The President's Council on Bioethics. *Human Cloning and Human Dignity: An Ethical Inquiry*. 2002.
The President's Council on Bioethics. *Beyond Therapy. Biotechnology and the Pursuit of Happiness*. 2003.
Price, D. *Legal and Ethical Aspects of Organ Transplantation*. Cambridge University Press 2001.
Purdy, L. (ed). *Ethics and reproduction, Hypatia* special issue 4:3 (1989).
Quante, M.; Wiedebusch, S. 'Overcoming the shortage of transplantable organs. Ethical and psychological aspects', *Swiss Medical Weekly* 136 (2006), pp. 523–28.
Qiu, R. *Bioethics – Asian Perspectives: A Quest for Moral Diversity*. Springer 2004.
Quinn, P.L. *Divine Commands and Moral Requirements*. Oxford University Press 1978.
Rachels, James. *The End of Life. Euthanasia and Morality*. Oxford University Press 1986.
Radcliffe Richards, J. 'Nephrarious goings on. Kidney sales and moral arguments', *The Journal of Medicine and Philosophy* 21 (1996), pp. 375–416.
Radin, M.J. *Contested Commodities. The Trouble with Trade in Sex, Children, Body Parts, and Other Things*. Harvard University Press 1996.
Rasmussen, L.M. *Ethics Expertise: History, Contemporary Perspectives, and Applications*. Springer 2005.
Ravelingien, A.; Krom, A. 'Earning points for moral behaviour. Organ allocation based on reciprocity', *International Journal of Applied Philosophy* 19:1 (2005), pp. 73–83.
Rawls, J. *A Theory of Justice*. Harvard University Press 1971.
Rawls, J. *Political Liberalism*. Columbia University Press 1993.
Regan, T. *The Case for Animal Rights*. University of California Press 1983.
Regis Jr, E. *Gewirth's Ethical Rationalism. Critical essays with a reply by Alan Gewirth*. University of Chicago Press 1984.
Rehmann-Sutter, C. 'Genetics, a practical anthropology', in: M. Düwell; C. Rehmann-Sutter; D. Mieth (eds). *The Contingent Nature of Life. Bioethics and Limits of Human Existence*, pp. 37–52. Springer 2008.
Reich, W.T. 'The word "bioethics". The struggle over its earliest meanings', *Kennedy Institute of Ethics Journal* 5 (1995), pp. 19–34.
Resnik, D.B.; Steinkraus, H.B.; Langer, P.J. *Human Germline Gene Therapy: Scientific, Moral and Political Issues*. R.G. Landes 1999.

Richardson, H. 'Specifying, balancing, and interpreting bioethical principles', *Journal of Medicine and Philosophy* 25 (2000), pp. 285–307.

Rippe, K.-P. 'Novel food and consumer rights. Concerning a food policy in a liberal state', *Journal of Agricultural and Environmental Ethics* 12:1 (1999), pp. 71–80.

Ritter, J. 'Landschaft. Zur Funktion des Ästhetischen in der modernen Gesellschaft', in: *Subjektivität: sechs Aufsätze*, pp. 141–64. Suhrkamp 1974.

Robertson, J. *Children of Choice: Freedom and the New Reproductive Technologies*. Princeton University Press 1994.

Roeser, S. *Ethical Intuitions and Emotions. A Philosophical Study.* Vrije Universiteit Amsterdam 2002.

Rollin, B.E. *The Unheeded Cry. Animal Consciousness, Animal Pain and Science.* Iowa University Press 1990.

Rollin, B.E. 'Animal pain: What it is and why it matters', *Journal of Ethics* 15 (2011), pp. 425–37.

Rolston III, H. *Environmental Ethics. Duties and Values in the Natural World.* Temple University Press 1988.

Ross, W.D. *The Right and the Good.* Oxford University Press 1930.

Roth, L.T. 'The moral construction of risk', in: S. Hitlin; S. Vaisey (eds). *Handbook of the Sociology of Morality*, pp. 469–84. Springer 2010.

Rothstein, M.A. 'Expanding the ethical analysis of biobanks', *The Journal of Law, Medicine & Ethics* 33:1 (2005), pp. 89–101.

Rowlands, M. *Animals Like Us.* Verso 2002.

Rudnick, A. 'A meta-ethical critique of care ethics', *Theoretical Medicine and Bioethics* 22:6 (2001), pp. 505–17.

Ruse, M.; Pynes, C.A. (eds). *The Stem Cell Controversy: Debating the Issues.* Prometheus Books 2006.

Rutgers, B.; Heeger, R. 'Inherent worth and respect for animal integrity', in: M. Dol; M. Fentener van Vlissingen; S. Kasanmoentalib; T. Visser; H. Zwart (eds). *Recognizing the Intrinsic Value of Animals. Beyond Animal Welfare*, pp. 41–52. Van Gorcum 1999.

Sandøe, P.; Christiansen, S.B. *Ethics of Animal Use.* Blackwell 2008.

Savulescu, J.; Bostrom, N. (eds). *Human Enhancement.* Oxford University Press 2011.

Scanlon, T. *What We Owe to Each Other.* Harvard University Press 1998.

Scheer, L. van der; Thiel, G. van; Delden, J.J.M. Van; Widdershoven, Guy. 'Theory and methodology of empirical ethics', in: Søren Holm; Monique F.J. (eds). *Engaging the World. The Use of Empirical Research in Bioethics and the Regulation of Biotechnology*, pp. 89–96. IOS Press 2004.

Scheffler, S. (ed). *Consequentialism and its Critics.* Oxford University Press 1988.

Scheler, M. *Die Stellung des Menschen im Kosmos.* Reichl 1928. English translation: *The Human Place in the Cosmos*, trans. Manfred Frings. Northwestern University Press 2009.

Schicktanz, S. 'Why the way we consider the body matters – Reflections on four bioethical perspectives on the human body', *Philosophy, Ethics, and Humanities in Medicine*, 2 (2007), pp. 2–30.

Schmitz, H. *Der Leib. System der Philosophie.* Bouvier 1965.

Schneider, I. 'Oocyte donation for reproduction and research cloning – The perils of commodification and the need for European and international regulation', *Law and the Human Genome Review* 25 (2006), pp. 205–41.

Schweda, M.; Schicktanz, S. 'Public moralities concerning donation and disposition of organs – Results of a European cross-cultural study', *Cambridge Quarterly of Healthcare Ethics* 17 (2008), pp. 308–17.
Schweda, M.; Schicktanz, S. 'Public ideas and values concerning the commercialization of organ donation in four European countries', *Social Science and Medicine* 68 (2009), pp. 1129–36.
Schwing, R.C.; Albers, W.A. *Societal Risk Assessment: How Safe Is Safe Enough?* Plenum Press 1980.
Scotch, R.K.; Schriner, K. 'Disability as human variation: Implications for policy', *The Annals of the American Academy of Political and Social Science* 549:1 (1997), pp. 148–59.
Scott, R. *Choosing Between Possible Lives: Law and Ethics of Prenatal and Preimplantation Genetic Diagnosis.* Hart 2007.
Seel, M. *Eine Ästhetik der Natur*. Suhrkamp 1991.
Shafer-Landau, R. *Moral Realism: A Defence.* Oxford University Press 2003.
Shakespeare, T. *Disability Rights and Wrongs*. Routledge 2006.
Shakespeare, T. 'Disability. Suffering, social oppression, or complex predicament?', in: M. Düwell; C. Rehmann-Sutter; D. Mieth (eds). *The Contingent Nature of Life. Bioethics and the Limits of Human Existence*, pp. 235–46. Springer 2008.
Shalev, C. *Birth Power: The Case for Surrogacy*. Yale University Press 1989.
Shannon, T.A. *Surrogate Motherhood: The Ethics of Using Human Beings*. Crossroad 1988.
Shenfield, F.; Sureau, C. (eds). *Contemporary Ethical Dilemmas in Assisted Reproduction.* Informa Healthcare 2006.
Sherwin, S. *No Longer Patient. Feminist Ethics and Health Care*. Temple University Press 1992.
Shrader-Frechette, K. *Risk and Rationality. Philosophical Foundations for Populist Reforms.* University of California Press 1991.
Shue, H. *Basic Rights. Subsistence, Affluence, and U.S. Foreign Policy*. Princeton University Press 1980.
Siep, L. 'Normative aspects of the human body', *Journal of Medicine and Philosophy* 28:2 (2003), pp. 171–85.
Silvers, A. 'A fatal attraction to normalizing. Treating disabilities as deviations from "species-typical" functioning', in: E. Parens (ed). *Enhancing Human Traits. Ethical and Social Implications*, pp. 95–123. Georgetown University Press 1998.
Singer, P. *Animal Liberation*. Ecco 1974.
Singer, P. *Practical Ethics*. Cambridge University Press 1797, 2nd edition 1993. 3rd edition 2011.
Singer, P. *Unsanctifying Human Life. Essays on Ethics*. H. Kuhse (ed). Blackwell 2002.
Singer, P. *One World – The Ethics of Globalization*. Yale University Press 2002a.
Singer, P; Mason, J. *The Ethics of What We Eat: Why Our Food Choices Matter.* Rodale Books 2007.
Skorupinski, B. 'The use of genetically modified plants and micro-organisms in agriculture and food production – an ethical reflection', in: V. Beekman; F. Brom (eds). *Proceerdings of the First European Congress on Agricultural and Food Ethics*, pp. 117–21. Wageningen Agricultural University 1999.
Skorupski, J. 'The definition of morality', *Royal Institute of Philosophy Supplements* 35 (1993), pp. 121–44.
Slote, M. *Morals from Motives*. Oxford University Press 2001.

Sloterdijk, P. 'Rules for the human zoo: A response to the *Letter on Humanism*', trans. Mary Varney Rorty, *Environment and Planning D: Society and Space* 27:1 (2009), pp. 12–28. German original: *Regeln für den Menschenpark. Ein Antwortschreiben zu Heideggers Brief über den Humanismus*. Suhrkamp 1999.

Slovic, P. 'Perception of risk', *Science* 236 (1987), pp. 280–85.

Smart, J.J.C.; Williams, B. *Utilitarianism – For and Against*. Cambridge University Press 1973.

Solbakk, J.H.; Holm, S.; Hofmann, B. (eds). *The Ethics of Research Biobanking*. Springer 2009.

Sorabji, R. *Animal Minds and Human Morals. The Origins of the Western Debate*. Cornell University Press 1993.

Spaemann, R. 'Gezeugt, nicht gemacht', *Die Zeit*, 19 January 2001. English translation: 'Begotten, not made', *Communio: International Catholic Review* 33 (2006).

Spallone, P.; Steinberg, D.L. *Beyond Conception: The New Politics of Reproduction*. Macmillan 1989.

Steigleder, K. 'Die Abenteuer der Bioethik – Ein kritischer Vergleich der Ethikkonzeptionen H. Tristram Engelhardts und Peter Singers', in: M.P.H. Wolff; Jean-Pierre Wils; D. Mieth (eds). *Ethik ohne Chance? Erkundungen im technologischen Zeitalter*, pp. 225–46. Attempto Verlag 1991.

Steigleder, K. *Die Begründung des moralischen Sollens. Studien zur Möglichkeit einer normativen Ethik*. Attempto Verlag 1992.

Steigleder, K. 'The moral status of potential persons', in: E. Hildt; D. Mieth (eds). *In Vitro Fertilisation in the 1990s: Towards a Medical, Social and Ethical Evaluation*. Ashgate 1998.

Steinbock, B. (ed). *Legal and Ethical Issues in Human Reproduction*, The International Library of Medicine, Ethics and Law. Ashgate 2002.

Steinbock, B. *Life Before Birth: The Moral and Legal Status of Embryos and Fetuses*. Oxford University Press 2011.

Steiner, G. *Anthropocentrism and Its Discontents: The Moral Status of Animals in the History of Western Philosophy*. University of Pittsburgh Press 2010.

Stephenson, P.; Wagner, M.G. *Tough Choices: In Vitro Fertilization and the Reproductive Technologies*. Philadelphia, 1993.

Stevenson, C. *Ethics and Language*. AMS Press 1944.

Stratton-Lake, P. *Ethical Intuitionism. Re-evaluations*. Oxford University Press 2002.

Strawson, P.F. 'Freedom and resentment', *Proceedings of the British Academy* 48 (1962), pp. 1–25. Reprinted in: John Martin Fischer; Mark Ravizza (eds). *Perspectives on Moral Responsibility*. Cornell University Press 1993.

Sumner, L.W.; Boyle, J. (eds). *Philosophical Perspectives on Bioethics*. University of Toronto Press 1996.

Sunstein, C. *Laws of Fear. Beyond the Precautionary Principle*. Cambridge University Press 2005.

Sunstein, C.R.; Nussbaum, M.C. *Animal Rights. Current Debates and New Directions*. Oxford University Press 2004.

Taylor, C. *Philosophical Papers*, 2 vols. Cambridge University Press 1985.

Taylor, P.W. *Respect for Nature. A Theory of Environmental Ethics*. Princeton University Press 1986.

Teuber, A. 'Justifying risk', *Daedalus* 119 (1990), pp. 235–54.

Thomson, J.J. 'A defense of abortion', *Philosophy and Public Affairs* 1:1 (1971), pp. 47–66.

Thomson, J.J. 'Imposing risks', in: *To Breathe Freely*, pp. 124–40. Rowman & Allanheld 1985.
Thompson, T.B. *The Agrarian Vision: Sustainability and Environmental Ethics*. University Press of Kentucky 2010.
Tierney, B. *The Idea of Natural Rights*. Emory University Press 1997.
Timmons, M. *Morality Without Foundations. A Defense of Ethical Contextualism*. Oxford University Press 1999.
Tong, R. *Feminist Approaches to Bioethics. Theoretical Reflections and Practical Applications*. Westview Press 1997.
Tong, R. 'Feminist ethics', in: R. Chadwick (ed). *The Concise Encyclopedia of the Ethics of New Technologies*, pp. 106–12. Academic Press 2001.
Tooley, M. *Abortion and Infanticide*. Clarendon Press 1983.
Trinkaus, C. *In Our Image and Likeness. Humanity and Divinity in Italian Humanist Thought*, 2 vols. Constable 1970.
Tronto, J.C. *Moral Boundaries. A Political Argument for an Ethic of Care*. Routledge 1993.
Tuck, R. *Natural Rights Theories. Their Origin and Development*. Cambridge University Press 1979.
Tversky, A.; Kahneman, D. 'Rational choice and the framing of decisions', *Journal of Business* 59 (1986), pp. 251–78.
Twine, R. *Animals as Biotechnology: Ethics, Sustainability and Critical Animal Studies*. Routledge 2010.
UNESCO. 'The universal declaration on the human genome and human rights', in: *Jahrbuch für Wissenschaft und Ethik* 11 (2006), pp. 377–85. Also in several languages on the UNESCO website: http://www.unesco.org/new/en/social-and-human-sciences/themes/bioethics/human-genome-and-human-rights/.
Unnerstall, H. *Rechte zukünftiger Generationen*. Königshausen & Neumann 1999.
UPIAS. *Fundamental principles of disability*. Union of the Physically Impaired Against Segregation 1976.
Varner, G. *In Nature's Interests*. Oxford University Press 1998.
Velleman, J.D. 'A right of self-termination?' *Ethics* 109:3 (1999), pp. 606–28.
Verstraeten, J. 'Narrativity and hermeneutics in applied ethics', *Ethical Perspectives* 1:2 (1994), pp. 51–56.
Vorstenbosch, J. 'The constitution of institutional animal care and use committees. A principled approach', in: M. Balls; A.-M. Zeller; Marlies E. Halder (eds). *Progress in the Reduction, Refinement and Replacement of Animal Experimentation*, pp. 1519–28. Amsterdam 2000.
Vries, R. de; Gordijn, B. 'Empirical ethics and its alleged meta-ethical fallacies', *Bioethics* 23:4 (2009), pp. 193–201.
Waal, F. de. *Good Natured. The Origins of Right and Wrong in Humans and Other Animals*. Harvard University Press 1996.
Waal, F. de. *Primates and Philosophers: How Morality Evolved*, S. Macedo; J. Ober (eds). Princeton University Press 2006.
Wallace, G.; Walker, A.D.M. (eds). *The Definition of Morality*. Methuen 1970.
Walter, J.; Küng, H. *Menschenwürdig Sterben. Ein Plädoyer für Selbstverantwortung*. Piper 1995. English translation: *Dying with Dignity: A Plea for Personal Responsibility*, trans. John Bowden. Continuum 1998.
Warnock, M. *A Question of Life: The Warnock Report on Human Fertilisation and Embryology*. Blackwell 1985.

Warren, M. Anne. *Moral Status. Obligations to Persons and Other Living Things*. Oxford University Press 1997.

Wasserman, D. 'Philosophical issues in the definition and social response to disability', in: G.L. Albrecht (ed). *Handbook of Disability Studies*, pp. 219–51. Sage Publications 2001.

Watson, G. 'Two faces of responsibility', *Philosophical Topics* 24 (1996), pp. 227–48.

Weber, M. 'Politik als Beruf', in: *Gesammelte Politische Schriften*, pp. 505–60. Mohr Siebeck 1988. English translation: David S. Owen; Tracy B. Strong (eds). *The Vocation Lectures: Science As a Vocation, Politics As a Vocation*, trans. Rodney Livingstone. Hackett 2004.

Weingart, P. 'Geman eugenics between science and politics', *Osiris*, second series 5 (1989), pp. 260–82.

Wiesing, U. 'Success rates in IVF', in: E. Hildt; D. Mieth (eds). *In Vitro Fertilisation in the 1990s. Towards a Medical, Social and Ethical Evaluation*, pp. 163–69. Ashgate 1998.

Wildes, K.W. 'The priesthood of bioethics and the return of casuistry', *Journal of Medicine and Philosophy* 18:1 (1993), pp. 33–49.

Wilkinson, T.M. *Ethics and the Acquisition of Organs*, Issues in Biomedical Ethics. Oxford University Press 2012.

Williams, B. *Ethics and the Limits of Philosophy*. Fontana Press 1985.

Wils, Jean-Pierre. *'Ästhetische Güte'. Philosophisch–theologische Studien zu Mythos und Leiblichkeit im Verhältnis von Ethik und Ästhetik*. Fink 1990.

Wimmer, R. 'Zur Eigenart moralischer Beurteilungen und ihrer anthropologischen Begründung', in: Jean-Pierre Wils (ed). *Orientierung durch Ethik? Eine Zwischenbilanz*, pp. 149–67. Mentis 1993.

Wimmer, R. 'Anthropologische Ethik. Erkundungen in unübersichtlichem Gelände', in: C. Demmerling; G. Gabriel; T.s Rentsch (eds). *Vernunft und Lebenspraxis. Philosophische Studien zu den Bedingungen einer rationalen Kultur. Für Friedrich Kambartel*, pp. 215–45. Suhrkamp 1995.

Wolf, S. *Feminism and Bioethics. Beyond Reproduction*. Oxford University Press 1996.

Wolpe, P.R. 'The triumph of autonomy in American bioethics: a sociological view', in: R. Devries; J. Subedi (eds). *Bioethics and Society: Constructing the Ethical Enterprise*, pp. 38–59. Prentice-Hall 1998.

Wood, A. *Kant's Ethical Thought*. Cambridge University Press 1999.

World Health Organization. *International Classification of Impairment, Disability and Handicap (ICIDH)*. 1980.

World Health Organization. *International Classification of Functioning, Disability and Health (ICF)*. 2001. (Available online: http//www.who.int/classifications/icf/en/.)

Wright, B. *Physical Disability: A Psychosocial Approach*. Harper & Row 1983.

Young, I. Marion. *Justice and the Politics of Difference*. Princeton University Press 1990.

Zimmerman, M.J. *An Essay on Moral Responsibility*. Rowman & Littlefield 1988.

Zimmerman, M.J. 'Risk, rights, and restitution', *Philosophical Studies* 128:2 (2006), pp. 285–311.

Index

Note: The reference 33n3 refers to footnote 3 on page 33.